Management and the Dominance of Managers

Routledge Series in Management, Organisation and Society

Management and the Dominance of Managers

An Inquiry into Why and How Managers Rule Our Organizations

Thomas Diefenbach

Routledge
Taylor & Francis Group
New York London

First published 2009
by Routledge
270 Madison Ave, New York, NY 10016

Simultaneously published in the UK
by Routledge
2 Park Square, Milton Park, Abingdon, Oxon OX14 4RN

Routledge is an imprint of the Taylor & Francis Group, an informa business

Typeset in Sabon by IBT Global.

Library of Congress Cataloging-in-Publication Data
Diefenbach, Thomas, 1965–
    Management and the dominance of managers : an inquiry into why and how
managers rule our organisations / Thomas Diefenbach.
        p. cm. — (Routledge studies in management, organisation and society ; 7)
    Includes bibliographical references and index.
    1. Management—Philosophy.   I. Title.
    HD31.D532 2009
    658.001—dc22
    2008045336

ISBN10: 0-415-44335-0 (hbk)
ISBN10: 0-203-87176-6 (ebk)

ISBN13: 978-0-415-44335-7 (hbk)
ISBN13: 978-0-203-87176-8 (ebk)

Contents

Tables and Figures

Tables and Figures

Acknowledgements

First and foremost I want to mention my partner in life Narin. This book would have not been possible without her. I owe a huge debt of gratitude to her for her love, support and belief in me. For this, and for so much else she has done for us, I thank her from the bottom of my heart. Narin has also actively contributed to the work on this book, particularly gathering data from literature and making these readily available for further use.

I would also like to thank Professor John Sillince, an outstanding scholar and true academic (which nowadays is not that common anymore, especially at business schools). Unfortunately, we only met as colleagues and started to discuss problems of organisations and society, social sciences in general and management studies in particular when the book was already well on its way. It would have been so much better if John had been involved earlier. However, the very stimulating discussions we had, his comprehensive knowledge and intellectual rigour motivated me time and again to at least trying to improve the argument I attempted to make in this book.Earlier this year we started a new research project on the 'persistence of hierarchical order' and the first results look promising.

I am also dedicated to Terry Clague, Senior Commissioning Editor at Routledge. In September 2006 he suggested that I might write a book about management—and the rest is, as they say, 'history'. For this initial impetus, but also for his support and patience during the past two years I would like to thank him.

Thomas Diefenbach
Glasgow, December 2008

Acknowledgements

1   Introduction

> The existence of an identifiable group of people who are labelled 'managers' has been one of the most significant aspects of the organization of work and society for well over a century.
>
> —Grey (1999, p. 561)

THE PUZZLE OF MANAGERS' DOMINANCE

When it is about organisations then it is about management. The organisations of our time are in essence *managerial* organisations (e.g. Grey 1999, Jacques 1996, Rosen 1984, Burnham 1941); even our societies are *managerial* societies. Our businesses and companies, both private and public sectors, our whole economy and society, even our private lives haven been conquered by yet another ideology—the ideology of management. As Thrift (2002, p. 19) put it: 'The awful thing about modern management discourse is that you can't escape it. It is on the walls, in people's mouths, creeping into every moment of human interaction.'

Management is everywhere; 'managerial bureaucracies are now to be found in government, in the City, the Church, the multinationals, the armed forces, the universities, the business corporations and every sector of public life' (Protherough / Pick 2002, p. 16). Management—and discourses about the roles and importance of managers and managing—is part of the prevailing *zeitgeist*. Apparently, it doesn't make much sense to be 'against' management either (Parker 2002, pp. 1–2); 'If we want to control nature and ourselves, and do so in a transparent fashion, then management is an obvious answer. It is the consolidation of order and efficiency, and who could be against order and efficiency?' (ibid., p. 4). What we have witnessed is not only the managerialisation of our private and public sector organisations, but of our society, our private affairs and even our personal lives (Alvesson / Willmott 1992a, p. 3). There is hardly anything left nowadays which doesn't need to be managed. Like myths and mythology in ancient times, Christianity in medieval times, Manchester capitalism in modern times, like cancer even, management has crawled into every fibre of our work and social life. It has reached hegemonic status—and it continues to spread. Even the serious flaws and limitations of orthodox management concepts do not stop its proponents from spreading the word and disseminating it further and further. There is an endless stream of strategy papers, mission and vision statements, (allegedly) 'new' business models, management concepts and change initiatives. There are an ever growing number of books and papers, conferences and workshops, meetings and projects all on management and managers. We live in 'the age of management'—and it seems likely that we will have to live with it for a long time.

But it is not simply buzzwords, fads and fashions, glossy brochures and management-speak. Managerialism produces *real* consequences—*very* real consequences. It has changed the world. From its early modern beginnings, it has been portrayed as a functional, even scientific approach, concentrating on the improvement of the 'technical' aspects of organisations and business (e.g. Kraut et al. 2005, Hales 1999, Mintzberg 1994, Taylor 1911/1967). It is said to be about increasing efficiency and productivity, shareholder maximisation and value for money, organisational objectives and strategies, structures and processes. But it is so much more. It has changed the way organisations operate. More importantly, it has changed the way people see, create, and solve problems—the way they talk and behave, think and act. After more than one and a half centuries of justification for management, for socialisation, conditioning, and indoctrination, people can hardly conceive of organisations without management. Moreover, management strongly contributes to the continuation of unequal and unjust social systems such as hierarchical organisations. It has created new social groups and classes, new layers of society and a whole new cosmos of social relationships. These aspects are crucial. Managerial discourses and their consequences may well create differences in technological terms, but even more so in socio-economical, organisational and socio-cultural terms. Hence, the interesting question is not so much "what is" management or "what is management about" in a functional sense, but what and who is *behind* management? For what purposes *exactly* is it used and what are the consequences? Who profits from it the most, and in which ways?

One part of the answer to these questions is straightforward. Managerial concepts, the managerial organisation and, overall, the ideology of management are primarily useful *for managers*.[1] As Hood (1991, p. 9) stresses, the introduction of management concepts in the public sector is primarily 'designed to promote the career interests of an elite group of 'new managerialists' . . .'. Senior and middle managers particularly have an interest in the 'legitimization of management for its own sake' (Deem / Brehony 2005, p. 220) since it strengthens and justifies *their* roles and privileges within organisations. According to Abercrombie et al. (1980, p. 135) managerial ideology 'is concerned to justify, not the ownership and rights of property, but the economic privilege and social power which the relatively property-less managerial stratum that controls modern industry wields.' More especially, it is not about the dominance of just *any* manager; it is particularly about the dominance of the new breed of 'all-purpose managers' (Protherough / Pick 2002, p. 16). These are the ones who don't care about the actual business their organisations do (and how they do it). They don't care about the employees who work for the organisation, the real value and sense of the products produced or services provided by their companies, or the overall impact all these aspects and activities have on individuals, our communities, society and the environment.[2] All they care about is the pursuit of their egoistic and career-oriented interests, the cynical and calculated use of their power and the further dissemination of their own narrow-minded and ignorant ideology of management.

These managers dominate organisations and business, the public sector and other parts of society. This epochal trend began in the early days of capitalism[3] and gained momentum in the second half of the 19th century. Although managers were already well established at this stage, by 1911 Taylor still felt the need to demand and justify management's prerogatives and dominance within organisations on a 'scientific basis' (Taylor 1911/1967, pp. 26, 32, 36–38). Just a generation later, Burnham (1941, p. 71) had already identified a transition 'from the type of society which we have called capitalist or bourgeois to a type of society which we shall call managerial. . . . What is occurring in this transition is a drive for social dominance, for power and privilege, for the position of ruling class, by the social group or class of the *managers* (. . .)'. Burnham predicted that capitalist society would be replaced by a managerial society (ibid., p. 29). Later, Petit (1961, p. 99) warned about the 'danger of coming under the domination of a management elite', and Galbraith (1977, p. 271) compared the dominance of managers to the earlier dominance of priests: 'These men of the technostructure [pioneered by Harvard Business School] are the new and universal priesthood. Their religion is business success; their test of virtue is growth and profit. Their Bible is the computer printout; their communion bench is the committee room.' This process is now complete. We live in a managerial world where 'propertied corporate elites have been replaced by property-less managerial elites' (Scott 2003, p. 159). Many even regard top managers as global leaders (e.g. Heames / Harvey 2006, describing the role of managers as 'undoubtedly a central one in all advanced economies and societies' (Poole et al. 2003, p. 1). In summary, within a century we have witnessed the creation and establishment of 'the managers' *as a new ruling social group, if not to say dominating class.*

By having their personal and group interests not only accepted, but actually institutionalised as the prevailing norms and values of organisations, managers have managed to establish and to advance their sectional interests as universally accepted, even as universal interests (Alvesson / Willmott 1992a, p. 6). With management, the modern organisation and business managers have managed to establish yet another group-based social hierarchy (Sidanius / Pratto 1999) primarily for the pursuit of their interests. In this sense, management is first and foremost about the power, interests, and ideology of management and managers; *managerialism is primarily not about management but about the dominance of managers!*

The prevalence of management over other discourses, the status and power of managers within organisations, and the institutionalisation of managerialism at a societal, even global level is all well known. Nonetheless, most investigations carried out so far into managers' roles have 'only' provided descriptions, analysis, or critique of managers' power. What we still need are *explanations*, theoretical concepts, to answer the question *"why and how do managers dominate our organisations?"* As Burrell (2002, pp. 32–33) put it: 'the growth of large-scale managerial hierarchies, coordinating diverse economic activities in the last century, is seen by many as one of the most significant politico-economic developments humanity has ever witnessed. How do we explain such developments?'.

The dominance of managers is a puzzle in at least three respects: historically, methodologically and theoretically.

Historically

In historical terms, it has been surprising that managers have become the rulers of organisations. Originally, as Marx described it, managers were 'special wage labourers' who were hired by capitalists to control and handle the new workforce of unskilled or semi-skilled workers. When the modern type of managers emerged, they had nothing:

- NO property, money, ownership or other legal rights (like the capitalists)
- NO titles or inherited privileges (like royals or aristocrats)
- NO spiritual or metaphysical leadership (like priests)
- NO special knowledge (like professionals or military leaders)
- NO strength in numbers (like the workforce)

Initially, managers' superior positions within (large) hierarchical organisations and their access to, and responsibilities for resources (including human resources) were enough to gain *some* influence. But it needs much more than this to become one of the dominant groups or ruling classes within society. In this long historical process, it is still surprising how dominant and hegemonic management and managers have become in the face of other aspirational social groups and professions. Although managers are still (special) employees (Jacques 1996, p. 87) and in the same formal contractual relationship with their employers (owners and shareholders) as they were many decades ago, they have made the transition from being the servants of capital to being (amongst) the new rulers. At this point in time, we still haven't really understood how comprehensive, differentiated and multi-dimensional the system which creates and guarantees the dominance of managers is. We still need to understand much more about the factors behind managers' epochal and global dominance.

Methodologically

Management and managers are nowadays so established that we take them for granted. The dominance of management and managers is apparently justified by their very existence; "management is necessary because things have to be managed and managers dominate organisations because organisations need managers". However, such 'explanations' are nothing else but a "naturalistic fallacy", i.e. the false assumption that things should be, because they are (as David Hume has explained in his 'Treatise of Human Nature' 1739–1740). In this sense the 'naturalistic explanation' (or even justification!) of management and managers—of *any* social institution or social event—does not hold sway. The prevalence of managers is neither self-evident nor necessary. *There is no necessity in the social realm!*

As indicated, managers came to power during a longer historical process. However, for the most of human history, large organisations and other social systems functioned (perfectly well) without managers. There are concepts and business models for organisations *without* dominating managers, and different contexts and times might produce very different understandings of what organisation and management (without managers) mean or could mean. Just because managers dominate so many of our contemporary organisations does not mean that this is, or should necessarily be the case. Hence, managerial dominance, and why and how managers rule, still needs to be explained.

Theoretically

Functional "explanations" (justifications) of management are not, however, convincing. Of course, from the very beginning the proponents of orthodox management and organisations studies have been keen to 'explain' and justify the prevalence of management and managers (e.g. Taylor, Fayol, Barnard, Dale, Drucker, Mintzberg, Porter). This is usually done by creating 'an image of the manager as a functionally necessary facilitator and coordinator of others' actions' (Willmott 1984, p. 353). Allegedly, managers' primary concern is getting things done in order to achieve the organisation's objectives. However, with regard to the phenomena they claim to explain, functional approaches are strangely narrow-minded and one-dimensional—a typical sign of positivistic approaches and attempts to provide science-like analysis.[4] Furthermore, the problem with all functional 'explanations' of social phenomena is that they, at best, describe the less important technical aspects of these phenomena. What they do not explain is why managers are there, why they do what they (allegedly) do or should do, why others do *not* manage, why others are *not* managers and why the relationships between managers and others are the way they are.

For example, for every functional 'explanation' of managers' roles, it could be said that either "others" could also fulfil these functions or that these functions could be organised in different, equally or even more efficient, ways. Functional approaches provide affirmative and normative descriptions of the status quo, but they rarely address the 'why?' (or 'why not?' or 'why not differently?'). However, such explanatory approaches (i.e. theories) are exactly what we need if we want to understand the reasons behind social phenomena such as organisations and (the dominance of) management and managers.

All in all, whether seen from a historical, methodological or theoretical point of view; the puzzle remains. *Why and how do managers dominate our organisations?* What is the basis for managers' success in the social competition of individuals and groups (within larger organisations)?

This book is about management, but even more about the dominance of managers. It will argue that the prevailing understanding of management and managers is only superficially about functional aspects. At its very core, management has been, and is, all about the power and control, interests and ideology of managers. It is about the dominance of managers over other groups of people. In order to investigate and explain this dominance, a multi-dimensional *'theory of social dominance of managers'* will be developed which is rooted in three explanatory factors: *power, interests and ideology*. These factors themselves will be analysed as comprehensive, multi-dimensional and interdisciplinary concepts in order to appropriately address the complex nature of managers' dominance.

There is a real need for such a theory. Since the early 1980s the concepts of *interests*, *power* and *ideology* have received less and less attention.[5]

- Individual and group 'interests' behind managerial decisions and attitudes are covered up by layers of so-called "functional" analysis.
- The 'power' of managers is largely ignored in orthodox management as a problematic issue and only addressed in Critical Management Studies and constructivist approaches.
- Mainstream management is allegedly "value-free", 'ideology' apparently something only communists, consumer groups, environmentalists or trade union representatives follow and use for their causes.

The idea that behind the orthodox understanding of management, managers' decisions and managers' actions lie very strong interests, power and ideology needs to be reinvigorated—particularly since managerialism has many devastating effects on organisations and people. In this sense, the book can be understood also as a polemic against social dominance, unjust social order, unjustified privileges and prerogatives, roles and social positions, power and influence of a particular group of people—*any* group of people. In so doing, this book contributes to attempts to look behind the obvious and tries to reveal some of the driving forces behind the ideology of management and the dominance of managers. In doing so, it contributes to the universal project of critical theory and enlightenment.

The whole line of argument developed here can be seen particularly in the tradition of Critical Management Studies (e.g. Brookfield 2005, Walsh / Weber 2002, Alvesson / Willmott 1992a, Willmott 1987, Knights / Willmott 1985), organisational politics approaches (e.g. Balogun / Johnson 2004, Cohen et al. 1999, Pettigrew 1992, Mintzberg 1985, Burns 1961), and a more general Weberian socio-philosophical reasoning (Weber 1921/1980). Sometimes, the argument made is also close to Social Dominance Theory (Sidanius et al. 2004, Sidanius / Pratto 1999). For more specific discussions it will primarily refer to

- multi-dimensional concepts of *power* (e.g. Clegg et al. 2006, Akella 2003, Courpasson 2000, Fincham 1992, Weber 1921/1980, Lukes 1974),
- socio-philosophical concepts of *ideology* (e.g. Thomas 1998, Hamilton 1987, Abercrombie et al. 1980, Therborn 1980, Weber 1921/1980) and
- socio-psychological concepts of *interests* (e.g. Darke / Chaiken 2005, Hendry 2005, Meglino / Korsgaard 2004, Ingram / Clay 2000, Miller 1999, Hindess 1986).

Based on these approaches, management and (the roles and activities of) managers will be investigated not as a set of 'neutral' functions, but as power-oriented, interest-driven, and ideology-based worldviews and actions of people within institutional settings.

For this, Chapter 2 will analyse the concepts of management and manager. It particularly provides a comprehensive description of managerialism in order to make the reader aware of how managerial our organisations (even our societies) have become and how serious the problem is. For this, a model of managerialism will be developed which identifies its core assumptions and elements. Based on this, it discusses positive and negative aspects of implementing managerialistic approaches in organisations. In addition, the chapter interrogates how 'the manager' can be defined and identified as a social construct within hierarchical organisations.

Chapter 3 provides a first set of explanatory variables for the dominance of managers. Here, the power of management and the management of power is systematically and comprehensively analysed. The social category of '*power*' is rarely openly addressed within discourses about managers. Often, it is either mystified or kept hidden under several layers of functional management ideology. In contrast, this chapter will demonstrate that most of managers' professional attitudes, decisions and actions can be explained (to some extent) by referring to the power-and-control dimension. To support this, several aspects of managerial power and control will be discussed, their implications investigated, and a complete, multi-dimensional concept of managerial power will be developed.

Another set of explanations for the dominance of managers can be found at the individual and group levels. Managerialism, like other social phenomena, does not come 'out of the blue'. Such a concept is formulated and justified, implemented and carried out by individual managers because they have an *interest* in it. For a whole range of reasons, managers want to dominate. In Chapter 4 therefore, it will be demonstrated that behind the dominance of managers lie very real and concrete interests. For this, a consistent and comprehensive concept of interests will be developed from a socio-philosophical perspective. It will be shown that managers' interests are not only about increasing a company's profit, market position or efficiency. In fact these are only the officially stated strategic goals. Managers care (even more) about their individual roles and careers, their position and influence within organisational politics, their personal background and aspirations, group interests and their influence within society.

Motives of managerial power and control (as well as managers' individual and group interests) are hardly attractive in terms of winning social and political support. When it comes to justifying their decisions and actions (as well as their positions and privileges in organisations), managers (like any other powerful group in history interested in pursuing their individual and group interests) are less keen to reveal the real underlying reasons. Hence, in order to conceal their real aspirations, they (have to) refer to 'higher values' e.g. increasing efficiency and productivity of the organisation; increasing the well-being of people; or securing the survival of the whole and the like. Against this backcloth, Chapter 5 identifies and analyses management as *ideology*. In order to do this, it investigates which definitions and criteria provide a sound basis for developing 'ideology' as a concept. Based on this, a whole range of ideological tools used by managers will be revealed, demonstrating how these tools together construct reality so that management is no longer even recognisable as ideology.

In Chapter 6 the three theoretical concepts of 'interests', 'power' and 'ideology' are drawn together into a *'theory of social dominance of managers'*. With the help of this theory, the full and comprehensive picture of managerial dominance becomes clearer. It will then be demonstrated that managers can be seen and portrayed as a dominant group within organisations, if not as one of 'the' ruling classes in our society.

Following this, Chapter 7 provides empirical evidence for the dominance of managers. It focuses on the ideologies, clashes of cosmologies, politics and power games played at senior management level during a strategic change initiative. It addresses managers' perceptions and sense-making, managerialistic strategies, attempts to centralise power and control, and cultural divides between powerful groups. It also critically reflects on the managerialistic concept of organisational change management, the justification of paternalistic leadership and managers' real interests behind strategic change initiatives. Finally, it sheds light on the consequences for employees, what organisational change and its management are really about and what people really resist.

Chapter 8 reflects, on a more general, socio-philosophical level, how organisations and management can and should be seen in a critical and enlightened manner. It explains what we need to do to free management from its ideological ballast and group interests in particular, and develop the study of organisations and management into a truly social science. Although the book does not explicitly address the possibility of alternatives to managerialism, Chapter 8 will at least mention some possible alternatives and what we can do in order to create less oppressive and more participative types of organisations.

To summarise, the first two chapters of the book together provide a *description and general analysis* of managerialism and the dominance of managers. Chapters 3 through 5 provide *explanations* for these phenomena by developing the concepts of managers' power, interests and ideology. These three concepts will be put together to a *theory of social dominance of managers based on interests, power and ideology* in Chapter 6. In this sense, Chapters 3 through 6 provide the theoretical framework for explaining and analysing managers' dominance within organisations. Chapter 7 will provide *empirical evidence* for the theory developed, while Chapter 8 provides some *critical reflections*.

What are the limits of the concepts and theory of the dominance of managers developed here? Firstly, it only encompasses the "Western", primarily US-American dominated understanding of management and managers. This may be justifiable since the bedrock of the ideology of management and the new breed of salaried managers can be seen largely in the United States (e.g. Shenhav 2003, p. 184, Protherough / Pick 2002, p. 10). Modern management theory has been developed and disseminated primarily by US-American management gurus (e.g. Taylor, Ford, Bearl / Means, Drucker, Porter, Chandler, Mintzberg), by US-American business schools via their MBA (master's of business administration) programmes (e.g. Harvard), and actively and aggressively promulgated through global US politics (European Recovery Programme, World Bank, Organisation for Economic Co-operation and Development [OECD]) (e.g. Barjot 2002, Grey 1999, p. 562). However, British, Australian, and Western European business schools have caught up since the early 1980s and have also become quite successful in spreading the word all over the world. Meanwhile, there are an increasing number of very successful business schools in Asia (particular in Hong Kong, Singapore, increasingly in India and China) which by and large follow the US-American and Anglo-Saxon model. In this sense, the book is a theory and critique of the "Western" / "Anglo-American" dominated understanding of orthodox management.

Secondly, this book should be understood as a *general* theory and critique of the dominance of managers and of orthodox management. The book does not address cultural, historical or regional differences. It does not investigate possible variations in managerial concepts because of different socio-economical, cultural or political conditions. And it also does not cover the possible variations in the explanatory basis, e.g. how the concepts of power, interest or ideology have emerged and have been interpreted within different cultural contexts. It therefore would be interesting to see work developed which concentrates more on empirical difference and which provides comparative analysis of these concepts in different cultural settings or historical context.

Finally, the book only provides a snapshot of the social dominance of managers, referring sparingly to historical processes and developments. It does not provide any basis for predicting future trends, societal or organisational conditions. Nonetheless, it is hoped that the book will be of some use to all who do not simply wish to contribute to an unjust, inefficient and narrow-minded present (or even to take advantage of such conditions), but see themselves in the grand tradition of enlightenment. Managers come and go, but the problem of unjust social conditions and social dominance still remains.

2 Managers and Managerialism

> The very idea of public institutions is under concerted attack. They
> need to be provided—and defended—collectively. Such things are
> anything but secondary. They are the defining characteristics of what
> it means to be a just society.
>
> *Apple (2005, pp. 18–19)*

INTRODUCTION

This chapter is about two problems: *What "is" a manager?* and *What "is"
management (about)?* Both questions have been answered primarily by prevailing orthodox management approaches, i.e. *managerialism*. Generally
speaking, managerialism is primarily concerned with two things: the establishment of management as a superior set of methods to solve problems and
the establishment of managers as superiors within social systems such as
private or public sector organisations. It is about emphasising *the primacy
of management* above all other rationales and activities and *the primacy of
managers* above all other groups within the organisation. According to this
view, managerial concepts and competencies are portrayed as superior to
any other concepts and competencies.

Moreover, according to orthodox approaches, management and managers are completely intertwined and co-existent. So it is especially managers
who benefit most from the introduction and dissemination of managerial
concepts—and most particularly 'the new breed of all-purpose "managers"' (Protherough / Pick 2002, p. 16). The primary interest of these managers is their concern with the 'primacy of management in organisations
and with the importance of management for management's sake' (Deem
/ Brehony 2005, p. 222). It is this 'equation of management with managers' (Grey 1999, p. 567) which draws the line in the sand, distinguishing between 'those who work, and those who plan, organize, coordinate,
and control work' (Kärreman / Alvesson 2004, p. 150). The image of 'the
manager' offers managers numerous opportunities to strengthen their position—in ideological as well as in practical terms. This is one of the prime
reasons why so many managers favour managerial concepts; they define
their social position and provide them with an ideological basis for their
claim that organisations shall and must be managed by managers (Deem
/ Brehony 2005, p. 221). What is officially portrayed as objective method
and functional analysis is in fact pure ideology, serving and advancing the
sectional interests of a specific group (Shrivastava 1986, p. 364, Burnham
1941, p. 25).

In this sense it doesn't come as much of a surprise that managers, like most other ruling classes or powerful groups of individuals, are first and foremost concerned with their individual status and influence and their aspirations and future prospects. There is empirical evidence that strategic change initiatives are used by many managers primarily to serve their individual ambition and tactical advantage, or for the advancement of their own personal interests such as career prospects, higher salaries or increases in their market value (Diefenbach 2005). Discourses about organisational change are to a large extent actually about the exercise of power and (centralised) control (Freiberg 2005, pp. 19–20, Hoggett 1996, p. 23). This is not only the case in so-called business or private organisations but also increasingly in public sector organisations. For example, Saunders (2006, p. 14) observed 'that our universities have been converted into political arenas in which this new generation of managers not merely compete and negotiate with one another for resources but also exercise powers their predecessors never had.' He also paints a very telling picture of this new breed of public sector managers (ibid., p. 14):

> For those who are neither dedicated teachers nor keen researchers, it is as if Moses had parted the Red Sea. Managerialism has created for such academics the means whereby they might not merely survive but thrive. Their entire way of life consists of mission statements, position papers and reviews of one sort or another; committee meetings, interviews and corridor discussions; phone calls, e-mails and memoranda amongst themselves; interstate conferences with other departmental heads and deans; graduation, prize and other ceremonies. Alliances are formed, favours are asked, deals are made, debts are owed, careers are advanced.

Who are exactly these managers? The purpose of this chapter is simply to provide a first rough sketch of management and managers together with some criticism of the core concepts of managerialism in order to introduce some ideas we explore in the rest of the book, including

- a concept for defining and identifying 'the manager',
- a brief look at some of the core ideas of (orthodox) management, and how managerialism fits into larger epochal trends,
- how organisational systems, structures and processes are designed to contribute to the management and control of organisations and
- how management and the managerial organisations transform employees into subordinates.

Finally, all these core aspects of managerialism will be put together into a single comprehensive framework. A comprehensive and thorough analysis of management and the development of a theory of managerial dominance then follow in Chapters 3 through 5.

A DEFINITION OF 'THE MANAGER'

This book is about *managers'* dominance, that is, it is about managers' power, interests and ideology. To a lesser extent, it is also about *employees'* lack of power and their compliance with managerial control against their other interests. Obviously, such a dichotomous view is not a true presentation of contemporary organisations and does not reflect the actual complexity of social systems. All larger hierarchical organisations (and societies) are factually much more differentiated than any dyadic view may suggest. Like every other ideology, the ideology of management creates, justifies and supports a whole micro-cosmos of social positions and their hierarchical relations. In the centre, there is usually 'the leader' and an inner circle of rulers, surrounded by a larger circle of still very powerful and influential leaders, which is in turn supported by an even larger, higher middle class quite distinct from 'the masses', which in themselves can be quite differentiated. And then there are 'the Others', i.e. outsiders and deviant people who nonetheless play a crucial part in and for the social system. Complex social systems and societies consist of several identifiable layers, often in double digits. Members of each layer therein are usually quite keen to distinguish themselves from lower layers while identifying themselves with the nearest and next higher layers. In the same way, complex organisations have many more hierarchical levels and possible groupings of social positions than simply 'managers' and 'non-managers'. The complexity of managerial organisations therefore raises the methodological question of *how to define the class of managers*[1] and *where the line can be justifiably drawn between managers and non-managers* (Grey 1999, p. 561, Zeitlin 1974, p. 1078).

The fact that the class of managers is highly differentiated in itself presents a further problem. They are not one coherent group and there are large in-group differences (e.g. Huddy 2004, pp. 950–951). For a start, managers are differentiated *horizontally*, i.e. along departmental and professional affiliations. For example, according to Willmott (1984, p. 350) 'managers not only meet resistance from subordinates but are often divided amongst, and even against, themselves . . . [based] upon their own sectional interests.' Some even identified that they had more 'internal struggles among managerial factions rather than with labor or external stakeholders' (Levy et al. 2001, p. 7). There is considerable empirical research on 'clashes of cosmologies amongst senior managers' (e.g. Diefenbach 2005) or competition and politics between managers at the same level and / or with different functions.[2] However, from a methodological point of view, the more important task is to identify and differentiate the class of managers *vertically*. By concentrating on vertical differences particularly within hierarchical organisations, it is possible to identify a continuum from the very top of senior management down to the lowest of all employees. And there are massive differences in managers' roles, responsibilities, power and influence depending on their position within the organisational hierarchy. We therefore need criteria to differentiate managers from non-managers hierarchically.

To start with, we can state that in any hierarchical system, a position is defined by its relation to the whole and its relation to others. The person holding this social role or position therefore has, or has not, responsibilities for the whole ('strategic responsibilities') and responsibilities for others ('line responsibilities'). 'Strategic responsibilities' mean the right and prerogative to be involved in making decisions which are relevant for the whole social system. This involvement can be at any stage of the process, either in the formulation or implementation of strategic issues. Strategic issues are about an organisation's purpose and aims ('mission and vision'); its strategic objectives ('how it does its business'); the allocation, use and development of resources within the organisation or organisational units (e.g. budget, tangible and intangible assets, structures and processes, functional units); and its performance measurement, management information and control systems. 'Line responsibilities' mean the set of official and formal rights to make decisions for others, i.e. one's subordinates. These decisions concern the nature, scope and relevance of subordinates' work and particular tasks. They involve setting criteria for making sense of, performing, controlling and assessing events, as well as the empowerment to use measures provided by the social system in order to influence subordinates directly or indirectly.

Most managerial responsibilities can broadly be subsumed under the headings of strategic responsibilities and line responsibilities. Hence, managers can be largely defined, and distinguished from non-managers by *their factual managerial responsibilities which come with their position within the hierarchical structure of an organisation*. All that comes along with such position and privilege accumulates to qualitative differences compared to other positions. The important divide,—at least when it comes to managers' dominance,—is between those who have managerial position and responsibility and those who don't.

According to this criterion, it is obvious that the senior management group also belongs to the class of managers. Top management's responsibilities are provided by organisational, and often even legal, regulations and requirements. The managerial elite (e.g. Pettigrew 1992, Hambrick 1989) represents the top level of every large organisation—private and public sector, governmental and non-governmental. These senior managers are identifiable through their titles e.g. Chairman, President, Chief Executive Officer, Managing Director, Division Managers, or any other 'Director of . . .'. Moreover, they represent quite a distinct group amongst all managers since they also operate as governance bodies (e.g. Board of Directors, executive committees, top management). It is *they* who formulate and decide (almost) all issues of strategic importance and communicate these further down the lines. And since senior managers are at the top of the organisational hierarchy, they are automatically provided with extensive line responsibilities.

Although also managers, 'middle management' in some respect is quite different. This group covers probably the most dispersed set of positions within the organisational hierarchy: from the lowest middle managers who have mostly operational tasks (e.g. shop managers, managers of small departments or other functional units); to the highest ranks of middle managers who are, indeed, members of the senior management team with all the associated functions and responsibilities (e.g. heads of larger departments, regional, product or brand managers, and the like). Middle managers are 'living in the organizational space between strategy and operations . . .' (Floyd / Wooldridge 1994, p. 50) and face role conflict and role ambiguity because of different, if not to say contradictory expectations (Currie / Procter 2005, p. 1351). When it comes to middle managers' roles in strategy development, Floyd / Wooldridge (1994, 1992) provide empirical evidence for their upward and downward contributions. Most middle managers are actively involved in the analysis and formulation of strategy (e.g. synthesising information and championing alternatives), as well as in the communication and implementation of strategy (e.g. facilitating adaptability, operationalising strategic objectives and measuring and monitoring performance etc.). Because of this 'broad participation in the strategic process' (Floyd / Wooldridge 1994, p. 51) and their related hierarchical positions and line responsibilities, middle managers therefore also belong to the class of managers.

In contrast, lower managers ('shop-floor managers') are not involved in the strategy process at all and have primarily operational roles. Most of them are solely occupied with operational tasks and are only equipped with the title of a manager in order to distinguish them from employees.[3] Their interests and concerns are mostly about the 'technical' aspects of their work. Their worldviews are likely to be much closer to employees than to middle managers, let alone senior management. Lower managers have got much more in common with other shop-floor employees, production-line workers or service personnel than with middle managers. Mentally (and often factually) lower managers belong more to the class of employees and workers than to the class of managers.

However, lower managers *do* have (some) line responsibilities. These managerial responsibilities are limited by the fact that they tend to manage their staff *directly and not through others*, i.e. they don't have line responsibilities over two or more hierarchical levels (Currie / Procter 2005, p. 1332). The direct nature of their managerial responsibilities and actions means that their power stems more from their task-oriented skills and experience or their personal attitudes. Nonetheless, even these limited line responsibilities put them into the formal position of a superior and provide them with managerial power. One might therefore also subsume lower managers into the class of managers.

In contrast, other groups may have strategic responsibilities, but not line responsibilities. For example, self-employed people, professionals, experts, project workers, even some project managers carry out the whole range of managerial tasks on a daily basis, and make important, often long-term and highly relevant decisions. These groups of people have strategic responsibilities but they are not formally superiors, i.e. they do not have line responsibilities. They are therefore not regarded as 'managers' according to the definition developed here.

All in all, managers can be defined via their managerial responsibilities within differentiated and hierarchical organisations. In this respect, regular involvement in strategic decisions, or at least having responsibility for linking strategic and operational issues is a good criterion to identify senior and middle managers. However, line responsibilities are a better criterion to comprehensively define and identify the whole social class of managers. In this sense, *a 'manager' is understood and defined as a person who has formal line responsibilities for at least one hierarchical level below him or her.* With this in mind, and for the sake of clarity, we here refer to 'managers' and 'employees'. As indicated above, the differentiation between 'managers' and 'non-managers' is used here only as an *analytical tool* to shed some light on the ideological construction and justification of the hierarchical order of organisations. In this sense, the analytical concept developed here doesn't claim that organisations factually comprise only two classes of people and are based on a strict division between management and worker (though this can be occasionally perceived in that way, e.g. during intensified industrial action); there is not a simple dichotomous divide between managers (who do the thinking and make decisions) and employees (who simply obey orders and do the work). Equally, there is no simple dichotomy that managers have (all) information, knowledge and freedom, while staff are tightly controlled by peer monitoring, self-appraisal, self-discipline and self-censorship. Depending on their hierarchical position, most managers are also being (closely) monitored and controlled, and have internalised self-discipline and self-censorship to such a large extent that it is only their "image" which seems powerful. Gabriel (1999, p. 186) rightly identifies that managers too 'are subject to organizations' totalizing controls, they too are colonized from within, they too are invited to buy in or get out, they too are subject to panoptic surveillance'. Managers are also part of the system (and also legally managers are employees, too). Therefore, in many respects managers are like everyone else; they are under the Damocles sword of externally set targets and indicators, internal control systems and measures, standards and procedures.

In this sense, when we talk about the 'dominance of managers' the social categories of manager / employee (or superior / subordinate) are not only meant in absolute, but more importantly in relational terms; within the hierarchical organisations there are many levels of superior / subordinate relationships. The division between managers and employees can therefore be better understood as a *continuum* along the hierarchy of roles and professional tasks. Along this continuum, prerogatives and privileges, responsibilities and resources, access to more crucial information and knowledge increase with the level of the position. The existence of this continuum means that the division (or great divide) between superior and subordinates is much more sophisticated and less obvious than in previous times or under different regimes. For example, employees much further down the organisational hierarchy actually believe that they are part of the same system, that they have real freedoms (within functional constraints) and that they even could do something else if they wanted. In reality, though, their work is planned and structured around management systems and their thinking remains set within the limits of the system.

However, to define and identify 'the manager' along the continuum of organisational hierarchy is one possibility. Another is to define them by how they see themselves—and accordingly act. Most managers have very similar sets of beliefs about the general ideas of management and managers, the associated image and responsibility, their roles, functions, positions and privileges, as well as how organisations and business (as well as employees) should function. Their *general* attitudes and professional behaviour are also very similar because they have similar individual life chances as managers and similar expectations (Nollmann / Strasser 2007, p. 384, Weeden / Grusky 2005, p. 141). More than their managerial position, which they have anyway, it is in fact *their managerial attitudes* which make them managers. At the same time, managers are all, like any other group, individually different. Their personal convictions, attitudes, beliefs and values, their power orientation, interests and how they think about managerial ideology can differ to a great extent. In fact, they can vary so much that they don't even see themselves as managers and, accordingly, do not demonstrate managerial attitudes—or at least not the ones orthodox management theory suggests. Not all managers believe in the usefulness and necessity of management as such, or in its basic assumptions, concepts and tools. However, since they are in a managerial position, they are still by definition managers—albeit possibly seen as incompetent managers (by themselves and others) compared to the currently prevailing orthodox image of 'the competent manager'.

This also draws attention to the fact that non-managers may or may not demonstrate managerial attitudes. If they don't do it they definitely do not belong to the group of managers. Probably more interesting is the case of people who are, at least initially, neither formally involved in strategic decision-making processes, nor have any line responsibilities. However, they may have internalised the ideology of management to such an extent, and adapted themselves to managerial attitudes, rhetoric and ideology with such intensity, that they can easily be regarded as managers. This could include professionals who may have made a "career-step" (or want to) and are now keen to demonstrate their "managerial skills and competencies" for whatever reason. Everyone has come across "political animals" within organisations who are very skilful at prowling the corridors, devising "important" initiatives and trying to motivate everyone in reach in order to demonstrate their "leadership" abilities. They can be found in every walk of life amongst professionals and knowledge workers, such as academics, lawyers or engineers, public sector workers or any other class of employees. These people use managerial concepts and believe in the ideology of management (at least publicly). They behave, talk and even try to walk like managers. Although this often may look quite funny, the underlying rationale, implications and consequences are more serious. But regardless of the outcome, this mindset and attitudes are sufficient reason to class such people as managers, or at least 'wannabee managers'.

All in all, there is the formal differentiation between managers and non-managers according to their position / line responsibilities. And there is also the mental differentiation between managers and non-managers according to their internalised values and belief systems and their demonstrated attitudes. The combination of both dimensions produces four possible categories, as the matrix below demonstrates.

Figure 2.1   A two-dimensional concept for the identification of 'the manager'.

Managers can be defined and identified via their position and / or their attitudes. In this sense, it doesn't make a difference whether managers are professional or incompetent. As long as they fulfil the formal criterion of position / line responsibilities, they still count as managers. In addition, the investigation into management and its dominance in this book also includes those people who are formally not managers, but whose value systems and attitudes make them managers—albeit 'wannabe' managers.

THE BUSINESS ENVIRONMENT—MANAGERIALISM AS PART OF AN EPOCHAL TREND

As indicated in the introduction, the ideology of management or managerialism has been around since the second half of the 19th century and has subsequently developed into not only an organisational but a societal value/belief system. The managerialistic or functionalist paradigm 'presumes the legitimacy of established managerial priorities and is dedicated to identifying more effective and efficient means for their realisation' (Levy et al. 2001, p. 1). This movement has been radical and total in its scope as well as in its intensity.

- It has been introduced not only into all *private* organisations but also into all *public* sectors including: government and governmental organisations, regional and local government, higher education institutions, health services, criminal justice system, police forces, the legal profession, and other professional service organisations (e.g. Kirkpatrick et al. 2005, McAuley et al. 2000, p. 89).
- It is an increasingly *global phenomenon* (Kirkpatrick et al. 2005, p. 13). It can be found in industrialised Western nations such as the United Kingdom and continental Europe, the United States and Canada, Australia and New Zealand (Torres 2004, Pina / Torres 2003, Mascarenhas 1993), but also in other industrialised and developing countries in South America, Asia and Africa (e.g. Lee / Haque 2006, Sarker 2005, Haque 1999).
- In the Anglo-Saxon and European countries at least, it has been supported by *all* (major) political parties and governments, e.g. by Republicans and Democrats, Conservatives and Labour, Liberals and even by the Green Party (e.g. Protherough / Pick 2002, pp. 19–27, Newman 2002, p. 234, Hood 1991, p. 6).

Managerialism seems to be capable of use 'in virtually any political setting, geographic region, or policy area' (Page 2005, p. 714). It had long ago reached *hegemonic status*. One of the reasons for this development is the fact that managerialism complements larger epochal trends which have dominated history for centuries. It represents the rationalisation of mankind's conduct of its own affairs, analysed so famously by Max Weber in 'Protestant Ethics and the "Spirit" of Capitalism' (1904/1993). This spirit achieved (very) material dominance in Manchester capitalism. The new order and new forms of production made traditional forms of controls (e.g. gang masters, physical punishment) increasingly insufficient and they required new, more efficient (sic!) forms namely management and the manager (Jacques 1996, p. 88). Out of this developed bureaucracy, war economies—which then changed into the large-scale production of consumer goods and service industries. Currently the trends are globalisation and neo-liberalism. But whatever the twist and turns of the changing and challenging business environment, whatever the epochal developments are, *more* management and *more* managers are (allegedly) always required. Management has been flexible enough to (actively) accompany all these developments and now fits perfectly to 'the new spirit of capitalism' (Chiapello / Fairclough 2002, p. 186), where even public sector organisations have to demonstrate market and profit orientation, professional management and the 'ethical change in governance from the traditional principle of public welfare to the commercial norm of value-for-money' (Haque 1999, p. 469). These changes in the ways organisations, people and whole societies now operate and function are part of a wider epochal societal trend—the "colonisation" or "economisation" of the lifeworld (Habermas, Fromm). Literally everything is, or has to be valued, judged and managed primarily according to its (factual or theoretical) market value. In this sense, managerialism simply supports the 'commodification of services' (Adcroft / Willis 2005, p. 386) and 'the commodification of every part of life' (Protherough / Pick 2002, pp. 156–157).

Proponents of managerialism do not only refer to such (alleged) environmental developments, they are also eager to portray them as natural forces at work within the natural order of things. The argument is whether or not someone likes what is going on in the environment, it is inevitable, irresistible and irreversible (Steger 2005, pp. 35–36). Private and public sector organisations *must* change in order to match the ever changing business environment; they must 'accept that they need to cope with the reality of change in order to be successful' (Karp 2005, p. 88). And, crucially, they can only change in the way managerialism and its proponents think is right because managerialism, too, is an "historical inevitability and necessity". What they don't usually mention is the fact that in the realm of social actions, institutions and society there is no such thing as 'inevitability'. Organisations as well as human beings *always* have a choice. Only ideologies refer to supposed 'laws of nature' that cannot (or should not) be changed or resisted.

Originally designed simply for managing and controlling the workforce within organisations, managerialism soon expanded to encompass wider external orientations so that it better reflected the organisational (business) environment and epochal trends discussed above (isomorphism). Three strategic outside orientations are usually emphasised:

1. *market and profit orientation* (commodification of services under the slogan of 'value for money'),
2. *stakeholder orientation* (meeting the objectives and policies particular of strong and influential external stakeholders) and
3. *customer orientation* (service delivery from a customer's perspective).

Of course, a greater awareness of developments in the environment and a greater responsiveness to such developments can indeed contribute much to improvements in organisations and their management. A market and profit orientation can help fit products and services better to requirements; a stakeholder orientation can contribute to higher levels of accountability; and a customer orientation might improve the quality of services. Nonetheless, the desperation with which the proponents of managerialism try to prove that their concept matches external prevailing values and institutions also produces some serious downsides for organisations.

For example, while creating new value along the lines of efficiency, quantification and monetarisation, managerialism at the same time ignores, reduces, damages or even destroys many other values. These include e.g. the collective organisation of work, traditional work ethos, and work-life balance. Moreover, for public services, it also destroys commitment to impartiality, social equality, integrity, equity and communitarian values, as well as a care for the qualitative dimensions and the uniqueness of each individual and individual case, and the socio-philosophical ideas of citizenship, representation, neutrality, welfare and social justice (e.g. Brookfield 2005, p. 165, Kirkpatrick et al. 2005, pp. 3, 48, Haque 1999, pp. 448–469, Hoggett 1996, p. 14). In doing so, it strongly goes against the idea that public services are 'universal entitlements and should be provided regardless of the gravity of need, cost or ability to pay' (Kirkpatrick et al. 2005, p. 46), and the ethos of 'provision of services on the basis of need rather than on the basis of ability to pay' (ibid., p. 167). This is such a devaluation of ethical values, goods and services, and of traditional private and public sector principles on such a large scale that it has historical dimensions.

The orientation towards stakeholders comes with similar consequences. Although the original concept identifies a whole range of internal and external stakeholders and suggests that their interests are addressed equally based on ethical values, a managerial or 'business-like' management of stakeholder interests (e.g. Johnson et al. 2006, pp. 181–182) differs quite significantly. It concentrates on meeting the targets and requirements only of strong and influential external stakeholders who have a vested interest in the organisation (e.g. the government or funding bodies). At the same time, less powerful and influential stakeholders, e.g.

(poorer) citizens, communities, NGOs representing social groups or the natural environment—get little or even no attention.

Finally, customer orientation is also quite problematic. It can be mere lip service—for example, when large quasi-monopolistic companies refer to private households, universities their students, or hospitals to their patients as '(our) customers'. However, the idea of a 'customer' of public services can be also meant seriously. In this case it is used in sharp contrast to the idea of citizen. A citizen is perceived more as a conscious and politically active member of the state and community. He or she is interested in public affairs, the welfare of the whole and others (Gabriel 1999, p. 404). Public sector organisations would have to do much more in order to address the multi-dimensional expectations of 'the citizen'. By contrast, the consumer simply demands the prompt delivery of a specific service for his or her own needs. And whereas the citizen could make his or her claims on the basis of broad set of philosophical values, the customer, again, can only claim on the basis of a narrowly defined 'supply/demand-concept' and the strength of his or her own position within this setting. The 'normative change from the democratic value of citizenship to the market criterion of customer satisfaction, . . . has shifted its attention away from the needs and concerns of common citizens to the demands and interests of affluent customers, especially the local business elites and foreign investors' (Haque 1999, p. 469).

All in all, managerialism's external orientations have already changed organisations quite dramatically. It has become all about products and services designed to the specifications of powerful stakeholders and offered to affluent customers who are willing and able to pay for them—and all within the narrowly defined settings of factual or artificially created market mechanisms in line with the epochal trends of capitalism and globalisation. This is even more regrettable when it comes to the public sector which has lost its administrative neutrality (Gawthrop 1999, p. 427):

> The language of buyer and seller, producer and consumer, does not belong in the public domain; nor do the relationships which that language implies. Doctors and nurses do not 'sell' medical services; students are not 'customers' of their teachers; policemen and policewomen do not 'produce' public order. The attempt to force these relationships into a market model undermines the service ethic, degrades the institutions that embody it and robs the notion of common citizenship of part of its meaning (David Marquand, cited in Apple 2005, p. 18).

But it is also true for many private organisations. In the context of managerialism, market, profit, stakeholder and customer orientations are flawed and limited concepts. With its external orientations and objectives, it serves very limited and artificially created aspects. Even at the level of strategic objectives, managerialism can barely deliver what it promises.

ORGANISATIONAL STRUCTURES AND PROCESSES OF MANAGEMENT AND CONTROL

Despite their own confidence, the proponents of managerialism are not wholly convinced that their claims for the primacy of management and managers (within organisations) are self-evident to everyone. Even references to 'natural' laws and development are not felt to be sufficient. This is the case with every ideology that tries to explain and justify an unequal hierarchical social order. Managerialism, therefore, is much concerned with *guidance* and *control*—specifically: *paternalistic* guidance and *top-down* control by managers (Kirkpatrick et al. 2005, pp. 68, 91, 161), and even the control of control (Sanderson 2001, pp. 301, 305). Most, if not all management systems within organisations are control systems. Such control systems and procedures derive from the very direct managerial control of the early days of capitalism: technological control along the assembly line, elaborated bureaucratic control systems up to today's sophisticated electronic performance management and measurement systems and the creation of the 'electronic panopticon' (Rothschild / Ollilainen 1999, p. 605, Jermier 1998, p. 246) in addition to all the other traditional systems still in use. The means may change, but the purpose remains the same.

With managerialism, organisational control and performance management and measurement systems have reached new highs (or lows, as we will see). There have always been bureaucratic systems of control and monitoring in organisations, but with the development of new management methods since the early 1980s, a whole range of additional systems and processes (of auditing, control, regulation, assessment, inspection and evaluation) were introduced. These have included industry and quality standards, 'best practice concepts', benchmarking, league tables, customer feedback mechanisms, Balanced Scorecard (and the like), quality assessments, performance reviews, staff appraisal, and so on. People nowadays live and work under a 'constant performance evaluation' (Kärreman / Alvesson 2004, p. 157).

Performance management and measurement systems always have both a *political dimension* (i.e. ideology, interests and power) and a *technological dimension* (i.e. functions, functionality). We will return to these issues in Chapters 3 through 5. Here, we discuss some of their core *methodological* aspects and implications. At first glance, there seem to be plenty of good reasons for using extensive performance management and measurement systems in private and public sector organisations. To systematically capture, measure, monitor and assess crucial aspects of organisational and individual performance will lead to positive consequences such as increased efficiency and effectiveness, productivity and cost-effectiveness, and higher performance and motivation (e.g. Freiberg 2005, p. 31). Additionally, explicit targets, standards and performance indicators ensure that management can be based on 'facts' and a rational basis. This increases opportunities to hold people accountable and to reduce 'illegitimate privileges'

(Courpasson 2000, p. 153). Overall, such systems seem (on the surface) to be much fairer than the 'old' systems of either no performance measurement at all, bureaucratic systems, or 'old boys / old girls networks'.

However, there seems to be serious problems with the whole idea. Just as in the heyday of Taylor's Scientific Management, there now seems to be kind of a *'measurement fever'*. Literally everything which can be measured will be measured and will be seen as relevant from a managerial perspective. Performance measurement and quantitative data: 1) set the agenda, 2) decide the objectives, 3) define what is relevant, 4) define what is *not* relevant and 5) shape how people (have to) think and act accordingly.

This *'measure mania'* has far-reaching negative consequences for organisations, the people who work in them and the services which are being provided (e.g. Butterfield et al. 2005). For example, despite serious attempts to develop multi-dimensional systems which capture more aspects than simply the financial or technical (e.g. Balanced Scorecard), the performance measurement approach is still limited both in its breadth and depth. Even with the most elaborated performance measurement systems, only a few intangible assets, core capabilities or value drivers can be quantified and measured by 'hard' indicators. Despite the modern design of such systems, they fall back on the prioritisation of very orthodox measures, such as efficiency and productivity, costs and technical performance (e.g. Kirkpatrick et al. 2005, p. 67, Pollitt 1990, p. 138). Managerial performance measurement systems are designed to capture and measure only *particular* aspects and results (measurable outputs), which are relevant only for *particular* strategic orientations and objectives (market and profit orientation). These correspond only with a *particular* understanding of performance, efficiency, productivity and accountability (quantitative absolute and relative results), which can and should be managed, achieved and controlled only in *particular* ways (top-down and linear) by a *particular* group of people (managers).

Such narrow-mindedness leads to further negative effects—especially for those aspects which are not quantifiable (Wilenski 1988, p. 218). Whether automatically ignored by the system or deliberately neglected by the proponents of managerial control systems, most of the intangible assets and traditional values are not captured by the performance radar. These include e.g. many aspects of human, social and organisational capital (i.e. skills and knowledge, forms of co-operation, knowledge sharing and development). And what about fairness, dignity, equality, justice, quality of life, security, freedom, representation, participation, commitment, trust or creativity? Or communities of practice, internal co-operation and (informal) knowledge sharing, innovation, social impact or usefulness of initiatives (Kirkpatrick et al. 2005, p. 67, Diefenbach 2004, Pollitt 1990, pp. 60, 138, Wilenski 1988, p. 218)? All of these, as well as similar aspects and values are seriously threatened by managerialism and may already have been significantly damaged (Pollitt 2000, p. 195). They are devalued and discredited, portrayed as not being important or only of instrumental use. They are ignored or treated as constraints and obstacles organisations have to overcome. The whole idea of efficiency and measurement devalues *any* qualitative values and aspects whatsoever. Due to this widespread efficiency and measurement fever, many services actually get worse. The *overall* performance of organisations does *not* increase (e.g. Butterfield et al. 2004, p. 413, Staw / Epstein 2000, Carson et al. 1999, p. 329);—on the contrary, it decreases.

All in all, it can be concluded that, despite the impressive designs and mountains of data gathered and generated, performance management and measurement systems do not deliver what the proponents of managerialism promise. On the contrary, most of the systems make things worse on the ground where the real work takes place, while at the same time giving different, if not in fact false impressions at the abstract level of generated and aggregated data.

Managerialism is also concerned with changing organisational structures and processes. According to its proponents, one of the primary objectives of re-structuring organisations is *de-centralisation* in order to achieve more flexible structures and less hierarchy. This is accompanied by a *concentration on processes*, particularly the intensification of internal cross-boundary collaboration, the acceleration of decision-making processes and of putting things into action. Thirdly, these attempts are supported by the *standardisation and formalisation* of strategic and operational management through widely accepted management concepts such as scenario planning, SWOT-analysis, business and unit plans, and the like. Again, there might be good reasons for such ideas, particularly if (rightly or wrongly) the "old" organisation is seen as a slow, over-formalised, compartmentalised, inefficient, red-tape-producing bureaucracy. According to such a position, many organisational structures and processes could be improved dramatically. Such changes would produce positive outcomes such as faster decision-making, reduced compartmentalisation ('silo-mentality') and internal barriers; intensification and improvement of internal communication and cross-boundary collaboration; and faster delivery of products and services.

However, although this looks good on paper, it seems, like many other concepts and great plans, to be too good to be true. Indeed, organisational reality is often very different from the official agenda. For example, change management initiatives on the basis of managerialism lead to de-centralisation only in a few areas—usually those areas and tasks which are operational, of secondary importance or unpopular (Pollitt 1990, pp. 55–57). At the same time, shifts towards the creation of operationally de-centralised units are accompanied by 'simultaneous attempt[s] to increase centralized control over strategy and policy' (Hoggett 1996, p. 9). There is widespread empirical evidence for the fact that 'contemporary managerial strategies try to create new forms of centralisation' (Courpasson 2000, p. 157). This is particularly true of activities which are crucial for the organisation as a whole (e.g. strategy, policy, planning, setting of strategic objectives, financial and performance targets, budget, standards, performance measurement and management information systems) (e.g. Diefenbach 2005, Hellawell / Hancock 2001, p. 192, Sanderson 2001, p. 300, Considine 1990, p. 169, Pollitt 1990, pp. 115–116). De-central-isation leads to centralisation, with more hardened structures (between the centre and the periphery) and more hierarchy. In short, it is about concentration and centralisation of *power* (Courpasson 2000, pp. 156–157).

The same paradoxical outcomes occur when we look at attempts to trim down bureaucracy and red tape, whether in over-complex standards and procedures or redundant structures and processes. Despite many well-meaning attempts, managerialism often generates even more of the plague it claims to be fighting. There is widespread evidence of the 'swelling tides of bureaucracy' (Protherough / Pick 2002, p. vii) *emerging* from new managerial structures and processes and increasing evidence for greater formalisation and bureau-cratic routines (e.g. Hoggett 1996, p. 23). As a direct result, frontline staff have less and less time to do their primary tasks (Butterfield et al. 2005, p. 335). For most staff in a practical sense, such systems simply mean additional work and a decline in efficiency and effectiveness. Hoggett (1996, pp. 27–28) gives quite a vivid description:

> Excessive formalisation has proved to be organisationally dysfunc-tional, creating new layers of bureaucracy engaged in contract speci-fication and monitoring, quality control, inspection, audit and review and diverting the energies of professional staff away from service and program delivery into a regime of form-filling, report writing and procedure following which is arguably even more extensive than that which existed during the former bureaucratic era.

Other findings support this. For example, Kirkpatrick et al. (2005, p. 115) describe 'numerous studies reveal how social workers now devote an increasing proportion to their time to administrative tasks associated with completing forms and recording information' and they criticise 'the grow-ing burden of red tape' (p. 175).

By referring to only a few organisational aspects such as (de-) centralisa-tion and (de-) bureaucratisation we again find evidence that managerialism produces real outcomes quite in contrast to its original claims and objectives. There might be some improvements in the reduction of compartmentalisation and internal barriers, in the intensification of internal communication and cross-boundary collaboration, and an acceleration of decision-making and putting things into action. But at the same time, these are more than neutra-lised by an increase in bureaucracy, formal requirements, and more complex relations between the centre and periphery, all of which lead to an increase in the mis-allocation of time and resources (e.g. Protherough / Pick 2002, p. vii, Hoggett 1996, p. 27–28). Combine this with organisational systems of managerial control and surveillance, and with performance and measurement systems, and the actual managerial organisation is far less impressive than it is portrayed.

TURNING EMPLOYEES INTO SUBORDINATES

Besides management (and managers themselves), the business environment and organisational systems, employees are the fourth big area of concern. The ideas of orthodox management and the role of managers have a massive impact on employees and on corporate culture; nowadays orthodox management makes the case for empowerment and subsidiarity. Staff is expected to develop 'business-like', pro-active, if not entrepreneurial attitudes. Modern organisations are, allegedly, very much about developing a supportive and enabling corporate culture, encompassing teamwork, knowledge sharing and cross-boundary collaboration. This is, of course, only one part of the story. The other part is less optimistic. There is empirical evidence of rising levels of stress (Kirkpatrick et al. 2005, p. 176) brought about because orthodox management concepts create much more challenging *internal* environments and working conditions (Newton 2003, p. 434). Many staff regard most senior management talk about new management and strategic change initiatives simply as paying lip service (Pollitt 1990, p. 85). They become disillusioned and cynical because 'for many staff the talk of a shared organisational mission, commitment to quality and customer responsiveness flies in the face of their experience of increased class sizes, inadequate nursing cover, disappearing job security, voluntary and compulsory redundancies, etc' (Hoggett 1996, p. 23). There is widespread demoralisation of employees and a deep resentment and suspicion of the way they are being treated by their superiors (Pollitt 1990, p. 178). Kirkpatrick et al. (2005, p. 5) come to the conclusion: 'Efforts to induce change have now lasted more than two decades, and the human and the financial costs have been large. One might point for example to the stultifying effect of new management systems for controlling and monitoring practice (. . .). Also of concern is the trend towards work intensification in many areas, rising levels of stress, staff demoralisation and employee turnover . . . .' In many organisations staff morale is at rock bottom. The deterioration of working conditions *because of* the introduction of new managerial methods has reached epidemic scales. People are simply fed up to follow yet another change initiative 'pro-actively'.

The reasons why these aspects are not more obvious and debated more intensively are several, but one is that people have learned to play the game. They *had* to learn to play the game; 'Clearly, many individuals and groups have become highly adept at impression management whilst others have become equally skilled in the art of performing to target, even though this may run counter to the need to do the right job' (Hoggett 1996, p. 24). People learn how to deliver the information required by 'the system', how to cope and deal with objectives, deadlines and indicators, how to give the right impression, how to demonstrate the attitudes which are required and how to manipulate the system (e.g. Butterfield et al. 2005, p. 338, Butterfield et al. 2004, p. 412, Zaleznik 1989, p. 105).

Although this might be interpreted as subversive, it is in fact exactly what the initiators and implementers of such systems want. Paradoxically, stressed and de-motivated, 'unable' and / or 'unwilling' employees fit very well into the ideological framework of managerialism! Such responses underline the necessity of *more* policies and procedures, of *more* systematic performance measurement and appraisal, of *more* monitoring and advising, of *more* 'leadership' and 'motivation'—and so completely underline the importance and necessity of managerial concepts and managers. It is always 'the staff' who are either not able or not willing to adapt to the new order, and it is therefore the responsibility of managers to improve their change capabilities (Karp 2005, p. 88). Resistance and dissatisfaction are seen by the proponents of managerialistic concepts as simply another reason and justification for applying more of their methods and for initiating yet another change initiative—and above all for the roles *they* play. As Willmott (1997, p. 1353) explained: 'Rubbishing the workforce as short-sighted and self-interested enables managers to secure and sustain their position and prerogative as the sole trustees and defenders of "business objectives" who, according to their self-serving rhetoric, are not "self-interested."' In this sense, managerialism has strong 'pedagogic' functions. It defines the frameworks within which people think and act. They shape people's attitudes and behaviour—what they strive for and in which ways, how they are evaluated, how they behave and even what they become (e.g. Kärreman / Alvesson 2004, p. 169, Hoggett 1996, p. 20). If properly guided and managed, employees can understand and fit into the new regime. All that is needed to make the new concepts work is more leadership and guidance, management and control. And all that is wanted is that people function, i.e. think and act *within* the boundaries set by the system. Managerialistic managers therefore want employees to function as true subordinates. For example, Saunders (2006, p. 17) draws the attention to the fact that 'the typical university in today's Australia wants staff who do what they are told rather than those who think independently or might behave in an eccentric or idiosyncratic way. "Collegiality" is lauded in theory but cronyism and conformity, even moral cowardice and sycophancy, are rewarded in practice.' In this sense, 'business-like' leadership and management are defined and understood as the hierarchical and paternalistic concepts of leaders who are knowledgeable, insightful and skilful—and those who aren't, hence, need 'guidance'. In the end, managerialism is not about empowerment but about the infantilisation of employees.

In summary, managerialism changes the corporate culture and working conditions for employees within private and public sector organisations much more and in a much more negative sense than it is claimed from its proponents. It changes employees much more than it is claimed or realised. Empirical findings show repeatedly and consistently that the impact of organisations on employees and corporate cultures comprises a whole range of negative psycho-sociological and organisational effects. For example, increases in occupational stress, illness, low morale, decline in job satisfaction and motivation, alienation, fear and resentment are quite common. This is compounded by the distorting intellectual effects of writing for audit, a competitive, adversarial and punitive ethos, and punishing as well as wasteful, stressful, over-bureaucratic and expensive audit procedures. These, and other conditions, lead to increased tensions, more distrust between people, forms of symbolic violence and institutional bullying and a rougher working climate, all brought about by an invisible net of managerial power and domination (e.g. Saunders 2006, p. 9, Diefenbach 2005, Morley 2005, p. 86–87, Parker / Bradley 2000, p. 126, Hoggett 1996, p. 24).

CONCLUSIONS

Managerialism might have been developed and disseminated for good reasons. It may have stemmed from initial ideas critiquing large bureaucracies, paternalism, the nanny state and the dependency culture (Newman 2002, p. 234), and a growing disappointment with the poor quality and high prices of goods and services offered by inefficient private and public sector organisations (e.g. Kirkpatrick et al. 2005, p. 53, Pollitt 1990, p. 138) combined with realistic hopes that organisations can function and be run in much better ways. Whatever the real reasons behind managerial concepts, their introduction in private and public sector organisations all over the world has led to quite a few, often dramatic improvements—particularly, when one compares managerial organisations with 'traditional' types of administration and bureaucracy (understood in a negative sense).

However, as this chapter has demonstrated, there are also many good reasons to criticise the concept. Orthodox management can firstly be criticised because of its many inconsistencies, one might even say hypocrisies. For example, on the one hand it aims at institutionalising the idea of change as an organisational capability ('change for the sake of change'). On the other, it also strives for standardisation and formalisation of strategic and operational management. Centralisation (of activities crucial for the organisation as a whole, e.g. strategy, policy, budget, standards or information systems) is simultaneously introduced with de-centralisation. More management layers are created at the same time as claims for less hierarchy. New regulations accompany plans for deregulation. The principles of empowerment and subsidiarity are announced even while more hierarchical structures and taylorised processes, formalised surveillance- and control-systems are being implemented. Staff are expected to develop 'business-like', pro-active attitudes. Yet at the same time, employees' tasks, attitudes and performances are more systematically defined, closely monitored, regularly appraised and tightly controlled by a new breed of managers.

In the following chapters we will see what lies behind such inconsistencies and hypocrisy. In this chapter, the aim was to first identify our basic assumptions and the core elements of managerialism. The following table provides an overview.

Table 2.1   Basic Assumptions and Core Elements of Managerialism

Area	Elements and assumptions
1. Management and managers	• establishment of a 'management culture': management is defined as a separate and distinct organisational function • emphasis on the primacy of management compared to all other activities and competencies • managers can be identified by their 'strategic responsibilities', but primarily by their 'line responsibilities' (formal differentiation), but also by their attitudes (mental differentiation) • 'managers' are defined as the only group and individuals who (can) carry out managerial functions (equation of management with managers)
2. Business environment	• managerialism has reached hegemonic status • managerialism fits well to epochal trends of capitalism, globalisation, commodification, and economisation of the lifeworld (isomorphism) • much more challenging and changing business environment • inevitability of external changes • market and profit orientation: commodification of services under the slogan of 'value for money' • stakeholder orientation: meeting the objectives and policies (only) of strong and influential external stakeholders • customer orientation: service delivery from a customer's perspective
3. Organisational structures and processes	• importance of paternalistic guidance and top-down control systems • standardisation and formalisation of strategic and operational management through widely accepted management concepts • systematic, regular and comprehensive capturing, measurement, monitoring and assessment of crucial aspects of organisational and individual performance through managerial control, performance management and measurement systems • management based on 'facts' and a rational basis because of explicit targets, performance indicators and measurable outcomes • very specific and narrow design of control and performance measurement systems • increased organisational efficiency, effectiveness, and productivity defined and measured (only) in technological terms • devaluation and neglect of many non-quantifiable aspects of social systems • de-centralisation and re-organisation of organisational units, centralisation of key functions
4. Employees	• staff is expected to develop 'business-like', if not entrepreneurial attitudes • idea of leadership and a new corporate culture

Managerialism is not only an inconsistent and poorly defined theoretical concept but also has very real implications and consequences for organisations and the people working there. Some of the major ones are the following:

- Management is established as a strong ideology dominating any other professional orientation. Managers are the main beneficiaries of the introduction of managerialism and simply see it as a great opportunity to further increase their power and control, influence and personal advantages.
- A limited understanding of organisational orientations (such as 'business-like' market, profit, stakeholder and customer orientations), narrow concepts of efficiency and productivity, effectiveness and cost reduction have superseded traditional values (such as public welfare, community and needs orientations, or public service ethos).
- Performance measurement and management systems have serious methodological and strategic problems. They concentrate on quantifiable, narrow, often inadequate indicators and contribute to a further ignorance, devaluation or even destruction of many intangible assets and values. In practical terms, they often simply add to an increase in workload and psychological pressures.
- Attempts to improve organisational structures and processes often lead to further increases in bureaucratisation, formalisation, and centralisation.
- The great majority of employees suffer because of greater workload and stress, declining motivation and work satisfaction, tighter regimes of management, advice, measurement, control and supervision. In many organisations, managerial concepts have led to a deterioration of the corporate culture, traditional work ethos and non-functional values.

In sharp contrast to the claims made by its proponents, management's serious negative consequences outnumber the positive outcomes by far. Despite all the buzzwords and promises, managerial approaches actually raise far more questions and problems for organisations and the people working for them than they solve (Carson et al. 1999, p. 329). For example, managerialism 'is in sharp opposition to the traditional democratic values of public administration, such as political democracy, public ethics and security of life and property' (Skålén 2004, p. 251). It is a 'sinister new orthodoxy' (Protherough / Pick 2002, p. vii), a so-called business-like strategy that bulldozes traditional ideas, values and attitudes that do not fit. As I have concluded elsewhere (Diefenbach 2005, p. 135): 'There seems to be little awareness amongst the proponents of new public management that strategic and change management approaches that seem to happen "according to the management books" *do not cope* with problems but *they are the problem*! The impacts of managerialism on and consequences for organisations, people, and whole societies might be even worse than we can see already.' At present we are witnessing the devaluation, if not to say destruction of values and goods at a global scale. At the same time, these negative developments are being used by many managers to introduce even more managerial methods, and, in so doing, to establish and further secure their own positions and interests. Once this vicious circle of causing problems and introducing so-called cures is set in motion, there can be only one result: *sustainable and (almost) irreversible damage to our organisations and societies.*

As we will see later, managerialism is a movement, an ideology particular for the advantage of its fiercest proponents and most uncritical followers. Career-oriented managers especially have vested interests in this concept because it primarily serves *their* interests and dramatically strengthens *their* position and influence. With the development and introduction of management during the past three decades, 'a new 'hierarchy of legitimation' has emerged in which discourses of 'managerialism and business' are now hegemonic' (Kirkpatrick et al. 2005, p. 3). In their current form, managerial concepts are not simply contrary to the interests of the large majority of people working in organisations, but to the interests of democratic societies. It is high time that we started to seriously question and challenge the claims and assumptions which the proponents of this ideology make. And it is high time to stop this ideology and look for alternatives. In Chapters 3 through 6 we will develop a framework and theory for explaining and analysing orthodox management and the dominance of managers. The validity of the theory will be demonstrated in Chapter 7 which will provide comprehensive and telling evidence in form of a case study. In Chapter 8 we will finally discuss how critical approaches can contribute to challenging prevailing ideology and power relations and help in the development of alternatives.

3   Power and Control within Organisations

> All national institutions . . . appear to me no other than human inventions set up to terrify and enslave mankind and monopolize power and profit.
>
> —Thomas Paine, 1794 (cited in *Kramnick* 1995, p. 175)

INTRODUCTION

One of the constituting principles of hierarchical organisations, perhaps of any social system, is *power*. Power forces people to do certain things in a particular way (or not to do certain things). Power controls people and it is power which keeps social institutions, structures and processes going—for better or worse. And power means *powerful* actors—who in the case of contemporary organisations are mostly managers.

The times when power in organisations was primarily based on crude physical and despotic means are, allegedly, long gone—at least in most business sectors and organisations in developed economies. With the emergence of the so-called new economy and the development of modern management since the second half of the 20th century, it seems that the concepts and means of power and control have changed to a great extent. According to the dominating orthodox / functional approaches within management and organisation studies (e.g. Zaleznik 1989, Chandler 1977, Drucker 1954, Fayol 1949), contemporary organisations seem to be almost 'power-free' (Lacey 2007, p. 131). They are portrayed as rationally designed enterprises, functioning smoothly because of established policies and procedures, elaborated structures and sophisticated processes. *Orthodox management and organisation studies* claim to cope primarily (if not solely) with the functional and technical aspects of organisations and management. They are predominantly about the efficient performance and management of systems and the whole organisation—all described and analysed in functional, and (allegedly) value-free, objective ways with little mention of power at all (e.g. Yanow 2007).[1]

Even when they are explicitly about people it seems that so-called modern concepts of managerial leadership (organisational learning, teamwork and projects, empowerment and 'intra-'preneurship) make the old concepts of power and control (almost) obsolete. For a large part of their time, most managers are allegedly concerned with 'leading', 'enabling', 'communicating' and 'supporting' their staff, their work and skills development. Yes, staff also have to be controlled and supervised, appraised, guided and sometimes even dismissed, but all this must be done in accordance with the organisation's policies, modern human resource management concepts and 'investors in people' standards. The main roles and functions of managers are largely not about power and control, but about initiating, facilitating and supervising in order to guarantee the efficient achievement of organisational objectives (Townley 1993, p. 223). Whether for structures or for people, according to orthodox management approaches, 'power' is *un-normal* (and unreal). It lies either with powerful leaders (who are so powerful and so distant from our ordinary lives and thoughts that we cannot grasp their power) or it enters our lives as a negative issue through the backdoor of organisational politics, to be dismissed and combated. In the 'normality' of organisational life (if there is such a thing), managers' power and influence are not "official" issued.

In contrast, Critical Management Studies explicitly addresses the issues of (managerial) power and control.[2] Their concern is to demonstrate that management is anything but value-free and neutral, and to reveal interests behind systems of power and control. For example, Rosen (1984, p. 305) explained that the very concepts of 'manager' and 'management' are 'social artifacts reflecting the social relations, or power order, in our society, based on hierarchical segmentation and value appropriation.' Managers particularly are identified as powerful actors who use a range of power in order to pursue their own and powerful stakeholders' interests. From a critical perspective, this is about the identification, critique and change of (dominant) ideologies, managerial power and oppressive social structures. Power has to be identified, unmasked and overcome. According to Max Weber's famous definition, power means 'any ability to impose one's own will in a social relationship, even against opposition, regardless of what this ability is based on' (Weber 1921/1980, p. 28, own translation). The 'ability to impose one's own will' is largely interpreted as the ability to control the actions and non-actions of others (e.g. Mechanic 1962, p. 351). In this sense, power is regarded as relative and relational. The so-called standard theory of power (Turner 2005, p. 2) thus sees power primarily as a constituent part of social relations between people, a structural component of any social relationship (e.g. Spierenburg 2004, p. 627, Zeitlin 1974, p. 1090), hence manager-employee or, more generally speaking, superior-subordinate relationships. Although this understanding still constitutes the core of theories of power,[3] multi-dimensional concepts have been developed. In his widely referenced conceptual analysis of power, Lukes (1974, pp. 11–25) has linked three different dimensions of power:

1. one-dimensional view (behavioural, i.e. one person's power over another person),
2. two-dimensional view (institutional, i.e. a person or group of people has managed to get their values and beliefs as the prevailing ones of a social system), and

3. three-dimensional view (hegemonic, i.e. even the subordinates think that the prevailing norms and values reflect their interests).

In this sense, it is not only understood that managers "have" the power in organisations (e.g. Watson 2006, p. 44, Akella 2003, Burnham 1941) and 'enjoy a monopoly over processes of decision-making' (Thomas 1998), but that managers are *institutionally* empowered. They are embedded in the hierarchical structures of organisational, social and economic relations which support the legitimacy of their roles and positions (Finkelstein 1992, p. 508, Willmott 1987, p. 253) and indeed the very *idea* of 'being a manager'.

These last points indicate that social phenomena such as managers' power are not a "given", but are socially constructed. In this sense, *linguistic, post-modern and constructivist approaches* contribute to our understanding of organisations as shaped by human perceptions and knowledge, discourses and rhetoric, organisational politics and struggles for dominance and power.[4]

From such a discourse analysis and interpretative perspective, managers' power is seen as based on systems of symbols, language, narratives, texts, perceptions, discourses, interpretations, sense-making, story-telling and communication (e.g. Clegg et al. 2006, Sillince 2006, Balogun / Johnson 2004, Walsh 1995, Hambrick / Mason 1984). These media are not neutral or mere technical devices, but elaborated systems of symbols indicating social status, responsibilities, social differences and influence. They contribute to the establishment and maintenance of hierarchical social systems and power differentials. In doing so, organisational systems of symbols, discourses and rhetoric create and shape not only the social construction of reality but also social action and practices. Managerial power is therefore deeply embedded in, and constructed by social institutions (Granovetter 1985), and takes place within the dialectical relationship of social action and structure (Giddens 1976, 1984). As Clegg et al. (2006, p. 300) explained: 'Foucault's perspective emphasizes the fact that an actor is powerful only within a particular discursive context as it is discourse that creates the categories of power within which actors act.' People's perceptions, (self-)images, social status and social actions are shaped by systems of symbols and discourse. People must know about their place within those systems and are expected to act and behave accordingly—managers as superiors, employees as subordinates. Such systems often reach 'an almost pathological intensity' (Thompson 1961, p. 496).

All in all, this first brief discussion indicates that managers' power can be identified and analysed in quite some different ways. Within all of the three approaches mentioned (functional, political and discursive), some strong theories have been developed which further our understanding of social and managerial power. However, what the approaches don't provide is *one* comprehensive and multi-dimensional framework for the analysis of managers' power. Because of specialisation, most concepts within these approaches concentrate on a few dimensions and particular parts of the problem. As a consequence, most of the relevant aspects have been investigated largely in isolation from each other. Hence the phenomena of managers' power (as such) as well as the reasons behind it are still not fully understood. In one word: We still lack a comprehensive and systematic explanation for why exactly managers are so powerful.

In this sense, the core thesis of this chapter is that *managers' power is based on very different sources which play together and, in so doing, create a comprehensive, elaborated, differentiated, and multi-dimensional system*. If we really want to understand the nature of managerial power within organisations (or social power in general) we need to systematically investigate the relevant preconditions, characteristics and explanatory variables as well as their relationships and interplay. In this chapter such a *comprehensive framework* will be developed, systematically capturing *all* aspects of managerial power and control within organisations.[5] This system comprises

1. social institution and institutional embeddedness (e.g. cultural and social capital),
2. organisational structures and processes of power (e.g. hierarchy, bureaucracy, modern forms of organisation such as teamwork or projects),
3. managers' prerogatives and the powerful manager (e.g. strategic objectives, management knowledge, leadership, personal skills and traits),
4. performance measurement and management systems (e.g. design, accountability, control),
5. (socio-)psychological traits of the conditioned employee (e.g. conformity and compliance, fears and conditioning, career-orientation, self-control and calculative mind, control of minds, normalisation).

With such a comprehensive framework for the analysis of managerial power, it will become clear(er) how multi-dimensional and multi-faceted the power of managers is—like the power of *any* dominant group or ruling class within any given social system.

SOCIAL INSTITUTION AND INSTITUTIONAL EMBEDDEDNESS

As discussed in the first chapter, managerial capitalism emerged in the last third of the 19th century. Step by step, managers became *the* central and dominant figures in larger organisations. One external factor contributing to this development has been the changes in social images and societal expectations. The ideas of 'management' and 'being a manager' became not only socially accepted, but associated with positive values such as professionalism, competence, realism, efficiency and so forth. At the same time, according to the idea of *isomorphism* (e.g. Ingram / Clay 2000, DiMaggio / Powell 1983, Meyer / Rowan 1977) organisations gained or increased their legitimacy when they created thick layers of management and demonstrated 'strong' leadership. 'Management' became one, if not *the* social institution of contemporary market economies and public services. This is a process and epochal trend which continues today and has spread like cancer not only into every corner of private and public organisations but also into our lifeworld. It is this institutionalised justification of the meaning and ideas of management and 'the manager' within organisation and throughout society which puts every manager automatically in a relative strong position; managers are institutionally empowered simply because of their embeddedness in structures of social and economic relations which support the status of their roles and positions (Willmott 1984, 1987, Granovetter 1985). To put it in a nutshell: Managers are powerful *because they are 'managers'*. This can be explained further.

According to the idea of *cultural capital* (Bourdieu 1983), individuals have power simply because they belong to that group of people which, for whatever reasons, represents the dominant values of a given society and occupies the most appreciated roles at a given time. These societal statuses and positions can be gained and developed by heritage, education, contractual arrangements, discourses, blunt lies, sheer force or any other means. Priests, knights, merchants, capitalists and now managers had and have power because their professions and roles became one of the core *social institutions* of their society. It is the social construct of status which makes individuals holding that position so privileged and powerful—however capable or incapable they actually are and whether they deserve it or not. A manager, *any* manager, already has a slice of power (in the eyes of him- or herself and of others) because he or she carries the label 'manager' and represents that social institution. And the more senior a manager is—ceteris paribus—the more impressive the image is he or she produces. "If you tell me you are a senior manager, or show it to me with your attitudes and status symbols, I fall on my knees!" This is 'the iconic status of management, a status legitimized on ontological grounds (managers as the bearers of the real world), epistemological grounds (management as the embodiment of expert knowledge), and moral grounds (managerialization being equated with greater justice, public accountability, democracy and quality in public services)' (Fournier / Grey 2000, p. 11). Simply being "on the right side of an epochal trend"—i.e. having a social position which belongs to the privileged ones in a given society—provides individuals with a head start for gaining, having and keeping power.

The institutional embeddedness of power does not only work in relatively abstract ways via social constructs of status and images. It also works in more concrete ways via the social relationships of and between actors, i.e. via *social capital* (e.g. Gant et al. 2002, Nahapiet / Ghoshal 1998, Bourdieu 1983, Granovetter 1973). Social capital does not only describe interpersonal relations or networks of people who know each other, but also the access to assets, resources, power, influence, advantages and potential linked to, and mobilised through such connections (Gant et al. 2002, p. 296, Coleman 1988, pp. 95, 102–105). All people working for an organisation have and / or develop interpersonal relations and, hence, social capital. However, it is particularly senior and upper managers who develop interpersonal relations with more important and influential external institutions, their representatives and stakeholders. These may include (e.g. Apple 2005, p. 20, Bolchover 2005, pp. 8–11, 75, Pina / Torres 2003, pp. 334–335, Haque 1999, p. 470, Willmott 1996, p. 326, Pollitt 1990, pp. 87, 134–135)

- owners of the organisation (family owners, large and powerful shareholders),
- suppliers and customers, competitors and business organisations,
- banks and other financial institutions (institutional investors, financial analysts, rating agencies, auditors, fund managers),
- consultancies, academic institutions, media,
- government and governmental organisations, political parties and
- supra-national institutions, non-governmental organisations (NGOs), associations and pressure groups.

Links and social networks between senior managers and these agencies can range from a mere functional fulfilment of contractual obligation and tasks, to more intense forms of collaboration (e.g. joint projects), interlocking directorates or multiple-board memberships (Pettigrew 1992, pp. 165 ff.) or even unofficial groupings (e.g. 'breakfast clubs'). Such relations represent a 'constellation of interests' (Scott 2003, p. 160) and, hence, strengthen a manager's position both within and outside the organisation.

Although many of the interests of these external stakeholders (Freeman 1983) can be quite different to those of managers, *all* stakeholders have at least one interest in common: they want to see the institution of management continued. Individual managers may change or may be exchanged every now and then. But the institution of 'the manager' and his or her power shall be kept intact. Stakeholders often do their utmost to actively support the idea of management and managers.

- Large corporations or individual capitalists support and collaborate in many ways with institutions which produce future managers or train current managers (e.g. universities, colleges, training institutes)— and particularly with those institutions which legitimise and uphold *orthodox* understandings of market economy, organisations and management (Rosen 1984, p. 319).
- Consultancies, management gurus and other players within the 'management fads-and-fashions industry' actively develop, promote and disseminate managerial concepts (Ramsey 1996, p. 166). The major-

ity of strategies, business concepts and models proposed by them might be technically different, but they nonetheless refer to the same set of explicit and implicit assumptions of the prevalence, importance and legitimacy of management (Protherough / Pick 2002, p. 61).

- The same is true concerning the output of many business schools and other higher education institutions. In their teaching and research they often simply reproduce, defend and justify the litany of (US-American) mainstream theories and concepts of orthodox management and business models without really questioning the underlying assumptions or multi-faceted implications of these concepts.

- Many governments are more than willing to introduce and strengthen managerial capitalism (Kirkpatrick / Ackroyd 2000, p. 527)—even in the public sector. In 1980, Michael Heseltine, the then British Secretary of State for the Environment, stated: 'Efficient management is a key to the [national] revival . . . . And the management ethos must run right through our national life, private and public companies, civil service, nationalized industries, local government, the National Health Service' (cited in Pollitt 1990, p. 3). This is only one, relatively early example for what has developed into a global trend for transforming public services under the buzzword 'New Public Management'.

- At a global stage, institutions such as the World Bank, the Organisation for Economic Co-operation and Development (OECD), the International Consortium for Financial Government Management and the International Monetary Fund contribute to the proliferation of managerial concepts and neo-liberal public administration principles (e.g. Pina / Torres 2003, pp. 334–335, Haque 1999, p. 470).

Despite their differences, these are some of the many, highly influential and powerful institutions which contribute actively to the institutionalisation and further dissemination of management and the manager—for whatever reason. Managers are often not just players amongst others but right in the centre of this "constellation of interests". For them, political and legal frameworks, investors, customers and business organisations as well as knowledge providers such as universities and consultancies provide an excellent playground for the formulation and implementation of strategies, tactical manoeuvres and shifting alliances. Flexible and changing constellations of external stakeholders who are basically in favour of management provide managers with a strong power basis.

To summarise, there are already some important external factors which contribute to managers' strong positions and power within organisations:

- the appreciation of 'management' and 'the manager' as a social institution (cultural capital),
- managers' embeddedness in networks and alliances (social capital), and

- the active interest of stakeholders in the (further) strengthening of managers.

Against the backcloth of longer epochal trends of capitalism, market economy and neo-liberalism, managers find extremely favourable circumstances for their activities, while at the same time doing their fair share to fit well into this institutional network.

ORGANISATIONAL STRUCTURES AND PROCESSES OF POWER

In this section we will start to look inside the organisation. Perhaps the most commonly cited type of managers' power is their *hierarchical authority* based on formal organisational structures (Finkelstein 1992, p. 508). A *hierarchy* can be defined as a socially constructed and institutionalised system of roles of superiority and subordination (Thompson 1961, p. 486). *Roles and social positions* are created and organised within that structure via hierarchy. These roles provide role-holders with 'statutory capital', i.e. with 'exclusive possibilities and responsibilities arising from, or linked to, such a position or role' (Diefenbach 2006, p. 412).

In hierarchical organisations a whole range of rights and duties are either formally ascribed to roles or come along with roles informally. These could include define and identify problems; set the agenda and objectives; make decisions and/or influence decision-making processes; communicate; evaluate and appraise performance; and promote, reward and sanction (e.g. Braynion 2004, p. 449, Jost / Elsbach 2001, p. 182, Jacques 1996, p. 120). These, and other similar tasks, are not only the responsibilities or prerogatives of the manager as such. Hierarchies define precisely the social position of any given person *in relation to others*. When Sidanius / Pratto outlined their Social Dominance Theory, they explained the nature of such 'group-based social hierarchies' as follows (1999, p. 31):

> At the very minimum, this hierarchical social structure consists of one or a small number of dominant and hegemonic groups at the top and one or a number of subordinate groups at the bottom. Among other things, the dominant group is characterized by its possession of a disproportionately large share of positive social value, or all those material and symbolic things for which people strive.

The way hierarchies relate social positions to each other constitutes the (official) social scaffolding for power and control; it makes managers superiors and employees subordinates. Hierarchically defined roles provide individuals with opportunities, if not to say prerogatives and entitlements which form large parts of his or her power base. Any person inheriting a position higher up an organisation's hierarchy is, ceteris paribus, provided with an increasing amount of power, i.e. with more tools for the hierarchical domination and control of subordinates (e.g. James 2005, p. 327, Thompson 1961, p. 494). In addition, everyone *must* be aware about their social positions as well as their place within that system and *must* obey this order.

> If left to their own devices, managers believe, people will descend into chaos because of irrational motives, conflicting interests, and unrestrained emotions. The imposition of structure and process will establish control and prevent a descent into chaos. Order will reign provided there is constant vigilance to guard against people's perverse tendencies. (Zaleznik 1989, p. 274)

In this sense, hierarchy is just another tool for uncertainty reduction—a very important tool. From a leader's perspective, the 'threat of uncertainty' can be very real. Getting things (and people) under their direct control is paramount. Organisations are seen by managers and bureaucrats 'as instruments of uncertainty reduction in their ability to secure stability, predictability, and precision' (Shenhav 2003, p. 201), i.e. as tools to gain and keep control over others. Every hierarchical social system therefore comes with its own elaborated systems of symbols indicating status, responsibilities and differences.

The responsibility for resources is another important factor contributing to managers' power (Turner 2005, p. 1, Burrell 2002, p. 39, Whitley 1989, p. 218). This applies equally to the well-known tangible resources (land, raw materials, semi-finished products, products, machinery and other means of production), or to financial resources (money, budget) or to the newly re-discovered intangible assets (such as legal rights, information and knowledge or human and social capital). Social positions higher up a hierarchical bureaucracy are attractive to many people exactly because they offer increasing access to, and control over resources. Willmott (1984, p. 361) made it clear: 'The power or powerlessness of any particular group or individual is directly related to their structurally limited access to the resources needed to secure compliance with their demands . . .'. In the case of managers it obviously is not necessary to actually own resources. According to Burrell (2002, p. 39) 'it was management's de facto access to the machinery of economic performance that gave them this tremendous advantage . . .'. It is sufficient to have the *functional responsibilities* for these economic resources, perhaps accompanied and secured by some sort of legal entitlements. Being in charge of resources is enough to establish and maintain a power basis. Furthermore, the allocation of power through access to resources and the distribution of the results stemming from the usage of these resources, quite often go hand in hand. Burnham (1941, p.

60) explained 'that the two chief factors in control [of resources] (control of access and preferential treatment in distribution) are closely related in practice. Over any period of time, those who control access not unnaturally grant themselves preferential treatment in distribution; . . .'. The owners may still have the *legal ownership* of the resources and get the lion's share of the profit accordingly. But managers have the *actual access* to the resources and hence get their lion's share of material and non-material advantages and returns *before* bookkeeping kicks in. Managers are not only privileged in their access to resources but also in the usage of organisational resources and the return stemming from the usage—which, again, increases their privileged position and power basis; a perfect positive feedback loop.

The nature of social positions within hierarchical organisations, and hierarchically differentiated control over resources, creates therefore almost automatically the tendency of role-holders to accumulate more and more 'responsibilities', which leads to a (further) concentration of power (Courpasson 2000, p. 157). In hierarchical organisations it is 'the centre' where most power sits. And power is like a magnet: power attracts more power. In this sense, most managerial strategies and change initiatives—initiated by senior management—are designed to contribute to a further concentration and centralisation of power. More precisely, they strive for more centralisation and centralised control over key strategic issues, policies and functions, while at the same time de-centralising operational responsibilities (e.g. Sanderson 2001, p. 300, Courpasson 2000, p. 155, Hoggett 1996, pp. 9, 18, Zaleznik 1989, p. 95). It is this constant battle between the centre and the periphery which converts organisational change programmes into political issues, with powerful managers as the main players (Diefenbach 2007, 2005). Hellawell / Hancock give quite a telling description of such a 'power culture' (2001, p. 192, the citation in the citation stems from Handy, 1976):

> 'This culture depends on a central power source, with rays of power and influence spreading out from that central figure. They are connected by functional or specialist strings but the power rings are the centres of activity and influence.' . . . The spider at the centre of the web of a power culture (. . .) is often keen not to 'micro-manage' so that the subordinates are allowed to have considerable degrees of autonomy. But the spider retains central control of the key threads (usually financial), which link the outer and inner circles of the web.

Of course, there are many senior and upper middle managers who make the claim for more de-centralisation and who fight the centre of their organisation in its strive for centralisation. But, at the same time, many of these managers continue to concentrate and centralise more responsibilities in *their* realms and fiefdoms. It is only the level of the power game that changes, not its nature!

The hierarchical relationship between centralised and de-centralised functions strengthens central power in another way. De-centralised units will often compete with each other (e.g. James 2005, p. 327, Hoggett 1996, p. 9) under the heading of 'internal markets'. And the more they compete with each other, the more powerful the centre remains. 'Competition can be thought of as an extremely powerful form of practice which shapes the behaviour even of those whose value systems embrace traditional notions of public service rather than the new values of public enterprise' (Hoggett 1996, p. 15). When it comes to resource allocation, strategic changes or just the usual organisational politics, de-centralised units particularly will invest even more time in monitoring, controlling and fighting each other. And the more busy de-centralised units are with fighting each other, the more factual power and control the centre has. This is true for units as well as individual managers.

Organisational structures and processes such as the ones just discussed (hierarchy, resource allocation and centralisation) are based on, and part of the standards and procedures, policies and regulations, formalisation and standardisation, rules and order—in one word: the *bureaucracy*. Bureaucracy is nothing new, as Weber's famous theory and analyses of the 'iron cage' indicates (Weber 1921/1980). It was invented and developed well before the emergence of modern management and managers. And since its early beginnings it has been used and instrumentalised by leaders to oppress and control the majority. This is for good reasons; leaders fear uncertainty, disorder and uncontrollability. Bureaucracy delivers certainty, order and controllability on a large scale, in a comprehensive manner and constantly. Managers' concerns and interests are the same: they want to have control over both the organisation and the people:

> If left to their own devices, managers believe, people will descend into chaos because of irrational motives, conflicting interests, and unrestrained emotions. The imposition of structure and process will establish control and prevent a descent into chaos. Order will reign provided there is constant vigilance to guard against people's perverse tendencies. (Zaleznik 1989, p. 274)

These concerns are shared by bureaucrats. There is nothing worse for a bureaucrat than people not obeying rules and procedures, and instead doing things their own way. So organisations are seen both by managers and bureaucrats 'as instruments of uncertainty reduction in their ability to secure stability, predictability, and precision' (Shenhav 2003, p. 201). For example, Weber's ideal type of bureaucracy has four guiding principles (Weber 1921/1980)—'functional specialization within a firmly ordered hierarchy; a comprehensive, impersonal body of rules and procedures; the precise definition of powers and responsibilities invested in each organizational role; formal equality of treatment regarding recruitment and promotion.' Managers are responsible for *all four* principles of bureaucracy—and, at the same time, their human product and incarnation. Managerial conduct happens more and more through bureaucratic forms of control (e.g. Jermier 1998, p. 235, Zaleznik 1989, p. 229). At the same time, precisely defined power and control responsibilities necessitate more regulations, particularly regulation of the allocation of power and of imbalances of power (Willmott 1984, p. 361). In other words, managers produce bureaucracy and bureaucracy produces managers. Both concepts share basic assumptions, are quite similar and have major objectives in common. This is another reason why so many managers became (partly) bureaucrats and so many bureaucrats also fulfil managerial functions. The bureaucratic manager and the managerial bureaucrat are the rule, not the exception in today's larger organisations.

Hierarchy, responsibility for resources, the idea of centralisation and bureaucracy are all typical aspects of orthodox organisations or other hierarchical social systems. They still form the backbone of most of our organisations. However, since the 1980s they have been increasingly supplemented by modern or even post-modern, (allegedly) 'non-hierarchical' and 'non-bureaucratic' forms of management and organisation. Management concepts such as lean management, business re-engineering, the knowledge or even virtual company have been accompanied at a more operational level by new work forms such as teamwork, projects, quasi-autonomous work units and profit centres. There are claims that these concepts have superseded the old forms of hierarchical power and control and, in so doing, have solved some or even most of the problems linked to these old forms. 'Many studies assume the commonly held and advocated view that the installation of team and family-style structures and processes reforms outdated bureaucratic workplaces, and uniform increases employee participation, commitment, motivation and empowerment, and organizational productivity' (Casey 1999, p. 156). In this sense, one might assume that modern work forms reduce managerial power to quite some extent.

However, there is strong empirical evidence suggesting that teams, projects, 'empowerment' and a so-called collaborative work environment put even *more* pressure and control on the individual than most of the external, hierarchical regimes (Jermier 1998, p. 248). The new work arrangements create, even necessitate, more informal and reciprocal control amongst peers. Casey (1999, p. 155), therefore, disputes 'the conventional view that the practices of the "new culture" and its purported reform of the hierarchical, specialized, conflict-ridden workplaces of traditional industrial organizations "empower" employees and provide "meaningful" relationships in the workplace.' Instead, he argues that 'these new "designer" cultural practices serve as processes of regulation, discipline and control of employee subject selves. Mutual monitoring of behaviour is simply a more "gentle" means of control and punishment (Foucault). They push team members and relieve management from much of its need for direct control (Rothschild / Ollilainen 1999, p. 605). Most managers, therefore, have simply modified their tactics of power and control to some extent. They are more engaged in team-working, setting up and managing teams, communicating, initiating projects and attending every meeting around. Not all managers will have been able to develop the necessary skills to thrive in these, more fluid power-and-control mechanisms. But most of them have been able to use these new strategies of indirect control to their own advantage. For example, Cour-passon (2000, p. 154) rightly mentioned that 'even in horizontal, flat, indi-vidualistic and flexible organizations, domination is the core of managerial strategies'. Even the most "anti-hierarchical" forms of work to some extent are mere managerial rhetoric which is primarily meant to obscure new and more intense forms of (indirect) control (Jermier 1998, p. 249) 'under the pretence of employee democracy and empowerment' (Akella 2003, p. 54). Managerial power and influence has not diminished but simply changed.

These new forms of indirect use of power and control are not only quite a strong substitute for formal rules and procedures but provide *additional* mechanisms. It is not so much that the modern forms of power and control have superseded the old, but that they are being added to the old forms; 'existing legitimate authority perpetuates itself by incorporating soft prac-tices and articulating these with hierarchical and formal bureaucratic practices' (Courpasson 2000, p. 142). In this sense, new organisations and workplaces are 'hybrid systems' of old *and* new control mechanisms (e.g. Sanderson 2001, p. 300, Casey 1999, p. 163), with the result that power and control in contemporary organisations are simply *more* (and more sophis-ticated). Modern organisations 'retain a need for the iron fist of strong and centralized control mechanisms, wrapped up in the velvet glove of consent' (Courpasson / Clegg 2006, p. 324).

Overall, hierarchical authority and social positions, responsibilities for resources, centralisation, bureaucracy and new forms of indirect power and control together create a comprehensive and thorough system of organisa-tional structures and processes. These structural components are so deeply entrenched in our understanding of what organisations look like—*should* look like—that we are hardly able to think about organisations *without* hier-archy, bureaucracy, privileged social positions—or *without managers*. Organ-isational structures and processes are *managerial* structures and processes, which provide managers with power and control no one can really challenge (at least, for the time being). They are designed to securing, strengthening and widening managers' power and influence, whatever the external and internal conditions are, and whatever the organisational form is.

MANAGERS' PREROGATIVES AND
THE POWERFUL MANAGER

As the previous section demonstrated, managers are massively empowered and privileged by organisational / managerial structures and processes. Like roles and role-holders, managerial hierarchy and managers relate to each other. Against this backcloth of analysis we will now investigate how managers as role-holders fulfil the expectations linked to the role of 'the manager'.

Because of their roles and position within orthodox hierarchical organisations, it is commonly assumed that managers' first and foremost task is to make decisions. Making decisions is the exclusive prerogative of managers. They therefore have, so to speak, a monopoly in decision-making, a monopoly which is even 'largely regarded as legitimate and necessary; it is felt natural that senior managers should take important decisions and, because they take responsibility for the decisions of others, they should also control them' (Thomas 1998). This monopoly is present at all levels within the organisational hierarchy. For example, senior managers particularly regard *strategic management* as their prerogative. They decide the official mission and vision statements of the organisation, its strategic objectives and strategy, budget and resources, performance management and measurement systems, and the main organisational structures and processes. And most managers are *very* keen to make these decisions. Deciding over strategic matters increases the manager's power base in several ways. One way is that the definition of what "is", or should be regarded as a strategic issue is confined to managers. Strategic management is defined as 'top level decision-making' (Shrivastava 1986, pp. 363, 369), with some limited involvement of middle management and communication further down the rank and file for the sake of political correctness. But it is only senior managers who set and control the agenda, who have, so to speak, the sovereignty over the strategy airspace. Controlling the agenda is one of the crucial preconditions for having power and influence within social systems where organisational politics play an important part. In addition, the *content* of strategic issues is also largely, if not solely defined and decided by senior managers. The actual strategies might be different depending on the environmental challenges an organisation faces, its organisational capabilities and personal preferences of powerful actors.

In addition, being able to set and control the strategic agenda as well as deciding its content provides managers with another powerful tool—*the power to silence*. Discourses about strategy can be used to suppress conflict, to ignore alternatives and to keep others quiet. This is particularly true of those ideas and concepts which do not provide challenges at a technical or functional level of strategic reasoning but question the very nature of managerial strategies, or even the status and privileges of managers. Lukes (1974, p. 38) described 'how political systems prevent demands from becoming political issues or even from being made' and rightly mentioned that 'the most effective and insidious use of power is to prevent such conflict from arising in the first place' (ibid., p. 23). For example, the concepts which are deeply embedded in the tradition of democracy and enlightenment, in empowerment and justice, equality and environmental concerns are systematically ignored. 'They are the controversial topics which go against the interests of powerful stakeholders: they do not engender support, they do not fit with the prevailing culture, they are not considered acceptable for discussion, so they are quietly sidestepped or suppressed or dropped' (Miller et al. 2002, p. 80). Managerial strategic discourse is very much about silencing other voices, particularly those airing grievances, interests, needs or requirements which already have little opportunity to be articulated (Braynion 2004, p. 453). And the proponents of alternative views, particularly those which challenge managerial supremacy, are being excommunicated—'excluded from further meaningful discourse as being insane, depraved, traitorous, alien, and so on. The excommunicated person is condemned, temporarily or forever, to ideological non-existence: . . .' (Therborn 1980, p. 83).

Therefore, there is a great chance that *all* strategies will be *managerial* strategies, as such underlining the importance of management and strengthening (senior) managers' roles. Strategies can be viewed 'as reflections of the values and cognitive bases of powerful actors in the organization' (Hambrick / Mason 1984, p. 193). Levy et al. (2001, p. 9) explained that 'strategy talk is not innocent. It is a powerful rhetorical device. It frames issues in particular ways and augments instrumental reason; it bestows expertise and rewards upon those who are "strategists"; and its military connotations reinforce a patriarchal orientation to the organization of work. In doing so, strategy demonstrates managerial rationality and legitimizes the exercise of power.' Strategies and strategic decision-making procedures are the institutionalisation of top management interests (Shrivastava 1986, p. 369). They are probably the most managerialist of all management tasks (Levy et al. 2001, p. 3),and some of its most powerful devices. In this sense, *strategic decisions are not only made by powerful managers—strategic decisions make managers powerful.* Without this more or less rational and justified prerogative, managers would simply do their operational job like anyone else—the job they actually do. Instead, they are made powerful by their organisation's strategy. This is because they set the agenda and shape the content of strategic discourses themselves, and it is part of the managerialistic ideology of our time that the task of making strategic decisions is portrayed as so important.

Although middle and lower managers' operational decisions may be less important compared to senior managers' strategic tasks, they nonetheless are powerful, too. Of course, lower managers' power and influence, prerogatives and privileges are quite small compared to the ones of senior managers. However, as indicated earlier, power is largely a relative and relational term. So, whereas middle and lower managers might have less power than senior managers, the principles of managerial power still apply to them. Within *their* areas of responsibilities, middle and lower managers are privileged in having the monopoly on decisions. Decisions at operational level particularly can be quite far-reaching and influential since it is here that 'the real deal' happens, and organisational reality largely shaped on a daily basis. It is the very nature of organisational hierarchy that middle and lower managers are, in principle, privileged in the same ways as senior managers—on a smaller scale and probably less glamorous, but nonetheless equipped with the same relational power and prerogatives. However we look at it, managers are in charge of organisations and are systematically empowered. But now, 'this system, with its sub-systems and its control mechanisms, is conceived of as one that has been designed by managers and, furthermore, it needs to be driven, continually maintained, and, from time to time, re-engineered by managers' (Watson 2006, p. 44).

Managers' prerogatives such as making decisions are justified primarily by reference to functional explanations, particularly to managers' specific knowledge and experience. It is claimed that their in-depth knowledge of their organisations and business, products and technologies enables them to make the right strategic and operational decisions. This is particularly true when they have already established a career in a specific industry or a particular organisation where their knowledge and experience are (almost) irreplaceable (Lazonick 1992, p. 450). In addition, the more senior managers are, the more access they have to crucial information (e.g. financial and production data). Senior managers know their organisation's strengths and weaknesses better than anyone else and can make their (strategic) decisions accordingly (Boyer 2005, p. 43). The power and control are not only gained because they know how to use managerial rhetoric, but 'because they, not the outside directors, had the knowledge, experience, and information required to make and implement the strategies essential to keep such enterprises profitable' (Chandler, 1990, cited in Rowlinson et al. 2006, p. 691).

However, it takes more than the 'mere' knowing of actual facts and details to make one powerful. For every specific question and problem, there are always other experts such as lawyers, accountants, consultants, engineers and secretaries. To a certain degree their specific and specialised knowledge might put them in a powerful position too, and might even threaten managers' dominance. Even the specific knowledge of the relevant industry, products and services may make managers simply successful, but not necessarily really powerful. It takes something different. Contemporary organisations, business, public and even social life, are all about managing. Managers, and other professions interested in their success, have been able to create a whole new universe of language and discourse about 'management' and 'managing'. Whenever it is about business or organisations, all key terms and core concepts are *managerial* in the sense that they define business and organisational problems from a management perspective and either suggest or ask for a 'management solution'; *only managers have the ('strategic') knowledge which guarantees the survival of the whole*—so they say. 'Management speak' underlines the importance of managers' roles and responsibilities, their positions and functions, interests and privileges. It is the managers, *and only the managers*, who have the necessary managerial knowledge to run the business and organisations *as such* (e.g. McKinlay / Wilson 2006, p. 661, Whitley

1989, p. 218)—at least this is how it is portrayed. They know the standard managerial concepts for analysing the external and internal environments of organisations, the stock concepts for structuring and organising work, functions and people. They know the language and rhetoric of management. And they know how to use it. This interpretation is further supported by the fact that many managers can and do work for different organisations and even industries very successfully. The specific knowledge counts only to a certain degree and can be obtained relatively easy. It is the more general knowledge and experience of managing that makes it so easy for managers to change organisations, industries, and even cross borders. *In this sense* managers are said to have expert power (e.g. Braynion 2004, p. 450, Finkelstein 1992, p. 508). 'Managers are in a similar position to the physician, who can be recognized as trustworthy from a professional or an individual point of view; in the first case, legitimization comes from knowledge, an impersonal sigh of legitimacy, and in the second case, from the professional's behaviour, and his/her past and crucial choices' (Courpasson 2000, p. 156). It is because of their position and tasks that managers can monopolise and use 'tactically relevant' management knowledge to their own advantage. This general management knowledge, in combination with specific knowledge about 'how things work' in their organisation and industry, is what makes managers powerful.

Such a knowledge-oriented "explanation" (and justification!) of dominance is not unusual. It was also constructed and used by druids, priests, merchants, aristocrats, communists and capitalists. Only they—at least according to them and their supporters—had or have the crucial knowledge to 'read the stars', 'interpret God's will', 'get goods from distant shores', 'impose war and peace', 'free the proletariat' or 'organise the factory'. As these examples show, it is the ruling classes' generation, monopolisation and dissemination of *particular* knowledge which shall explain and justify their superior expertise in dealing with issues that are, allegedly, crucial for 'the whole', i.e. for the organisation, country or nation. This time, it is about 'knowing how to manage' which supports a particular group of people's claim for power and influence.

By setting the agenda and deciding on 'important' strategic issues, managers also try to provide guidance. In other words, they are keen to demonstrate *leadership* (Jacques 1996, p. 164) and to be seen as 'leaders'. This image is deeply embedded in societal images of superiors, i.e. expectations that "the ones at the top" (or simply above oneself) demonstrate that they are capable of setting directions, making decisions and guiding everyone else. Obviously, this is a very specific understanding of leadership—it is *hierarchical* leadership (Kerr / Jermier 1978, p. 375). Only leaders can and shall lead. All others, because of their lack of knowledge, skills and motivation, need guidance. In this sense, the mainstream understanding of leadership is quite paternalistic. It almost automatically makes the ones 'at the top' stronger and puts others into a position of psychological and factual dependency. As superiors within hierarchical organisations, managers are, quite understandably, increasingly anxious to portray themselves as 'leaders' and to see the "kite mark of leadership" being attached to their style of management. Only managers "know" what is going on in the social system's environment, in which direction the organisation should go, how the ambitious objectives can be operationalised and what needs to be done so that these can and will be achieved. This interpretation of leadership has further implications. If a particular activity is portrayed as so important, then the people, who carry out this activity must also be of crucial importance; if 'leadership' fails, the very survival of the organisation is at stake. Hence, managers, who are leaders, are crucial. It is they, *and only they*, who can guarantee the very survival of the organisation—allegedly. Amongst other things, this means that they need and deserve all the means available to carry out their selfless tasks and that their decisions must be supported, their instructions followed and their will obeyed. And they must not be challenged! To criticise the leaders is to put the whole collective at risk! Obviously, communicating such an image, acting 'pro-actively' and demonstrating 'strong leadership' strengthens and justifies managers' social positions, power and influence to a considerable extent.[6]

If a manager manages to be seen as a leader in such a way (by important stakeholders, some of his peers and his subordinates), he or she will gain a new quality of *legitimacy*. The higher up a position is located, the more competent and experienced the role-holder is (allegedly). Thompson (1961, p. 492) described this phenomenon even more dramatically: 'the amount of prestige attached to hierarchical position increases as we go up the hierarchy at what would appear to be an "abnormal" rate. The status system appears to have a "quasi-neurotic" character'. But this is obviously good for the ones higher up the social ladder. Ruling based on power alone is fairly inefficient since it requires comprehensive resources to create and maintain systems of surveillance (Tyler 2005, p. 212). In contrast, ruling based on legitimacy, however weird and irrational this might be on closer inspection, is quite efficient, since it almost automatically creates pro-active support, or at least quiet obedience on the side of subordinates. Legitimacy is further gained and increased by the official image and assumptions about the competences of the leader. They *must be* competent because otherwise they would not be a leader. As Brookfield (2005, p. 47) explained: 'After all, if the fittest really do survive then the ones who are in positions of power must be there by virtue of their innate strength or superior intelligence since this has obviously allowed them to rise to the top.' In a nutshell, leaders are leaders because they are leaders—the circle is closed.

The status of the leader is further enhanced and protected by an '*aura of mystique*'. And the higher superiors are, the more mysterious it gets. There is 'an increasing vagueness as to the activities at each level as one mounts the hierarchy, and this vagueness supports the prestige ranking which we call the status system' (Thompson 1961, p. 493). Senior managers particularly are portrayed as distant and powerful leaders, so distant and powerful that we only can imagine what they are really capable of, what their skills and knowledge are, what they really do and how they do it. This is 'because [power] is potential, ... is usually impossible to see. Furthermore, where it exists it tends to be deliberately hidden; those who sit among the mighty do not invite sociologists to watch them make their decisions about how to control the behaviour of others' (Kahl 1957, cited in Zeitlin 1974, p. 1085). When Kärreman / Alvesson carried out their empirical research concerning the management of knowledge in a large consultancy they found widespread evidence for information asymmetry exactly because of a hierarchical organisation. As one of their interviewees explained (2004, p. 157): 'We have a well defined hierarchy. And you are extremely small to partners. They are at the top and you have no idea of what they are doing—perhaps they are selling or cashing in the profit or whatever, I don't know. I don't have the faintest clue about what they do in their everyday business.'

This great hierarchical divide in our organisations and society is not a coincidence. To allocate knowledge, which is portrayed as crucial, at the top end of a social system and while making people further down the hierarchy believe that they know less, is a powerful tool. Mystique has been created and used by the powerful throughout the centuries because the unknown scares people and makes them more manageable and controllable. The *'mystique'* of business and management, leadership and managerial skills (Zaleznik 1989) is created and upheld *deliberately* by upper managers (and other interested parties) in order to gain, keep and increase power and control—*their* power and control. It is one more of the inconsistencies surrounding leadership, social dominance and power. On the one hand, it is the very intention of superiors to make their leadership and its legitimacy clear to everyone. On the other hand, what this leadership is really about, on what exactly it is based and how exactly it is performed and carried out by the leaders, will be kept secret. Though inconsistent from a logical point of view, this works well in reality. The concept of leadership and leaders as described above is a powerful tool for managers. It not only establishes, but also justifies, strengthens and protects their position.

Although all the rhetoric about managers' prerogatives, management knowledge and leadership already contributes the lion's share to managers' power, there is more needed and expected from managers: the job requires certain *personal skills, traits* and *attitudes*. And, because of the exceptional nature of these tasks, exceptional personal characteristics are required. Managers keen to play a (more) powerful part and to increase their influence within the organisation particularly need to have the following psychological and personal characteristics—or at least give the impression that they have them.

- The first is *action orientation*, or having the personality of a *'doer'*. Zaleznik (1989, p. 10) has explained this in detail: 'The cardinal rules in modern management are to be active rather than passive and to master rather than acquiesce to events. If a manager remains

passive in an authority structure, whether in relation to an immediate superior or to a surrogate staff executive, the manager relin-
quishes autonomy. And in relinquishing autonomy, the manager
jeopardizes integrity and career.' Portraying oneself as a 'doer' and
'achiever' sends strong signals in all directions. It corresponds with
prevailing social expectations and, hence, contributes to the (further) justification and strengthening of the manager's position.

- Equally, if not more important for the manager is a *power orientation*.
Power can be compromising, for male and female careerists equally. As
Henry A. Kissinger once famously stated (1974, cited in Frank 2001,
p. 629): 'Power is the ultimate aphrodisiac'. The *will for power*, some
would even call it the 'greed for power' or 'perverse need for power'
(Zaleznik 1989, p. 168) is a necessary precondition for becoming powerful within a hierarchical context. It is only of secondary importance
whether this will for power stems from, for example, an urge to please
infantile power fantasies, or fears of not being in control or striving
to avoid the feeling and sense of helplessness (Zaleznik 1989, pp. 162,
202, 224). If someone does not have this political and power-oriented
mindset and related attitudes, he or she will simply lose out at some
stage and will not climb up the power ladder.

- In addition, action orientation and power orientation need to produce results. However, results can be produced, shaped, interpreted
or explained in many different ways. What is even more important is
how the actions taken by the manager are perceived by others. It is the
image that counts. Hence, for career-oriented people, an *image orientation* is far more important than result orientation. The latter is only
significant as part of the creation of the appropriate image. Again,
this image has a lot to do with social expectations, with the official
and unofficial rules concerning appearance, attitudes and style, language and communication, and with demonstrated personality and
character. If a manager manages to produce all the "right" types of
these aspects, he or she can increase his or her social position and,
hence, can gain great influence and privileges.

- Finally, *role and morale flexibility* are a must, i.e. the ability to act
like a chameleon in a hierarchical and competitive environment. A
manager with far-reaching career aspirations must be, or become a
political animal. People with strong ethical values and moral principles will find it hard, if not to say impossible, to adapt to the social
milieu of a hierarchical organisation. In contrast, people who only
care about their personal progress and the games being played will
prosper in such an environment and become powerful players themselves. 'Seemingly, no better place exists for this flexible personality than large organizations. There are no demands for loyalty, but
there are enormous rewards for people who are good role players,
who know how to calculate, who can shift their stance, who adopt

the coloration of their surroundings, and who understand how to play the game of control and compliance' (Zaleznik 1989, p. 186).

All in all, prerogatives concerning setting the agenda and formulating the strategic objectives of an organisation, impersonating the image of a great leader and having or developing the relevant attitudes and personal traits, such as action orientation, power orientation, image orientation and morale flexibility, are the core ingredients of probably quite dysfunctional but powerful managers.

PERFORMANCE MEASUREMENT AND MANAGEMENT SYSTEMS

The two previous sections shed some light on power related to organisational structures and processes (such as hierarchy, bureaucracy or post-modern work forms) and to actors (such as managers' prerogatives, management knowledge, leadership and personal characteristics). However, there are more dimensions and sources of power for managers available. In this section we will first concentrate on performance measurement and management systems (PMMSs) of organisations.

Due to changes in society (information and consumer society), business environment (globalisation, increased competition) and technology (information and communication technologies), managers as well as employees need increasingly more data, information and knowledge on a daily basis. For this, multi-dimensional PMMSs were developed in the early 1990s, for example: Balanced Scorecard (Kaplan / Norton 1992), EFQM Excellence Model (EFQM 2003 a, b), Intellectual Capital Index and Skandia Navigator (Edvinsson / Brünig 2000, Sveiby 1998, Nonaka 1991). These are only the latest examples of a long tradition of measurement systems and processes of control, regulation, assessment, inspection and evaluation, such as (double-entry) bookkeeping, budgets, audit systems, industry standards, best practice concepts, benchmarking, or league tables (e.g. Kärreman / Alvesson 2004, Hoggett 1996). Although they differ to quite some extent, all PMMSs have in common that they are designed to capture and measure what someone did and / or what happened, i.e. activities and performances, inputs and outputs. The idea behind all PMMSs is simple: making something visible also makes it controllable and governable (Townley 1993, p. 224), i.e. 'What you measure is what you get!'—as the old adage goes. The idea is to capture *all* aspects of an organisation which are relevant for its management in a systematic and comprehensive way. In the case of socio-productive organisations, this means financial aspects, tangible assets such as commodities, buildings and machinery, but also an increasingly broader definition and understanding of intangible assets such as human, social, cultural, organisational and intellectual capital (Diefenbach 2006).

PMMSs, therefore, play a crucial role in organisations, in *any* organisation and in *any* context. This raises the question: how and where exactly does managerial power come in when it is about organisational performance measurement and management systems?

Most, if not all PMMSs can be seen in the tradition of 'technocratic concepts'. According to such approaches, organisations are viewed as rational, neutral, but instrumental input-transformation-output machineries (Hoggett 1996, p. 23, Shrivastava 1986, p. 371). With the development of the 'Scientific Management' approach F.W. Taylor formulated the modern rationale which is still valid today: 'In the past the man has been first; in the future the system must be first' (Taylor 1911/1967, p. 7). Consequently, the management of organisations should be based on exact data provided by measurement systems and on clearly defined laws, rules and principles. Over time, PMMSs create and represent a new reality. As Zaleznik (1989, p. 106) has observed:

> The control systems in corporations are universal in design, language, and use. They exist apart from the language of products, markets, and manufacturing methods. They are so powerful in framing problems and perceptions that they can easily take on a reality they do not deserve. It is astonishing to observe the reality ascribed to these reports and the numbers on them.

What becomes easily forgotten is the fact that these systems are designed by humans. In the case of organisational PMMSs, they have been designed, developed and decided by managers high in the hierarchy and specialists who get paid for supporting the managerial agenda (e.g. accountants, corporate lawyers, chief engineers, organisation experts and the like). It is particularly senior and upper middle managers' prerogative to decide about the basic design of a PMMS, i.e. its leading principles, primary objectives, indicators and measures. Setting the parameters of socio-productive social systems is much more than deciding about 'mere' functional aspects of strategic importance. Creating a new PMMS is creating a new cosmos, deciding what is on the agenda (and what is not). It therefore decides what is regarded as important and what is regarded as not important, and what is of value and, hence is measured—and what is not, and therefore is not valued. Only what is being measured and acknowledged by the system is part of the (official) organisational reality. Anything else is not only neglected—it doesn't in effect exist. In this sense, a PMMS defines and shapes (organisational) reality—and it is the managers who are behind this. Being entitled and privileged to set the very objectives and indicators of a PMMS, to design, define and implement such a system and, hence, to design, define and shape organisational reality provides that person with great power and influence.

The fact that it is (senior and middle) managers' prerogative to design such systems provides the ground for a second type of managerial power related to PMMSs. Such systems represent useful tools for supporting and deepening the division between those who think (about the grand themes and strategic issues) and those who work (i.e. carry out operational tasks). This has always been an issue between different groups of people, or classes, throughout history and in different societies (e.g. Sidanius / Pratto 1999). In this case it is about managers and employees. Taylor (1911/1967, p. 36) provided the blueprint for this practice:

> Under scientific management the "initiative" of the workmen (that is, their hard work, their good-will, and their ingenuity) is obtained with absolute uniformity and to a greater extent than is possible under the old system; and addition to this improvement on the part of the men, the managers assume new burdens, new duties, and responsibilities never dreamed of in the past. The managers assume, for instance, the burden of gathering together all of the traditional knowledge which in the past has been possessed by the workmen and then of classifying, tabulating, and reducing this knowledge to rules, laws, and formulae which are immensely helpful to the workmen in doing their daily work.

And he explained further: 'Thus all of the planning which under the old system was done by the workman, as a result of his personal experience, must of necessity under the new system be done by the management in accordance with the laws of the science; . . .' (ibid., p. 38). Although our contemporary societies and, hence, our organisations are much more differentiated, the structure and rationales of any PMMS reflect and follow closely the hierarchical order of the organisation. Which kind of information is analysed in what ways, and who has got access and other user rights depends on his or her social position within the organisational hierarchy. In this sense, employees and lower managers are kept busy with gathering, collecting and providing an endless stream of single data and information at operational level. For employees further down the organisational hierarchy, there remains only the feeling and impression that they are in charge of their own work. In fact, their thoughts and work are pre-defined, shaped and limited by the parameters and data flow of the system. In contrast, middle and senior managers are being provided with access to increasingly aggregated data. The provision of more crucial information and knowledge increases with the level of the position; the higher up someone is positioned within an organisational hierarchy, the more entitled and empowered he or she is to make use of increasingly crucial and important data. People higher up the hierarchy are therefore in much better positions to make sense of events via data provided by the PMMS. They can use it in much more intelligent and sophisticated ways, and use this knowledge and these insights to their own advantage, including the maintenance of their power over others. The differences in the scope and range of intellectual freedom, cognitive privileges and access to knowledge between employees and lower managers on the one hand, and middle and senior managers on the other, means therefore differences in power (Jacques 1996, p. 106). In this sense, PMMSs play a crucial part in further cementing socially embedded power.

When performance measurement and management systems are implemented and produce the data they are designed for, a third source of power emerges for managers—holding people accountable. 'Accountability' comprises the specification of duties and measurements as well as reports on actual outcomes and possible reasons for these. As part of their position, managers are not only responsible for accountability—they are *specialists* in accountability and holding people accountable. There are two reasons for this. One is that managers themselves are being held accountable all the time. Over the years, they have therefore developed the appropriate skills, knowledge and experience to deliver data and information as required by the system, by their superiors and / or their peers. And when the sums do not add up, they are usually quite able to provide all sorts of explanation and / or to play the blame game. Again, the higher people are in the organisational hierarchy, the more experience they usually have in organisational politics and playing the system. This knowledge and experience translates into power. Secondly, managers are superiors and therefore hold others accountable, particularly their subordinates. Again, because of their experience and their position managers are usually quite skilled at holding others accountable. Michael (2005, p. 101) called this 'the vital political power gained from the ability to punish. Without accountability, there can be no punishment—and without punishment, there can be no power.' In this sense, PMMSs provide managers with systematic, comprehensive and detailed opportunities to control the work process—if not the whole organisation (e.g. Kirkpatrick et al. 2005, p. 161, Sanderson 2001, p. 305, Jermier 1998, p. 246, Pollitt 1990, p. 177).

With regard to employees, PMMSs provide another type of power source for managers—they are great devices for 'managing' the workforce. This is due to several characteristics of such systems.

- Objectives and performance measures controlling relevant activities and outcomes are being provided "by the system". Hence, they are conveyed in de-personalised, allegedly neutral and objective ways. This de-personalisation makes management, particular the direct management of people, much easier. For the many things a manager wants his or her employees to do, he or she now simply refers to the system. In many cases, even the direct involvement of the manager is not required anymore since contemporary information technologies provide staff automatically with the data needed to be achieved. Staff is managed by the touch of a screen.
- PMMS-based management contributes to the further division of the labour force (Protherough / Pick 2002, p. 131). For example, league tables, 'employee of the month' and all sorts of lists of daily, monthly, and annual performance data create (artificial) differences between

employees and put them in quasi-competition amongst each other. It is the old Roman Empire's notion of 'Divide et impera!' which simply comes now in the new design of institutional and organisational measurement systems.

- PMMSs are not only systems for continuous evaluation but they also fulfil "pedagogical" and "educational" roles. By (openly) feeding back results and outcomes to all parties involved, the system shows not only how individuals have performed, but how they are as people—how they need to act and behave, and what is needed in future (Kärreman / Alvesson 2004, p. 169). In doing so, PMMSs provide the basis for all forms of punishment of deviance, non-compliance and for disciplining the individual (McKinlay / Wilson 2006, p. 657)—which is then, of course, the duty of managers (Taylor 1911/1967, p. 83) and / or the training and skills development department.

- The endless lists of various performance measures, evaluations and accountability 'manage' employees in another way—they simply keep them busy. They keep them busy with trying to understand how the system works, what 'it' requires and how to either deliver or to find ways around the system. For example, Hoggett (1996, p. 28) explained that these new PMMSs 'create new layers of bureaucracy engaged in contract specification and monitoring, quality control, inspection, audit and review and diverting the energies of professional staff away from service and programme delivery into a regime of form-filling, report writing and procedure-following which is arguably even more extensive than that which existed during the former bureaucratic era.' In a nutshell—as long as people are kept busy with fighting forms (and each other) they cannot fight the rulers.

Finally, PMMSs provide managers with another power dimension (probably the most powerful)—they make power and control (almost) invisible. This is mainly due to two aspects. One is that new technologies make monitoring and observation of behaviour, which would normally be recognised as such by the observed, more and more undetectable. Most PMMSs nowadays are part of an organisation's electronic information systems. Data are being generated automatically while employees work at the check-out, at the conveyor belt or use their PCs filling in excel sheets. It is an 'electronic panopticon' (Rothschild / Ollilainen 1999, p. 605) through which all-seeing managers control and have power over staff (while at the same time being controlled through the same systems and trying to get around them like anyone else does). Secondly, PMMSs and the whole notion of 'performance measurement', 'monitoring', 'auditing' and 'controlling' are so deeply embedded and institutionalised in our organisations—and increasingly in our whole society—that they have simply disappeared from the radar. They are part of a new form of authority—'normalisation' (Courpasson 2000, p. 153). Classification, standardisation, routines and pre-formulated performances are now the norm. It is one universal system (Jacques 1996, pp. 113–114) in which we all have to perform according to pre-defined expectations. Even our creativity and individuality are already set within parameters. Anything more or different is 'deviation' (and will be punished accordingly!). According to Jacques (1996, pp. 115–116):

> Normalization is maintained through the apparently neutral objectivity of externalized rules and practices which have authority, not because they are supported by the power of this or that individual, but because they have been empirically derived by experts and certified by 'the scientific method.' They are not presented as forms of power or as values and preferences, but as forms of truth. It is normalizing practices which produce the ubiquitous, disembodied 'they,' as in 'they won't let us do it any other way.'

In this sense one might even talk about 'the normalisation of norm-alisation', i.e. the transformation of externally pre-formulated standards into un-reflected routines as the way things normally are. PMMSs are therefore, not only powerful tools but also a good example of the concept of *embedded power*, i.e. power that is not ascribed to a particular person or position but which is "somehow" related to abstract mechanisms and procedures. Although managers, and even senior managers, are also part (and victims) of the system, they are nonetheless to a larger part its designers and engineers. And they are its biggest winners; power and control are strongest if they are not seen or perceived as power and control.

All in all, as demonstrated in this section, performance measurement and management systems provide managers with several types of power and control:

a) It is particularly senior and middle managers' prerogative to make decisions about the basic design of the systems, i.e. its leading principles, primary objectives, indicators and measures. In doing so, they define and shape organisational reality.
b) Reflecting the organisational hierarchy, PMMSs provide people with different levels of access to data and user rights. They therefore contribute to a further differentiation in the scope and range of intellectual freedom, cognitive privileges and opportunities to use crucial knowledge ('strategic thinking versus operational tasks').
c) PMMSs provide managers with systematic, comprehensive and detailed opportunities to control the work of others. On the basis of the data delivered by the measurement systems, managers can hold subordinates accountable.
d) PMMSs present excellent opportunities to 'manage' the workforce (indirectly and impersonally), i.e. primarily by instructing them via the provision of data, by creating (artificial) differences, by feeding back performances and by keeping people busy with additional tasks.

e) Performance measurement is largely invisible and happens automatically through electronic systems and normalisation, i.e. without even being realised and recognised (anymore) by employees.

(SOCIO-) PSYCHOLOGICAL TRAITS OF THE CONDITIONED EMPLOYEE

One would assume that the big machinery of the managerial organisation already provides a sufficiently broad range of sophisticated power and control mechanisms. Managers' power is deeply embedded in, and supported by external institutions as well as organisational hierarchical structures and processes, legitimised by their prerogatives, privileged roles and responsibilities, and accompanied by comprehensive performance measurement and management systems. Taking the full scope and depth of managers' power into account, there seems to be little need for more measures. Indeed, within hierarchical organisations, most of management's power and control over employees can be achieved through external rules and procedures, incentives and punishment. However, this system is still relatively inefficient since it usually requires quite developed control and sanctioning mechanisms. A more efficient way is to transfer managerial power and control *to* subordinates, i.e. to *internalise* power and control.

With this additional focus on the (socio-) psychological aspects of power and control mechanisms over subordinates, one of the great puzzles of society becomes again obvious: subordinates often support, even actively contribute to the very system of social dominance which oppresses them. Hierarchical systems such as the managerial organisation are maintained by the coordinated and often joint activities of both superiors *and* subordinates (Sidanius / Pratto 1999, p. 45). And it is the rule—not the exception!—that subordinates collaborate with their superiors quite actively and willingly. The question, therefore, is: *Why do subordinates so often actively contribute to the functioning, stabilisation and even further development to the very hierarchical social order that disadvantages and oppresses them?* Obviously, "old" explanations of 'false consciousness' and 'ideology' cannot (fully) explain this paradox. But they at least indicate that there must be additional factors *within* subordinates which contribute to their willingness to comply with, and support hierarchical systems.

This internalisation or psychologisation of control mechanisms takes place in several ways. The first aspect is *compliance*, i.e. employees' compliance with current structures and processes. It is about accomplishing organisational control 'through the self-positioning of employees *within* managerially inspired discourses about work and organization' (Alvesson / Willmott 2002, p. 620, emphasis added by author). This is nothing new—simply the tried and tested practice of all rulers. Sidanius / Pratto (1999, p. 44) gave a clear description of this idea:

Within relatively stable group-based hierarchies, most of the activities of subordinates can be characterized as cooperative of, rather than subversive to, the system of group-based domination. Furthermore, we suggest that it is subordinates' high level of both passive and active cooperation with their own oppression that provides systems of group-based social hierarchy with their remarkable degrees of resiliency, robustness is not maintained primarily by the oppressive behaviour of dominants, but by the deferential and obsequious behaviour of subordinates.

In this sense, *it is the first and foremost task of every employee to fit and to function well in the world of managerial dominance and supremacy.* At this comparatively still basic and unsophisticated stage of internalisation, it is not so important whether subordinates obey orders willingly or unwillingly, enthusiastically or grudgingly (Gabriel 1999, p. 193). The only thing that matters is that employees *by and large* and *publicly* comply with the regulations and formalities.[7] Their compliance is largely about accepting organisational structures and processes, acknowledging managers' prerogatives, demonstrating willingness to fit into the system, functioning according to external expectations and collaborating and co-operating with fellow employees *and* managers—all within the boundaries of the current social order, simply because 'it is more rewarding to do what is expected than to deviate from standards of behaviour' (Zaleznik 1989, p. 49).

However, employees' compliance doesn't simply exist out of the blue. Constant reminders of what *could* happen if the employee doesn't comply with all requirements (at least, officially) will help. In other words, subordinates must have a constant feeling of *fear*. Within hierarchical organisations, comprehensive control systems and actual punishment put individuals in a constant state of fear and, hence, keeps them in line. For the most part, however, symbols, indicators and brief demonstrations of power and prestige are usually enough to 'manage' and intimidate employees, particularly well-socialised employees. The managerial organisation is plastered with signs, symbols, rhetoric and discourses which permanently remind everyone about the importance, legitimacy, superiority and prerogatives of management and managers. This communication and demonstration of privilege and power is perceived and interpreted constantly and shapes our behaviour, attitudes, actions and even thinking to a much greater extent than we normally realise. Subordinates' fears and internalised conditioning mirror the portrayed and displayed powers of their superiors. In this sense, fears will help to shape and regulate most of subordinates' behaviour towards a more thorough compliance with external rules and a stronger acknowledgement of superiors' power. It is not so much factual external measures, but mostly internal guesswork about *possible* negative reactions of superiors which increases their power. Superiors' power is largely based on subordinates' mind-games. The individual is in constant fear of losing what he or she has got, is keen to fit into the systems and conform (officially) with the rules, feels guilt when he or she does not fit and does not meet the expectations and overall tries to get the most out of this constant battling and balancing. And the individual may even be happy in this sad state of human conduct (although unhappy enough at the same time in order to keep going). Whether it is through real fear, deeply held anxieties or simply an increased tiredness, the more experienced people become in the workplace, the more they accept the (self-classified) boundaries within which they have to function and the more they are keen to demonstrate the values, views and identities which they are required to demonstrate (Akella 2003, pp. 47–48). People want to conform and to meet external expectations at the workplace probably not because they agree with them but because public compliance makes life easier. Over time, people cease to question the existing order—the whole system of unjust and unjustified privileges, advantages and discrimination. They are happy to exist within the current system and to live their working lives within its boundaries (Brookfield 2005, p. 191). Immanuel Kant, the great German philosopher, gave a telling example of the power of (internalised) fear and conditioning (Kant, I.: What Is Enlightenment?, 1784, cited in Kramnick 1995, p. 2):

> After the guardians have first made their domestic cattle dumb and have made sure that these placid creatures will not dare take a single step without the harness of the cart to which they are confined, the guardians then show them the danger which threatens if they try to go alone. Actually, however, this danger is not so great, for by falling a few times they would finally learn to walk alone. But an example of this failure makes them timid and ordinarily frightens them away from all further trials.

Most of our organisations and institutions are designed as large machineries to hold the individual in a constant state of fear, to intimidate and to shrink human beings to cattle. It is the "abnormal normality" of hierarchical social systems that fits the negative psychological traits of humans so cunningly into the oppressive mechanisms of these systems, even constituting them in the first place on such traits. Without fear there would be no managerial organisation.

Within the hierarchical organisation, external systems and punishment, together with internal control mechanisms such as compliance, conditioning and fears, can already guarantee most of the smooth interaction and mutual reinforcement of subordinates' obedience and superiors' power. However, at the same time as their well-functioning and (demonstrated) obedience, subordinates do not comply with all of the rules of the system on a daily basis. They even (dare to) challenge authority now and then. There will be no consequences as long as this happens within the boundaries of what is socially accepted / tolerated by the system. In contrast, if the subordinates' "mal-functioning" or "inappropriate behaviour" crosses the boundary of the socially accepted and is recognised as such, measures need to be taken—and they will be taken in most cases. If the boundary crossing becomes public, the individual has to demonstrate his or her awareness of this fault. In this sense, the "appropriate" reaction of the individual at being caught crossing boundaries without permission is the demonstration of feelings, even consciousness, of *guilt* (e.g. McKinlay / Wilson 2006, p. 671, referring to Foucault).[8] Guilt is a further stepping stone for the individual on his or her way to (full) internalisation of social dominance. But guilt, and the handling of this feeling, can only be of help if the individual doesn't leave the organisation. In other words it is paramount to keep the individual within the reach of the system. For this, there is a powerful tool at hand which can provide the missing link between an individual's guilt and "the system's interests" (which are in fact the superiors' interests)— *confession*. Confession is the more or less public demonstration of the individual's guilty conscience (Abercrombie et al. 1980, p. 81). In so doing, the individual acknowledges his or her own deficits, the legitimacy of the system, the rightfulness of the superiors and the individual's willingness to better him- or herself. For example, Casey (1999, p. 173) gave a telling and vivid analysis of an organisation based to a large extent on a culture of confession. He revealed: 'These public admissions of fault, displays of remorse, and promises to do better next time ostensibly serve to alleviate guilt and failing, and to build group harmony and solidarity. Reconciliation strengthens team bonds and identification.' Like all the other factors discussed so far in this analysis of managers' power, confession is basically not a new invention. Of course, the system of confession (and encyclopaedic summas / systematic catalogues of sins and their punishments, Abercrombie et al. 1980, p. 80) developed and used by the medieval, particularly Catholic Church was crude and appalling. In contrast, contemporary private and public sector organisations have a much more sophisticated and humane arsenal of 'confession weaponry', e.g. management by objectives and annual career reviews, mentoring, self-examination, performance appraisals, team-reflexion and the like. Such systems and tools nowadays provide quite sophisticated and elaborated instruments to identify sins and extract confessions from the employee. Despite massive "technical" differences, supervision used by superiors and contemporary organisations does not differ *in principle* from its meaning in the medieval and even modern Catholic Church. Such organisations are keen to keep individuals inside the reach of their power, structures and processes, to have them functioning smoothly, to work on the individual in the case of "mal-functioning" and / or deviance and to offer "solutions" for its betterment—provided the individual accepts his or her "guilt" and confesses "sins". From a managerial point of view the idea of formal and regular confessions is clear; 'the successful control of an object . . . requires a degree of understanding of its forces, its reaction, its strengths, and weaknesses. The more it is known, the more controllable it becomes' (Garland 1987, cited in Akella 2003,

p. 48). Equally important is that 'something' happens with the individual. As Gabriel (1999, p. 187) explained:

> Even if an individual has nothing to confess, the transformation of the workplace into a confessional, with the implicit acceptance that there are right and wrong attitudes, appropriate and inappropriate behaviors, measurable performances, etc., and that the individual must continuously monitor him/herself against such standards, creates pliable, self-policing, self-disciplining individuals, who lack the words (or discursive resources) to oppose or shake-off the invasive tyranny of power / knowledge.

It becomes clear that the whole notion of a culture of confession does not only mean the public demonstrations of one's feelings of guilt and urge for betterment. Perhaps most of it even happens within the individual; to confess 'sins' during formal managerial procedures, at meetings with his or her line-manager or even in front of colleagues / work team is one thing. More importantly, employees need to "confess" their faults, poor performance, mal-function or non-compliance *to themselves*. In this sense, confession is 'a form of emotional atonement which infantilizes the individual, creating a perpetual sense of guilt and dependence, and paralyzing his/her will to resist' (Gabriel 1999, p. 187). Nonetheless, the individual is not being left alone with his or her internal struggles. At the end of the day it is *always* the superior (priest or line manager), *and only the superior*, who has got both the authority and competence to hear the confession, impose punishments and provide (ab-) solution. Only the tightly regulated combination of subordinates' confession and superiors' punishment can provide the much needed spiritually cathartic effects (Abercrombie et al. 1980, pp. 80–81). In so doing, priest and church-goer, manager and employee work together "in perfect harmony".

This indicates that it is apparently more and more to the advantage of the employee to internalise external power and control mechanisms provided by the managerial system. At least this is how it is portrayed by the proponents of the system. Employees, therefore try to become even more part of the organisation. It is about their *desire, even need to fit* into 'the system(s)'. In the early days of hierarchical (capitalist) organisations, it was largely about *making people fit* into physical and bureaucratic systems like Taylor's Schmidt—if not to force them into inhuman conditions by almost any means. The ideas of contemporary organisations and managerial power are much more sophisticated. This time many people *want to fit*. Fitting into a stable structure means that subordinates know what is required from them, what they need to do, and what they are allowed to do. In a rather strange way, power and control structures and processes, the regular behaviour of the powerful, official policies and rules give many employees some kind of *security*, or at least the feeling of security—'lacking other forms of power, they can use rules to limit what others can do to them' (Jacques 1996, p. 111). On top of this, people want to belong to a greater social entity, they want to be appreciated and socially accepted. If employees demonstrate the appropriate attitudes of the well-conditioned employee who behaves within the boundaries, the managerial organisation will give them the feeling of fit.

The need, even desire to fit in and to comply with the rules and regulations of the system indicates that there are not only negative reasons for employees' acceptance of managers' power. Compliance with hierarchical systems and their rules and requirements can have positive consequences—even for those who are systematically disadvantaged and oppressed. In the long run, subordinates' 'appropriate' behaviour and performance will be to their advantage. In the context of hierarchical and competitive organisations this often means *career*, i.e. promotion or progression to another hierarchical level. The 'career' is yet another invention of the bureaucratic and managerial society of the late 19th century (e.g. McKinlay / Wilson 2006, pp. 657, 673, Watson 1982, p. 271 referring to Bums 1961). But even after all the talk of 'lean management', 'team- and project-based' work organisation and 'post-modern organisation', horizontal differences in social position are still one of the fundamental principles of the managerial organisation. And with a position higher up the hierarchy comes a whole range of factual or perceived advantages, such as: higher status, more prerogatives and privileges, responsibilities and resources, better and / or more intelligent tasks, financial, sociological and psychological aspects. In the case of the managerial organisation, this means that employees can even become managers—and many will. Indeed, upward mobility on this comparatively widespread and large scale is a relatively new feature of both our societies and organisations. Such opportunities for advancement create and nurture the individual's imaginations and desires, goals and aspirations. Career conditions people's thoughts and actions—many people are willing to do and accept almost anything for being promoted. Amongst a whole range of advantages and downsides for both the organisation and employee alike, this basically means employees accept the hierarchical order (Lukes 1974, p. 49) as well as the whole cosmos of values and attitudes that come with it. Arguably at least within bureaucratic and hierarchical organisations, the career is 'the primary disciplinary mechanism in its efficiency and enforcement of self-regulation . . .' (McKinlay / Wilson 2006, p. 662).

Career, therefore, is a double-edged sword. On the one hand, it is attractive to many employees and managers since it offers them opportunities for development and satisfaction. On the other hand, career-oriented members of organisations can pursue their personal interests only by accepting (at least, officially) the organisation's values and rules (probably by denying some of their own convictions and personality), by demonstrating unrestricted loyalty and by acting accordingly. In other words, although subordinates might be successful in bringing their personal aspirations and organisational interests together, they nonetheless primarily exist to fulfil organisational, i.e. managerial requirements. In this sense, the individual simply reinforces and reproduces established power and control mechanisms. Superiors are quite aware of these aspects. Subordinates' desire for individual progress is therefore often welcomed and (in principle) encouraged by managers higher up the hierarchy; 'it is through an appeal to subordinates' instrumental self-interests that the powerful routinely seek to strengthen their control' (Knights / Willmott 1985, p. 25). It may threaten the superior's position to a certain extent because aspirational subordinates theoretically or even factually are after their job and position. However, superiors understand this and know most of the possible actions their subordinates may take in order to achieve this, simply because they have been there before and 'know the game'.

Hence the possibility of career is seen more as a useful tool to manage and even co-opt (potentially threatening) employees, to create willing internal elite sub-groups, even 'nursing and educating the potential rebels, and then, transforming them into selected aspirants and successors' (Courpasson / Clegg 2006, p. 328). On balance, managers prefer career-oriented employees because career-oriented opportunists and conformists are much easier to manage and to handle than, e.g. value-oriented idealists and non-conformists. As Fincham (1992, p. 752) has explained: 'Career is both carrot and stick—the rewards of promotion and the fear of failure both motivate managers. Career represents a kind of "control on credit" for the organization in that rivalry for a single promotion can keep several managers on their toes.' The powerful of our time have understood well the usefulness of self-interest for *their* course. In this sense, managers are both victim and offender. Like other employees, managers are trapped in the career game according to the hierarchical position they have reached by their personal skills and aspirations. On the other hand, because of their roles as line managers, and also the strong roles they play in internal communication and organisational politics, managers are powerful gatekeepers for people's career aspirations (as well as a whole range of other concerns). Managers have the power to promote and to select; selection 'represents the formalization of the patronage powers of senior incumbents, crucially legitimized by bureaucratic rules of rationality' (Fincham 1992, p. 752). Being amongst the ones who decide people's future (for better or worse) puts managers in a strong and powerful position.

The two previous points made it clear that control is much more efficient when subordinates have developed positive opinions about, and attitudes towards, the very system and its representatives that oppress them. It is about *control of the hearts and minds*. Controlling the language and discourses contributes to managers' attempts to control the minds of others. The language, knowledge and moral justification of management create social reality not only for managers, but for everyone, particularly for employees and external stakeholders interested in the conduct of business and organisations. In doing so, managers shape the ways people perceive their environment, the ways they think and act. Lukes (1974,

cited in Braynion 2004, p. 455) asked the rhetorical question: 'Indeed
is it not the supreme exercise of power to get another or others to have
the desires you want them to have—that is to secure their compliance by
controlling their thoughts and desires?' For any power-and-control system this is one of the most crucial, at the same time most difficult, aspect
to achieve. Efforts to control and manage beliefs, meaning, norms, and
interpretations of others might be seen as socio-ideological forms of control (Kärreman / Alvesson 2004, p. 152). Braynion (2004, p. 455) provided one of the best descriptions of this phenomenon:

> This shaping process helps define people's realities and helps justify and
> maintain the current systems of power. This shaping of the individual
> means the exercise of ultimate power, to shape how individuals identify
> what their desires are, and control their hopes and thoughts. This level
> of control leads to compliance as the individual only strives for those
> things that the "defenders of status quo" want them to strive for, thus
> there is no conflict or rebellion. Energies are poured into seemingly
> individual pursuits which people are told they want and they come to
> believe this is what they want. Thus actual conflict is not necessary for
> power to be exercised. The supreme use of power is through ensuring
> that individuals only ask for what those in power want to give them.

In this sense, managerial discourses are often closely linked to ideology as
well as hegemony, power, social domination and interpretative processes of
(managerial) oppression and resistance to it (e.g. Clegg et al. 2006, p. 294).
The language of management is comprehensive. It does not only control
organisational reality; it defines this reality for everyone *according to managers' views*, supports *their* claims for power, helps to mystify their and
others' interests and to suppress subordinates' resistance (Knights / Willmott 1985, p. 29). Managers' power is based on, and works *only* within
systems of managerial symbols, rhetoric, and discourses. As Clegg et al.
(2006, p. 300) explained: 'Foucault's perspective emphasizes the fact that
an actor is powerful only within a particular discursive context as it is discourse that creates the categories of power within which actors act.' The
ability to control the perceptions and opinions, minds and worldviews of
others (even regarding their own thoughts and interests) makes the difference between leaders and followers—and it makes the difference between
ruling and being overthrown. Managers, therefore, have vested interests in
gaining and keeping the 'sovereignty over the rhetorical airspace' because
this puts them in a much better position to pursue their own interests and
to make sure that they can do so also in future—'Discourse is power!'

The socio-psychological aspects of managers' power described so far do
not only mean internalisation of *some* rules by individuals; it is the mould-
ing of a new human being (Gabriel 1999, p. 187). Gabriel also provides an
excellent description of it (ibid., p. 180):

Corporate culture has emerged as an infinitely more subtle form of normative control, one that transforms each employee into a self-regulating, self-policing subject, one who is almost unable to achieve any political, critical, or moral detachment from his/her employer's power practices. This subject is hardworking, flexible, and docile; it is a subject that breaks easily into a smile when meeting the organization's customers, a subject that experiences guilt and shame with alacrity, but has no sense of justice or injustice. It is a subject that is constitutionally unable to turn his/her malaise and despair into resistance, a subject that has developed the utmost psychological, social, and material dependence on the corporation; it has become a nonsubject.

This new type of employee is grounded primarily in a permanent state of *self-control* (e.g. James 2005, p. 326, Hoggett 1996, p. 10). This is convenient and advantageous for the managerial organisation and managers' interests in efficient power and control mechanisms; with this new type of employee, 'control by others is replaced by self-control, as social norms and values are internalized and become part of the individual's own desires concerning how to behave' (Hoffman 1977, cited in Tyler 2005, p. 212). And this is not a one-off, but *a routinely maintained and reinforced process*. Employees are permanently reminded that only employees who observe and monitor their own actions and performances can improve and achieve their own goals—which are not quite their own goals. Self-surveillance is—allegedly—very much in the interest of the good (i.e. well-functioning and successful, productive and efficient) employee. As soon as self-surveillance and self-discipline, self-control and self-censorship have begun to work, there is not really a need anymore for superiors (the dominant group or ruling elites) to use their power or control—their subordinates do all of this by and to themselves. This is quite a cunning twist. The ultimate idea is not only that external power and control aren't recognised as such anymore—the idea is that subordinates' control is generated, maintained and applied by the subordinates themselves. It is in the individuals' own interest to control themselves—without even recognising this as such. Managerial power and control are not only in the best interest of employees—they are their self-interest.

With self-control permanently turned on, the individual has reached the final stage of his or her internalisation of external control: the *calculative mind*. The underlying principle is that of 'hard work and subordination now, bonuses, status, and autonomy later' (Kärreman / Alvesson 2004, p. 168). This principle is little more than the modern version of the old 'protestant work ethic and the spirit of capitalism' (Weber 1904/1993). Amongst others, it comprises the idea of so-called 'rational' decision-making, i.e. assessing one's options, the possible outcomes and consequences of each of them, and deciding which promises the best result. The calculative mind is attractive to dominating groups. Subordinates permanently seek their advantages within the existing system—and only within the existing system. In doing so, they actively contribute to strengthening it. To put it slightly differently: subordinates with a calculative mind strengthen the prevailing order simply because they see it as in their interest. According to Zaleznik (1989, p. 51) 'self-interest and indifference are the foundations of a psychology of power and control that dominate modern corporations. They create the politics of compliance, the heart of the managerial culture.' In this sense, managerial power and control is yet another example of 'how control is exercised through the "manufacture" of subjectivity' (Alvesson / Willmott 2002, p. 622). It is 'identity regulation' (ibid, p. 621) at the highest level—because it is done to a great extent by the individual itself. The ideal subordinate is this new type of self-controlling and self-controlled employee who enthusiastically does all the managerial control him- or herself—even without realising it. The modern employee comes along in one functional, easily manageable package of the calculative mind.

This notion of the calculative mind (or calculative selfishness) has become the ideal and standard not only for our organisations but for our society. It has become a societal value. It is communicated and internalised a million times every day. It has been disseminated and has become such a dominant part of our social and organisational lives that it has reached hegemonic status, i.e. it is often even not realised anymore. And employees as well as managers do their utmost to live up to this notion. As Brookfield (2005, p. 44) described: 'The dark irony, the cruelty of hegemony, is that adults take pride in learning and acting on the beliefs and assumptions that work to enslave them. In learning diligently to live by these assumptions, people become their own jailers.' Management is such an established institution, and reminds people of this every day through the actions of managers and countless numbers of organisational arrangements, that employees have lost the ability to think and act outside this box. They are trapped in a 'mental cage' of socio-psychological control which supplements the 'iron cage' of hierarchical and bureaucratical structures (Kärreman / Alvesson 2004, p. 165); 'the most supreme exercise of power would be where it is possible to shape the perceptions, cognition, and preferences of individuals so that they accept the existing nature of things either because they can see or imagine no alternative or simply because they consider it natural and unchangeable or as divinely ordained and beneficial' (Akella 2003, p. 47). The most sophisticated—and most efficient—form of power is when it is not present anymore; it has reached *hegemonic control*, defined as the process where 'the intellectual, moral, and philosophical leadership provided by the class or alliance of class and class fractions which is ruling successfully achieves its objectives of providing the fundamental outlook for the whole society' (Bocock 1986, cited in Akella 2003, p. 47). In such a state, all traditional means of power and control are still present and still being used. But for large parts, i.e. for the (apparent) normality of daily routines, the maintenance of social order and prevalence of commonsense wisdom they are not really needed—simply because people are more than willing and keen to continue and to defend the way things are. According to Stoddart (2007, p. 201),

> hegemonic power works to convince individuals and social classes to subscribe to the social values and norms of an inherently exploitative system. It is a form of social power that relies on voluntarism and participation, rather than the threat of punishment for disobedience. Hegemony appears as the 'common sense' that guides our everyday, mundane understanding of the world. It is a view of the world that is 'inherited from the past and uncritically absorbed' and which tends to reproduce a sort of social homeostasis, or 'moral and political passivity' (Gramsci 1971:333).

Nowadays, this is exactly where managers' power sits; it is not only a comprehensive and multi-dimensional system but in most parts so socially accepted that it is not visible and recognised anymore. The managerial organisation has become the norm and normality, including managers' power and subordinates' absence of concern about it. Managers' power doesn't need to intervene anymore because it is so embedded in the daily routines of individuals and the design of the whole social system that it has simply disappeared as an identifiable issue or entity. In our contemporary managerial organisations, most employees function not only because they want to function, but because they can't even imagine alternatives, let alone try to change things. *Why should they?*

All in all, one of the strongest pillars of managers' power is the modern employee—because he or she is usually receptive to the internalisation of (socio-) psychological power and control mechanisms. The most relevant mechanisms are the following:

1. *Compliance:* this involves acceptance of contemporary organisational structures and processes, acknowledgement of managers' prerogatives, demonstration of willingness to fit into the system and function according to expectations which one does not necessarily like or support.
2. *Fear:* fears of actual or possible punishment help to shape and regulate most of subordinates' behaviour towards more thorough compliance with external rules and a stronger acknowledgement of superiors' power.
3. *Guilt and confession:* if boundaries are being crossed in unaccepted ways, the demonstration of feelings of guilt is required. In addition, the individual will confess "inappropriate" behaviour. By this eagerness to confess, the individual acknowledges his or her own deficits, the legitimacy of the system, the rightfulness of superiors and willingness to improve with the help and guidance of superiors.
4. *Desire and need to fit:* individuals want to conform with external expectations at the workplace probably not because they agree with them but because (publicly demonstrated) compliance provides a sense of security and other advantages.

5. *Career:* subordinates' 'appropriate' behaviour and performance will produce positive results for them. In the context of hierarchical and competitive organisations this mainly means (self-) development, progression, promotion—in one word: career.
6. *Control of hearts and minds:* the ability to control the perceptions and opinions, minds and worldviews of others (even regarding their own thoughts and interests) makes the difference between leaders and followers—and it makes the difference between ruling and being overthrown.
7. *Self-control:* social norms and values are internalised and become part of the individual's own desires concerning how to behave.
8. *Calculative mind:* the pursuit of one's own advantages within the existing system are based on a so-called rational assessment of options, the possible outcomes and consequences of each of them, and choosing the one which promises the best result.
9. *Hegemonic control:* power doesn't need to intervene anymore because it is so embedded in daily routines of individuals and the design of the whole social system that it has simply disappeared as in identifiable issue or entity.

Together, the (socio-) psychological power and control mechanisms described in this section constitute a continuum. It spans from forces imposed on the individual from outside (i.e. request for compliance, socialisation through institutions) over negative notions (i.e. raising fears, guilt and confession) to positive aspects (i.e. desire and need to fit, focus on career). They converge and culminate in the most internal and, hence, most effective forms of power over others and control of subordinates; control of the hearts and minds, self-control and the calculative mind. Together, they constitute hegemonic control. Modern management's (and managers') approach to managing and controlling the internal aspects of employees rather than (only) their directly visible behaviour makes sense. To extend managerial power and control *into* subordinates is a much more efficient strategy. Hoggett (cited in Sanderson 2001, p. 301) also found that '"hands-off" control can often be more effective and powerful than "hands-on" regulation'. This is one of the more cunning—and cynical—aspects of such oppressive systems like the managerial organisation; they are *deliberately* designed for transforming external "objective" systems of control and dominance into internal subjective mechanisms. They are now part of the individual's psyche and value system. Power and control have disappeared as externally imposed regimes.

THE SYSTEM OF ORGANISATIONAL SOURCES
AND MEANS OF MANAGERIAL POWER

The previous sections revealed that managerial power and control are based on many more pillars than only, say, their hierarchical position.

The table below provides an overview of the whole system of organisational sources, means, and objects of managerial power and control.

When discussing modern forms of organisations, some claim that new forms of power and control such as rhetoric have been substituted for older forms such as hierarchical and bureaucratical means. In contrast, others, e.g. Kärreman / Alvesson (2004, p. 151) drew attention to the fact that new forms rarely substitute for but complement existing forms and systems. Even when new forms of work organisation are being introduced, managers' previous rights and responsibilities remain largely intact (Rothschild / Ollilainen 1999, p. 594). Such a view implies that power and control mechanisms not only get more sophisticated but accumulate over time. Whether 'substitution' or 'accumulation' is the

Table 3.1   The System of Organisational Sources and Means of Managerial Power

Category	Sources, means and objects of power and control
1. Social institution and institutional embeddedness	• social institution (cultural capital) • networks (social capital) • stakeholders' active support
2. Organisational structures and processes of power	• hierarchy, roles and social position, rights and prerogatives • responsibilities for resources • centralisation and de-centralisation • bureaucracy, rules and order, structures and processes • teamwork, projects
3. Managers' prerogatives and the powerful manager	• setting the agenda / content of strategic issues, power to silence • management knowledge • leadership, mystique • personal skills, traits and attitudes
4. Performance measurement and management systems	• basic design of the systems, i.e. its leading principles, primary objectives, indicators and measures • differentiation in the scope and range of its usage • systematic and comprehensive opportunities to hold people accountable • indirect 'managing' of the workforce • invisibility through electronic panopticon and normalisation
5. (Socio-) psychological traits of the conditioned employee	• compliance • fear • guilt and confession • desire and the need to fit • career and selection • control of the hearts and minds • self-control • calculative mind • hegemonic control

more appropriate description for modern managerial and organisational forms of power and control, by and large, both might be a correct observation to describe specific *means* for power and control—particularly the ones which are based on technologies. There are definitely changes, innovations and "improvements" in how power and control are being constructed and carried out, as is the case with every technology, since humans are 'innovation-oriented animals'. Just as archives of physical files and folders have been substituted by electronic databases which can handle much more data, so has physical punishment of subordinates by their superiors been substituted by management by objectives and human resource policies which can provide a much broader spectrum of positive and negative sanctions.

Nonetheless, when it is about the *dimensions* of power and control (like the six dimensions described and analysed above and the strategies for using them) the picture is different. By developing the system it becomes clear that there is not a single or one-dimensional explanation of why managers rule organisations or why a social class dominates a society. *Managers' dominance is based on a multi-dimensional framework of sources and means of power and control.* Power was *always* embedded in institutions, structures and processes, ascribed to roles and role-related tasks, controlled by performance measurement systems. It was *always* internalised by subordinates, thereby always allowing their superiors to dominate in defining and shaping social reality via language and knowledge, rhetoric and discourse. Basically, *all* forms and dimensions of power and control have been around ever since human beings set up social systems and social relations—at least, so far. *When it is about power and control in principle, it is not substitution or accumulation but persistency which is in the centre of the problem.*

In this sense, there might be some considerable differences in the sophistication of power and control systems: in their design, how they are portrayed and how they are perceived. It is worth investigating these specifics since they reveal insights into how social relationships, organisations, and societies function, how they are designed and how they could or even should be changed. But many crucial aspects of social systems often, if not always, remain the same. The technical means and level of sophistication by which ruling classes dominate subordinates may change, but the dimensions of power and control relationships *as such* remain largely the same—even in what may be at first glance very different types of organisations or other social systems. Hence, it is not so much about whether management and contemporary organisations as regimes of control tend more towards George Orwell's iron fist of "1984" or Aldous Huxley's velvet glove in 'Brave New World' (Jermier 1998, p. 241). The real interest lies in revealing common patterns in both (and other) systems and how they are combined in particular power and control systems such as those designed and run by managers.

CONCLUSIONS

The analysis in this chapter has demonstrated that management is not (only) a set of organisational functions but a *multi-dimensional system* of power, authority and control (Willmott 1987, p. 254). It has also been suggested that power and control are much more widespread and intense in our contemporary organisations than ever before, particularly *managerial* power and control. One might say that it has reached hegemonic control in our organisations—and to a large extent also in our societal institutions, society and private lives. Although power and control have always been an issue in human history, it has become clear that modern forms of organisations and definitions of management have created multi-dimensional realities of power and control rarely seen before—at least not in this 'modern', and often sophisticated combination of the different dimensions and means. Since the late 19th century, orthodox organisations have become increasingly dominated by one social group: managers. And this group has become so powerful that only few could have imagined it. Even the long-ruling classes of aristocrats, merchants and capitalists with all their experience in playing societal power games for their own advantage, could not have foreseen how organisational responsibilities would put managers in such a strong position and that managerial power would be so deeply embedded in literally all organisational aspects and affairs.

Moreover, contemporary organisations are largely based on a 'low-trust managerial culture dominated by power interests and the elaborate system of organizational and ideological controls that it generates' (Reed / Anthony 1992, p. 602). They provide managers with a whole range of means of power and control which they can use as an elite minority to pursue their own interests even further (Lacey 2007, p. 133). And since managers are the ones who are responsible for the design of the systems, structures and processes which embed power dimensions, even if change is introduced, managers will make certain that they and their group will keep, if not increase their shares of power and influence (Zaleznik 1989, p. 114).

4 Managers' Interests in Dominance

> Not ideas, but material and ideal interests directly govern men's conduct.
>
> —Max Weber, 1920

INTRODUCTION

In the previous chapter it became clear that managers have the power within organisations. What is less clear is *why* they want it. The obvious answer is that they have an *interest* in dominating. Neither an individual nor a group of people could have and keep power over any longer period of time if they were not at least interested in doing so. Many people and professions do *not* want to dominate and rule—and, hence, they will not rule. Being interested in gaining, keeping and increasing power is a necessary, though not sufficient precondition for social dominance.

That managers have an interest in being powerful seems to look like an explanation, or at least part of it—but it isn't. It simply raises the question: *why are managers interested in dominating?* Why *should* they be interested in it? Some answers to these questions come immediately to mind:

- Managers might be interested in domination because they are expected to be powerful.
- Managers need to be powerful leaders because of functional or political reasons.
- People with particular character traits have an interest in dominating and therefore become managers.

Perhaps there is some truth in all of these answers. And there maybe other reasons—as we will see in the following. Unfortunately, research into the motivations behind managers' aspirations for dominance has so far has been limited and insufficient.

Orthodox management and organisation studies (e.g. Zaleznik 1989, Chandler 1977, Drucker 1954, Fayol 1949) are not only (almost) 'power-free' but also 'interest-free'. 'The manager' is largely portrayed as a task-oriented person who simply does what is required from her or him (albeit of course, in pro-active, innovative and most efficient ways). Only one strand explicitly addresses the issue of interests: neoclassical rational choice and agency theory. This assumes that particular self-interest is a major factor in determining attitude formation, decisions and actions of individuals. Based on this assumption, managers and their behaviour are analysed as rational actors (e.g. Hendry 2005, Grossmann / Hart 1983, Williamson 1975, Alchian / Demsetz 1972). In 'principal agent models' this strand provided some important insights into the basic problem that subordinates' (i.e. managers') interests can conflict strongly with superiors' (i.e. owner's or shareholders') interests. However, in general, neoclassical concepts are based on such narrow and rigorous assumptions about human decision-making and action that they are only sufficient for some game-theoretical reasoning. Because of their limitations, fundamental inconsistencies and methodological problems, they are often simply misleading if one wants to make sense of social phenomena such as people's interests. As a whole, orthodox management and organisation studies prefer to hide managers' interests under functional analysis and make (deliberately?) simple assumptions about managers' individual 'non-functional' motivations.

In contrast, Critical Management Studies make more or less explicit and realistic assumptions about managers' interests. In particular, it addresses the main reasons behind organisational politics—e.g. that managers have vested interests in managing as well as in the idea of 'the manager', gaining and keeping power and control, being responsible for ever more resources (including the whole organisation or parts of it) and increasing the areas they are responsible for (e.g. Brookfield 2005, Courpasson 2000, Alvesson / Willmott 1992a, b, Pettigrew 1992, Hindess 1986, Mintzberg 1985, Abercrombie et al. 1980, Burns 1961). Although such views may be quite helpful for a realistic investigation into managerial and organisational phenomena, this approach is largely confined to an analysis of the political aspects of organisations and management.

Finally, classical psychological attitude theories (e.g. expectancy value models, behaviourism or utility theory) investigate interests from an individual and psychological perspective (e.g. Darke / Chaiken 2005, Meglino / Korsgaard 2004, Miller 1999). Such contemporary approaches also take situative and social aspects into account, i.e. they address both psychological *and* socio-psychological approaches. As a result, they provide valuable insights into human interest-oriented decision-making. Most of these, however, stem from carefully designed experiments carried out under highly controlled conditions. Psychological theories hardly cope with the multi-dimensional embeddedness of people in complex organisations where many intervening variables clash with each other and cannot be separated from each other.

All three approaches described above have particular strengths in their areas of analysis and reveal important facets of the specific aspects they investigate about (managers') interests. But exactly because of their foci they provide too little for a comprehensive understanding of the phenomena. As a consequence, managers' interests are either being taken for granted, investigated in too limited ways, considered as not being worthy of analysis or are deliberately not being addressed at all—for whatever reasons. In contrast, this chapter provides a comparatively systematic investigation into managers' interest in dominance. The basic assumption is that the work of managers should not be portrayed as a set of 'neutral' activities (Willmott 1984, p. 350) but *as interest-driven actions of people within complex institutional settings*. The idea, therefore, is to identify the whole range of factors which are crucial for constituting and shaping managers' interests in becoming, being and staying powerful. For this, a comprehensive framework will be developed which comprises and addresses major areas of possible explanatory variables. The framework outlines a set of structural, organisational / functional, psychological, socio-psychological and sociological drivers shaping managers' interests within an organisational context. In doing so, the chapter will not provide one single hypothesis or an artificially reduced one-dimensional explanation. The analysis will shed some light on very different types of interests (as well as their constituting factors) and will show the complexity of the problem of interest-driven human existence, particularly interest-driven dominance of managers within organisations.

The following section provides a brief discussion and definition of the concept of interests. Based on this, the following sections develop a comprehensive model that identifies and differentiates between several types of interests of managers in an organisational context. It comprises the following:

1. Interest links between the organisation and its environment
2. Functional dimension, roles and organisational politics
3. Interests of managers as a group
4. Managers' individual and personal background
5. Subordinates' interests

The model acknowledges freedom of will and individual behaviour, and not only provides descriptions of several types of interests but also a basis for understanding the underlying driving forces in a comprehensive, systematic and thorough way. The final section draws some conclusions from the analysis.

THE CONCEPT AND DEFINITIONS OF INTERESTS

All human decisions are based on interests. Powerful and influential people, such as managers, are even more aware of their interests and so pursue them more consciously and thoroughly than less privileged or less influential people. Moreover, managers' decisions about option A or B are not (solely) based on an abstract strive for 'profit maximisation' or 'efficiency' (or whatever is portrayed as 'the interest of the organisation') but on what they regard *from a personal and individual point of view* as in *their* interest.

Based on this assumption, we will follow an individualised concept of interests. It is assumed that people do things for a purpose. This is not an unusual idea; on the contrary, Adam Smith may not have been the first, but he is the most cited proponent of the market economy. He famously stated: 'It is not from the benevolence of the butcher, the brewer, or the baker, that we expect our dinner, but from their regard to their own interest. We address ourselves, not to their humanity but to their self-love, and never talk to them of our own necessities but of their advantages' (Smith, A.: 'Inquiry into the Wealth of Nations', 1776, cited in Kramnick 1995, p. 507).[1]

Are managers any different from other human beings? Are they less self-interested than the butcher or baker in their small high street shop? Managers' decisions and actions within (social) structures are linked to their interests like any other system of human actors' decisions and actions within (social) structures. Managers make a conscious decision for something because *they have an interest in it.* Interests shape how people see and interpret the world, their ideas and intentions, attitudes and actions. In this sense, 'interests' provide the crucial explanatory link between people, their decisions and actions, and their social structure (e.g. Meglino / Korsgaard 2004, pp. 946, 953, Hindess 1986, p. 116)—as the Latin word for "to be in between" ('inter-esse') suggests. Hence, the concept of interests can be used to explain the intentional relationship between subjects and objects or objectives—e.g. between a current and a future state, between what one has and what one wants, between a need or desire and its satisfaction. According to this view, 'interest' is defined here as: *a person's or group of people's conscious attraction towards a certain object or objective.* This can either mean a (non-instrumental) curiosity in something or an (instrumental) desire or aspiration to achieve something, whereby the understanding of the object or the realisation of the objective is deemed by the person or group of people as useful or advantageous for them after due consideration.

This definition, and the assumptions on which it is based, can be explained further:

1. Only living beings with a consciousness can have interests (in something), i.e. human beings and probably many higher developed animals.[2] In the context of human society, this means that 'interest' is understood solely as a *people-oriented concept.* In this sense, it is *not* possible to say that an organisation "has got an interest" that something is or is not, should or should not be the case. Organisations and institutions, structures and processes—whether they are natural like an ecological system or man-made like a business organisation—can neither have nor express any kind of interest! It is always, and only, people who can have interests or make the claim that something is 'in the interest' of a particular natural or social system.

2. 'Interest' is meant here in a broad sense including not only self-interest (Ingram / Clay 2000, p. 528, Miller 1999) but also interest in others, i.e. egoism *and* altruism. Egoism relates to those interests which are only concerned with one's own advantages. Altruism refers to interests based on ethics (or 'ethical reasoning'), which refer to higher values, i.e. the sake of the whole group or system, epochal or even universal ideas (Darke / Chaiken 2005, p. 864, Rutledge / Karim 1999, p. 175).

3. There is individual judgment and personal freedom in the pursuit of one's interests (e.g. Fincham 1992, p. 749, Whittington 1992, p. 696, Stubbart 1989, p. 329). Managers, like any other people, are not the slaves of their or others' interests—at least not necessarily. As Hindess (1986, p. 120) put it: 'Interests are the product of assessment. They do not appear arbitrarily out of nowhere, they are not structurally determined, and they cannot be regarded as fixed or given properties of actors.' And he added (p. 129): 'Actors are not mere creatures of their position in sets of social relations, . . .'. Roles and organisational context, individual background, belonging to a particular group, epochal ideologies and interests of others—as strong as they seem to be—do *not* mean determinism.[3] Within structures or institutions there is room for individual discretion and interpretations (Dent / Barry 2004, p. 10); 'actors pursue their interests by making choices within constraints"—as Ingram / Clay (2000, p. 527) aptly put it.

4. In addition, *'after due consideration'* means that a person's interest is not 'only' an immediate urge, basic need, unconscious routine or reflex (Bresser-Pereira 2001, p. 365). Nor is it about a differentiation between people's 'real' and 'false' interests. 'Interest-driven' decision-making simply means that people are aware of possible alternatives, and think consciously about them, their implications and assumed consequences.[4] It is the 'rationalisation of acting . . . through planned adaptation to interests' (Max Weber 1921/1980, p. 15, own translation). As Stubbart (1989, p. 330) explained: 'Managers take strategic actions mainly for reasons, neither as a habit nor as a mindless repertoire'. To have an interest in something is a *conscious, thoughtful and reflective aspiration* towards one particular object or objective and its implications and consequences, and against any other alternatives, and their implications and consequences.

5. 'Due consideration' leads to the aspect of *rationality*. This is probably one of the most contested issues of Western reasoning and society. The concept as discussed here is *not* meant in the neoclassical economics sense where the central model of homoeconomicus wrongly portrays an image of human beings as 'rational maximisers' of their own 'self-interest' (du Gay 2005, p. 391). In

contrast to such heroic assumptions, human reasoning and decision-making are interpreted here in a much more realistic way. This
means the following:

a) People have neither got all information, nor are able to cope
with all information available, and nor is all of this information consistent and certain. As Hendry (2005, p. 58) has
explained: 'The world of business is . . . confused, uncertain
and unpredictable. The information on which decisions have
to be based is both insufficient and overwhelming, and can be
full of contradictions.' It is not possible to say with certainty
what the best decision or strategy is or what is 'in the best
interest' of a person, a group of people or an organisation.
People's judgment of (their) interests happens on the basis of
bounded rationality (Simon 1979, p. 502).

b) Rational decision-making cannot be reduced to a mathematical problem. Human reasoning, consideration and decisions
do not happen (only) on quantitative data or within one-dimensional frameworks. Like the concept of value, interests
can be everything which is deemed from a subjective point of
view to be of benefit—whether it is quantifiable or not (e.g.
Hindess 1986, p. 112). It is an assessment and comparison of
quantitative *and* qualitative aspects whereby final decisions
are always a *qualitative* judgment.

c) In this sense, rationality or rational decision-making cannot
be understood to be 'optimising'. Rational' "only" means
that a person has considered the alternatives, their opportunities and risks (Meglino / Korsgaard 2004, p. 946). It is
understood as 'calculative' in the sense that human beings
try to make a rough assessment of whether a certain decision
bears more positive or negative possible outcomes and consequences for themselves. Human goal-oriented reasoning is
about finding out what is *assumed to be* in one's 'best' interest, not finding some mathematical optimum.

6. The concept of interest is used here solely as a methodological tool.
Miller (1999, p. 1053) states that in Western cultures at least 'the
assumption of self-interest is not simply an abstract theoretical concept but a collectively shared cultural ideology'. It is the *ideology
of self-interest* which dominates our thinking and that we regard as
probably one of the highest goods (Moore / Loewenstein 2004, p.
195). It may even function 'as a powerful self-fulfilling force. The
assumption of self-interest contributes to its own confirmation . . .'
(Miller 1999, p. 1059). In contrast to the ideology of self-interest,
the concept of interest used here does *not* claim to describe human
nature or proclaim how humans *should* reason and act in a certain
way. It is meant as a methodological tool to reveal and analyse

influential factors *amongst others* which influence human decision-making and behaviour.

Based on this definition and further specifications, the next four sections develop a framework which systematically and comprehensively identifies sets of interests which influence managers' interests within an organisational context.

INTEREST LINKS BETWEEN THE ORGANISATION AND ITS ENVIRONMENT

The first factors which significantly shape managers' interests are *external* factors, i.e. those in the environment of the organisation. Managers are usually aware of what happens in those areas outside their organisation which they deem to be relevant. They take into account crucial events and (future) developments in their organisation's political, economic, social, technological, environmental and legal environment—and they are strongly encouraged to do so by management and organisation theories (e.g. Johnson et al. 2006, pp. 65–87). Of course, the environments of organisations may differ markedly depending on what industry and markets the company does its business in, and these differences may be regional and cultural as well as situative. In addition, managers receive information which largely corresponds to their organisational positions and functions. So their perceptions and worldviews, the ways they interpret the environment and make sense of events in it can differ quite drastically (e.g. Balogun / Johnson 2004, Staples et al. 2001, Melone 1994, Isabella 1990, Stubbart 1989, Daft / Weick 1984). Acknowledging these differences, the question is how managers' interests fit in between an organisation's factual (or perceived) environment on the one hand, and the managing of the organisation on the other hand.

According to new sociological institutionalism and its idea of "isomorphism", any given system must conform with, and internalise, the leading principles, institutional pattern and forces of its environment (e.g. Coopey / Burgoyne 2000, Ingram / Clay 2000, DiMaggio / Powell 1983, Meyer / Rowan 1977). This means that there *must be* isomorphism between prevailing values and trends in the environment and an organisation's values and strategy since otherwise in the long run the organisation would disappear. Organisations *have to* incorporate elements which are legitimised externally, rather than developing their own individual set of criteria in order to gain legitimacy (as well as political, financial, and cultural support) (Staw / Epstein 2000, p. 524, Meyer / Rowan 1977, p. 348). Many empirical examples can be found which appear to support this position.

However, the idea of isomorphism can be also quite misleading. No social system can "adapt" itself to institutions in its environment or adopt prevailing values and customs. Social systems such as organisations do not "exist" like an organism—such ideas are only metaphors. Organisations do not "perceive" their environment, "interpret" information, "make" decisions or "take" action—*only human beings can do this*. It is always the members of an organisation who, as its representatives, demonstrate their interest in (doing) something via their views, decisions and actions (or non-decisions and in-actions). In this sense, talking about an organisation's interests and actions with regard to its environment is misleading. In such an extreme form, institutionalism is nothing more but anthropomorphism.

In its less extreme form, the idea of isomorphism is implicitly present in many perceptions of the environment. External challenges and changes are often portrayed by managers as inevitable. According to Ellis (1998, p. 231) 'very few businesses have the power or ability to resist the competitive pressures they face . . .'.[5] Even if managers wanted to, they could not do otherwise—so they say. "The reality" has to be accepted as it is. Spencer-Matthews' (2001, p. 56) citation of one manager is typical: 'I don't understand why people are hell bent on shooting the messenger—we don't have a choice—we are being pressured into doing this from outside—if we don't do it we won't be around as a university for very long'. However, this human actor-oriented version of isomorphism is, again, misleading. There is no necessity in the social realm! Even if all managers within a particular industry come to the same conclusion and decide on the same business model, they still could do something else—and they often do. For example, entrepreneurs *deliberately* start or steer their business against conventional wisdom and prevailing forces. An entrepreneur, by definition, has an interest in *not fitting*, and being successful "against the odds". There are always innovators who come up with very different strategies and business models which turn existing industries upside-down or even create new industries (and there are even more who fail). Isomorphism cannot explain, or cope with the (successful) behaviour of entrepreneurs. It can only explain (and / or justify) why *conservative* managers are keen to fit into existing and prevailing value systems. In this sense, isomorphism is not a valid representation of reality or the relation between an organisation and its environment as such. It is a conservative look at things. In doing so, it gives an idea of how *some* managers' perceptions and interests are shaped by this concept—and how such managers use it (at least in their official rhetoric) in order to adapt their organisation to whatever is currently portrayed as 'the iron laws of the market', 'the demands of society', 'political requirements' or the like—*at that time*.

This last point also indicates that theories such as isomorphism cannot cope sufficiently with the dynamics of social systems, i.e. the changing relationships between the greater system (e.g. a society) and its parts (e.g. business sector). And it cannot cope sufficiently with human interests, decisions and actions within these interlocking systems and their dynamics. This is particularly an issue for business, markets and the world of managers. With the emergence of the 'managerial society' in the second half of the 20th century, management concepts are formulated and disseminated at increasing speed. Examples like shareholder orientation, lean management, TQM, business re-engineering, Balanced Scorecard, Corporate Social Responsibility, knowledge management and the like are all parts of an endless chain of trendy new concepts which have collectively come to be known as 'managerial fads and fashions' (e.g. Staw / Epstein 2000, Ramsey 1996, Abrahamson 1996). Managers are aware of these fads and fashions within their organisation's environment. Many managers even appreciate the widespread availability of such latest management concepts because they deliver ideas, models, explanations and frameworks which provide order in a confusing world (Kieser 1997, p. 67). They can be used for the formulation, introduction and justification of yet another strategic change management initiative, and they provide relatively simple and straightforward solutions. The ways in which managers see and approach business and organisational issues, not to mention their own curiosity, aspirations and interests, are considerably shaped by managerial fads and fashions.

Simultaneously, their environment *expects* managers to use the latest concepts and management techniques (e.g. Staw / Epstein 2000, pp. 547–548, Abrahamson 1996, p. 257).[6] Their use and application is perceived as yet another sign of managerial, if not to say entrepreneurial skill. The 'ideology of good management . . . associates managers with the introduction of new ideas, new organizational forms, new techniques, new products, or new moods' (March 1981, cited in Kieser 1997, p. 65). 'Joining the bandwagon' and similar 'herd behaviour' (Carson et al. 1999, p. 321) makes a lot of sense for managers. In doing so, they can demonstrate (and prove to everyone, including themselves) that they are using the 'latest cutting-edge techniques'.

Unlike isomorphism, following the latest terminology and concepts is actually seen as 'innovative', or at least 'pro-active' management. It is therefore very much in managers' interest to follow managerial trends and fashions, since this corresponds to the currently prevailing ideology about what managers (allegedly) do and how they should do it. In doing so, managers follow and meet societal expectations, i.e. to do what is recommended and required. They simply do what everyone else does—this can't be wrong! If managers stick to what is portrayed by interested parties (as well as the managers themselves) as 'professional management' and behave as 'professional managers', they will belong to the "in-group" and can avoid the sanctions associated with deviance (Carson et al. 1999, p. 322). In this sense, following trends is not so much a mechanical adaptation of organisations to their environment in response to "natural laws", but a more or less conscious decision by managers because it is in *their* interest!

To suggest that managerial fads and fashions shape managers' interests and that it is in managers' own interest to follow them is a valid point. However, it still doesn't explain how these abstract entities and developments relate to, and influence managers' interests. This becomes clearer when one includes in the analysis other identifiable actors who are also in the environment, i.e. external stakeholders (Freeman 1983). According to the stakeholder concept, managers particularly take into account the interests of those people and institutions which are regarded as of great relevance to business, and to the purpose and existence of the organisation. The interests of owners, shareholders, investors, analysts, business associations, media, government, governmental organisations, employee representatives and pressure groups can be a considerable influence on both organisations and managers. For example, Abrahamson (1996, p. 261) explained that 'if managers do not appear to use such techniques, then stakeholders' expectations that the organization is run rationally will tend to be disappointed, and stakeholders will tend to withdraw their support from the organization, thereby increasing the likelihood that this organization and its managers will fail.'

There might be many reasons why managers care about stakeholders. The important point to make is that managers' reactions are, again, not *'mechanical' but interest-driven*. How managers *actually* perceive, and respond to different stakeholders and their vested interests depends on the underlying rationale, i.e. by whatever criteria stakeholders are seen and judged. Perhaps the most widespread version of the stakeholder approach draws attention particularly to dependency and power relations (e.g. Savage et al. 1991, Freeman 1983). Johnson et al. (2006, pp. 181–182) suggest managing different stakeholders on the basis of their identified power and interests: i.e. the more powerful stakeholders are, and / or the more interest they have in the organisation, the more attention they should receive. Following this rationale it seems that managers, like members of other groups with power, are more sensitive to vested interests the more stakeholders potentially or factually are able to make a positive or negative impact on the organisation—which basically means *managers'* positions and interests. Many managers seem to try to increase their image and external value exactly along the lines of this rationale. In their decision-making and tactical manoeuvres, managers take the interests of stakeholders into account in proportion to the stakeholders' actual or potential influence and power. So managers primarily try to meet the expectations of powerful stakeholders (e.g. banks, investors, government, big customers), and will only secondarily try to satisfy and inform those stakeholders who are not that interested (e.g. business associations, other organisations) or not that powerful (trade unions). Finally, under the cover of buzzword-like "concerns" and cynical lip service, managers will simply ignore all those stakeholders who seem to be of little or no threat to their position and interests (e.g. smaller suppliers, less important customers, employees, local community, the public and society in general). The following four sub-sections discuss how some very relevant and influential stakeholders support and strengthen managers' dominance. These are

- business organisations,
- government, (non-) governmental organisations and mainstream politicians,
- consultancies, management gurus and business media, and
- business schools.

Business organisations

It is well-known that managers, particularly senior managers, have managed to establish large and strong networks beyond organisational boundaries—e.g. via interlocking directorates, 'old-boys' / 'old-girls' networks, or simply via more or less regular collaboration with suppliers, customers, bankers or even their competitors. Much of this networking is about creating 'win-win situations', granting favours and building trust (e.g. Carroll 2007). The more influential of these networks within the realms of business and industries are initiated and run by managers of larger corporations, as well as financial institutions such as banks and other institutional investors. Scott (2003, p. 168) gave an excellent description of this situation:

> The structure of this elite was characterised by a pattern of bank centrality . . . . It is the bank boards that are central to the whole structure of interlocking directorships and to patterns of economic decision-making. The leading banks occupy strategic positions at the centre of clusters of connected enterprises, and their boards operate as crucial intermediaries in the flow of information from one enterprise to another. . . . Bank directors, then, form the core of a corporate elite with system-wide interests.

Managers of business organisations may compete with each other intensively over market shares, customers and access to resources. They may also all have fundamentally different interests compared to those of financial investors (e.g. long-term oriented strategic objectives vs. short-term oriented shareholder maximisation). However, there is a 'constellation of interests' (Scott 2003, p. 160) concerning one issue amongst *all* managers: that the prevalence of management and the prerogatives of managers shall prevail. This is an important societal factor for managers' dominance. Even if individual managers fail, all that will happen is that they will be replaced by yet another manager, and perhaps with some rudimentary changes in regulatory frameworks, strategy, or at operational levels. At the end of the day, even the most appalling scandals of managerial malfunction and criminal energy do not and cannot hurt the institution of management as such and, hence, the class of managers. Managers come and go, the institution of management remains. It is the commonly shared ideal and interest of all business-related stakeholders that management *and* the notion of 'the manager' shall be kept intact—by (almost) all means.

Government, (non-) governmental organisations and mainstream politicians

It is not really surprising that finance and business, as well as managers across industries and even national boundaries, have this basic interest in the dominance of management in common. What has been quite a new development in the past quarter of a century is the scope and intensity with which governments of almost all political colour support not only 'the economy' but especially managerial capitalism (e.g. Kirkpatrick / Ackroyd 2000, p. 527). 'Big business' and (better) management in particular are seen and portrayed by politicians and senior managers alike as of 'national interest': 'What is good for business is good for the country!' Politicians are therefore more than willing not only to praise the abstract idea of 'managerial professionalism' (Abercrombie et al. 1980, p. 135) but to actively support and strengthen the societal position and power of managers as well—both in the private sector and increasingly in public sector organisations (e.g. Apple 2005, p. 20, Cohen et al. 1999, p. 484).[7] The reasons for this are not necessarily related to political convictions—as recent Labour governments demonstrate. It has more to do with similarities in mindsets. For example, the interests of political elites in gaining and keeping power and control are very similar to managers' interests (Kirkpatrick / Ackroyd 2003, p. 527). Senior politicians' and senior managers' careers are quite similar; both have to fight their way up hierarchical organisations, both have to be very power-oriented, both need to have similar personalities and personal attitudes for surviving organisational politics. Although their businesses are different, politicians and managers essentially speak the same language and talk about the same things. They understand each other because they are of the same breed. There is a constellation of interests between politicians and managers which is publicly much about business and organisations as well as more deeply about similar mindsets and acting within environments perceived and created as challenging and hostile.

Consultancies, management gurus and business media

One group with a probably even stronger interest in upholding and disseminating the idea of management as well as serving managers is the management fashion-setting community, i.e. business and management consultants, management gurus and business media publications. It is specifically their business to sell ideas and concepts to, as well as about managers and management. Ramsey (1996, p. 166) captured this notion well: 'As organizations, consultancies clearly have a vested interest akin to that of suppliers of automobiles or consumer durables: to offer replacements frequently enough to sustain their growth as firms, and attractive enough to appear worth ditching or adding to the old technique for.' This is the commodification of knowledge for the management knowledge market (Abrahamson / Eisenman 2001). And the most important group of customers in this market are the managers themselves, particularly those in the upper echelons. As with any other commodity, it is not about how valuable or useful managerial concepts actually are, but how well they are perceived (and bought) by those managers. It's therefore not very surprising that managerial concepts are particularly tailored towards the needs, self-images and positions of managers. They are made for managers, they are about managers' prerogatives and they are developed for *their* needs (under the camouflage of functional language). According to Protherough / Pick (2002, p. 61) business consultants hit the nail on its head: 'They "act as organisational myth-makers or story tellers" and part of their success is because they deliberately set out to give legitimacy to the aspirations and status-claims of the managers who buy and read their books.'

It is therefore no surprise that contemporary business and management consultancy is predominantly about the prevalence, importance and legitimacy of management and managers. Business and management consultants have (pro-) actively developed, promoted and disseminated managerial concepts which are all based on the same assumptions (Ramsey 1996, p. 166):

1. Managers are responsible for organisations.
2. Only managers can do management.
3. If an organisation needs to be more x ('x' stands for any buzzword and latest management fashion), then it is managers' responsibility that 'y' is done.
4. Since only managers can guarantee this, managers' roles and responsibilities need to be strengthened accordingly.

With such an agenda, business and management consultants have contributed a great deal to the development of the 'ideology of the manager' as well as to the institutionalisation of managers as one of the dominant classes.

Business schools

Particularly in the past three decades we have also witnessed a boom in management education, academic business research and management consultancy provided primarily by academics at business schools. There are some claims that the outcomes of such academic activities have a relatively small impact on actual business practices and have little relevance to the concerns and actions of practicing managers (e.g. Smallman 2006, Pfeffer / Fong 2002). There might be some truth in this. On the other hand, the theoretical foundations, conceptual narratives, systematic elaboration and ideological justifications of managerial concepts are largely developed and disseminated in the realm of academia, i.e. at business schools, in academic publications and at conferences. And there is a massive demand for it. Business education has become 'big business' and a 'cash cow' at most universities (e.g. Pfeffer / Fong 2002).

Most of what has been said about consultants is therefore also relevant to business school academics, particularly mainstream business- and manager-oriented academics. The knowledge they generate and disseminate is officially about organisations and the improvement of their efficiency and effectiveness (e.g. AACSB 2007 or the Academy of Management's 'Code of Ethical Conduct', referred to in Baldridge et al. 2004, p. 1066). In reality, it is mostly about managers and *their* problems. And these problems are seen from a certain cultural and ideological perspective. In both their teaching and research, business schools simply use, reproduce, defend and justify the litany of (US-American) mainstream theories and concepts of orthodox management without questioning the very assumptions on which these concepts are being based.[8] As early as 1982 Watson (p. 259) had realised that a 'great deal of organizational theory and research has been limited in its critical analytical potential as a result of its having been closely associated with the interests of people whose primary concern has been with the management of organizations.' Since then, mainstream business school academics have become even more focused in studying business, organisations and management mainly, if not exclusively from the viewpoint of (senior) managers. Such a perspective primarily, if not exclusively supports managers' interests, power and ideology. It is about speaking '*about* employees, *to* managers *as* professional experts' (Jacques 1996, p. 93).

In addition, and perhaps even more importantly, (mainstream) business school academics shape the worldviews and mindsets of *future* managers through their teaching and management education, i.e. younger students in undergraduate and post-graduate courses as well as experts and lower managers in MBA courses. In doing so, business schools lay the foundation for the making of future managers and contribute massively to the further shaping, if not to say conditioning of current managers. They do this at a scale and intensity which we have never seen before. It has societal dimensions and implications; business schools play a large part in the making and development of the social class of managers. Moreover, business schools crucially provide the knowledge and justification as well as the concepts and tools for dominating. Without business schools and their activities, the class of managers could not dominate both within organisations and society, and could not regenerate itself and perpetuate its basis of social dominance.

All in all, managers' views, interests and decisions are considerably influenced by developments in their organisation's environment. Usually, the environment is too complex and too multi-faceted to create a straightforward and direct link, let alone a cause-and-effect relationship between external factors and managers' interests in dominating. The legal and regulatory frameworks, societal values, cultural and economical trends, expectations and behaviour of stakeholders and so on only set the scene—and the limits—for most managers' perceptions, interests and choices. This ever- changing framework provides sufficient room for managers' discretion. However, despite the complexity of today's world and its varied, often contradictory trends, there is nonetheless quite a strong tendency towards conformity amongst managers. But this is *not* due to (quasi-) natural laws or a mechanically operating isomorphism. It is because of managers' interests in demonstrating that their organisation 'fits' to its environment, a half-conscious, half-unconscious following of managerial fads and fashions, and particularly an appreciation of powerful and / or otherwise influential stakeholders. Managers' views and interests are strongly shaped by these ideas of "best fit", "fads-and-fashions" and "stakeholder orientation". Moreover, they are keen to demonstrate that they know their respective relevant business environment, that they are up-to-date with latest trends and developments and that they address concerns and prevailing values being formulated and brought forward by powerful and influential stakeholders. Most managers, therefore, tend to be interested in the same managerial concepts which address, demonstrate, underline and support this notion.

As the examples above demonstrate, managers are not the only ones who have vested interests in maintaining the dominance of managers. Managers are well-served and well-supported by powerful and influential players within the realm of business, including

- managers of companies, banks and institutional investors,
- governments, political parties of all colours and non-governmental organisations,
- consultancies, management gurus and business media, and
- (mainstream) business school academics.

They all contribute immensely to the dominance of managers as a social class. Although there might be occasional clashes, the common interests and worldviews of these players usually prevail. There is a *'structural constellation of interests'* amongst major stakeholders and key players in economy and society. Managers are right in the middle of a *power web* which is constituted and supported by the range of vested interests listed above including not least, business school academics. Because of managers' synergetic and mutually beneficial relationships with these actors and institutions, they are in a strong position to justify, strengthen and deepen their positions and influence.

FUNCTIONAL DIMENSION, ROLES AND ORGANISATIONAL POLITICS

In contrast to the previous section we will now concentrate on possible reasons for managers' interests in dominating organisations. The first section addresses internal factors of organisations such as (so-called) functional aspects, managers' roles and organisational politics. We will later concentrate on more psychological factors within managers themselves.

The prevailing orthodox theory of the firm makes the *functionalistic* claim that organisations exist for a purpose which goes beyond any individual. Therefore, the first and foremost of all objectives is the survival of the organisation. Organisations 'are viewed as neutral, rational, technical, instrumental systems designed to convert inputs into outputs, and strategy is conceived as the determination of ends and the selection of means for achieving ends' (Shrivastava 1986, p. 371). Accordingly, orthodox management theories portray managers as functionally necessary facilitators and coordinators of others' actions and the whole organisation. The objectives of both managers and their organisations are said to be closely linked together and managers are therefore regarded 'as the guardian[s] of the overall purposes of the organisation' (Pollitt 1993, cited in Kirkpatrick et al. 2005, p. 66). Managers' sole, or at least primary, interest is to achieve the best outcome for the organisation and what is in the general interest of all (e.g. Pettigrew 2002, p. 97, Alvesson / Willmott 1992, p. 1). They therefore pursue management tasks solely for the sake of the whole, and to improve the efficiency and functionality of the units they are responsible for. In this sense, their decisions and actions are portrayed as 'impartial and uncompromised by self-interest or class-interest, motivated only by the seemingly universal virtues of efficiency and effectiveness' (Willmott 1996, p. 326).

In Chapter 5, we will see that this 'functional' image of managers, management and the managerial organisation is anything but 'neutral' and 'value-free'; it is *ideology*. But even if we remain for the time being within the confines of the functional view, it quickly becomes obvious that managers' interests are *not* primarily about the impartial pursuit of organisational purposes. According to the functional approach, managers' first interests are to be responsible for the management of organisations—and indeed to be the only ones who are responsible for it. As the internal and external representatives of the organisation, managers specifically see it as their task to be the final arbiters on all important issues of within the organisation; i.e. setting and measuring strategic objectives, values and vision, as well as supervising the operational realisation of those objectives. It is about setting the agenda, the crucial issues against which everything else is finally judged and valued, and who controls that; it gives managers *the prerogative and exclusive right to manage*. It therefore is one of managers' highest interests to secure, justify, even strengthen these prerogatives by (almost) all possible means. Managers will therefore opt for the same managerial concepts since they support and reproduce *their* ideas and understandings of strategic management (Baker 2005, p. 699). This indicates that the functional approach is anything but 'interest-free'. It is in fact a comprehensive, thorough, and elaborated blueprint for the formulation and justification of individual and sectoral interests.

However, managers do not want to decide on strategic issues purely for the sake of deciding on them. They also have vested interests in what is decided. An organisation's primary objectives can be interpreted as 'reflections of the values and cognitive bases of powerful actors in the organization' (Hambrick / Mason 1984, p. 193). Managers, like other groups within an organisation, are proponents of cosmologies who are keen to get their interests represented through the organisation's primary strategic objectives. 'At issue here is the question of organizational discourses: which agenda is seen to hold sway?, Whose interpretations are defining organizational reality?' (Cohen et al. 1999, p. 492). They understand the importance of having their ideas reflected in the strategic objectives and values of their organisation—the more one is identified, or can identify with the prevailing objectives and values of a social system, the stronger and safer his or her position is. Managers therefore prefer strategic objectives, vision and mission statements where they can see their functional and personal interests being reflected the most. Managers' interests in securing their functionally justified prerogatives are even more understandable. These are not only about rhetoric. Having the privilege and responsibility to make managerial decisions has got *factual* consequences; such decisions 'are likely to threaten existing patterns of resource-sharing' (Pettigrew 2002, p. 98). Even when we concentrate solely on functional aspects (and leave organisational politics and psychological factors until later), we can say that within the organisational context, managers' interests are very much about *their* responsibilities for, and access to resources (Swedberg 2005, p. 371, Hales 1999, p. 345). This is particularly relevant to financial resources (budget), organisational resources (departmental and functional realms), human resources (staff), other intangible assets (intellectual and social capital) and physical resources. Because of their (self-) image and the societal status ascribed to their position (as well as material advantages), managers are keen to get their hands on as many resources possible, not only by securing and maintaining access to existing resources, but by procuring a comparatively larger share of what else is available in future—hence their interest in being involved in the formulation of any strategy and policy.

Most of managers' prerogatives and (resource) responsibilities are formally defined and fixed in their *roles*. A role can be defined as an 'organized pattern of behaviour in accordance with the expectations of others' (Thompson 1961, p. 486). According to role theory, to a large extent roles prescribe what people usually do (Biddle 1986, 1979). Much more, roles tell people which problems need to be solved and how—particularly organisational roles within differentiated hierarchical organisations (Simon 1991, p. 126). Roles therefore shape people's interests immensely. In a business context, one's primary concerns and interests are often linked particularly to one's professional role. What influence people's interests most are the main objectives, key tasks and expected outcomes laid out in the job description and reproduced in daily routines and tasks. There is convincing

evidence that managers' interests are shaped considerably by these functional aspects and their related rewards and penalties (e.g. Waller et al.
1995, pp. 948–949, 964). The role model for managers is clear: 'Norms
of managerial rationality are societal expectations that managers will use
management techniques that are the most efficient means to important
ends' (Abrahamson 1996, p. 256–257).

If managers do not use managerial concepts and strategies, they are simply seen (and blamed!) as 'unprofessional'. Managers are therefore keen not
only to carry out their tasks in accordance with the role prescription, but
to create and communicate a public image of the manager as a functional
power figure, an image of performance, mastery and command. This portrait is 'a highly partisan and partial narrative. It is designed to be impressive, to affirm and naturalize the power of dominant elites' (Scott 1990, p.
18). Scott developed and called this concept of ruling elites 'public transcripts' and concluded (ibid., p. 70) that the powerful 'have a vital interest
in keeping up the appearances appropriate to their form of domination.'

This is even more important since in hierarchically organised social
systems, roles divide people not only horizontally but vertically. In addition to their functional aspects, they also define *social position* (Biddle
1979, pp. 89–93, 103–110). Managers' roles and positions are embedded in a system of interrelated roles and hierarchically organised positions (Simon 1991, p. 126). Thanks to career background and experience,
managers are very aware of this fact. They are also therefore sensitive
about their roles and positions, as well as events and changes which may
have an impact on them—particularly to *their* own areas of responsibilities and influence.

Of course, since managers' roles and positions differ widely, their role-
related interests are also quite distinct. The division of labour between managers has some of the same consequences of any differentiation between
(groups of) people. The division of labour and structuring of jobs 'creates
sectional interests, each with their own needs and priorities. . . . once organizational groups are given different tasks they begin to formulate their
own sets of norms and goals. They either reinterpret objectives or construct personal goals which serve their own interests' (Miller et al. 2002,
p. 79). For example, *departmental affiliation*, professional background and
expertise play a large role in shaping managers' strategic and operational
interests (Melone 1994, p. 452). This does not simply mean that a marketing or sales director will necessarily (always) opt for a more market-oriented strategy, or a finance director for a more cost-oriented strategy. There
are very few human resources directors who really care about people. But
there is sufficient empirical evidence which suggests that managers tend to
see problems from their own areas of responsibility and that they develop
viewpoints which are more consistent with the goals and activities of the
unit or function they are responsible for (Melone 1994, p. 439, Walsh 1988,
p. 875). Many managers will (also) compare options on the basis of what

they regard as their units' interest: i.e. what are the implications of the company's strategy for the area they are responsible for? What will be required from this unit? Which resources will it get? What might be possible opportunities and threats? Because of these departmental priorities and sectoral interests, managers tend to prefer options which, overall, will provide more advantages than disadvantages for their area of responsibility.

As a result of these different prerogatives, responsibilities, roles, sectoral and departmental affiliations, managers may have different interests and understanding of strategic and managerial issues. Managers of an organisation are not one homogeneous group but vary considerably. They represent different sectional interests, have different personal backgrounds and compete with each other in their perception of what the strategy and management of the organisation should be about. So managers come up with different strategies, business models, interpretations of strategic objectives, perceptions of change initiatives or operational aspects (Diefenbach 2007, 2005)—and they try to make their respective views and interests heard. In one word, it is about *politics*—organisational politics, or the internal politics of organisations (Burns 1961). Amongst managers, even, or perhaps particularly in the upper echelons of the organisation, there is (open or hidden) conflict, clashing worldviews, internal struggles, and shifting coalitions (e.g. Balogun / Johnson 2004, p. 544, Miller et al. 2002, p. 80, Levy et al. 2001, p. 7, Fincham 1992, p. 743). These happen on a daily basis, but intensify and become even more obvious when strategic and managerial decisions are on the agenda such as: a new strategy or business model; mission and vision statements; budgets; and major changes in structure, processes or resource allocation (e.g. Staples et al. 2001, Samra-Fredericks 2000, Cohen et al. 1999, p. 473, Coopey et al. 1997, Melone 1994, Isabella 1990, Stubbart 1989, Walsh 1988, Daft / Weick 1984, Hambrick / Mason 1984).

According to Levy et al. (2001, p. 2), 'Strategy can be viewed as a set of practices and discourses which promotes instrumental rationality, reproduces hierarchical relations of power, and systematically privileges the interests and viewpoints of particular groups.' The position of (senior) managers within an organisation usually encompasses—rightly or wrongly—high status and authority with great influence and power, but at the same time it can be quickly threatened or damaged. Managers therefore consider the implications of such decisions very carefully (Miller et al. 2002, p. 80)—particularly from *their* own perspective and considering their own interests. They focus on three areas: a) the primary objectives of the organisation (who achieves his or her objectives and to what extent?); b) access to organisational resources (who gets what share of the budget and other resources?); c) power and influence (who can keep or even increase his or her power and influence?).

During major change initiatives, managers can re-shape the organisational configuration of power and renew their claim for leadership (e.g.

Clegg / Walsh 2004, pp. 230–231, Kieser 1997, p. 66). Such periods are particularly crucial; present patterns of responsibilities and privileges as well as their personal future are at stake. Managers' battles are therefore about competing paradigms of governance, power and control. It is about imposing one's worldviews and will on others, struggling for power and influence and providing meaning and guidance for others (e.g. Walsh 1995, p. 290). It is about ideologies, i.e. which (and whose) belief system will reign. But most importantly, *it is about personal interests and individual aspirations.* The actual strategic issues are relegated to secondary importance, if any—buzzwords and technicalities may and will change anyway. The prime issues and concerns are to secure, if not to increase one's influence and responsibilities, fiefdoms and financial rewards. Organisational politics can therefore be seen as a tool for managers to gain, keep or increase their internal position, influence and control (e.g. McAuley et al. 2000, p. 87, Kieser 1997, p. 67, Zaleznik 1989, pp. 45–46). Given what is at stake, it is of primary interest to be involved in these activities. Moreover, *it is even expected that managers engage in politics.* Playing and staying in the game is in managers' interest because it indicates, guarantees and strengthens their very status as managers. It is in effect part of the organisational function of managers.

We can now summarise what the analysis of managers' interests has revealed in this section. According to the *functionalistic view* of orthodox management and organisations theory, a manager's prime interest is the pursuit of organisational objectives. Even accepting this view, it becomes clear that managers have strong individual interests within this functional framework. Firstly, they have very strong interests in securing and justifying decisions and the management of *strategic and operational objectives as managers' prerogatives.* This interest in organisational responsibilities extends into their interests in the content of strategic decisions, and securing or even enlarging their access to, and responsibilities for *budget and other organisational resources.* In addition, many managers are also keen to develop the *roles and public image* of a functional power figure through functional performance and mastery. And since their interests might differ considerably from other managers because of *sectoral interests and departmental affiliations,* most, if not all managers are actively involved in or*ganisational politics*—in fact they have to be as part of their organisational functions. Clearly, the claim that managers' involvement in functional aspects of organisations is 'interest-free' is not valid; on the contrary, organisational functions and managers' interests are inseparably linked.

INTERESTS OF MANAGERS AS A GROUP

In the previous sections, managers' interests were discussed primarily from an individual manager's perspective. However, despite major differences, organisational politics and potentially intense competition, managers have also *common interests*. Because of this, it is possible to see managers as a *group* to a certain degree.[9] As early as 1908, Georg Simmel, a famous German sociologist wrote (cited in Swedberg 2005, p. 369): 'Socialisation is the form . . . in which individuals grow together into a unity and within which their interests are realized. And it is on the basis of their interests—sensuous or ideal, momentary or lasting, conscious or unconscious, causal or teleological—that individuals form such unities.' Watson (1982, p. 264) came to a similar conclusion: 'individuals relate themselves to others in objectively similar circumstances to defend or advance shared interests.'

What are managers' prime shared interests? Probably one of their most common interests is 'being a manager' (and all what comes with it). According to social identity theory (e.g. Ullrich et al. 2005, Ashforth / Mael 1989, Tajfel / Turner 1979), the gaining and development of a *social identity* (or social identi*ties*) is one of the constitutional factors for the individual as a social being. It is 'the individual's knowledge that he belongs to certain social groups together with some emotional and value significance to him of this group membership' (Tajfel 1972, cited in Hogg / Terry 2000, p. 122). As members of a (strong and successful) group, individuals can develop a positive social identity (self-enhancement), distinguish themselves from others (self-distinctiveness) and continue to develop their self-concept (self-continuity) (Elstak / Van Riel 2005, p. E2). 'Being a manager' provides such an opportunity to develop a positive social identity. It also provides the basis for seeing managers as a group. For example, Hartley (1983, p. 16) claimed that 'a group may be defined through social identification rather than through social interaction'. Managers have a fundamental understanding of what it means to be a manager, a sense of group belonging and group identification (Jost / Elsbach 2001, p. 183). Despite their daily battles and organisational politics, managers in the same organisation may even have a stronger common understanding, whether this has developed 'naturally' or was created by countless vision statements, corporate identity buzzwords, training seminars and artefacts. Particularly with respect to their functions and areas of responsibilities, managers have enough in common to develop some group coherence (van Dijk 2006, p. 119, Swedberg 2005, p. 367). Managers have vested interests in common simply because they share the same socially defined role of a 'manager'.

In addition, belonging to a group makes sense because individuals usually fare better when they co-ordinate their activities to some extent— "together we are stronger". It is a fundamental truth of groups that the individual pursuit of interests is easier in the long run when interests are being organised socially, i.e. on the common ground of shared or similar values, co-ordinated action and collaboration. This is also true for managers. Watson (1982, p. 266) gave a vivid example:

The impression gained from talking to these managers and from sitting in on management meetings led by the Castings Director was that the group as a whole was committed to achieving the intended changes in large part because it would assist their future advancement as individuals. Their common interest was one of gaining individual advancement—or at least avoiding effective demotion—through group achievement of successful change.

Managers usually know that they can achieve their personal interests often better when they work together—at least, to a certain degree and depending on the situational circumstances. In addition, being in a group provides further advantages in larger social systems which comprise different groups. In this situation, actors not only have interests concerning and within their own group but also in relation to other groups (e.g. Hindess 1986, p. 123). Within hierarchical and competitive settings such as the managerial organisation, social identity transforms into *striving for social dominance*. Managers are keen to secure, if not to increase their superiority within asymmetrical power relations (Levy et al. 2001, p. 2, Feldman 2000, p. 624). This produces at least two outcomes managers have to balance. On the one hand, as the analysis in Chapter 3 has revealed, managers' power is supported by and embedded in networks of powerful and influential stakeholders, in particular shareholders, professional bodies, middle managers, and employees or their representatives. They are therefore interested in meeting those stakeholders' expectations and to collaborate with them (depending on the stakeholders' ability to make an impact on managers' and the organisation's course). On the other hand, they simultaneously have vested interests in pursuing their own interests (and to increase their power and influence) at the expense of, and *against* such external and internal stakeholders. O'Brien / Crandall (2005, p. 1) draw attention to the fact that:

> Human societies tend to be structured as group-based hierarchies in which dominant groups possess a disproportionately large share of positive social value such as political authority, power, wealth, and social status, whereas the subordinate groups possess a disproportionately larger share of negative social values including low power, low social status, and poverty . . . .

This is particularly the case when values and institutions are inherently competitive (e.g. the market economy, hierarchical or managerial organisations) and when resources are limited. In such cases, 'dominant groups possess a disproportionately large share of positive social value, subordinate groups possess a disproportionately large share of negative social value, . . .' (Sidanius / Pratto 1999, pp. 31–32). These social values can be anything, either abstract (e.g. status, privileges and responsibilities) or highly material (e.g. goods and financial advantages). As a group, managers are not only keen to increase their slice of the cake, they strive for supremacy and social dominance: within organisations, within the world of business, and—as the past two decades have shown—increasingly in the public sector and all other areas of society. In this sense, the most general, and yet the most crucial interest of managers as a group is to promote their common interest in upholding the idea management, the idea of 'the manager', their group status and dominance that come along with these concepts, to demonstrate coherence and, hence, to strengthen their position as a group against any other group.

In order to keep and increase their position and influence, it is important for managers that their tasks, roles and positions are not only widely accepted as societal institutions but regarded as important, if not as *the most important aspects of the social system*. However, managers, like other dominant groups, know that they cannot succeed (in the long run) if they try to pursue their personal and group interests (too) openly and too confrontationally. Although our society upholds the image of the "successful" self-interested careerist, it usually goes against political correctness and societal values to openly acknowledge the selfish and egoistic nature of such endeavours. It therefore helps managers if they can portray their personal and group interests as the organisation's common interests.[10] One way to achieve this is the *universalisation of group interests*. Strategic and managerial discourses are excellent opportunities to reproduce the status of managers and provide managers with an ideological basis for their claims. They can be used for linking their sectional interests to the prevailing objectives and values of the organisation. In doing so, managers, as the dominant group, can pursuit their interests and can maintain their dominant positions and influence without being blamed for, or accused of selfish behaviour. Levy et al. (2001, p. 2) e.g. revealed 'the manner in which strategy constitutes certain problems as "strategic" and legitimizes specific groups of people as the "strategic managers" capable of addressing them, thus universalising the sectional interests of senior managers and stockholders, while securing the reproduction of organizational inequalities.' Attempts to hide one's individual or group interests, and to portray them instead as universal interests is a typical sign of ideology (e.g. Deem / Brehony 2005, p. 221, Sidanius et al. 2004, p. 868). Hence, what looks like functional analysis is often, in fact, pure ideology serving and advancing the sectional interests of the specific group of managers (Burnham 1941, p. 25). But it works! So managers mainly promote concepts and strategies which underline the dominance and importance of management and managers per se. Even more, they will opt for concepts which do not address and reveal their personal and group interests directly. Instead they use a functional or 'neutral' language, which (allegedly) meets the concerns and expectations of 'the public' or influential stakeholders. *It is the very interest of the group of managers that their interests are not being seen as individual or sectoral interests, but as ("serving of") the common interest.*

In summary, managers do have shared interests in dominating as a group (against and over other groups). Belonging to the group of managers establishes a great part of social, or at least organisational identity, and conveys high social status and privileges. Despite their political struggles, managers therefore have a common interest in strengthening the institution of management as well as their position in comparison to, and against other groups. The specific objectives are to:

a) underline and maintain the importance, necessity and primacy of management,
b) secure managers' prerogatives in agenda-setting and decision-making,
c) ensure their personal and group interests are reflected in the organisations' primary objectives, vision and mission statements, norms and values, and
d) portray their group interests as universal interests.

MANAGERS' INDIVIDUAL AND PERSONAL INTERESTS

Having looked at managers' interests in dominance from an external, functional and group perspective, this section will now concentrate on the *individual and personal background* of managers—particularly those aspects which may go against the functional image of managers and their work as portrayed by orthodox approaches. Although acknowledging that many managers (might) have an honest and real interest in their work and its strategic and operational problems, and even that managers might be intrinsically motivated (e.g. Zaleznik 1989, p. 197) to find 'the best' solution to problems, we will concentrate here on the "darker sides" of individuals' aspirations within an organisational context.

The underlying assumption in this section is that managers do not purely assess managerial options with regard to functional or political aspects, but also assess them, perhaps primarily, with regard to their individual and personal background. Like other people, managers make sense of events and developments in their environment within the framework of their previous experiences, personal beliefs and worldviews. To put it slightly differently: the way people think, the way they perceive and assess situations and possible alternatives, is shaped by their previous experiences and individual situation. They look at the world how they have learned (or have been made) to look at it. For example, most managers have progressed through the ranks primarily through applying managerial strategies—otherwise they would not have reached the level and position they inhabit. So they make sense of problems and formulate possible solutions primarily on the basis of their own experiences and managerial concepts. Managers think and act in managerial ways because this is what has worked for them over the years and this is how they were socialised in their professional education and careers. Even if managers choose 'innovative' strategies or 'revolutionary new business models', the fundamental assumptions of the new concept will not be far away from the manager's individual experience and previous concepts. It will be based on what has worked successfully in the past (at least in the eyes of the manager) and what fits his or her internalised traditions, i.e. his or her understanding of what business, management, and organisations are about or should be about.

In addition to the more unconscious contributions of learned reactions, managers' sense- and decision-making is also influenced by considerations about their present and future position. Most managers have put years of effort into reaching their current position. Providing they have not already reached the end of their business life and / or have become completely cynical, they are usually quite concerned about their present situation, particular the security of their job and career prospects. Like many other employees, their first allegiance is *not* to the company they are working for, but to their careers, private lives and their profession. If they had not put their personal and career interests first—and everything else, including their employer companies, second—most managers would not have reached their positions (and will not make future progress). Bolchover (2005, p. 79) explained that 'political manoeuvring and patronage, not ability or productivity, are the engines of individual progress, hence the constant advertising of loyalty and conformity by the use of business-speak and other methods.' Hence, managers also judge managerial problems on the basis of their personal career orientation. As high-status individuals they will often prefer options which underline their status, help their career aspirations and are therefore necessarily of managerial nature (Thompson 1961, p. 491)—otherwise they would be soon 'out of the game'. In the context of organisational politics discussed earlier, it is in managers' interest to be involved in such activities. Indeed, it is even required and expected from them as part of their managerial tasks and functions. Even if they don't want to, managers *have to* be aware of their own as well as others' interests and are obliged to play the power game (at least to some extent). The "typical" manager is a 'political animal': he or she *must* develop these skills since otherwise they will lose out. Vickers / Kouzmin (2001, p. 105) provide quite an explicit, but not unrealistic description of this type of actor:

> the modern careerist epitomizes the 'damaged' organizational actor, who appears to say and to act as is required through a process of adaptation which is beneficial for career advancement but disastrous for emotional health. This is evidenced by the apparent promulgation of 'automatons' . . . colourless, dull and unimaginative individuals characterizing the quintessential 'organization man' . . . an essentially calculating animal pursuing the necessities of organizational life.

Nonetheless, there is room for freedom. It is up to the individual manager, his or her personality, ethical convictions and attitudes to what extent to push his or her own agenda and careers and by what means. Some managers may participate in organisational politics more as 'habitual patterns of thinking and behavior' and less as 'a conscious conspiracy to exert their influence' (Shapiro / Matson 2007, p. 202). Dugger (1980, cited in Shapiro / Matson 2007, pp. 202–203) described this less pushy type: 'The habits of thought of most political officials are those learned in performing, or in preparing to perform, corporate roles. These political officials are not corrupt. They are not conspirators. They do not have to be. They simply follow the motives, goals, and ideals they have learned, and in doing so they also use the means they have learned.'

And there is a type of manager who is truly concerned about his or her work, about the people he or she is responsible for, who cares about the implications and consequences of his or her work in a multi-dimensional and ethical manner and who avoids playing political games. However, with the status and level managers have reached in hierarchical organisations, *personal advantages (material and non-material)* usually play a more important role. For example, Boyer (2005) provides convincing empirical evidence that the compensation of managers, particularly senior managers, has increased dramatically specifically in the past two decades. This is *not* closely linked to the *actual* performance of the companies they are working for. The remuneration of senior managers has reached a level in absolute as well as relative terms which is neither justified nor justifiable anymore. Anyway, senior managers' prerogatives and privileges are only anecdotal evidence at the extreme end of a comprehensive and thorough system of inequalities. The whole managerial organisation is based on the principle of increasing privileges and prerogatives, and material and non-material advantages along the lines of the hierarchical division of labour. Because of this, personal advantages within hierarchical systems are as much absolute as they are relative. According to Zaleznik (1989, pp. 53–54), managers therefore 'calculate their relative advantage. They become precise in thinking about their job and discipline themselves to do what is necessary to secure favourable judgments from the constituencies that count.' As soon as one has begun to taste the privileges of the level one has reached within a hierarchical social system like the managerial organisation, there is no way back. The only way is up to the next level. Managers usually have a strong interest to keep and protect, indeed to increase, what they have achieved for themselves so far. This includes position and social status, prerogatives and privileges, salaries and other material benefits, as well as their individual market value, their career aspirations and all the effects and consequences which come with the package. In the light of their highly personal interests, they want to dominate as much as possible in order to protect their present advantages and to get the best "package" and deals in future.

Finally, managers' interests, decisions and actions, like anyone else's, are also influenced by 'negative' psychological and emotional aspects. There is empirical evidence that many managers are deeply anxious and feel vulnerable and insecure (Antonacopoulou 1999, p. 5). Watson (cited in Willmott 1997, p. 1346) found in his empirical research 'human angst, insecurity, doubt and frailty' among managers, and that 'they have all the human frailties and anxieties of the other people whom they seek to influence.' These are quite understandable reactions since people higher up the hierarchical ladder act in a competitive environment—competitive *within* the organisation. Many managers therefore have an interest in controlling as much as possible (including themselves!). They usually prefer to make decisions on the safe side, not taking too many risks or supporting weak causes. 'Do as the Romans do' is reassuring for both stakeholders and the managers themselves. McAuley et al. (2000, p. 96) pointed out that managerialism represents a moment of certainty, order and rationality in an uncertain and threatening world. Psychological reasons such as fears and anxieties, or possible threats caused by internal competition mean that many managers prefer strategies which will provide them with the feeling or impression of being in control and being safe. They look for certainty and security as much as possible—particularly *for themselves* and *their position*. Managers, therefore, tend to opt for managerial concepts and strategies which are widely accepted. These psychological traits will drive most managers towards the same conformist behaviour, just like the fads-and-fashions behaviour we explored earlier. Although this behaviour largely contradicts the image of managers as 'doers' and 'entrepreneurs', it nonetheless helps to strengthen and develop their position and dominance.

In summary, there are very strong individual and personal reasons why managers want to dominate. Based on previous experiences, managers think and act in managerial ways. In addition, their present position and future career aspirations make it more likely that they will choose managerial options and demonstrate managerial approaches in their behaviour in order to strengthen and justify their position. This becomes even more obvious when one thinks about the personal interests, advantages, and material and non-material privileges of management. All these individual dimensions combined with the pursuit of personal interests are strong motivations for managers to behave and act like the orthodox concept of 'the manager'. This image also corresponds with most managers' personality and self-image. Managers higher up the hierarchy particularly like to see themselves, and to portray their image as 'doers', 'strategists', 'leaders', even 'entrepreneurs'. Although negative psychological traits such as anxiety, fear and conformism seem to contradict such images, they can be still be upheld on the surface, adding to managers' demonstrations of dominance.

SUBORDINATES' INTERESTS

This chapter is primarily about *managers'* interests in dominating. However, the very nature of managerialism is inclusive—it tries to convince as many stakeholders as possible that managerialism also serves their interests—and one group of stakeholders is their employees. Of course, employees are not as powerful and important as other stakeholders, but managers nonetheless need to keep an eye on them and manage them. For this, manager provide subordinates with sufficient reasons and 'explanations' that it is in *their* interest—and *in their best interest*—to function smoothly within the managerial organisation and to fit into the very societal and organisational conditions which make them subordinates. In some ways, it's surprising *how* accepted the managerial organisation and the supremacy of managers are. Since this has much to do with 'ideology', we will analyse this phenomenon thoroughly in Chapter 5, which focuses on the ideology of management. Nonetheless, this section explores briefly the idea that managers' dominance seems to be also in the employees' interest and that it is (allegedly) in their interest to support management.

This compliance and the apparently smooth functioning of the majority of employees and other subordinates might stem from a fear of negative consequences, e.g. punishment of deviance. Indeed, for many employees there is the very real fear of losing their job. As Collinson (2003, p. 532) has explained:

> For many workers, a fundamental source of insecurity is the material and economic realities of selling one's labour power in return for a wage. In capitalist organizations hiring labour as a purchasable and disposable commodity is not only the means for creating value and expanding capital, but is also a central feature of workplace discipline. Job insecurity can create material and symbolic anxieties for workers. The fear of losing one's economic independence can be interwoven with more symbolic anxieties. To lose one's job . . . can erode one's sense of autonomy and self respect. . . .

Managerialism and the managerial organisation have a range of aspects which simultaneously provide both insecurity and security, raise and reduce uncertainty, and offer positive incentives and negative sanctions (mostly within power and control dimensions, as demonstrated in Chapter 3). Fear is one of the important factors contributing to the phenomenon that subordinates (e.g. employees) regard their superiors' (e.g. managers') interests as their own interests.

In addition to more or less concrete and present fears, most employees are already thoroughly conditioned by their (work-related) life-long socialisation. Societal conditioning and professional socialisation have already largely taken place (particularly in learning and education institutions) and continue to happen while employees work for organisations (both in the workplace and in training). Although these processes can obviously generate a whole range of welcomed and less welcomed outcomes, one of the most important ones is that people are being trained to fit into, and accept institutions, including management as an institution. Employees have been taught *not* to think about their power to challenge the system (or managers) and seek fundamental change but only to use their power to perform within (and for) the system. In this sense, employees are *disem*-powered and *em*-powered *at the same time*, but they are only made aware of the latter. Hence, employees' self-concept provides them not only with their "appropriate" place within organisations (e.g. Hogg / Terry 2000, p. 124) but also with the pre-disposition to be amenable to managers' interests. Alvesson / Willmott (2002, p. 619) cast some light on 'how employees are enjoined to develop self-images and work orientations that are deemed congruent with managerially defined objectives.' Because of their conditioning or 'learned helplessness' (Van Vugt 2006, p. 361), most employees automatically regard managers' superiority as part of the "normality" of organisations and life. And it is therefore in subordinates' interest to accept and to support this.

Another outcome of their pronounced interest in supporting and maintaining the hierarchical system of managerial organisations is employees' obedience. Many employees even actively contribute to the very social system which makes them subordinates. This might even be labelled a 'rational' interest and behaviour since there is a whole range of factual advantages for those who function appropriately. These might include

- psychological advantages (belonging to a greater, strong and successful entity which gives the subjective feeling of security or offers factual career perspectives),
- concrete advantages due to the division of labour (doing one's job more efficiently and with less input required),
- actual material advantages (usually higher wages, better overall remuneration packages and fewer working hours compared to other organisations or opportunities to earn a living) and / or
- physical advantages (better health-and-safety policies).

For most employees, trapped in their daily lives and routines, with bills to pay, and who seek to continue or improve their standard of living, the hierarchical organisation and the system of managers' dominance offer to them advantages and opportunities they could not get easily somewhere else. The managerial system provides them—within limits—with purpose and order, with opportunities to meet their interests and with protection against some of the misfortunes life can bring. Employees will benefit from these advantages *as long as they function within the boundaries of the system*. Smooth functioning within the boundaries of a hierarchical, unjust and oppressive social system of managerial organisations makes considerable sense for the individual.

Subordinates, therefore, do not function only because they are not 'conscious' and 'reflective' enough but also because it makes sense to them. It is mainly about the socially dominating value of *'calculative selfishness'*, i.e. the strange combination of instrumental individualism, goal-oriented pragmatism and narrowly defined functional rationalism (all converging in the ideal model of the homo oeconomicus). Calculative selfishness and its instrumental use obviously have not only a power dimension but also an interest dimension. Constant provision, marketing and internalisation of the now dominating societal values of calculative selfishness have made it one of the strongest *interests* of most people within our contemporary societies and organisations. It works well for *both* the employee *and* the manager *at the same time*. The employee develops strategies to get the most out of an organisation while reducing his or her input and keeping any frictions with and within the system to a minimum—and managers do the same. However, as superiors they can 'count' on this calculative behaviour from their subordinates (because managers think and act in the same way) and can use it to further their aims and ambitions. In fact, managers' dominance *depends* to a great extent on this ability to count on the calculative (and therefore predictable and manageable) behaviour of their employees, while it is in the employees' own interest to demonstrate such behaviour. And most subordinates even *want* to care primarily and mostly about their own personal affairs and well-being. They have largely lost, amongst other things, the interest in challenging managers' power and unjust hierarchical systems. Most people primarily concentrate on functioning smoothly within institutional boundaries in order to gain individual advantages. They have *very explicit and conscious* interests in functioning smoothly because this is much more advantageous for them and the pursuit of their interests than questioning or challenging managerial power and authority. On balance, for the majority of employees the hierarchy and social system of the managerial organisation is acceptable—at least sufficiently acceptable that they have an interest in seeing the hierarchical social system continue. In this sense, calculative selfishness plays into the hands of dominating groups and ruling classes, and in the case of managerial organisations it strengthens the dominance of managers.

More rationally than paradoxically, subordinates actually support their managers' struggle for social dominance. Even if employees have hidden forms of resistance, they largely avoid open confrontation with managerial structures of authority (Scott 1990, p. 86). But even low-level compliance and smooth functioning are already enough to support managers' interest in dominating. However, most employees have a more affirmative interest in functioning within the hierarchical organisation. They willingly accept, even pro-actively support management because, on balance, the advantages of working for the managerial organisation are greater than the downsides.

THE CONCEPT OF MANAGERIAL INTERESTS

Why are managers interested in dominating? Which factors are mainly responsible for, and shape this interest? The previous sections shed some light on different areas of interests managers take into account when they make decisions and take actions. Table 4.1 summarises these areas.

Table 4.1   Aspects Influencing Managers' Interests in Dominating

Area	Aspect
1. Interest links between the organisation and its environment	• isomorphism • fads and fashions, conformity • external stakeholders and their (possible) influence (interests and power)
2. Functional aspects, roles and organisational politics	• functional approach • strategic and operational objectives as managers' prerogatives • content and implications of managerial decisions, budget and other organisational resources • role and public image • sectoral interests • organisational politics
3. Interests of managers as a group	• group of managers and group interests • social identity • inter-group collaboration • social dominance (compared to and against other groups) • universalisation of managers' interests as a group
4. Managers' individual and personal interests	• previous experiences • career aspirations • personal advantages (material and non-material) • negative psychological traits
5. Subordinates' interests	• interests behind subordinates' compliance, conformity and obedience

How do these different areas influence managers' views and decisions as well as their interest in dominating? The key points of the analysis undertaken in this chapter can be summarised as follows:

1. The vast majority of managers seem to be interested in responding to influences from the external environment in the same way. Whether it is the idea of 'best fit', 'fads and fashions' or 'stakeholder orientation', in order to meet external expectations, they will opt for essentially the same concepts—those which underline the importance of management and managerial solutions.

2. Internal functional influences are more differentiated. Because of their sectoral interests, departmental affiliation, responsibilities for resources and organisational politics, managers can have very different views, objectives and interests. They often compete with each other for influence and dominance, and attempt to reduce other managers' power. However, this still takes place within the confines of the notion of management, managerial prerogatives and images.

3. As a group, managers have enough in common (and common interests) to pursue and emphasise the dominance and importance of management and the "group" of managers in particular—particularly against other groups. The interest of social dominance and the universalisation of their individual and group interests (hidden under functional and allegedly 'neutral' language) are the common denominator of (almost) all managers.

4. Based on their previous experiences and socialisation, managers think and act in managerial ways. Furthermore, the pursuit of personal interests and advantages, material and non-material privileges and future career aspirations, as well as individual psychological traits all compound their interest in securing their present positions of high social status and dominance.

As the analysis has revealed, the overwhelming majority of influential variables point in the same direction. Managers will opt for broadly the same managerial concepts, apply the same managerial techniques and share the same, more or less conscious interest in protecting and developing managerial dominance within organisations and within the wider society. There are plausible reasons for this. Managerialism is an ideology which is about power and control, dominance and supremacy. It legitimises 'the interests of management in how organisations are managed, stressing the role and accountability of individual managers and their positions as managers' (Lawler / Hearn, 1996, cited in McAuley et al. 2000, pp. 95–96). It is therefore quite understandable that most managers have a strong interest in not only keeping and nurturing their roles and positions within that hierarchy but also in defending and maintaining the whole managerial system. Even when managers' interests clash—e.g. in the formulation of new strategies, major change initiatives, allocation of departmental resources or budgets—they will nonetheless compete with each other only within the framework of organisational hierarchy and managerial ideology. Managers may challenge each other's positions and privileges but they will never ever challenge the social system of management and managerial supremacy as such. This is simply because they know that they can only pursue their own interests and continue to use their power and privileges as long as management prevails and the hierarchical social system continues.

In an empirical study on managers' decision behaviour, Palmer / Barber (2001, p. 110) came to the following conclusion: 'our results are consistent with what Perrow (1972) called the "tool view of organizations," according to which top managers are actors, corporations are instruments, and top managers use these instruments to pursue their interests in proportion to their capacities'.

Managers, therefore, will be very keen to ensure that *any* strategy will *always* correspond first and foremost to *their* ideas, interests, positions and privileges. Even so-called innovative business models/fads/fashions and dramatic organisational changes are not fundamentally different, but are in reality only slight technical differentiations. The basic managerial assumptions are kept intact. The mechanisms are simply modifications and the consequences for the people involved are the same as ever. Managers decide for managerial strategies because it is in their social nature to do so. 'Managers have too much invested in managerialism to make them likely to rebel en masse. They have identities, qualifications, salaries and status through being what they are, a full dinner-pail, so why should we assume that they will wish to disinvest and join movements for reform?' (Parker 2002, p. 189). In contrast, real changes would require very different ideological mindsets (Zammuto et al. 2000, p. 262)—but that is another story. Although there might be a few internal reasons which could force senior managers to choose very different strategies (e.g. departmental affiliation, organisational politics), the overall result is quite clear: *Managers will (almost) always decide for managerial concepts that fit current managerial ideologies, support their claims for dominance and underline the importance of management as such. This is because expectations from their organisation's environment, functional necessities and strong individual as well as group interests suggest it should be so.*

CONCLUSIONS

By taking an interested-oriented approach like the one developed here, it is possible to gain a better understanding of (some of) the mechanisms behind managerial phenomena within an organisational context. It provides systematic explanations for managers' interests in dominance and draws attention to some of the most relevant aspects which often remain neglected. In particular it reveals that managers' aims and objectives, decisions and actions are 'rational'—but not in the sense usually claimed by the proponents of orthodox management studies (and many managers themselves)! It shows that they are rational primarily *from the managers' perspective*. Managers decide according to whichever of their functional, personal, and group interests are most relevant to them at the time of their decision. Whatever the specific situative conditions and particular reasons are, managers are definitely much more interest-oriented than any functional theory wants us to think. In contrast, an interest-oriented approach provides an opportunity to uncover hidden reasons behind human actions. It helps to dismantle ideologies which wrongly portray managers' and leaders' decision-making processes and actions as 'rational acts of unselfish services for a greater good'. By investigating managers' conduct within organisations in a much more realistic way, we are able to identify reasons and formulate explanations for why managers do certain things in certain ways and why managers don't do certain things.

In this sense, an interest-oriented approach may help empirical research in another way. It helps by concentrating on the individual (or individuals).

It is manager A or manager B who makes certain decisions which can make so much of a difference for better or for worse to others (and to themselves). In the face of increasingly more abstract mechanisms and structures, we need to concentrate more on the individual. This is particularly the case for senior managers. It is their job to make decisions and they get paid for it. Most of these decisions are strategic, with far-reaching implications and consequences—decisions which can have the severest consequences for other people, the environment and society. The higher managers are, the more power they have to make decisions—and the more opportunities they have to abuse their power. Willmott (1997, p. 1339) explained that

> opportunities and incentives for "misbehavior" among managers are often much greater than for other employees: Because the scope for private gain is often so great (. . .), and because of the high degree of discretion associated with most positions, the problems of discipline and control may well be far greater in the case of managerial labor than with routine employees.

Managers therefore must be much more accountable in their daily conduct of business. It is not about attempts to contain 'white-collar criminality' but to reveal the daily routines and actions of managers which are highly questionable yet still within the range of legitimate 'corporate' privileges, as justified and condoned by the contemporary ideology of neo-liberalism and 'elbow-society' (Willmott 1997, p. 1339). For example, Boyer (2005) drew attention to the serious problem of controlling senior managers and linking their remuneration to their performance and to the consequences of their decisions and actions. According to Whittington (1992, p. 708), management research should, therefore, 'investigate how individual leaders constitute and sustain their authority within different social systems, . . .'. The concept of interests is particularly closely related to the aspects of responsibility and accountability (Hales 1999, p. 342). *Managers, particularly the very senior managers of organisations, must be held much more accountable for what they do (or don't do), how they do it and the consequences their decisions and actions bear.* Unfortunately, the issues of personal and group interests, power and organisational politics have received less and less attention in organisational studies and management research. This is particularly the case in general management, strategy and change management, decision-making and organisational learning (e.g. Ferdinand 2004, p. 435, Coopey / Burgoyne 2000, p. 869). It is high time that we changed this.

5   The Ideology of Management

> The ideas of the ruling class are in every epoch the ruling ideas: i.e.
> the class which is the ruling material force of society is at the same
> time its ruling intellectual force . . . the class which has the means of
> material production at its disposal, has control at the same time over
> the means of mental production, . . . The individuals comprising the
> ruling class . . . rule also as thinkers, as producers of ideas, and regu-
> late the production and distribution of the ideas of their age.
>
> —Karl Marx / Friedrich Engels, in
> 'The German Ideology', 1845
> (cited in Brookfield 2005, p. 41)

INTRODUCTION

As the previous two chapters have demonstrated, the dominance of managers
is based on a very comprehensive, multi-dimensional system of power and
control as well as a whole range of individual and group interests—all of
which keep this system going. However, despite the cunning design of organisations and managerial concepts, most of the factual interests underpinning
managers' decisions and actions are anything but attractive. If these were
more widely known, subordinates would function less willingly and start to
question social reality; who would pay tribute to a naked King (or Queen)?
Therefore, dominant groups are particularly anxious to "justify", even cover
up their actual interests and power, ambitions and social practices. One way
to achieve this is overlaying them with additional, more "convincing" layers
of sense-making and sense-giving systems. We are talking about *ideology*.

Ideology is one of the strongest tools available to promote, and at the
same time to conceal, interests and to maintain and strengthen power and
domination (Deem / Brehony 2005, p. 218). Many social practices can be
traced back to ideologies. For example, John Maynard Keynes (1953, cited
in Goshal 2005, p. 75) explained:

> The ideas of economists and political philosophers, both when they are
> right and when they are wrong, are more powerful than is commonly
> understood, . . . Indeed the world is run by little else. Practical men,
> who believe themselves to be quite exempt from any intellectual influ-
> ences are usually the slaves of some defunct economist. . . . It is ideas,
> not vested interests, which are dangerous for good or evil.

Already in 1974 Winter realised that managerialism was about to become
the prevailing ideology. Since then, 'management' has developed into one of

the strongest, most elaborated and successful ideologies mankind has seen so far. It is arguably as strong and powerful as the ideology of Christianity, monarchy, communism or capitalism. This is also due to the fact that it is not only managers and economists who uphold management. A whole range of interested parties have contributed actively to the development of 'managerialism'—the 'generalized ideology of management' (Parker 2002, p. 10); shareholders and institutional investors, 'business-oriented' academics, consultants and politicians.

However, in common with the ideologies of most other dominant groups, orthodox management and organisation theory strongly rejects the idea that it is ideological. As we saw in Chapters 3 and 4, this approach claims to address only functional and technical aspects of organisations and management. According to its proponents, it is predominantly about managers' activities, strategy, organisational structures and processes—all described and analysed (allegedly) in functional, value-free and objective ways. Since the second half of the 19th century, orthodox management and organisation studies have been developed in the tradition of positivism, with Taylor's Scientific Management (1911/1967) as a first famous (or infamous) milestone. Donaldson's view (2003, p. 42) nicely mirrors the main rationale, passed on through generations of orthodox and conservative business researchers: 'Organizational science aims to create valid explanations that capture how the organizational world really operates, rather than to broadcast views that may better accord with values but which are not accurate characterizations of the world as it exists. Thus organizational science is value-free and may be quite tough-minded in some of its aspects.'

This position has not been without criticism. In sharp contrast to the functional approach, Critical Management Studies (CMS) assumes that 'the horizontal and vertical differentiation of tasks between individuals and groups cannot adequately be explained by references to functional imperatives' (Willmott 1987, p. 254). CMS therefore seeks to reveal the interests behind systems of power and control, analyse political behaviour particularly of powerful actors / stakeholders (as we saw in Chapters 3 and 4) and demonstrate that management overall is anything but value-free and neutral (e.g. Brookfield 2005, Alvesson / Willmott 1992a, b, Therborn 1980, Abercrombie et al. 1980, Burns 1961). CMS sees phenomena such as the dominance of managers as the result of social conflict. In the tradition of organisational behaviour (e.g. Mintzberg 1979, Cyert / March 1963, March / Simon 1958), corporations are therefore regarded as 'political organisations' (Burns 1961, p. 258). From such a perspective, organisations and management are seen to a large extent as the products of (clashing) values and beliefs, ideology and (overt or covert) 'ideological conflict'. Superiors' and subordinates' views, perceptions, actions and attitudes are largely shaped by (their) ideology, but particularly by the 'dominant ideology' (Abercrombie et al. 1980, pp. 1–2). According to Brookfield (2005, p. 67), 'Ideology is the system of ideas and values that reflects and supports the established order and that manifests itself in our everyday actions, decisions, and practices, usually without our being aware of its presence.' Critical theory in general, and CMS in particular, wants to identify, criticise, challenge and change any (dominant) ideology which tries to convince people that unequal social relationships are a normal state of affairs (Brookfield 2005, p. viii).

In addition, the principles and mechanisms of social dominance and oppression as well as (managerial) power and control are embedded in managerial rhetoric. One dimension, again, therefore moves to the centre of attention: the dimension of language and communication, knowledge and perceptions, rhetoric and discourse. According to such concepts, social reality (and, hence, phenomena such as managers' dominance) is largely seen as socially constructed, i.e. shaped by human perceptions, interpretations and discourses (e.g. Sillince 2007, 1999, Clegg et al. 2006, Vickers / Kouzmin 2001, Alvesson, M. / Kärreman, D. 2000, Isabella 1990, Daft / Weick 1984). However, such analysis reveals more than just 'mere' perceptions and rhetoric. Every hierarchical social system comes with, and is based on, elaborate systems of symbols indicating social status, responsibilities and, most importantly, differences. These systems develop over time to the point where they often reach 'an almost pathological intensity' (Thompson 1961, p. 496). People's perceptions, (self-) images, social status and social actions are shaped by systems of symbols and discourse—and people must know their place within those systems and are expected to act and behave accordingly. Symbols, rhetoric and discourses create and shape not only the social construction of reality (Berger / Luckmann 1966), but also social action and practices within it as well as the continuation or change of hierarchical social structures and social differences. As soon one develops the 'right' language and corresponding type of discourse, and monopolises the essential knowledge, it is no longer that difficult to legitimise and justify the prerogatives and privileges of a specific group. On these grounds, people can be made believe that the reason for social domination is not power itself, but its rightness legitimacy (Courpasson 2000, p. 141). Clearly, rhetoric and discourse are a fertile ground for ideology.

In this chapter, we will investigate how ideology contributes to the dominance of managers and investigate the ideological nature of management. This ideology is not only relevant to 'grand strategies' carried out by great leaders and / or the inner elite circles of corporate power. It is more about 'normal' management and how it is understood and carried out in quite an un-dramatic manner on a daily basis. Seeing management as an ideology provides an opportunity to reveal its philosophical, cognitive, psychological, sociological and methodological dimensions and functions *beyond* its more mundane appearances and functional meanings. Accordingly, the following discussion analyses and demonstrates how multi-dimensional, sophisticated and elaborate the ideology of management really is—and how much managers gain from it. In order to do this, we first discuss some of the most relevant definitions and concepts of ideology. Based on this, step by step the most important dimensions of ideology will be identified and interrogated which systematically capture all aspects of managerial ideology and its impact on people, organisations and society. All in all, this chapter provides a comprehensive framework of the ideology of management with regard to the following main areas:

1. Societal dimension (e.g. references to institutions and the social world, stakeholders, epochal trends such as neo-liberalism, globalisation)
2. Functional aspects and cognitive dimension (e.g. provision of 'explanations', meaning, justifications concerning how the world is and or should be)
3. Socio-psychological and sociological dimension (e.g. group formation, social order)
4. Psychological dimension (e.g. scaring, frightening, addressing anxieties and hopes)
5. Methodological and logical dimension (e.g. comprehensiveness, inconsistencies)

DEFINITIONS AND CONCEPTS OF IDEOLOGY

What "is" ideology? Most people may think immediately about (extreme) political programmes and (radical) social movements. Or they may even regard religious, moral, economical or scientific worldviews and theories as ideology. Either way, the term 'ideology' (and all that is related to it) is often understood and used in a rather negative sense; 'ideology consists of those opinions of others which differ from our views!' Ideology is often used to describe or criticise 'false' or 'irrational' belief systems which we believe provide followers and supporters with a distorted view of the world (e.g. Krauss 2006, p. 1221, Hartley 1983, p. 10).

In contrast, in this chapter 'ideology' will be used as a *neutral* term but in a more complex sense. For this, ideology can be defined as 'collective knowledge structure[s]' (Walsh 1995, p. 291) about the human world and nature. According to Hamilton (1987, p. 38), ideology is 'a system of collectively held normative and reputedly factual ideas and beliefs'. In this sense, ideology is seen as a 'normal' part of our construction and sense-making of the world—as part of the social construction of reality (Berger / Luckmann 1966). Mitchell (2005, p. 244), e.g. defined ideology as a 'shared pattern of more abstract ideas that serves to manage and make sense of the flow of information that we have about the world'. However, ideology only encompasses 'factual' knowledge or 'correct' information to a certain degree. It also comprises perceptions, emotions and other subjective aspects. Although ideologies can be about "the whole world", at their core they are about society and its structure, people and their relationships.

They are about 'particular pattern[s] of social relationships and arrangements, and/or aimed at justifying a particular pattern of conduct, which its proponents seek to promote, realise, pursue or maintain' (Hamilton 1987, p. 38). Chiapello / Fairclough (2002, p. 187) gave a more specific description of this socio-political core:

> An ideology is a system of ideas, values and beliefs oriented to explaining a given political order, legitimizing existing hierarchies and power relations and preserving group identities. Ideology explains both the horizontal structure (the division of labour) of a society and its vertical structure (the separation of rulers and ruled), producing ideas which legitimize the latter, explaining in particular why one group is dominant and another dominated, why one person gives orders in a particular enterprise while another takes orders.

Finally, there are logical and methodological issues which are relevant for any ideology, particularly the comprehensiveness and consistency of the assumptions which the ideology is based on. We will come to these aspects later. All in all, 'ideology' might be defined as a *value-based belief system about the (sense of the) world, social systems and human beings, people's relationships and their being in the world.*

Based on this definition, 'managerialism' will be analysed in this chapter as ideology, moreover, as *dominant* ideology (Brookfield 2005, p. viii). The dominant ideology represents 'the beliefs which dominant groups hold and disseminate' (Abercrombie et al. 1980, p. 130). These beliefs focus mainly on values and practices that strengthen and reproduce existing social structures and processes. As Marx and Engels once wrote in their famous 'German Ideology' (cited in Abercrombie et al. 1980, p. 7):

> The ideas of the ruling class are in every epoch the ruling ideas: i.e., the class which is the ruling material force of society, is at the same time its ruling intellectual force. The class which has the means of material production at its disposal, has control at the same time over the means of mental production, so that thereby, generally speaking, the ideas of those who lack the means of mental production are subject to it.

In the case of managers, the ideas focus mainly on organisational and managerial structures and processes in the widest sense. Abercrombie et al.'s 'dominant ideology thesis' (1980, p. 1–2) captures the nature of the ideology of management very well:

> The major conceptual components of the dominant ideology thesis can be summarised in the following terms. The thesis argues that in all societies based on class divisions there is a dominant class which enjoys control of both the means of material production and the means of mental

production. Through its control of ideological production, the dominant class is able to supervise the construction of a set of coherent beliefs. These dominant beliefs of the dominant class are more powerful, dense and coherent than those of subordinate classes. The dominant ideology penetrates and infects the consciousness of the working class, because the working class comes to see and to experience reality through the conceptual categories of the dominant class. The dominant ideology functions to incorporate the working class within a system which is, in fact, operating against the material interests of labour. This incorporation in turn explains the coherence and integration of capitalist society.

The ideology of management and managers is the dominant belief system for private and public sector organisations, in neo-classical economics and orthodox business and management studies, and increasingly in our whole society and at a global scale. Managerialism is an ideology primarily *about and for* managers, in order to explain and justify their authority and positions, prerogatives and responsibilities (Hartley 1983, p. 11). In one word: *managerialism is the ideology about the dominance of managers.*

SOCIETAL DIMENSION OF THE IDEOLOGY OF MANAGEMENT

The ideology of management dominates all current discourses about management—in business organisations, public organisations and many areas of our private and public lives. It can be seen as part of the 'economisation of the lifeworld' (Habermas). However, despite its widespread dominance and dissemination, 'management' is not the most dominant or only dominating ideology in our societies; it 'merely' dominates certain areas within institutions and amongst other ideologies. One requirement for dominant ideologies, therefore, is that they must correspond with the institutional settings of their society. In this section it shall be demonstrated that 'management', indeed, fits in very well with contemporary society and other existing ideologies.

Since the ideology of management has evolved (particularly in Western Europe and North America) from the middle of the 19th century onwards, by and large it has been consistent with the 'spirit of capitalism' (Weber 1904/1993). Capitalism itself is quite a flexible ideology. It prospered during the heydays of monarchies and 'Manchester capitalism', under nationalism and fascism, and became even more dominant under the conditions of representative democracies and regulated market economies. Chiapello / Fairclough (2002, p. 187) explained that

> one of the main characteristics of capitalism as a social order is that it constantly transforms itself. Capitalism in the general sense is capable of

assuming highly variable historical forms, which continue to be capitalist through the continuity of a number of central features (wage-labour, competition, private property, orientation to capital accumulation, technical progress, the rampant commodification of all social activities). The 'spirit of capitalism' is therefore an ideology which serves to sustain the capitalist process in its historical dynamism while being in phase with the historically specific and variable forms that it takes.

The ideology of management is of similar nature. As current examples of Russia and China as well as many developing countries demonstrate, the ideology of management is so flexible that it can prevail and prosper in almost any institutional setting, from the most developed welfare-states (e.g. Sweden) to the cruellest dictatorships (Zimbabwe)—and all countries within that continuum. This is also true in regard to socio-economic conditions, i.e. the level of industrialisation and technicalisation, or the levels of poverty, education, equality or lifestyle. The ideology of management has emerged and spread in just and unjust societies, "Western" and "Eastern" economies, tightly regulated and open organisations, and any combinations thereof.

The relationship between socio-economic institutions and ideology works in both ways. Managerialism is firmly rooted particularly in the institutions and bureaucracies of the market economy. At the same time, managerialism feeds back into, and provides further meaning and justification for those, and other institutions (Pollitt 1990, p. 28). The proponents of managerialism were very successful in demonstrating its suitability for the economy and society. Here we are talking about *isomorphism*, i.e. the way a system fits the institutional rules of its environment which in turn provide its legitimacy (Suddaby / Greenwood 2005, Staw / Epstein 2000, DiMaggio / Powell 1983, Meyer / Rowan 1977). As Coopey / Burgoyne (2000, p. 873) have explained: 'To achieve legitimacy an organization needs to mirror the institutional patterning generated in the environment, often in a variety of social fields. These effects result not only from direct control mechanisms (e.g. as exercised by central government) but also through constitutive processes created by environmental meaning systems.' Although isomorphism is largely applied to organisations and their fit to their institutional context, it can be also applied to belief systems such as ideologies. Here, too, it is about gaining and / or enhancing legitimacy and cultural support by adapting—at least, officially—to larger meaning systems and institutions and to function 'in a manner consistent with broader myths, narratives, or cultural accounts . . .' (Suddaby / Greenwood 2005, p. 59). This indicates that isomorphism does not necessarily mean a real fit. For example, managers may openly support democratic systems, but there is very little, if any, democracy within their organisations. Business praises free market and competition, while at the same time it calls for regulations and does everything in its business practices to reduce or even impede competition and market forces. Paying lip service is usually sufficiently enough at an ideological level, as giving the right impression is often enough for achieving isomorphism.

However, as we saw during the analysis of managers' power and interests, the idea of isomorphism describes in a more abstract way a possible fit or misfit between the organisation and (abstract) institutions. In reality it is more about the concrete fit (or misfit) of the perceptions, worldviews and agendas of (powerful) actors which represent, run and shape these institutions. Ideologies, like many other intangible constructs, do not emerge and relate to other meaning systems and institutions on their own. All these constructs are being formulated, communicated, implemented and supported *by real people* (with a whole range of interests on their agenda and powerful tools at their hands). Behind every ideology there are real people with certain interests, power and influence.[1] In this sense, it is probably even more important that managerialism not only suits managers but fits a whole range of influential stakeholders in managers' and their organisations' environments. The following sub-sections give a brief idea about the broad range of stakeholders supporting the ideology of management.

BUSINESS AND FINANCES

Traditionally, owners, shareholders and institutional investors are regarded as some of the most important stakeholders of (big) business. In line with neo-classical theory, they robustly uphold and communicate the *ideology of shareholder maximisation*. There are, therefore, strong expectations that management orientates its agenda, and that of the whole organisation, towards this objective—whatever the actual business model and latest management concept is. To a certain extent managers must and will meet these expectations; managerialism *must* fit to the fundamental understandings and objectives of business. This was clear from the very beginnings of modern management, i.e. since the middle of 19th century. Managers were hired to guarantee increases in productivity and efficiency, to run their large organisations in a business-like manner and to control the workforce for the sake of profit (maximisation). This hasn't changed even in these times of multi-dimensional performance measurement, management systems and elaborated Corporate Social Responsibility agendas. At the end of the day (and the fiscal year), it is the bottom line that counts. Mainstream management theory is, and so far always has been, *managerial capitalism* (e.g. Abercrombie et al. 1980, p. 129).

Of course, investigations based on moral hazard- and principal-agent theory have demonstrated that there can be very strong differences between the objectives of shareholders / investors and (senior) managers. Senior and middle managers try to maintain capital in the organisation and often tend to increase their own privileges and remuneration packages at the expense of investors. All parties involved are aware of their different interests. Generally, there are legal, governance and consultancy mechanisms in place which by and large stem the problem and cope with discrepancies sufficiently. In exceptional circumstances, such differences escalate to a level where open war breaks out between the parties and actors involved (such as Enron). Usually, shareholders and managers find a common basis and understand that their two main interests—to secure managers' position and shareholders' returns on their investments—overlap to a large extent. Hence, despite basic differences in some areas of interests, both sides find sufficient commonalities at an ideological level to collaborate in practical ways.

GOVERNMENT, GOVERNMENTAL ORGANIZATIONS, POLITICAL PARTIES

Business, particularly 'big business', and managers usually get strong support from government and political parties of every colour. They are often seen as of national interest; 'what is good for business is good for the country!' Once more, managers are expected to run businesses as efficiently as possible, but this time not only for the sake of the owners, but for the sake of the national economy (and society). Again, the ideology of management is flexible enough to meet these political expectations. Although there can be also differences and tensions between government and business, common interests (*not* common sense) dominate and usually prevail. Throughout modern history, most governments have regarded the agendas and activities of merchants, capitalists, and now managers as mostly in line with the so-called 'national interest'. Concerns about (international) competitiveness of national industries, or open and hidden protectionism are only a few examples of the 'business orientation' (which, in fact, is largely 'big business orientation') of most of current governments. And despite, perhaps even because of globalisation managers are quite good at 'playing the national card' when it suits their interests. There is a broad common basis government and management can use and develop for mutual benefit.

What is probably new since the early 1980s are the political expectations and aspirations for public sector organisations; they, too, shall be run by managers and managed like business organisations. Governments and political parties all over the world increasingly expect, praise, and strongly support so-called managerial professionalism (Abercrombie et al. 1980, p. 135). Michael Heseltine, the then British Secretary of State for the Environment, said in 1980 (cited in Pollitt 1990, p. 3): 'Efficient management is a key to the [national] revival. . . . And the management ethos must run right through our national life, private and public companies, civil service, nationalized industries, local government, the National Health Service'. Since then, the *ideology of managerialism* has entered all public services, even public and private life, on a global scale (e.g. Kirkpatrick / Ackroyd

2000, Cohen et al. 1999). Government and public sector have internalised large parts of managerial ideology and language, while businesses have applied governmental and bureaucratic systems and procedures to a great extent. The ideologies of management and governance can easily cross the trenches between managers and politicians.

CONSULTANTS AND MANAGEMENT GURUS

A third group of highly relevant stakeholders for the ideology of management are management consultants and so-called management gurus. Their ideology is quite simple—to sell whatever can be sold at the highest price possible. In this sense, we might talk about the *ideology of consultancy maximisation*. In this respect, 'management' is one of the best products ever invented; it is a whole universe of concepts and terms vague enough to be applied to every problem within any context. At the same time, it is specific enough so that buyers think they are getting something for their money. And it can be changed easily, so that customers constantly feel they have to buy the latest fashion. As Ramsey (1996, p. 166) explained: 'As organizations, consultancies clearly have a vested interest akin to that of suppliers of automobiles or consumer durables: to offer replacements frequently enough to sustain their growth as firms, and attractive enough to appear worth ditching or adding to the old technique for.'

Consultants and management gurus are part of the 'management-fashion-setting community' (Protherough / Pick 2002, p. 61), a community which is eager and very successful in producing and disseminating the myths of managerial genius. At the same time, managers have a whole range of personal, group, political and tactical reasons to buy into these managerial fads and fashions. Consultants and managers might in reality see business problems from different angles simply because of their different functional responsibilities. However, they nevertheless share the same ideology (of management) and play the same game of managerial fads and fashions. In practical terms, they often collude in an almost symbiotic relationship because they know that the more they collaborate, the more they can gain from each other, and create a win-win situation.

BUSINESS SCHOOLS AND MANAGEMENT DEPARTMENTS

Although usually less glamorous, less eloquent and quite late compared to consultants and management gurus, business school academics also contribute to the production and dissemination of the ideology of management—and on an industrial scale. Business schools have turned into medium-sized enterprises (Worthington / Hodgson 2005, p. 96) offering a whole range of products (management and business degrees) in different market segments and on an increasingly global scale. At the same time, their research produces an endless stream of managerial theories and concepts, replacing old theories with new ones, and providing empirical evidence for the dominance of the factual. The teaching and research delivered by academics at business schools have a much greater impact than ongoing discussions about their relevance suggests. This is because the actual product of business schools is not degrees or theories—it is managers. Business school academics provide current and future managers with the worldviews and mindsets, theories and models, skills and attitudes which enable them to become "professional" managers. Conditioning people, shaping their ways of thinking and acting, has always been the real product of schools.

Of course, at almost every business school and within almost every programme, there are the usual references to interdisciplinary, multi-dimensional, critical and reflective thinking. Issues such as business ethics, corporate social responsibility, global warming and emotional intelligence are often part of the curriculum. However, they are mostly additional embellishment, not core. These 'nice-to-haves' are too little and too dispersed to really make any difference, or to balance, challenge or change the hard core of economics and business studies (i.e. mainstream management and strategy concepts, accounting, finance, operations, marketing and human resource management [HRM]). There are no major theoretical or practical differences between the ideology of management developed and taught by the vast majority of business schools academics and the ideology of management upheld by most managers. Business schools teach and research managerial orthodoxy in the same manner that schools in medieval European monasteries once taught Christian orthodoxy and, in doing so, primarily served the upper echelon of the Catholic Church.

SUPRA-NATIONAL INSTITUTIONS, NON-GOVERNMENTAL ORGANISATIONS (NGOS), THINK TANKS, PRESSURE GROUPS

Finally, there is a whole range of supra-national institutions, NGOs, think tanks, and pressure groups which may also be influential and have an impact on the ideology of management. Larger organisations such as the Organisation for Economic Co-operation and Development (OECD), World Bank, International Monetary Fund, U.S. Agency for International Development, and the Commonwealth Secretariat (Pina / Torres 2003, pp. 334–335, Haque 1999, p. 470) actively advocate and disseminate market and business ideologies. They require that organisations—and even whole countries—commit themselves to these principles and put them into action as quickly and comprehensively as the circumstances allow. So there are no clashes with the ideology of management;—on the contrary, it is actively promoted.

It might be different across the spectrum of NGOs, particularly think tanks and pressure groups. There is not one consistent set of core assumptions which can be identified because of the wide range of possible ideological backgrounds. The relationship with the ideology of management, hence, can be either affirmative or challenging. However, conservative business associations and think tanks are usually most efficient in getting their agenda through.

The examples above clearly demonstrate that managers are not the only ones who believe in, and actively promote, the ideology of management. Shareholders and institutional investors, governments and political parties of all colours, consultants and management gurus, business schools academics, supra-national institutions, conservative business associations and think tanks all contribute massively to the formulation, justification and dissemination of the ideology of management. They all contribute to 'the development of a body of knowledge that largely ignores the (contradictory) relations of domination and exploitation that are a medium and outcome of what managers do' (Willmott 1996, p. 326). There is a 'structural constellation of interests' (Scott 2003, p. 160) amongst the major stakeholders and key players in economies and societies concerning the promotion of the ideology of management. Moreover as demonstrated, the ideology of management is flexible enough to fit conveniently with most of the stakeholders' other ideologies, concerns and agendas (e.g. the ideology of shareholder maximisation or neo-liberalism); 'once it has been learnt, management can be applied anywhere, to anything and on anyone' (Parker 2002, p. 5). Managers are therefore able to justify, strengthen and deepen their positions and influence because they have successfully positioned themselves within social systems, into networks of powerful stakeholders and right in the heart of an ideological network. In a nutshell, the ideology of management does not strengthen managers' dominance simply because it is developed and communicated by managers *to* others, but *with* and *amongst* others.

Furthermore, the ideology of management is not a static but a dynamic phenomenon. As in any other ideology, there are a few *non-negotiable* core assumptions. These include private property and profit orientation, inequality, managers' responsibilities and prerogatives for managing organisations, class structure, anti-democratic organisations, exploitation of the many by the few and other similar assumptions. This is the protective belt. The proponents of managerialism do not have any problem with shifts and changes in any parts which do not belong to the protected ideological core of management. On the contrary, there is a constant strive to change the external appearances and themes of the ideology as much as possible. Business-oriented media, hero managers, management gurus, consultants and business school academics are particularly keen to produce, actively promote and disseminate a constant flow of latest managerial fads and fashions. Yet interestingly, despite all the different contributions from this variety of interested parties, and despite all the different issues raised and tackled, neither the community nor the ideology of management evaporates. This is mainly due to the forces of conformity, i.e. what Carson et al. (1999) called 'herd behaviour' or 'bandwagon-effect'. 'Jumping on the bandwagon, even at the later stages of a management fad, may be perceived as a form of innovation when it is contrasted with the more passive act of ignoring industry trends or the more active stance of rejecting them altogether' (Staw / Epstein 2000, p. 528). It is also due to the similarities in interests and ideologies of the powerful players involved. Managerial fads and fashions are not completely random—they orbit around the hard core of the ideology of management and the related dominating ideologies of neo-liberalism and globalisation (Steger 2005, p. 33). The ideology of management develops and proceeds along the larger epochal trend of capitalism with its changing narratives (nationalism or globalisation, protectionism or neo-liberalism).

The way in which the ideology of management fits with both longer epochal trends and shorter fads and fashions provides it with another important dimension—a historical perspective. Proponents of orthodox management are keen to trace it back even as far as ancient Greece, or are happy to identify it in medieval societies as well as in the predecessors of modernity (e.g. Bracker 1980). And anything from the middle of the 19th century onwards is history, (almost) with necessity and inevitability. This is a very typical characteristic of ideologies—their portrayal as the (natural) outcome of a long historical development. As Jacques (1996, p. 146) explained: 'Where historical perspective is not ignored completely, it is most often used to explain the supposedly steady "evolution" of a nearly perfected body of thought. If not, it is likely to be used to show the constancy through time of currently accepted belief or the repetitive cyclicality of the order of things.' Such a portrait implies, or is used to imply, a kind of 'historical inevitability' (Steger 2005, p. 34). Jacques (1996, p. 14) provided an excellent analysis of this aspect of ideology, cited here in full:

> Open any introductory American text in organization studies and, if it contains a history of management thought, the story will almost certainly be linear, progressive, teleological and truth-centered. It is *linear* in that management is presented as a continuous thread running through civilization; 'Would you believe that organization theory issues were addressed in the Bible? Well they were!' (Robbins, 1990:36). It is *progressive* in that management knowledge is portrayed as becoming increasingly perfect over time. Pre-industrial societies may have been 'largely biased against the concept of managing organizations effectively and efficiently' (Bowditch and Buono 1994:7), but knowledge has 'evolved' from that primitive point. The term 'evolution' appears almost universally in these stories, but not in a sense strictly in accordance with Darwin or current biology. Rather, it has what is called a *teleological* connotation, the idea that knowledge is not just adapting

but improving relative to a final goal. The goal in this case is a paradigmatic science of behaviour in organizations. Were this day to arrive, behaviour in organizations could be assessed with reference to rules of interaction analogous to the periodic table of chemistry or the gas laws of physics. In this sense, such histories are *truth-centered.*

Finally, like every other ideology, the ideology of management also looks forward. It has ultimate objectives, ideal states, utopias of perfect conditions, processes and outcomes. In the case of the ideology of management, this is mainly about transforming organisations into perfect machinery for profit maximisation, optimal efficiency and productivity. It is about best fit (sic!) between an organisation's business environment, its strategy and organisational capabilities. It is about finding the secrets of achieving sustainable competitive advantage, or a highly motivated and skilful workforce which always delivers outstanding performance on a daily basis. In this sense, the ideology of management is teleological (Suddaby / Greenwood 2005, p. 46).

In summary, the ideology of management has managed to achieve isomorphism with

- current structures (institutions, socio-economic conditions, powerful stakeholders),
- current processes (fads and fashions, epochal trends),
- previous structures and processes (historical perspective)
- and future structures and processes (utopian ideal of the organisation).

As its proponents would say, managerialism has been inevitable in the past, is irreversible at present, and is irresistible in future (Steger 2005, pp. 35–36). It is a very typical characteristic of ideology to link past, present, and future—to portray the present as a natural outcome of the past, and as the basis for a possible and, of course, better future. The final piece of the ideological jigsaw is that it is only the proponents of the ideology who can guarantee this continuity. It is therefore essential that management remains the dominant force and is supported by all influential actors.

FUNCTIONAL ASPECTS AND COGNITIVE DIMENSION

The previous section showed some of the links between the ideology of management and its (present, past and future) environment. This and the following sections are about managerial ideology within organisations as well as discourses about organisations. The analyses will concentrate first on functional aspects. According to orthodox management concepts, management and managers primarily address organisational problems from a functional perspective. Their particular concerns are to

1) increase profitability, shareholder value,
2) outperform market criteria (such as competitiveness, value-for-money, customer satisfaction),
3) increase economic efficiency and cost-effectiveness of goods produced and services delivered,
4) achieve improvements in functional rationality, technological efficiency, productivity, quality, flexibility, risk reduction or speed of organisational structures and technical processes,
5) make managerial decisions as efficiently as possible and
6) ensure the well functioning and efficient control of staff.

Because of this, management is said to be solely concerned with functional aspects of organisations and based on purely functional, 'value-free' concepts for the sake of the whole and the general interest. Correspondingly, managers are portrayed as '"professionals", impartially carrying out the universally and technically defined functions of management' (Willmott 1984, p. 355).

It can be agreed that orthodox theory does indeed comprehensively describe and analyse the functional and technical aspects of organisations in great detail. It also provides a range of useful ideas, theories and concepts for how to organise work, how to organise the production of goods and provision of services (better), how to keep organisation functioning and how to make them, as well as whole value chains and industries more efficient. The world would be, indeed, a less developed place without the functional and technical concepts and approaches, theories and technologies of managerialism.

However, management's main principles and objectives for organisations (e.g. profit-maximisation, shareholder value, efficiency, productivity or customer orientation) are *value statements*. Orthodox management and organisation studies apodictively state what *should*, even *must*, be the main objectives of organisations, how they *should* be organised and according to which principles managers *should* make their decisions and take action. At the same time, other values are excluded from the core of organisational discourses and realities (largely on allegations that they are 'not realistic', 'not business-relevant' or 'ideological'), and only placed at the periphery, if at all, for the sake of political correctness. These are values such as the following (e.g. Kirkpatrick et al. 2005, pp. 41, 74, 167, Michael 2005, pp. 104–105, Skålén 2004, p. 251, Gabriel 1999, p. 404, Haque 1999, p. 469, Hoggett 1996, p. 14, Abrahamson 1996, p. 262, Pollitt 1990, p. 60):

1) public and individual welfare, stakeholder concerns,
2) liberty, civic virtues, community norms, communitarian values, social usefulness,
3) equality, social justice,
4) fairness, ethics, quality, integrity and morality of social processes,

5) democratic institutions, decision-making, representation of employees at all levels,

6) empowerment and development of staff as citizens.

Obviously, compared to these values, the orthodox agenda is about very
specific, if not to say narrow-minded organisational values (profit), structures (hierarchy) and processes (managerial decisions). This, paradoxically,
might be even an advantage—at least for some groups of people. By focus-
ing on the managerial value system, managers are in a position to dominate
and manage both the discourses about organisations and management as
well as factual events; 'whoever is in a position of power is able to create
knowledge supporting that power relationship' (Brookfield 2005, p. 137).
The language generated, used, and disseminated by superiors defines, even
creates phenomena, how they are seen and have to be seen, and whose
knowledge and competences are relevant in what ways. In this respect,
managers (together with other interested parties), have been successful
in creating aspects of organisational and managerial reality by creating
and shaping the language of business. To list but a few of the buzzwords
and 'management-speak' concepts: 'efficiency' and 'productivity', 'market
orientation' and 'customer orientation', 'leadership' and 'management',
'business re-engineering' and 'TQM' (total quality management), 'knowledge management' (sic!) or 'learning organisation'. Literally all key terms
and core concepts are *managerial* in the sense that they define organisations and organisational problems from managers' perspective and either
directly demand or indirectly imply the need for (more) management and
(more) managers. Since these terms and concepts are in the centre of any
(mainstream) reasoning about management, organisations, business and
markets, and since managers are trained in using these concepts, it is the
managers who are in the strongest position to get the best part of discourses around and about organisations and, because of this, often the best
part of material consequences. Like other ruling elites, managers are keen
to control the language and concepts of their fiefdoms and to dominate the
discourses both around and about management and organisations.

Having decided on the grand narrative and discourses of the managerial
world, it is then possible to *explain* this world with the help of the ideology
of management. According to Hartley (1983, p. 23), an ideology provides
'beliefs about the causes and processes of events and their contiguity, the
relationships people perceive among events (. . .) and the explanations they
furnish to explain these relationships'. An ideology is a system of explanations for everything that can be, needs to be, and shall be explained—
including explanations why some things can't be explained. For example,
Therborn (1980, p. 18) mentioned that every ideology involves three fundamental modes of ideological interpellation: 1. what exists, and its corollary,
what does not exist; 2. what is good, right, just, and its opposites; 3. what
is possible and impossible.

The ideology of management states the following:

1. The only things which exist are those which can and should be measured, managed and optimised because they are relevant for the overall objectives of management and organisations. Everything else is irrelevant and, hence, is simply not on the radar.
2. Out of all manageable and measurable events only those which are important and which help to achieve the overall objectives are good, i.e. profit-maximisation, increases in efficiency and productivity. Issues not in line with, or even against this holy trinity are bad and wrong.
3. Everything is possible—as long as it is properly managed. Theoretically, there are only two things which are impossible: an economy not based on market principles and business or organisations not based on management principles of private property and without management—impossible at least according to the proponents of the ideology of management.

In this sense, managerial ideology explains the (socio-economic) world we live in, including challenges and changes in the environment, what and how organisations have to do in order to achieve desired outcomes and the roles of management and people within these settings. And, according to the ideology of management, it is managers' prerogative to develop and provide these explanations (which they may have got from experts and information sources); managers, and only managers, have the official status and "task" to define what counts as true.

Those who provide explanations also provide *meaning*. As Protherough / Pick (2002, p. 141) explained: 'For many people, meaning is no longer given to everyday life by the churches, by the language of Bible and prayer-book, but by the modes and cultural assumptions adopted by the powerful economic and political movements. . . .' In the world of business and organisations it is management, and only management, which can ascribe meaning to events. This is of crucial importance for managers because they are aware of the fact 'that the struggle for power in an organization is often a struggle to impose and legitimate a self-serving construction of meaning for others' (Walsh 1995, p. 290). Managers, therefore, are keen to get meanings 'right'. Literally everything that exists within or concerning organisations—be it socio-economic aspects, strategies, organisational structures and processes, or people—must be interpreted in line with the ideology of management and managers' interests. The world is seen and interpreted from a management perspective. Things are only meaningful when they relate and contribute to the overarching strategic objectives and grand managerial rationale—or at least, when it can be portrayed in that way.

However 'real' or 'unreal' the explanations and meanings may look to an outsider, every ideology is concerned with 'the reality'. It is about human beings, their place in society and what they do either to preserve or change the current situation and practices. Ideologies try to link the world, society, institutions, objectives, actors, reasoning, decisions, actions and consequences in a meaningful way. The ideology of management is no different. It is probably one of the most *practice-oriented* ideologies humankind has witnessed and experienced so far. In addition to its rhetorical arsenal, it is a practical toolbox for managers to solve managerial problems and achieve managerial objectives (Braynion 2004, p. 454). Managing organisations, their structures and processes within challenging environments, as well as people within organisational settings in order to achieve specific objectives and outcomes almost automatically necessitates a strong reality and action orientation. However, the ideology of management does not address the whole reality. The organisational and managerial reality constructed through the lens of managerial ideology is both limited and biased. It is a world of the functional and instrumental, of measurable and largely one-dimensional factors—nothing more, nothing less. Only in its own logic and worldview is it comprehensive and consistent.

According to this understanding, organisational reality can, and is structured only in one way; *hierarchically*. Hierarchy is the structural incarnation of the functional / orthodox worldview and its comprehensive and consistent principle of organising social activities within organisations and even societies. As we saw in Chapter 3, hierarchies define and institutionalise roles and social positions of superiors and subordinates. Of course, the social structure of complex organisations is much more differentiated than the categories of 'managers' and 'non-managers' imply. Nonetheless, by using this distinction as an analytical tool, it becomes clear *that the managerial construction and justification of organisational reality is primarily about creating and protecting social differences*. It is the very definition of the hierarchical organisation that there are few at the top, some more in the middle and the vast majority at the bottom—and it must *always* be that way! This principle is applied throughout the whole social system and in all its parts. It is present not only in the hierarchical structure, but also in projects, teams or other forms of organisation. With this principle, the ideology of management creates and contributes to the design and explanation of all structures and processes of the social system; it constructs and justifies a whole system of unequal societal relationships. It gives organisations not only a functional but, more importantly, a *political order*; 'consequently, the concepts and method of the management discipline are a social classification system, . . . For example, the very concepts of "manager" and "management" are social artifacts reflecting the social relations, or power order, in our society, based on hierarchical segmentation and value appropriation' (Rosen 1984, p. 305). Managerial ideology then legitimises the existing hierarchy and power relations within and beyond managerial organisations. It even 'explains' why the horizontal structure (division of labour) and vertical structure (the separation of rulers and ruled) are necessary, 'why one group is dominant and another dominated, why one person gives orders in a particular enterprise while another takes orders' (Chia-pello / Fairclough 2002, p. 187). In doing so, the ideology of management justifies *authority* (Baker 2005, p. 699, Zammuto et al. 2000, p. 263). With the ideology of management, managerial authority became an acceptable and accepted institution.

The principle of hierarchy also clarifies another important aspect of the ideological justification of organisational social structures and process-es—the justification of *social inequality*. 'Hierarchy means inequality', as Zaleznik (1989, p. 152) said so decisively. The establishment of inequalities and differences between social groups is only in certain respects an end in itself (e.g. to increase the privileged people's self-esteem and to provide them with a feeling of importance, success and superiority). The ideological con-struction of organisational reality in form of social inequalities establishes, justifies, secures and maintains *factual* differences between social groups, particularly the following (e.g. Levy et al. 2001, p. 10, Pollitt 1990, p. 6, Shrivastava 1986, p. 365, Abercrombie et al. 1980, p. 130): structural

- power asymmetries at institutional level,
- exclusion of lower managers and non-managers from participation in strategic decisions,
- higher status and privileges of dominant groups,
- fewer opportunities, access to resources and outcomes for lower ranks, unequal distribution and allocation of resources,
- (large) differences in rewards and remuneration.

Although there is an endless stream of fashion-oriented modifications of this structure, the basic principle of managerialism remains intact: through hierarchy, social positions and status, rights and duties, as well as contribu-tions and returns are allocated unequally amongst members of the social system. For example, in the managerial organisation some of the main pre-rogatives and responsibilities are exclusively reserved for (senior) managers; to define and identify problems, to set the agenda and objectives, to make decisions and / or influence decision-making processes, to control, to evalu-ate and appraise performance, to promote, and to reward and sanction (e.g. Braynion 2004, p. 449, Jost / Elsbach 2001, p. 182, Jacques 1996, p. 120)—all of those decreasing in both breadth and depth from the top to the bottom of the hierarchy.

As the examples listed above demonstrate, inequality usually leads to tangible differences and advantages. Social differentiation is largely about providing members of privileged and more powerful groups with much bet-ter positions and opportunities to pursuit their own *individual and group interests* compared to members of less powerful groups (Sidanius et al. 2004, p. 848). Ideology is all about giving more to those who have, and less to those who have not. The managerial organisation is no different—it 'gives a great deal at the top and very little at the bottom' (Thompson 1961,

p. 495). In this sense, the ideology of management is nothing new. It is the same old story of the hierarchically differentiated society or system, ensuring the division between 'those at the top' and 'the people', between 'them' and 'us'. 'Organisations become two-class societies: the upper class consists of the people who are expert, or on their way to expertise, in the arts of calculation, and the lower class consists of the dependents, the people who either do not understand the tactics of calculation or who emotionally cannot participate' (Zaleznik 1989, p. 157).[2]

However, this consciously designed system of social stratification and inequalities needs to be explained and justified. And, indeed, it is justified—in a functional way: 'Managers are those people given official responsibility for ensuring that the tasks undertaken in the organisation's name are done in a way which enables the organisation to continue into the future' (Watson 2006, p. 167). Nonetheless, proponents of the functional approach usually feel that it is not enough to simply re-state the obvious—that managers are superior(s). It still remains to be explained why organisations are, and should be, based on the principle of hierarchy and hence why people have different responsibilities and possibilities to act within the system. Basically, the legitimacy and justification of the whole system of the managerial organisation, and with it the dominance of managers, is at stake.

Since the proponents of the functional approach cannot base their claims publicly on ethical grounds (because this would go against the claim that the functional approach is value-free), there is only one way to deliver a practice-oriented explanation and justification—by reference to 'natural laws', i.e. to biology, or, more precisely, socio-biology (Wilson 1975). For example, Zaleznik (1989, p. 149) tried to portray social inequalities and unequal treatments as an almost natural law: 'Ranging from the animal kingdom to human groups, relationships form into a hierarchy.' And he explained further (p. 150): 'In human groups hierarchy in the distribution of power is a general tendency that has been verified in many observations and experiments. In study after study of group formations in work and "natural" groups, leaders and followers align themselves into a remarkably predictable relationship with few at the top and many at the bottom of the power pyramid.' It is, allegedly, not only a functional necessity but 'the nature' of social relationships that they are organised hierarchically. In a similar example, when Van Vugt (2006) attempted to shed some new light on 'the origins of leadership and followership in humans' he came up with the same 'insight' that 'whenever a group of people come together, a leader-follower relationship naturally develops' (p. 354).

The problem for the socio-biologist is not only to explain why subordinates should accept this so-called natural order but why they should willingly and happily support the hierarchical structure and everything what comes with it. According to Brookfield (2005, pp. viii–ix) an ideology's 'chief function is to convince people that the world is organized the way it is for the best of all reasons and that society works in the best interests of all.' This is yet another one of the primary functions and concerns of ideology—particularly conservative ideologies. It is a typical characteristic of these ideologies that they try very hard to convince particularly subordinates and the less privileged of the legitimacy and advantages of the system in order to get their consent (Thomas 1998). If successful, it leads to *voluntary deference* to the directives of authorities and rules and acceptance, even active support of the system of inequalities. And socio-biology provides the explanation for this, as Van Vugt (2006, p. 358) stresses:

> In this view, the occupation of leader and follower roles is explained entirely by the relative positions of individuals in the dominance hierarchy of a group. Dominance hierarchies are the product of competition among group members for scarce resources (. . .). Because some individuals are more successful than others in gaining access to these resources, hierarchies emerge in which those at the top of the hierarchy enjoy greater reproductive success than those at the bottom, the notorious pecking order.

According to functional and socio-biological ideology, hierarchical social order is not only 'natural', but 'advantageous' and 'just' for everyone. We all, therefore, deserve to be where we are in the hierarchy because this is the natural order of things. People at the top are simply better, stronger, and / or more intelligent than the rest of us. On this ground, the ideology of management not only explains and justifies how organisations are run and organised, but how they *should* be run and organised. It tries to justify the 'existing social and organizational relationships as natural and / or unavoidable' (Fournier / Grey 2000, p. 19). Parker (2002, pp. 8–9) described this as 'one of the largest institutional legitimation and public relations campaigns in the history of thought.'

All in all, this socio-biological / functional 'explanation' and 'justification' of hierarchy and managerial structures has had considerable success. And indeed, not only managers but most employees buy into it. Unfortunately, many people often forget that functional approaches based on socio-biological or similar theories are very limited in their ability to explain social systems. Biologism, evolutionism and the like are powerful, well-developed and often tested theories which provide good explanations for *un-reflected* behaviour of living organisms, animals and humans. They can also explain the emergence and behaviour of leaders and followers under specific social conditions (e.g. totalitarianism, mass hysteria or some extreme forms of group dynamics). However, such approaches are not designed to cope with issues and situations which are *not* determined by genetically pre-defined programmes, instinctive or un-reflected behaviour. *Where people have choice, i.e. are able to make up their mind and to make decisions based on a (more or less conscious) assessment of the situation and their possibilities, socio-biological / functional approaches fail.* Trying to explain and justify un-determined social events and situations with so-called natural laws is a typical characteristic of ideology, and in particular conservative ideologies. Whereas dominant groups come and go, the justification for their dominance, and for the oppression of the many, seems to remain the same.

Proponents of the functional approach may be aware of this and understand that the official aims and objectives of an ideology still might not be enough to convince people fully. Explanations, meaning and justifications of social reality based on ideology only become really convincing when they also comprise "positive" and "voluntary" aspects—something people can appreciate and strive for (of course, under the guidance of their superiors!). The usual tactics for achieving this are references to higher values and institutions. Throughout mankind's history there has been no shortage of institutions and values to be referred to—be it oracles, God(s), monarchy, money, 'the party' or 'the nation'. And there is no shortage of cynical individuals and groups of people to misuse them; e.g. priests, clergy, queens and kings, knights and aristocrats, capitalists, communists and fascists. The challenging task for any ideology is to successfully and convincingly link its beliefs and worldviews about (unequal and unjust) social reality to a set of higher and indeed highest values. Burnham (1941, p. 186) made this quite clear:

> They must at the same time be so expressed as to be capable of appealing to the sentiments of the masses. An ideology embodying the interests of a given ruling class would not be of the slightest use as social cement if it openly expressed its function of keeping the ruling class in power over the rest of society. The ideology must ostensibly speak in the name of 'humanity', 'the people', the race', 'the future', 'God', 'destiny', and so on.

He also found empirical evidence that groups when competing with each other during organisational change to get their agendas and values through, were all insisting that their ideologies 'are universal in validity and express the interests of humanity as a whole; . . . ' (ibid., p. 25). Nowadays it is all about economy and companies, management and managers. Accordingly, the higher values are all about wealth and progress, efficiency and productivity, profits and competitiveness. As we discussed earlier, the ideology of management has already incorporated all these values since it must demonstrate its closeness and fit to the epochal trend of capitalism. As with any other ideology, there is *a massive discrepancy* between the highest values referred to and the real interests, activities and factual behaviour of the dominant proponents of the ideology:

- Whereas managerial ideology is officially about shareholder maximisation, senior managers particularly fill their pockets on a scale never before seen.

- Whereas officially it's about organisational effectiveness and competitiveness, in reality it is about managers' fiefdoms and egos.
- Whereas officially it's about customer orientation and empowerment, it actually is about managers' prerogatives and privileges and keeping subordinates under control.

Once more, the ideology of management demonstrates a cynical use, misuse and abuse of higher values. But all of this is quite typical of ideologies and rulers—*why should it be different this time?*

We can now summarise our investigation into how the ideology of management tries to explain and justify organisational structures and processes on the basis of the functional approach. The analysis above has shown that claims that the functional approach is 'value-free' and is only concerned with so-called functional aspects of management and organisations cannot be sustained. The provision of functional 'explanations' and 'meaning' about organisational reality constructed by managerial discourses fails to convince. Managerialism is primarily concerned with the creation of a specific managerial discourse and, hence, organisational reality which disguises managers' power and interests. It is even biased towards managers' perspectives and interests. The functional approach towards organisations and management is fundamentally concerned with the establishment and justification of hierarchical structures, the prerogatives and responsibilities of superiors, and the tasks and duties of subordinates. This is partiality obscured by so-called rational explanations, by appealing to people's intellectual abilities to judge through what is portrayed as 'rational' argumentation and sense-making. However, its references to socio-biology in order to justify the hierarchical order, strongly suggest that ideology is at work. The functional approach primarily tries to explain and legitimise a hierarchical social order which strongly favours managers and oppresses employees. Since this reality is not quite the perfect world described by theory, and managers' factual interests and power orientations differ considerably from the officially portrayed aims and images, the ideology of management uses higher values in attempts to make it look more convincing. Also in that sense managerialism is quite a typical and developed ideology.

IDEOLOGICAL JUSTIFICATION OF MANAGEMENT AND MANAGERS

Closely related to attempts to justify the social structure of the managerial organisation is the idea of justifying management itself. And, probably more importantly, it is about convincing people of the legitimacy, if not to say necessity, of managers' positions and authority. According to the proponents of the ideology of management, managers are responsible for the whole. Therefore, it is first and foremost their task to concentrate on those issues which are portrayed as being of general relevance and crucial importance for the organisation. Usually these issues are defined as 'strategic', i.e. official mission and vision, strategic objectives and strategy, strategic decisions and strategic management, performance management and measurement systems, organisational structures and processes. In addition, managers are also responsible for the whole range of managerial tasks, e.g. representation of the organisation, operational functions, or managing (people) in general. Managers' responsibilities are not only 'technicalities' but the basis and tools for their power and influence. Managers, therefore, know how important it is to get their ideas and agendas adopted as the leading and guiding principles of the organisation—and they usually achieve this, either in the form of management concepts or as daily 'hands-on managing'. So the managerial characteristics of an organisation become largely reflections of the interests and values of the powerful actors, i.e. managers (e.g. Daft / Weick 1984, p. 285, Hambrick / Mason 1984, p. 193).

At the same time, others are excluded from these managerial responsibilities. Employees, experts, knowledge workers and professionals are not allowed to make managerial decisions. They contribute with their work, experience and / or knowledge to the overall outcome, but they are not involved in managerial routines. In this sense, managerial issues are not only managers' responsibilities but *prerogatives*. The ideology of management presumes 'the legitimacy of established managerial priorities' (Levy et al. 2001, p. 1), and it defines and protects the "rights" and privileges of managers. This is another typical aspect of ideology—to identify and secure certain zones of sense- and decision-making and make them to 'no go areas' for others. But in this instance, it is not on religious, aristocratic or political grounds on which claims for supremacy are being made—it is on *functional* grounds. This time the higher values are not divine destiny, royal pedigree or party membership but management knowledge. The ideology of management's "explanations" and "justifications" of the prerogatives and dominance of managers are primarily *political statements*. Managers, and only managers, can generate and apply the knowledge which is needed to run our organisations, businesses, indeed the whole economy and society. *The whole functional approach is actually about managers' problems and objectives, social roles and responsibilities, their positions and functions, interests and privileges.*

It therefore doesn't come as much of a surprise that most, if not all managers are very much in favour of the functional approach. It justifies *their* prerogatives, privileged positions and actions; it describes organisational reality with respect to *their* interests while at the same time shaping it accordingly; and it gives *them* great power while at the same time disguising it. Orthodox management theory concentrates largely on (the importance of) superiors and their interests whereas it only concerns subordinates in their (mal-) functioning. Managerialism deliberately creates social reality in a very specific way while denying doing so—which is exactly what ideologies do.

Management means privileges. But an even greater, and more important, prerogative for members of the dominant group of managers is *leadership*. There is an endless stream of proponents of management ideology keen to either contribute to the theoretical foundation of leadership or to provide empirical 'evidence' for its importance and necessity. For example, an American Management Association survey carried out in 1994, revealed that the keys to successful strategic change are 'first and foremost leadership' (Gill 2003, p. 309). This is hardly a surprise since the survey was taken from senior managers. What still needs some explanation is the fact that so many academics were and are more than willing to support the ideological claim for leadership. For example, Stewart / Kringas (2003, p. 676) cite findings which state that 'numerous studies suggest the importance of leadership in bringing about successful change' and that 'the "package" of competencies possessed by leaders is correlated with the degree of cultural change'. And, of course, there is the endless caravan of business consultants, management gurus and even politicians who all praise leadership as both a value in itself and as a panacea for almost every (strategic) problem. Added to this is the countless number of handy airport bookstall guides which 'reveal' the 'right set' of personal and professional skills and attitudes for leadership and success—wherever, whenever, and however.

'Leadership' has often been one of the core elements of ideology. But it is usually a very particular understanding of leadership; it is *hierarchical* leadership (Kerr / Jermier 1978, p. 375). The question, therefore, is 'how [do] individual leaders constitute and sustain their authority within different social systems' (Whittington 1992, p. 708)—whereby all these different social systems simply mean different forms of hierarchical systems. Proponents of conservative ideologies have been very productive throughout the centuries developing checklist-concepts of what constitutes a leader, particularly 'grand', 'powerful' or 'successful' leaders. There are endless lists of personal criteria, psychological traits, attitudes and behaviour. In addition to biological, genetic, sociological and psychological aspects, they are concerned about what these leaders do and how they do it. Chiapello / Fairclough (2002, p. 202) provide some typical examples: leaders "sense problems and weaknesses', exhibit 'curiosity', 'create', 'imagine', 'improvise', 'dream', have 'visions', 'shake up' reality and their own thinking, . . . They are charismatic: they 'inspire' others, and 'raise aspirations' with their visions, they 'wake people out of inertia', . . .'. And so on, and so forth. Whatever the specific leadership-approach is, they all have one thing in common: What exactly constitutes a leader, how leadership actually can be done, and what 'outstanding' leaders precisely do in order to be so successful *is and remains a mystery*. Of course, there are training courses, certificates, and even degrees for (prospective) managers and leaders. Curricula and textbooks provide a comprehensive and systematic coverage of the whole field of management including leadership. Lecturers, researchers and consultants transfer management knowledge from the theoretical realm to practitioners, and practitioners feed their experience back into the system. Every aspect is covered a hundred times from every possible angle. But above a certain level, information gets sparser and vaguer. In the context of senior management and leadership, (apparent) lack of knowledge and confusion reinforce each other. We are told defensively that 'managers do a large number of different things' (Salaman), that these 'defy description and analysis', and that 'remarkably little is known about the particular skills or competencies required by managers' (Barry). The role of management is apparently 'to integrate a complex set of human and organizational variables' (Freedman), while '"diversity makes it far from easy to generalise about what managers do, or indeed to make any coherent sense of management at all" (Sjostrand)' (Protherough / Pick 2002, pp. 77–78). Meanwhile, 'the leader' is simply a mythical figure, far away from our daily sense-making and routines. A plethora of symbols, physical signs, barriers, cultural and behaviours indicators, psychological and sociological stereotypes and, of course, willing servants who surround 'Him' or 'Her' all contribute to supporting this mysterious image. These are all part of the deliberate attempt to *create* myths and mystique around the institution of leadership as well as around leaders which is described in almost religious modes (Soloveitchik, 1983, referred to in Friedman et al. 2005, p. 26) as inexplicable mysteries and wonders in the mundane and rational sea of daily business. As Friedman et al. (2005, p. 26) explained: 'From the spiritual perspective, order, causal explanation, and instrumental concerns are not an end but rather a starting point from which to engage and experience deeper mysteries. The desired state of affairs for a spiritual consciousness is awe and wonder.' Hence, leadership is *not* a mystery because the things leaders do are so different to other human behaviour and actions. Nor is it a mystery because of the individual skills and personal qualities of leaders—leaders are humans like you and me. Leadership is and remains mysterious because it is *socially constructed as mystery*; an 'aura of mystique' is created both by leaders themselves and their willing servants. Fournier / Grey (2000, p. 12) also described this phenomenon: 'the manager has been depicted as a mythical figure requiring a rare blend of charismatic flair which cannot be routinized and codified in rules transferred through scientific training. This aura of mystification and glory with which managers (of the right kind) have been sanctified by the popular literature has served to increase the potential power and status of management . . .'

This is the half conscious, half unconscious mystification of people higher up in organisational or societal hierarchies and class systems—for the sole and simple reason that they are higher up the hierarchy. 'Incumbents of high office are held in awe because they are in touch with the mysteries and magic of such office; . . . Since one knows less and less about the activities of superordinates the farther away on the hierarchy they are, the more the awe in which he holds them and consequently the greater their prestige or status' (Thompson 1961, p. 493). Basically, leadership is all about creation of an image and getting this into people's mind so that they do things which they otherwise would not do. This is the whole "secret of leadership"— nothing more, nothing less. Without the social and cultural creation of 'leadership mystique' there would be few leaders or leadership. Without the social creation and nurture of the ideology of leadership the whole thing would simply disappear—and we all would be much better off.

All in all, there seems to be a great divide in reasoning about management. When talking about 'normal' management, all dominant theories and concepts are based on rational approaches and make sense for managerial and organisational issues in rational and functional ways (allegedly). But as soon as we talk about leadership and senior management, for whatever reason, rational and functional approaches don't seem to apply anymore and the language changes into a kind of quasi-religious jargon of mystery. This is a specific terminology and jargon constructed not for experts but adepts. Only the ones who belong to this 'circle of the elected few' apparently know the secrets.

MANAGERIAL IDEOLOGY AND THE GROUP OF MANAGERS

It is worth remembering that the core parts of every ideology are developed, implemented and maintained by and for a particular group of people or even a social class. Hence, despite their very regular appeals and references to general values, ideologies reflect mainly the very *specific interests, values and objectives of a particular group or social class* (e.g. Baker 2005, p. 692, Deem / Brehony 2005, p. 221, Burnham 1941, p. 25). And dominant ideologies, by definition, reflect the interests, values and objectives of the prevailing group(s). But they don't usually do this in a straightforward manner since the dominant group's real interests don't address the concerns of the majority of people. In fact they are likely to be in stark contrast. So the dominant ideology reflects a dominant group's interest only indirectly, disguised by references to more general and more attractive values as explained earlier. This usually means that the majority of people don't realise the partiality of ideology, or even recognise the ideological nature of the concepts at all. Sidanius et al. (2004, p. 868) provided some explanation for this: 'Because of their control of the means of intellectual production (e.g., mass media, universities), the "ruling classes" are able to convince non-elites of the moral and intellectual righteousness of social policies, especially allocative policies that primarily serve the interests of the owners of the means of production rather than the interests of the workers and lower classes (. . .)'.

Throughout the world, rulers are not stupid. Their regimes of symbols and language, attitudes and actions may look ridiculous to an outsider, or to anyone who hasn't (yet) internalised the regime, if not to say brainwashed by the constant indoctrination. But when it comes to individual and group interests, power and their ideological cover-up, the practical intelligence of rulers and their top supporters is well above average. In their understanding as well as their actions, they are much more sophisticated and professional than it appears or than their critics may think.

For example, members of the dominant group are very aware of the relationships and differences between their own interests and the ideology they publicly represent. For them, it is important to obey and uphold officially the general values and objectives of the ideology, and that they demonstrate publicly a common understanding of its values and coherence. If they wouldn't uphold the public image of the system, they can't pursue their personal interests and enjoy their privileges to the extent they would like to. Scott (1990, p. 55) therefore stressed the fact that 'most ruling groups take great pains to foster a public image of cohesion and shared belief. Disagreements, informal discussions, off-guard commentary are kept to a minimum and, whenever possible, sequestered out of sight . . .'. This is also true for managers and the management ideology. Despite all their possible different perceptions, interests and objectives, managers share a common interest in the ideology of management in itself. This shared understanding (and its public demonstration) plays a crucial part in group formation and integration, and for *group locomotion and cohesion*. Ideology integrates groups (Baker 2005, p. 699)—even groups of the most selfish and egoistic members. The integrative power of dominant ideology also explains that groups might be defined more 'through social identification rather than through social interaction' (Hartley 1983, p. 16). Although managers are more individually oriented, and may not even believe in the ideological positions (Apple 2005, p. 20), the ideology of management nonetheless gives them a common ground for identification (as a manager) and a strong feeling of belonging to the group of managers (van Dijk 2006, p. 119). In this sense, the ideology of management does not only produce a collective cognitive map, mindset or shared mental representations amongst managers (Walsh 1995) but it also represents and produces the social group of managers.

Of course, the factual interests behind the ideology of management can be quite varied and complex. Nonetheless, the prime ideological interest supported by all managers is a concern with the 'primacy of management' and with the 'importance of management for management's sake' (Deem / Brehony 2005, p. 222). Managers' first and foremost ideological interest is to achieve general acceptance that managers, *and only managers*, do management. It *must be generally accepted* that managers are the ones responsible for managing, for strategic issues and strategic decision-making, for the design and maintenance of the organisation, for guidance and control. This has high sociological relevance since this general acceptance means this special group's interests are institutionalized as the leading principle for a whole social system. Managers' work, problems and concerns will, even must, be seen by everyone as of supreme significance. Having achieved this, managers can then 'maintain their hegemonic control and perpetuate domination' (Shrivastava 1986, p. 364). The ideology of management does not only support and justify a particular group's sectional interests, values and objectives—it portrays them as universal ones. It is yet another tool for 'more or less conscious efforts to defend or advance sectional interests in the name of a universal interest' (Alvesson / Willmott 1992, p. 6). The ideology of management means the *universalisation of sectional interests* (Hamilton 1987, p. 23, Shrivastava 1986, pp. 366, 369).

However, although the ideology of management is hegemonic, institutionalised and universally accepted, managers—like any other rulers—can never be sure about the security of their dominance. The ideology of management is particularly vulnerable since it has not changed the basic characteristics of orthodox organisations. In principle, they are just as anti-democratic, exploitative, unjust and class-centred as organisations were in previous centuries. In fact, management and the ideology of management even actively contribute to the ongoing reproduction of exploitation, injustice and inequalities. One of the core functions of ideologies is to offer 'legitimizing myths' which 'provide intellectual and moral justification for either greater or smaller levels of group-based social inequality' (Sidanius / Pratto 1999, p. 234)—there is always a need for ideology to develop, justify and disseminate a certain set of interests and values in the light of more or less obvious inconsistencies with the factual situation people are in. Hence, the universalisation of sectoral interests can only work when those who are privileged by the ideology can either 'convince' others of the necessity and advantages of their dominance or can produce enough propaganda that the majority of people simply doesn't realise the discrepancies between ideological claims and (their) social reality.

Managers need to find a convincing way to explain why the universalisation of their sectoral interests should be accepted, and even supported by everyone—or at least not recognised as a problematic issue. It is usually assumed that managers' actions are *not* (self-) interest-driven and they are keen that their work is perceived 'as impartial and uncompromised by self-interest or class-interest' (Willmott 1996, p. 326). It must be believed that their work, decisions and actions are only motivated by the desire to increase an organisation's efficiency and productivity—by universal values and virtues. Even more, managers' roles and responsibilities, objectives and interests, prerogatives and privileges need to be portrayed as being in the interest of the whole organisation and for the good of the social system as a whole. As Willmott (1996, p. 325) explained: 'If "subordinates" can be persuaded that managers simply perform a role, task or function within the division of labour that is necessary to maximize efficiency and effectiveness, resistance to managerial authority appears to be irrational and anti-social—it threatens to undermine the capacity of management to do what, allegedly, is in the universal interests of everyone concerned.' This corresponds nicely to the fact that managers, like anyone else, want to see themselves as concerned with the selfless improvement of the whole, rather than primarily driven by career aspirations and political struggles over budgets and resources (Pfeffer 1981, referred to in Willmott 1996, p. 325). Managers are simply doing what is expected from them as the guardians or servants of the organisation they are responsible for. One is touched by so much selflessness.

Nonetheless, there is a further twist. Managers claim that they can only do their job best if they are provided with sufficient resources and are in a strong position to make all the right decisions and to take all the necessary actions for improving an organisation's competitiveness, efficiency and productivity. Hence, the organisation, and even its stakeholders, must do everything to strengthen and support management. And managers have to contribute to this, too! In order to use their full potential for the organisation and to perform at the highest level possible, managers must put all their efforts into the pursuit and development of *their* knowledge and skills, individual situation and progress. For this, managers must first make sure they secure their own position and to strengthen management in order to "serve" the organisation, society or the country in the best way possible. They must do so both as individuals as well as members of the dominant group. The better the dominant group is established and provided with the means to fulfil its tasks, the better it is for the whole. This, again, fits nicely to the self-image of members of the ruling group. They do not only think that they deserve what they've got, but that their material and other interests are for the good of the whole.

This is one of the cynical strategies of almost every ruling group. They not only claim that it is for the interest of the whole that they 'serve' so selflessly—they claim that their partial interests are good for the whole, that their egoistic pursuit of advantages and privileges is a necessary precondition for the positive development of the entire social system! According to this view, the dominant group's sectional interests should not only be the leading principles and values *of* the whole organisation, but are good and necessary *for* the whole organisation. Ideologies like managerialism portray the pursuit of individual and group interests as advantageous for the whole; *what is good for managers (or the Royal family, aristocrats, or other upper echelons of any type of hierarchical organisation) is good for all of us!* This is ideology 'at its best' (or at its worst!), i.e. turning things upside down in a dialectical spin and making people believe that it is in their interest if dominant groups largely pursue only their own interests while at the same time cynically using and abusing generally accepted higher values and virtues.

SOCIALISATION AND CONDITIONING— THE PSYCHOLOGICAL DIMENSION OF IDEOLOGY FOR SUBORDINATES

The hierarchical nature of the managerial organisation means that the large majority of people are excluded from any sensible form of participation in decision-making processes, the management of the organisation and the overall outcomes of the collective effort. Compared to the dominance of managers, the well-functioning collaboration, even submissiveness, of 'non-managers' (employees, lower management and professionals) might be an even greater puzzle. This has been a central question with regard to many social systems. Jost / Hunyady (2005, p. 261) suggest the following explanation of this rational / irrational behaviour: 'Many people who lived under feudalism, the Crusades, slavery, communism, apartheid, and the Taliban believed that their systems were imperfect but morally defensible and, in many cases, better than the alternatives they could envision.' This phenomenon can also be found in hierarchical organisations, in relation to the dominance of managers and the obedience of non-managers. As Sidanius et al. (2004, p. 869) comment: 'Although subordinates will often not endorse the hierarchy-enhancing and system-justifying ideologies and myths with the same degree of enthusiasm as will dominants, this endorsement will often still be of sufficient magnitude and breadth as to lend net support to the set of hierarchically structured group relations (. . .).'

The fact that so many people further down the pecking order do not oppose the dictates of hierarchical organisations and managerialism, and do not seek alternatives more actively requires considerable explanation (Protherough / Pick 2002, p. 41). This crucial question arose when we began to analyse managerial power and interests, and it emerges again now in the context of management ideology: *Why do the members of disadvantaged groups support the very ideologies and systems which oppress them and only benefit a small elite? Why does the majority, dominated by the few and subjugated to their unjust social systems and institutions, perceive this as legitimate and 'normal'?*

The paradox of subordinates' compliance cannot be resolved here entirely: it would require a much more comprehensive and thorough investigation of different types of oppressive systems, and in different historical and cultural circumstances. However, 'ideology'—like power and interests—seems to play quite a crucial part. As Burnham (1941, p. 25) explained: 'Ideologies capable of influencing and winning the acceptance of great masses of people are a indispensable verbal cement holding the fabric of any given type of society together.' It 'functions to secure the participation of subordinate classes in exploitative relations of production' (Stoddart 2007, p. 196). Further down we will see how ideology addresses a whole range of (basic human) psychological functions primarily to achieve and secure subordinates' obedience and compliance.[3] The analysis will also reveal some similarities with the functions of power and interest concerning subordinates' behaviour.

Before we begin to investigate the mechanisms of ideology concerning subordinates within organisations, it might be worth remembering that individuals have already been *socialised and conditioned* well before they enter the world of (business) organisations. People are conditioned in many different ways by a large number of institutions of primary and secondary socialisation, including family, peer groups, school, Army, and further and higher education institutions. It is part of the life-long process of socialisation and conditioning, i.e. the externally initiated and supported internalisation of dominant values and beliefs, acceptable behaviour and attitudes by new and in-coming members of a particular group or social system. Of course, all these institutions are *not* "one grand ideological state apparatus" but differ considerably; they each have their specific ideas about which values and beliefs they want to pass onto individuals and in what way. Equally, the individuals' responses and developments are very different. Nonetheless, it can be said that most conditioning and socialisation is about *obedience to order, rules and dominance*. This does not necessarily mean 19th and early 20th century-style strict discipline and submissiveness (though there are still large parts of it in most forms of conditioning). There are also more sophisticated and subtle methods. Media events such as 'Big Brother' or 'The Apprentice' demonstrate that sticking to the rules (even in a non-conformist way) brings success—and that deviance or underperformance (measured by criteria set by the system) will result in the inevitable ruling: 'You're fired!'.

Whatever the actual means, socialisation is about rewarding or punishing individuals for their acceptance or disregard of existing social arrangements (i.e. values, attitudes and behaviour) (Abercrombie et al. 1980, p. 2). The primary aim of socialisation is to ensure that members of a given social system function unconsciously and smoothly within its boundaries and without reflecting too much on those boundaries. From the cradle to the grave, individuals have to learn the meaning of restrictions and how to behave and function well *within* those limits. The child has to learn to accept boundaries set by their parents, the kindergarten and the school system; the apprentice needs to learn to accept willingly or grudgingly his bosses' instructions; and the student must learn to be clever *within* the framework of curricula and assignments. Throughout these years, people's awareness is steered into directions and types of behaviour which are portrayed as 'realistic'. One day they will be convinced that it simply doesn't make sense to go for 'unrealistic' options such as a fundamental change of the social system (Scott 1990, pp. 73–74). "Little strokes fell big oaks!" Sooner or later, most of them will have learned their lesson.[4]

This means that by the time people start their first job, they've already had 16 or 20 years of socialisation and conditioning. So most employees are already socialised and (pre-) conditioned enough to accept managers' dominance and managerial systems *before* they have even joined the organisation. The workplace is just another link in the chain of life-long societal conditioning and (professional) socialisation. In addition, during their professional careers most people work for a number of different organisations. And with every change of workplace, employees carry yet another bag of experiences of more or less successful adaptation with them and, based on this, will behave (more) accordingly in the next job—which largely means being more conscious about "how to fit in" and how to avoid negative reactions. And if this isn't enough, there are sufficient measures awaiting the new employee. From the very first day, he or she is faced with introductory procedures, HRM policies, training and seminars, and myriad formal and informal hints. This adds to the steady daily interaction with both (line) managers and colleagues will further socialise and condition the employee. One of the many "insights" the employee gains from this permanent experience is that there is no escape from the need to behave "appropriately" and to adapt to "the system". Although initially this is often simply a tactically motivated public demonstration of certain behaviour and attitudes ("playing the game"), over time it nonetheless shapes and changes individuals' thinking, behaviour and acting. It changes their personality, values and orientations to a great extent. As a result, subordinates conform and comply not because they need to but because they want to.

In hierarchical organisations, socialisation, conditioning and indoctrination get even worse. Shaping employees' identities, beliefs, emotions, attitudes and behaviour via top-down ideologies, managerial attitudes and comprehensive power and control systems have been around for a long time. Weber's famous naming of organisations / large bureaucracies as the 'iron cage' poignantly catches the very nature of hierarchical systems. As we saw in Chapter 4, control nowadays is less physical, less bureaucratical and less crude. Power and control systems which force people to do certain things in certain ways (or not to do certain things) are more quiet, intangible, virtual and sophisticated. Similarly, ideology nowadays is not blunt propaganda anymore, but more cunningly designed and communicated messages. It is now the *mental* iron cage, i.e. the ideologies of management and leadership, of hierarchical governance and social dominance which hold our organisations and society in their cold grip. Understood in this broader sense, the 'iron cage' metaphor provides a realistic picture also of contemporary organisations and their institutions. Despite all the hysteria about change management and the window-dressing talk about the 'learning organisation' and 'empowerment', contemporary organisations haven't changed much—and, probably more important, they look unchangeable to the individual. For subordinates, one of the strongest ideologies imaginable is the steady force of the factual shaping of the unconscious functioning of the individual. It is 'the way things are'—and the way they must be accepted. Jost / Banaji (1994, cited in O'Brien / Crandall 2005, p. 5) explained: 'Once a set of events produces certain social arrangements, whether by historical accident or human intention, the resulting arrangements tend to be explained and justified simply because they exist.' The individual is only willing and able to function within the machinery and within the dominating settings, because he or she has lost the ability to think about alternative settings. One might call this unconscious functioning 'automatic obedience'.[5] It describes the unconscious functioning of subordinates because of the steady force of the factual. Automatic obedience leads to a self-stabilising and re-occurring process which contributes to the further strengthening of the existing system; 'The more that people believe in such ideologies, the more likely they are to behave in ways that reinforce the hierarchical nature of group relations' (Sidanius / Pratto 1999, p. 262). Moreover, automatic obedience contributes to the automatic dominance of the rulers, in our case managers.[6] Non-managers accept the ideology of management simply because it is present throughout the whole organisation, in all of its structures and processes, both in abstract systems and in concrete human attitudes and behaviour. And managers dominate because the system runs smoothly. Ideology is at its strongest when simply accepted without reflection and upheld in daily routines.

However, superiors can never be sure of the automatic obedience of their subordinates. If the steady force of the factual doesn't work (fully), the ideology of management has a broad repertoire of means to make employees aware of their deviant behaviour, if not to say 'malfunctioning'. During the discussion of power and control, we saw that a lot of these mechanisms are there to put pressure on subordinates. The same applies to ideology; one of its major psychological functions is *to scare and frighten* people. Kieser (1997, p. 61) made the following point: 'The origin of myths is above all the fear of disaster and helplessness in the face of the unexplained.' What had previously been evil-minded Gods and monsters in ancient and medieval societies is nowadays portrayed in much more sophisticated, even rational ways. There is a recent, well-known and quite vivid example. In September 2002, the former Prime Minister of the United Kingdom, Tony Blair, stated in his foreword to the document 'Iraq's Weapons of Mass Destruction: The Assessment of the British Government':

> What I believe the assessed intelligence has established beyond doubt is that Saddam has continued to produce chemical and biological weapons, that he continues in his efforts to develop nuclear weapons, and that he has been able to extend the range of his ballistic missile programme . . . I am in no doubt that the threat is serious and current, that he has made progress on WMD [Weapons of Mass Destruction] and that he has to be stopped . . . And the document discloses that his military planning allows for some of the WMD to be ready within 45 minutes of an order to use them.

Clearly, scaring people remains one of the strategies and tactics of the powerful in order to convince people in more or less 'rational' ways. Especially in politics, the theme of danger occurs again and again (Starr 2004, p. 390). Foreign nations, foreigners or other external forces—allegedly—threaten the nation, national economy or national culture (whatever this actually is). And if there are no identifiable dangers outside the social system, there is always the opportunity to "identify" internal threats to stability. Either way, the identification of threats is a useful tool to achieve wider support for any kind of politics (Lieven 2005, p. 11). Scaring people has worked throughout the centuries, under many different societal conditions, because it addresses and reinforces strong emotions in the human psyche such as uncertainties, anxieties and fears. The ideology of management is typical in this sense. Mainstream management, particularly when it concerns strategy, strategic or change management, starts by frightening people. A much more challenging and changing environment (e.g. competition, globalisation, technological change, fashion trends) puts great pressure on the organisation and, of course, its management. Allegedly, the very survival of the organisation is at stake! It is widely known amongst leaders and managers that an 'enemy outside the organisation' is of great use in getting their agenda through, e.g. imposing tough measures on the system and the people, or justifying power and privileges. In such cases it is almost irrelevant whether this enemy really exists, is as powerful and dangerous as described or is indeed non-existent, like the 'bad witch' in fairytales. The important thing is that managers, particularly senior managers, are portrayed as the ones who are aware of all the dangers out there, have knowledge about the nature and scale of danger and, of course, are the only ones who can find a way out of this threatening situation. It is immaterial whether employees and other subordinates really believe (senior) management's story or not; the possibility of external threats to the system is often enough reason to follow management, to accept their dominance and to support (or at least not oppose) them in their unselfish endeavour to fight the forces of evil and to protect the system.

But the "forces of evil" are also within the organisation and must be fought there, too. Most of these forces can be found amongst subordinates. Most employees function well within the organisational structures most of the time, carrying out tasks according to what they are being told and performing with regard to the criteria set by their line managers. To achieve and guarantee this, the ideology of management has managed to co-opt the traditional work ethos of the working class and to combine it with modern models of the highly motivated, aspirational, empowered, even 'entrepreneurial' employee. To cement this, "performance orientation" has become one of the dominant values both at the workplace and within our societies. It is about 'achieving', '(out-) performing' and 'delivering'—which primarily means that people have to function and can be held accountable if they don't function. And they will be held accountable—by their direct superior / line manager, colleagues or third parties. As performance orientation covers (almost) all activities, usually sets quite demanding tasks and is multi-dimensional, managers can relatively easily identify 'under-performance' and demonstrate that the employee hasn't (yet) met expectations. This will have consequences for the employee, and can be made even more threatening because parts of the job are often linked to 'performance-oriented' criteria such as probationary periods, promotions or remuneration.

Secondly, individuals can be held accountable internally, i.e. they judge themselves. Very little is written about how people within organisations judge themselves, yet they do it literally every moment, with constant fears and reflections about how they carry out their tasks, how they perform and which consequences might happen. Since this performance orientation—and other images and ideals closely linked to it—is widely internalised, this constant internal judging is probably the more intense aspect of "ideology at work". Whether externally or internally initiated, most employees develop a sense of *guilt* when confronted with allegations, evidence or mere doubts that they haven't performed as required. Over a longer period of time, they may even blame themselves if they do not meet the expectations, or are not good enough and are not successful because they have not reached the next carrier level. For example, Lasch (1979, cited in Frank 2001, p. 114) explained that 'ruling classes have always sought to instil in their subordinates the capacity to experience exploitation and material deprivation as guilt, while deceiving themselves that their own material interests coincide with those of mankind as a whole'. It is only then a small step from guilt to *punishment*. Once more, this can be both external and internal, i.e. in the form of

- official punishment, e.g. 'feedback' and its consequences from the line manager on the basis of management by objectives, training and skills development, human resource policy-based procedures,
- collegial punishment, i.e. more or less sublime forms of social interaction,
- self-punishment, e.g. a whole range of psychological mechanisms ranging from temporary feelings of unease up to the development of chronic psycho-somatic diseases and / or self-harming behaviour.

Initiating feelings of guilt and establishing comprehensive punishment procedures and mechanisms for those who do not function properly is one of the cornerstones of the ideology of management. Together, fear of punishment and feelings of guilt lead to 'forced obedience'. It usually is very effective; guilt and punishment work.

This threatening aspect of ideology nicely complements another set of psychological functions. In a world portrayed as scaring and frightening where people feel guilt and are punished, ideology provides *security, reassurance, certainty and order* (e.g. Watson 2006, p. 224, Chiapello / Fairclough 2002, p. 188); it offers certainty in an uncertain world, security in the face of danger, order to overcome chaos and reassurance where there is doubt. Ideology provides answers and solutions, and the way out of the misery to the Promised Land. However, there is a major difference between these two sets of psychological functions. The first set (public threats and fears) is addressed solely to subordinates, whereas the second (reassurance and certainty, security and order) is intended for superiors *and* subordinates. Leaders have the particular knowledge, skills and methods to search for and find solutions for all challenges. In contrast, followers are provided with the reassurance that the leaders will care for them—as long as they follow and believe in them (and as long as the leaders don't plan to sacrifice some of their followers for whatever "higher" reason). This distinction is also quite easy to identify in the case of the ideology of management. It specifically provides *managers* with the certainty that they have the right strategic and operational concepts to respond to external challenges, that they can 'engineer' organisational structures and processes, and that they can manage people and organisational change. Managerial concepts give managers a feeling of order and security in a chaotic and multi-dimensional environment—a sense of certainty in an uncertain world. And they are reassured that they will remain on top of the game as long as they stick to these managerial concepts, the assumptions they are based on and the recommendations they generate (e.g. Watson 2006, pp. 222–223). At the same time, managerial ideology reassures *employees* that management will do everything to secure the survival of the organisation in the light of external challenges and threats. Managerial ideology explains to employees the social order and their place and tasks in this natural order. It gives them a feeling of security and certainty—as long as they do not leave their post, do what is required and as long as they do not start to question or challenge the managerial order as the best of all possible worlds. Once more, the ideology of management keeps the distinction, if not to say the great divide between leaders and followers intact.

So employees have every reason to function smoothly. It is even in their interest. This unconscious smooth functioning corresponds with the human *psychological need* to support and strengthen existing social orders, and to defend and justify the status quo.[7] As Jost / Hunyady (2005, pp. 261–262) explain it: 'People who possess heightened needs to manage uncertainty and threat are especially likely to embrace conservative, system-justifying ideologies (. . .). More specifically, uncertainty avoidance; intolerance of ambiguity; needs for order, structure, and closure; perception of a dangerous world; and fear of death are all positively associated with the endorsement of these ideologies'. System-justifying ideologies are designed to take advantage of these psychological needs. They particularly address, develop and strengthen those psychological traits within people which stabilise the system and make people accept almost everything simply to avoid uncertainty, change and disturbances for themselves; 'people are motivated to justify and rationalize the way things are, so that existing social, economic, and political arrangements tend to be perceived as fair and legitimate' (Jost / Hunyady 2005, p. 260). Of course, there are people, perhaps often even the majority, who openly or quietly disagree with the existing social order, who want to change the ways things are and who develop strategies of opposition and resistance. However, if an ideology has done its work as successfully as the ideology of management has over several decades, then all the disagreement shown by people is more or less of merely 'tactical' nature and can usually be dealt with by and within the system. In fact, the *overall* interest of non-managers working for the organisation is much more about keeping things the way are. They want to be reassured about the security of their jobs, they want to see their work as part of a larger order and they want to belong to a greater system which can provide them a sense of identity, belonging and future. And, most importantly, they want to see the managerial organisation continue because one needs his or her work and income. This notion might be called 'dependent obedience', i.e. obedience stemming from psychological and factual needs for security, certainty and order.

But ideologies do more than condition people's minds and views to current orders and practices. They address deeply held human desires for a better future; ideologies promise and give hope. An ideology *must* address genuine desires and hopes for a better future in order to be attractive (Brookfield 2005, p. 78). This is even truer since so far in the history of mankind there have been few larger social systems which were just and good and could live up to the ideals and promises put forward by their ruling elites. In fact, a just and good social system with a ruling elite is an oxymoron. It is therefore particular crucial that every dominant group's ideological system gives hope to those who live under unjust conditions and are being excluded from most opportunities. Again, it works. It is both amazing and sad at the same time to see how long people can be misled by ideologies and even how strongly they support the unjust conditions and lies that suppress them simply because it is their human nature to hope for the better. However, concerning the aspect of hope, management ideology is somewhat different to other ideologies. Whereas many ideologies only offer a hope after death (most religions) or in some distant, unspecified future (communism), managerial ideology, like capitalism, provides hope for today, or at least for a future within reach. 'From rags to riches!' is the battle-cry of the army of hopefuls who want "to make it". If you have internalised the morals of the market, i.e. being egoistic and greedy, and have internalised the rationale of hierarchical organisations, i.e. to simultaneously function and do organisational politics, then you can be successful right now *in this life*! Indeed, in sharp contrast to other ideologies, capitalism and the ideology of management are 'true' in a certain way; indeed, people *can* achieve what has been promised! In this sense, there are positive reasons why the ideology of management works so well even for the majority of people at the lower end of the organisational and societal hierarchy. It is, or at least it can be, both *attractive and convincing*. Abercrombie et al. (1980, p. 135) made this point with regard to late capitalism: 'By emphasising the importance of individual mobility and achievement, in particular the opportunity for anyone with the ability and the motivation to rise through the occupational and income hierarchy, the ideology makes inequality appear to be the result of natural law, while income differentials appear as fair and just'. Proponents of the ideology of management can refer to examples of its many successes and advantages. Managerialism in certain ways makes organisations more efficient and productive, more successful and competitive. And it can be advantageous for the individual, too. Everyone who applies (the latest) managerial theories, models and concepts will be much more successful in whatever he or she manages or wants to achieve—whether it's about private or public organisations, departments, projects, teams, family, relationships or even oneself. In following and applying the concepts of managerialism, employees can even become managers—factually or theoretically. The ideology of management promises success, career, money, self-enhancement, happiness and fulfilment. It stretches over all five levels of Maslow's pyramid. Many employees, therefore, show a kind of 'happy obedience' because in certain ways the ideology of management is (partly) attractive and convincing.

It gets even better (or worse). As indicated, the ideology of management promises career and other advantages to those who are *able and willing*: i.e. those who have the skills to take or even create opportunities for themselves and who are willing to put sufficient effort into their attempts. For example, getting a post-graduate degree in management, trying hard to climb up the managerial career ladder and do things "the managerial way" in both their work and private lives. Theoretically, and practically, everyone can be able and willing. Hence, even non-managers feel that the ideology of management could be for them. This is quite typical for successful ideologies; they integrate subordinates to a certain degree and give them the belief and aspirations, perhaps even some limited opportunities, to progress and perform—albeit, of course, within the prescribed ideological framework and closely controlled by its proponents. This is largely done in order to win consent and to gain widespread support for an ideology which actually privileges only a few. It is yet another strength of the ideology of management that in large part and on a daily basis, it is very popular (in the true meaning of the word) and inclusive.

This part of the ideology of management corresponds to major shifts in the core values in society. Since at least the early 1980s, the dominant values in Western societies have largely focussed on career orientation, egoism and opportunism, functioning within organisational settings and taking personal advantage of institutions and situations. The ideology of management can provide all of this. It particularly addresses those people amongst managers and non-managers who are aspirational, who want to achieve and perform and, at the same time, who are willing to do (almost) everything for this. For those who are keen to obey, and contribute to 'the rules of business' pro-actively, the ideology of management provides the perfect framework. The opportunities it promises and the contemporary values and attitudes of career-oriented and egoistic people, fit very well together. The ideology of management has changed the nature and culture of our organisations—many individuals are now keen to function and perform within the social order before guilt and punishment, even before direct incentives kick in. Such attitudes are a sort of 'anticipatory obedience', i.e. a pro-active willingness to support and contribute to an existing order which exactly requires this—a happy, willing submissiveness.

Such obedience is not without reasons; on the contrary, the majority of employees actually have considerable advantages in most managerial organisations, such as

- psychological advantages (belonging to a greater, strong and success-ful entity which gives its members a feeling of security, belongingness or offers factual career perspectives),
- concrete advantages due to the division of labour (doing one's job more efficiently and with less input required),
- material advantages (usually higher wages, better overall remunera-tion packages and less working hours compared to other opportuni-ties to earn a living) and
- even physical advantages (better health and safety policies).

Employees may benefit from these advantages as long as they function according to the requirements set by management and within the boundar-ies of the system. Hence, subordinates do *not* function because of a "false consciousness", or because they "do not reflect enough on their situation". This is something critical theory has always got wrong. *Exactly the oppo-site is true!* Most subordinates (nowadays) function because they have done their maths consciously and have reflected on the situation they are in. Most employees have an *explicit and conscious* interest in functioning smoothly because this is much more advantageous for them than it is to question or challenge managerial power and authority. This part of the reason for subordinates' attitudes might be called 'calculative obedience', or the 'cal-culative mind'. It relates to another trend in society which has become pre-dominant. Many people nowadays are not only egoistic and opportunistic, but they also literally judge everything (goods, other people, ideas, work, career, private life) on the basis of their own individual input / output anal-ysis: *"What do I gain from x if I put effort y into it?"* This shift in values and sense-making has also taken place at the workplace. Employees are now 'calculative actors with instrumental orientations to work' (Barley / Kunda 1992, p. 384). They know the advantages of well-functioning and they know how to avoid the impression of mal-functioning.

Anticipatory obedience and a pro-active willingness to function exist as long as the trade-off is advantageous for the individual. Such an approach represents a realistic and pragmatic agreement with the dominant values of management ideology. It guarantees the non-manager enough oppor-tunities to pursue his or her own interests and, overall, to be much better off—as long as he or she plays by the rules (or at least gives the impression of doing so)! Moreover it is perfectly in line with superiors' expectations; 'The actuality of obedience and satisfactory role-performance is all that dominant groups require of subordinates, not the internalisation of an ideology' (Abercrombie et al. 1980, p. 142). According to this logic, the calculative mind plays even more into the hands of the ideology of management and its proponents than most other aspects. Employees' calculative obedience actively contributes to the maintenance and further strengthening of the very social system which makes and keeps (most of) them subordinates. This might be even called a 'rational' interest and behaviour, since a whole range of factual advantages exists for those who function. Smooth functioning within the boundaries of the hierarchical, unjust and oppressive social system of managerial organisations delivers the greatest advantage for the individual. It is the utmost form of selfishness and egoistic behaviour.

Finally, ideology represents the managerial organisation as a cosmos, an order where the power and interests of different groups and people are in balance. One of the main ideological functions of managerial ideology concerning subordinates is to give them the impression that the social reality of hierarchical organisations is *normal*, that managerial organisations are how typical organisations appear—and *should* appear. The managerial organisation of business and work, even life and leisure, is the way things are, the way things should be, the way people *must* act, behave, even think (otherwise *they* are not 'normal'). Moreover, the ideology of management provides subordinates with sufficient reasons and 'explanations' that it is in *their* interest—*and in their best interest*—to function smoothly within the managerial organisation and to fit into conditions which make them subordinates. As Brookfield (2005, p. 95) explained:

> The important thing to remember about hegemony is that it works by consent. People are not forced against their will to assimilate dominant ideology. They learn do this, quite willingly, and in the process they believe that this ideology represents their best interests. Hegemony works when people actively welcome and support beliefs and practices that are actually hurting them.

The ideology of management portrays the managerial organisation as the norm and normality—of business, society, private lives, of everything.

All in all, an ideology's psychological sophistication and appeal do not simply come from its ability to address specific human feelings. Its real power of persuasion stems more from the fact that it triggers a whole range of psychological responses. The ideology of management is no different. In particular, it

- contributes to the further socialisation and conditioning of employees,
- tries to achieve an unconscious functioning of employees via the steady force of the factual ('automatic obedience'),
- scares and frightens, addresses uncertainties, anxieties and fears,

- creates and enforces within subordinates feelings of guilt and punishes them externally or internally ('forced obedience'),
- provides security, reassurance, certainty and order,
- addresses psychological needs for order and security ('dependent obedience'),
- meets desires for a better future, promises and gives hope,
- is attractive because it can offer a whole range of specific advantages ('happy obedience'),
- is able to create a pro-active willingness of subordinates to support the system and function because of egoistic interests ('anticipatory obedience'),
- contributes to the development of the calculative mind ('calculative obedience') and
- portrays all of this as the norm and normality of organisational, societal and private lives (hegemony).

According to the proponents of the ideology of management, employees have every reason to function well within the managerial organisation. However, the analysis in this section has revealed that this is not because the managerial organisation is designed for employees—of course, it is not! It is more due to the fact that the ideology of management has developed a whole battery of psychological means to socialise and condition, intimidate and manipulate employees. In so doing it has been so successful that most employees even think that it is in their interest not only to function but to willingly and actively support this social order. This is the utmost an ideology can achieve. As Brookfield (2005, p. 140) explained: 'In both hegemony and disciplinary power, the consent of people to these processes is paramount. They take pride in the efficiency with which they learn appropriate boundaries, avoid "inappropriate" critique, and keep themselves in line. Both constructs emphasize learners' collusion in their own control and their feelings of satisfaction and pleasure at successfully ensuring their complete incarceration.' In addition to pursuing individual goals within the boundaries of the system, employees simultaneously contribute to its stabilisation and further strengthening. In doing so, employees contribute to the dominance of managers at least as much as the managers themselves—but that is exactly the idea of hegemony.

METHODOLOGICAL AND LOGICAL DIMENSION OF IDEOLOGY

In this final section of the analysis, we will discuss some main methodological and logical aspects of the ideology of management. It primarily addresses the major inconsistencies which, again, are a typical sign of ideology.

First it is about the scope of the ideology of management. On the one hand managerialism is very *comprehensive* and *systematic* (Hartley 1983, pp. 14–15). 'Management' covers literally every aspect of an organisation, both at the strategic and the operational level in general, as well as in all specific functional areas. It gives meaning to all of this in one complete framework. As Pollitt (1990, p. 6) put it, 'ideology is not simply a summation of a set of attitudes, but consists of some kind of relatively systematic structuring (though the structuring may be psychological rather than logical)'. By being comprehensive, the ideology of management is also hegemonic. It is embedded in institutions, structures and processes, in people's daily routines, decisions, actions, and practices—even in their thoughts and worldviews. It is so deeply embedded in everything that we are usually unaware of its presence (Brookfield 2005, p. 67). At the same time, the proponents of the ideology of management are very keen that core areas and issues it copes with are confined and approached in particular ways. Only *certain* views, values, objectives and outcomes are portrayed as 'relevant' for management. These mainly concern functional, instrumental, financial and technological aspects of organisations which emphasise efficiency and productivity for the sake of profit orientation and competitiveness. Because of this focus, a whole range of highly important and relevant issues are deliberately excluded from the core repertoire of management, for example: environmental and social values, inequality, conflict, power and politics, domination and subordination, ideology and manipulation, fairness, justice, representation, participation, empowerment, profit-sharing and social citizenship (Ferdinand 2004, p. 435, Levy et al. 2001, p. 10, Coopey / Burgoyne 2000, p. 869, Willmott 1997, p. 1330, Jacques 1996, p. 5, Pollitt 1990, p. 138). These issues usually paid mere lip service, are only addressed for the sake of political correctness, but practically treated as constraints in the pursuit of 'business-oriented' objectives. Critics, critical approaches and truly alternative concepts are largely ignored, silenced by micro-politics within the field of business and management studies, or are barely tolerated at the periphery of discourses and actions. The ideology of management is very *comprehensive* and *systematic*—and (also) very *exclusive and ignorant*.

Secondly, proponents of the ideology of management want to be very *specific and apodictive* about those areas they regard as of great importance for the organisation—and even more for managers. Creation of value and profit for shareholders, accounting, governance, operations and legal issues are some of these areas. Management consultants and business schools put considerable efforts into creating ever more sophisticated models and tools managers can use. And even in the 'softer' areas such as strategy, marketing or HRM, the concepts got more and more sophisticated and apodictive. On the other hand, its proponents want the ideology of management to be as *general* as possible (Hamilton 1987, p. 24). It should be applicable to very different situations, changing environments and must be suitable for the pursuit of very different strategic and operational aims and objectives. Burnham (p. 191) realised this as early as 1941: 'Cultural background, local history, religion, the path taken by the revolution, the ingenuity of individual propagandists will permit a considerable diversity in the new ideologies, just as they have in those of past societies.' 'Conceptual ambiguity' also secures greater popularity, consensus and support (e.g. Hartley 1983, p. 20). The more general the language, the more attractive an ideology can be, and the more its ideas and methods will be accepted: '(potential) users can eclectically select those elements that appeal to them, or what they interpret as the fashion's core idea, or what they opportunistically select as suitable for their purposes' (Benders / van Veen 2001, pp. 37–38). Who, for example, would not be in favour of 'increased efficiency', 'greater productivity' and—perhaps most importantly—'better management'? In this sense, the ideology of management is *apodictive and specific as well as quite vague and general at the same time.*

There is an even greater inconsistency. On the one hand, attempts to produce apodictive and specific knowledge are based on the notion to generate a body of *'objective'* management knowledge (Watson 2006, p. 222). Managers can then use it to design and manage organisations 'rationally' like engineers design and maintain machinery. As known, this belief is strongly based on the tradition of Scientific Management (Taylor 1911/1967) with its ideal of management as applied science. There still seems to be a strong conviction among the proponents of management ideology that business and organisations are based on natural laws, and that these laws can be discovered, made available to managers and applied by them. *Managerialism is positivistic.* Indeed, in core areas of management and business studies, concepts have been developed which state theories and laws which are both applicable and even falsifiable. There is a large body of approved knowledge for all functional areas of organisations, e.g. accounting and finance, production, logistics and operations, even marketing, HRM and strategy. However, as revealed above, when it comes to strategic management, leadership and other 'prerogatives' of senior management, the ideology of management, again, provides a countless set of theories and concepts. But here, the ideology of management itself concedes that these crucial aspects are firstly about 'ingenuity' and 'brilliance', experience and tacit knowledge. At the end of the day, how to run a business (successfully) and how to manage an organisation remains a secret which only the elected few 'know'. It is obvious that such a position is anything but 'scientific' or 'rational'; *it is deliberately anti-positivistic.* In its very core, management is based on unverified and unverifiable knowledge (Hamilton 1987, p. 33). Burnham (1941, p. 25) made it absolutely clear: 'An ideology is *not* a scientific theory, but is nonscientific and often antiscientific. It is the expression of hopes, wishes, fears, ideals, not a hypothesis about events—though ideologies are often thought by those who hold them to be scientific theories'. On the one hand the ideology of management claims that it has developed scientific approaches concerning the management of organisations, on the other it claims that the management of organisations is an art and mystery which cannot be expressed as verifiable or falsifiable knowledge. Hence, it is both *positivistic and non- or anti-scientific at the same time.*

In both its positivistic and anti-scientific manner, the ideology of management primarily focuses on the provision of 'functional' concepts and knowledge. People who believe in the ideology of management have been very successful in developing and providing an uncountable number of concepts and models which can be applied in every organisation, for every industry and market, and which work in (almost) every contextual and transactional environment. In this sense it could be argued that they are functional, objective and 'value-free'. However, like any other tools, managerial theories, models, concepts and methods are made for particular purposes, for particular reasons and objectives. They are only accepted and used when they contribute to achieving the strategic objectives of the organisation. Despite all the window-dressing, the objectives formulated for organisations are usually quite specific, narrow-minded and tailored to the interests of selected stakeholders (e.g. shareholders). Managerial tools are not as objective and value-free as they look. In fact, the concepts and methods can really only be practice-oriented, practical and applicable if they come with information / recommendations concerning their actual implementation, measurement and control within real situations. This information is not value-free but prescriptive and normative. This becomes even more obvious when one starts to reveal and critically discuss the explicit and implicit assumptions on which the 'functional' concepts are based, and the objectives for which they are made. It then becomes clear that these concepts are quite normative; they express principles, morals, values and interests which might not be obvious at first glance. For example, models and concepts often propose types of ideal or optimal states which could be achieved (at least approximately) if the concepts were applied. This is prescriptive in itself as it implies that people and organisations *should*, even *must* strive for 'best practice' and 'perfect' solutions. Managers are explicitly encouraged via these principles and best practices to organise and do business in a very specific way—and only in that way. "If you want to be a successful manager (and who doesn't?), you *must* apply this concept in that way because this will increase shareholder value and the efficiency and productivity of your business!" How much more value-based and normative can it get? The ideology of management is *at the same time functional and prescriptive, 'value-free' and normative.*

Moreover, the concepts and methods recommended by the ideology of management are not only normative; they are *partisan*. The ideology of management doesn't question managers' prerogatives and organisational reality. On the contrary, its proponents are keen to justify, support and strengthen existing power and control relationships. Managerial concepts are specifically designed as tools for managers, for their particular concerns, interests and objectives. Managerial concepts therefore reflect only certain worldviews and agendas while maintaining the appearance of objectivity. And it is not only selectivity but an affirmative judgment of managers' interests and prerogatives, a justification of literally everything that is formulated, decided and pursued by them. Time and time again, this selectivity leads to partiality. It leads to a totally undifferentiated conservative-affirmative justification of existing rights and privileges and of orthodox and narrowly formulated objectives for hierarchically designed organisations. It justifies orthodox structures, control- and punishment-oriented performance measurement systems and confirms the systematic oppression and obedience of subordinates. The ideology of management is a typical 'justifying ideology'. It is a narrow and one-sided partisanship in favour of the interests of managers (and other 'business-oriented' groups such as shareholders, institutional investors, consultants, business media and business school academics).

Perhaps because of its positivistic and affirmative nature (in addition to its prescriptive, even partisan characteristics), most of its opponents are of the opinion that the ideology of management is not critical. However, this is only true in a certain sense. We cannot undertake a comprehensive discussion about what it means to be critical here. Instead, I will simply use Horkheimer's criteria (referred to in Carr 2000, p. 211). According to him, a theory is critical when: a) it explains what is wrong with current social reality, b) it identifies actors to change it and c) it provides clear norms for criticism and practical goals for the future. In relation to these criteria, orthodox management and organisation theory or management ideology could be said to be critical because: a) time and again it shows when organisations are not efficient, not productive or otherwise not good enough, b) it regularly identifies managers, consultants, project leaders or other parties as change agents and c) with its functional concepts and theories it definitely has clear norms and ideals of how organisations should be, what needs to be changed and what needs to be done in order to achieve better performances and results.

In this sense, *mainstream management concepts and conservative organisation theories are very critical towards the social reality of both management and organisations.* However, if this is true for these theories, then it is true for (almost) every social theory—more or less. They all "somehow" criticise social malpractices and refer to certain people who can change this. The usual demarcation of critical from non-critical is not clear; it simply doesn't work. It's more fruitful to differentiate between 'technically critical' and 'in-principle critical' social theories. Here, the question and crucial criteria to distinguish both is not just being critical (or not) but *being critical about what?*

One might say that, technically, critical approaches are critical about means / ends relationships and the performance (by whatever standards) of such relationships. The idea is to develop knowledge about these relationships and how to manage and improve them (e.g. Fournier / Grey 2000, p. 17, Alvesson / Willmott 1992a, p. 4). In contrast, critical theories principally question not only the ends and means as such, but also the underlying explicit and implicit assumptions, implications and consequences beyond such ends / means relationships (e.g. whom they serve, whom they do not serve). The aim is to develop knowledge about all those aspects which privilege, restrict or disadvantage people as well as the knowledge which can liberate them. Obviously, according to this dichotomy, the ideology of management is technically critical but not critical in principle. In this sense, it is both critical *and* un-critical.

However, and perhaps slightly surprisingly, the ideology of management is quite honest in many respects. It is frank about what the objectives of organisations should be and how they should be measured and achieved. It explicitly prescribes how organisations, their systems, structures and processes should be designed and how people should decide, act and behave—even how they should think. And it is honest about the overall result of all of this—the bottom-line. Moreover, it is absolutely clear that managers are in charge of all, that their positions, privileges, power and responsibilities are justified and that subordinates have to function. At the same time, however, the ideology of management covers up important aspects. This is mainly due to the 'pretentiousness of managerial language' (Protherough / Pick 2002, p. 58); making employees redundant is called 're-engineering' or 'downsizing', disciplining the workforce is called 'supervision', or giving people simply more work is called 'empowerment'. Strategy and marketing language speaks of shareholder value, corporate social responsibility, ethics, concerns for the environment and, above all, "employees are our greatest value". Strategic consultancy papers, mission and vision statements, and internal memoranda are a never-ending source of 'business-speak'. It is cynical wordplay, a mendacity—disguising whether those managers using 'management-speak' really believe their own official half-truths or are completely aware how misleading this sort of language actually is. The ideology of management *is simultaneously honest and deceptive.*

A final example demonstrates that the ideology of management is also inconsistent in crucial core parts of its content. According to structural contingency theory (Lawrence / Lorsch 1967), managers do nothing more than adapt organisations to their environments in the best way possible. Because of 'quasi-natural objective forces' (such as 'the market', 'the environment' or 'organisational / technological imperatives'), they do not really have a choice. Managers *must* and will decide for the most effective option. They simply carry out 'the universally and technically defined functions of management' (Willmott 1984, p. 355). As Zaleznik (1989, p. 229) explained: 'In its pure form, management mystique is a denial of personal influence. At every level of the hierarchy power is impersonal. Thought and action are directed by some structure, system, or procedure, not an individual'. According to this view, managers do not have power. On the other hand, particular senior managers are often portrayed as *powerful leaders* (e.g. Kanter 1989) who can shape entire organisations and even whole industries almost at their will. According to leadership theory, managers are powerful because of this special combination of hierarchical position (and the responsibilities, influence and resources that come with them) and personal skills, experience and ingenuity. Zaleznik's 1989 'The Managerial Mystique—Restoring Leadership in Business' is probably one of the best examples for this idea. According to him (p. 181), 'Management as a profession has accumulated its own "book of rules" how to use power and how to influence people's thoughts and actions'. Managers' power is only mentioned with a sense of awe, but not really addressed in an analytical sense. To sum up, managers' power is negated because of environmental / functional imperatives yet simultaneously elevated beyond any normal understanding. However, both functional denial and mystical elevation lead to the same result: managers' power is, in fact, largely "defined out" of functional analysis—of *any* analysis of management or organisations. This example could be evidence of attempts by the proponents of managerial ideology to create and use inconsistencies deliberately in order to avoid or confuse certain issues, rather than to address and analyse them. And these seem to be exactly the issues which are crucial for the dominance of managers.

As this chapter has demonstrated, the ideology of management is a fully developed ideology. In literally all its dimensions (environmental, cognitive, psychological, socio-psychological), it tries to provide both explanations and justifications for the dominance of a particular social group—managers. It explains why their interests and worldview should prevail, why others should obey and why the elaborated hierarchical structure of the social system known as "organisation" is 'the best of all possible worlds'. At the same time, its proponents know that 'the "best" ideology is one that cannot be recognized as such' (Hartley 1983, p. 21)—or, as Althusser put it (1971, cited in Brookfield 2005, p. 73): 'ideology never says, "I am ideological".' Hence, when managers are asked about their power and influence, about business and strategy, organisational aspects or how organisations should be designed, all we often get is 'management-speak' and 'socially expected answering behaviour'. In this sense one can say that the ideology of management is simultaneously *ideological and not ideological*.

We can therefore conclude that the ideology of management is also a typical ideology in its methodological and logical dimension. It is highly inconsistent and many of its core assumptions and values are mutually contradictory: on the one hand it tries to be comprehensive, covering every aspect of the management of organisations, even spreading into every corner of our social even private lives. On the other hand it is highly exclusive and ignorant of values and issues which do not fit with managers' interests or their view of the world. In order to serve these interests, the ideology devises an endless stream of theories and concepts which cover many organisational areas in a targeted and specific manner. Yet at the same time, managerialism is quite general and vague, particularly strategy and management-speak. In its attempt to provide managers with effective tools, it tries to be scientific, even positivistic. However, many of its basic (mostly implicit) assumptions are non- or even anti-scientific. Therefore, its attempts to deliver functional ('value-free') instruments and advice to managers are quite limited. Most of its assumptions, objectives, analysis and recommendations are highly normative. Even more, they are deliberately partisan, tailor-made for managers' concerns and interests, primarily supporting their objectives and strengthening their power-base. In terms of roles, it is quite honest. Nonetheless, managers' specific individual and group interests as well as the ideology of management's interests are usually obscured beneath cynical layers of ethical and moral rhetoric, misleading terms and window-dressing language. The ideology of management constantly portrays itself as not ideological whereas in fact it is ideological through and through.

THE IDEOLOGICAL CONCEPT OF MANAGEMENT

The previous sections have systematically revealed the conceptual nature of the ideology of management. The following table summarises the main aspects of each area and, hence, the entire ideological concept of management.

Just as with managers' power and interests, the ideology of management is well-established in society. It is strongly supported, upheld and promoted *by powerful and influential stakeholders*. One of the reasons for this is the fact that the ideology of management is primarily about the *ideological justification of the prime objectives, social structures and processes* of organisations, i.e.

- political order (legitimisation of the existing hierarchy and power relations),
- authority (explanation and justification why one group dominates others),
- social inequality and stratification (justification and maintenance of differences between social groups) and
- preferences of group interests (members of privileged and more powerful groups are in a much better position to pursue their own individual and group interests).

The managerial organisation is a reflection of the hierarchical order of society. In addition, the ideology of management particularly defines and

Table 5.1 The Ideological Concept of Management

Area	Aspect
1. Environmental dimension	• isomorphism with social institutions and socio-economic conditions
	• powerful stakeholders
	• fads and fashions, epochal trends / historical perspective / utopian ideal
2. Functional aspects and cognitive dimension	• claim that functional approach is 'value-free', value statements and exclusion of other values
	• creation of specific managerial language, rhetoric, discourses and, hence, organisational reality and practices, disguise of power and interests by use of functional language
	• provision of functional 'explanations' and 'meaning' concerning socially constructed reality
	• specific orientation towards social and organisational practices
	• legitimisation of hierarchy (based on biologism) in order to establish political order, justify authority and institutionalise social inequality
	• reference to higher values (e.g. profit maximisation, efficiency, productivity)
3. Management and managers	• justification of management and managers' positions, responsibilities and prerogatives (e.g. setting the agenda, [strategic] objectives, making decisions, . . .)
	• leaders and leadership
	• mystery, mystique, mystification
4. Group interests and ideology	• interests of a particular group
	• group cohesion and locomotion
	• universalisation of group interests
	• for the sake of the whole
5. Psychological dimension of ideology for subordinates	• socialisation, conditioning, indoctrination
	• automatic obedience (unconscious functioning because of the steady force of the factual)
	• scares and frightens, addresses uncertainties, anxieties and fears
	• forced obedience (guilt of mal-functioning and punishment)
	• provides security, reassurance, certainty, order
	• dependent obedience (psychological needs for order and security)
	• addresses desires, promises, gives hope
	• happy obedience (attractiveness of managerial ideology)

(continued)

Table 5.1   (continued)

Area	Aspect
5. Psychological dimension of ideology for subordinates (continued)	• anticipatory obedience (pro-active willingness, support and contributions because of egoistic interests) • calculative obedience (calculative mind) • hegemony, normalisation, normality
6. Methodological and logical dimension	• comprehensive and exclusive, ignorant • apodictic and vague, specific and general • positivistic and non- or anti-scientific • functional ('value-free') and normative, even partisan • critical and un-critical • honest and deceptive • not ideological and ideological

justifies *managers' prerogatives*, primarily their positions and respon-sibilities, their claim for leadership and the mystification of leadership. Managers are, and always will be the dominant group. According to this view, the ideology of management is specifically designed to support the *interests of the management group*. It

a) reflects mainly the specific interests, values and objectives of the group of managers,
b) integrates the group of managers and supports group cohesion and locomotion,
c) strongly supports the universalisation of the sectional interests of managers and
d) tries to convince others that the pursuit of managers' individual and group advantages and privileges is for the sake of the whole.

For this, it develops a whole set of instruments for *the socialisation and conditioning of non-managers* in order to achieve and guarantee their obe-dience. It explains and justifies the cosmos of domination and obedience, superiors and subordinates as one consistent and just order.

CONCLUSIONS

As became obvious in this chapter, ideology is not only "big speeches" or staged performances by 'grand leaders', the rhetoric of glossy party pro-grammes, manifestos, strategies, or vision and mission statements. All of this can readily be identified and dismissed as ideology. In addition to these instruments, and more importantly, ideology is a comprehensive and differentiated belief system, comprising environmental, cognitive, psychological, socio-psychological, sociological, as well as methodological and logical dimensions. Brookfield (2005, p. 76) was right when he said that ideology does not just comprise 'secret cabals of capitalist mind manipulators skilfully selling to gullible masses conspicuously false and distorted ideas which serve to secure the power elite's continuing supremacy.' Dominant ideologies are an (almost) inseparable part of societal institutions, enmeshed within their social structures and processes. As the analysis in this chapter has revealed, management ideology is a multi-dimensional concept which is deeply embedded in our daily lives and routines, in the ways people see the world and act within its control. It is in our perceptions and thinking, attitudes, decisions and actions so that we are usually not aware of its presence and impact.

The same is true concerning the ideology of management. With regard to management and organisations, Thomas asked in 1998: 'So how do senior managers secure their continued dominance in organizational decision-making, even when their employees believe them to be inept, misguided or positively villainous? . . . How are the dissatisfactions of employees diffused to the extent that they accept situations which they believe to be irrational or even plain wrong?' Part of the answer has been provided in this chapter. The whole body of management knowledge is not a mere 'technique' made for everyone, available to everyone for understanding and solving problems in a balanced, reflective and ethically comprehensive and differentiated manner. It is especially made for managers, designed for strengthening *their* position, prerogatives, power and dominance within hierarchical organisations and networks of stakeholders. It is an ideology particularly designed to portray managers' individual and group interests as the interests of the whole. In doing so, it institutionalises managers' power and interests as well as the duty of subordinates to acknowledge managers' prerogatives and behave accordingly. The ideological construction of managerial reality plays a crucial part in managers' dominance. Managers can only pursue their own personal and professional interests if people are unaware they are doing it, i.e. as long as managers act behind a cloud of functional management-speak. It is therefore one of their primary interests within organisations to do everything to ensure that their interests do not become obvious. This is again very characteristic of a dominant group or ruling elite.

Obviously, the ideology of management is a typical example of a conservative ideology. It is nothing new, but simply part of the same old story since history began: the dominance of the few over the many. In achieving this, the ideology of management is as developed, comprehensive and dominant as the Christian religion once was.

6 A Theory of the Dominance of Managers

> The danger is not that a particular class is unfit to govern. Every class is unfit to govern.
>
> Lord Acton, 1881 (cited in Frank 2001, p. 114)

INTRODUCTION

Chapters 3 through 5 investigated managers' dominance via three analytical concepts—power, interests and ideology. These concepts have not only analytical usefulness, but also strong explanatory power. For example, it was demonstrated that managers' dominance is not "only" due to their privileged position, responsibilities and access to resources within hierarchical organisations. Instead, it turned out that their power, interests and ideology are constituted and shaped by several areas which comprise very different variables (as summarised in Tables 3.1, 4.1, and 5.1).

Power of dominant groups and individuals is embedded in social institutions, structures and processes; ascribed to roles and role-related tasks, supported by various kinds of performance measurement and management systems, and internalised and re-produced by subordinates through their daily routines. It is only because of this multi-dimensional nature that power shapes, even defines and creates social reality for all people involved, particularly superiors and subordinates.

It also became clear that managers need to have a strong *interest* in dominating. This interest, again, does not have a one-dimensional basis but is influenced by a multi-dimensional variety of factors. Managers' interests result from societal values, expectations and trends, and stem from their functional responsibilities, departmental affiliations and organisational politics. In addition, their interests are strongly shaped by individual aspirations, personal backgrounds and psychological aspects. They are also influenced by the primary objectives, norms and values of both the dominant and the subordinated group(s).

In addition, the analysis revealed that managers' power and interests need to be justified and protected by a comprehensive and differentiated *ideology* which is capable of addressing *all* possible human concerns. The ideology of management explains the whole (business) environment and links the past, present and future via epochal trends. In doing so, it provides (allegedly) rational explanations, meaning and justifications. In addition, it refers to uncertainties, scares and frightens while at the same time provides reassurance, hope and solutions. The ideological system addresses a whole range of socio-psychological and sociological issues. These include managers' interests and prerogatives, non-managers' obedience, order and authority within hierarchical and unjust social structures, as well as providing a methodological and logical context.

In this sense, the analysis carried out so far has demonstrated that explanations for managers' dominance, for *any* kind of social dominance and hierarchical social order, cannot be one-dimensional. The concepts of power, interests and ideology which explain managers' dominance are influenced by multi-dimensional sets of influential factors and variables. Figure 6.1 provides an overview of the approach developed so far (the areas and variables shaping and influencing managers' power, interests and ideology had been summarised in Tables 3.1, 4.1, and 5.1 in Chapters 3 through 5).

However, so far we have interrogated managers' power, interests and the ideology of management separately and largely in isolation from each other. In social reality, though, the three dimensions are closely linked—particularly in the context of dominating groups. In Figure 6.1, this is indicated by the arrows between power, interests and ideology. In other words: *managers dominate because their personal and structural power, their individual and group interests, and the ideology of management are closely related*

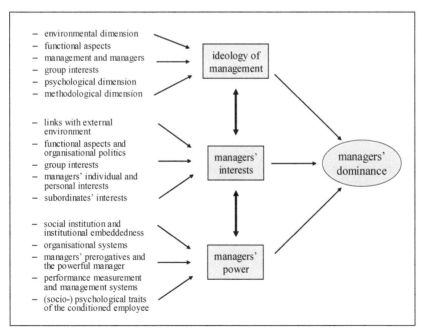

Figure 6.1 Managers' dominance based on power, interests and ideology.

to each other and together create a comprehensive and multi-dimensional system of social dominance. This theorem is central. It represents the prime rationale of the 'theory of the social dominance of managers'; only if the three concepts of power, interests and ideology are linked and seen together can managers' dominance be fully explained and understood.[1] This idea will be further developed in the next section.

THE THEORY OF SOCIAL DOMINANCE OF MANAGERS BASED ON POWER, INTERESTS AND IDEOLOGY

If we look closer at the areas of variables which influence managers' power, interests and ideology as analysed in Chapters 3 through 5, some commonalities become obvious.

Firstly, managers' dominance seems to be supported by the *environment* of organisations. Specific social institutions and external stakeholders as well as more general epochal trends, fads and fashions support and strengthen managers' positions considerably. Particularly important and influential stakeholders such as financial institutions, politicians, academics and media have very strong interests in the continuation of managers' power. Amongst other things, they provide large parts of the value system, theories and concepts for the dominance, justification and continuation of management.

Secondly, *organisational structures and processes* provide another set of factors which support, even create parts of managers' power, interests and ideology. Organisational hierarchy—whether in its more traditional or more modern, if not post-modern forms—provides managers with their roles, rights and responsibilities for resources. Bureaucracy, formal and informal rules, as well as organisational processes of centralisation and de-centralisation may limit the influence of individual managers but nonetheless strengthen the position of managers as such.

Thirdly, there are the *managers* themselves. Only they have—and must have—managerial responsibilities and prerogatives such as setting strategic and operational objectives (including setting the agenda and power to silence), participation in decision-making, controlling and punishing. Only they have (allegedly) the appropriate and necessary management knowledge, and are permitted, even required, to demonstrate leadership. Only managers have the personal skills, traits, attitudes and previous experience which enable them to be superiors in organisations—according to them and other proponents of management. And all these factors are further strengthened by managers seeing themselves as a group. Belonging to the group of managers provides social identity, group cohesion and locomotion, inter-group collaboration, social dominance (compared to and against other groups), and contributes to the further universalisation of managers' power, interests and worldviews. In the context of business, organisations or almost any other issue, managers are central—at least according to their own worldviews and self-image and the social reality of contemporary societies and organisations.

And fourthly, there are the *non-managers*, most of them *employees*. Due to their socialisation, conditioning and indoctrination, they demonstrate views and attitudes which largely mirror, support and complement managers' power, interests and ideology. With their obedience, uncertainties, anxieties and fears within an organisational context as well as their career orientation and other personal goals many employees contribute to the institutionalisation of management and managers. There is often even a pro-active willingness to function and behave well which, together with the other factors, converge towards the creation of the 'calculative mind'.

In this sense, the system of managers' dominance is based on four main elements[2]: superiors (managers), subordinates (employees), structures and processes (organisation), and the wider environment:

a) *Superiors:* roles and responsibilities, prerogatives and privileges of the dominant group and its individual members,
b) *Subordinates:* roles and tasks, functioning and obedience, compliance (and sometimes resistance) of inferiors,
c) *Social system:* hierarchical and unjust construction of the social system, structures and processes,
d) *Environment:* references and links to external aspects (greater forces, nature, socio-economic or cultural aspects), epochal trends and eternal laws, powerful stakeholders (and enemies) within the environment.

These four elements represent all factors necessary for creating any (persistent) system of social dominance. As indicated above, the theory of social dominance of managers assumes that the interplay of power, interests and ideology creates and maintains social dominance. The following sections demonstrate how power, interests and ideology relate to each of the four elements.

SUPERIORS—INDIVIDUAL MANAGERS AND THE GROUP OF MANAGERS[3]

If a group of people dominates, or strives to dominate, its individual members as well as the group as a whole are usually (much) more power-, interest- and ideology-driven than other groups. Their worldviews and perceptions are more focused, if not to say single-mindedly, on everything which relates to *their* objectives and concerns. Dominating groups and their members are primarily concerned with their own affairs and agenda (though their public image implies exactly the opposite—that's an aspect of their dominance). Literally everything about that particular group and its members comes first and foremost. The world is seen and interpreted solely in relation to *their* concerns (yet simultaneously their public talk is about "serving" the greater good).[4] The group and the individual member *is* the world (at least perceived as the subjective and factual centre of the world), and the whole social, political, economic and cultural system is viewed as being solely at the group's disposal. This is also the case with most managers, particularly more senior managers and 'their' world. They are not only managing the organisation—they *are* the organisation. It is their concerns which need to be addressed. It is they, and only they, who care for the organisation and can guarantee its very survival. Their power, interests and ideology are therefore vital for the sake of the whole.

Whether officially acknowledged or not, the individual manager, and group of managers, therefore, must have *power*. This is primarily because of their roles, responsibilities, positions and privileges within orthodox hierarchical organisations. It is also because of their prerogatives over so-called strategic decisions and responsibilities. Their power derives from setting the agenda and formulating the official mission and vision statements of their organisation; deciding its strategic objectives and strategy; allocating budget and resources; controlling performance management and measurement systems; and devising the main organisational structures and processes. Furthermore, managers—and only managers—are allowed, even expected to demonstrate leadership, particularly *hierarchical* leadership. Such an understanding corresponds strongly with personal traits of power-, decision- and image-oriented people, *regardless of their actual capabilities and skills.*

But individual managers and the group of managers do not simply dominate because of the power deriving from their privileged roles and positions. They have power because they have an *interest* in dominating—and they *must* have an interest in it. If managers—or any other dominant group of people—weren't interested in dominating, they either would not get the power in the first place or they would lose it sooner or later. It is one of the very basic principles of 'being a manager' that he or she is interested, and must be interested in gaining, keeping and executing power. This is in sharp contrast to many other professions. For example, the 'classical' engineer is primarily interested in finding technical solutions to technological problems, the 'classical' academic is mostly interested in research and teaching and the 'classical' accountant wants to get the bottom-line right—nothing more or less. Only the 'classical' manager is basically interested in dominating (so-called managing). Of course, managers as individuals are as different as anyone else is. Equally, in every social system and amongst people of all walks of life there are political animals who have personal interests in gaining power and / or becoming a formal or informal manager, a formal or informal leader. But only some social roles like the one of 'the manager' require this interest, if not to say this urge for power, *by definition* and *with necessity*. Other historical and contemporary examples for social roles and professions which need to be power-oriented per se are aristocrats or politicians. But within an organisational context it has only been the group of managers who have developed that strong interest in gaining, having and executing power (so-called managing). In addition, because of their experiences climbing up the career ladder, and their current position and future ambitions, individual managers are keen to keep and extend their power. Personal interests and advantages, material and non-material privileges, social expectations, self-images and psychological traits such as anxiety, fears and conformism—these are all strong drivers for managers' desire and drive for power. Even more so, the group of managers also have an unspoken common interest in keeping and increasing their dominance in a variety of ways. They are keen to underline the de facto primacy of management, to secure managerial prerogatives and to pursue their personal and group interests both within organisations and the organisational environment. All in order to strengthen the roles, image and power basis of 'management'—which is quite understandable; a manager is nothing without managerial power, and the group of managers would not dominate. *Managers have vested interests in obtaining, keeping and extending their power within and even beyond organisations since only then they can pursue their individual and group interests.* Generally speaking, if a social group is competitive and wants to dominate, then interest and power *must* come together. The mutual reinforcement of interests and power is a necessary precondition for individuals' or a group of people's social dominance.

Furthermore, the power and interests of individual managers and the group of managers are strongly supported and 'justified' by an *ideology of management*—they *must* be supported, if not to say concealed by a thick layer of ideology. The power and interests of dominant groups are usually anything but attractive or advantageous for the large majority of people. The power and interests of the dominant group must therefore be twisted and shaped until they look like the power and interests of the whole. Managers' privileges and interests are reflected in, even portrayed as, the organisation's primary objectives and main rationale (concealed by functional language and managerial fads and fashions). The prevailing norms and values of organisations therefore mainly reflect the specific interests, values and objectives of the group of managers. They contribute to the further universalisation of their sectional interests, and portray managers' individual and group prerogatives, advantages and privileges as necessary for the sake of the whole. Managers, and other proponents of the ideology of management, have developed a comprehensive and elaborated system of meaning—an ideology, which 'explains' and 'justifies' manager's dominance and provides so-called functional reasons why managers should keep and even extend their power. It can therefore be said that managers not only dominate because they have the power and have strong interests in being powerful, but also because they have been very successful in 'convincing' people of the importance of management and managers. *The history of management is the history of concealment of managerial power and interests by grey and dull layers of functional analysis and by colourful and glossy images of managerial excellence and success stories.*

To sum up: it already becomes obvious that when it concerns individual managers and the group of managers 'as such', power, interests and ideology relate to and strengthen each other in order to establish and justify managers' dominance. In fact they *have to* mutually reinforce each other—as soon as one of the three pillars starts to crumble, the other two will also collapse. With less power, managers would be less capable of pursuing their interests, and fewer people would be interested in contributing to the ideology of management and keeping it alive. If managers had no interest in being or becoming (more) powerful, their power basis would soon be claimed by other ambitious individuals or parties, and would vanish. Finally, if the ideology of management were no longer convincing, people would start to understand how unjust and unjustified managerial power is. They would start to question managers' interests and to challenge managers' power. Even many of the managers themselves would lose their interest in being a powerful manager or leader, since this interest is partly generated by an ideology which portrays managers in certain ways. In short: the dominance of managers works and continues to work only as long as managers' power, interests and ideology are strong and, more importantly, strongly support and mutually reinforce each other.

SUBORDINATES—INDIVIDUAL EMPLOYEE AND EMPLOYEES

The analysis of managers' power, interests and ideology showed that these concepts are also supported, or at least accepted by most employees. Social dominance is a *relational* concept. By definition it necessitates the existence of master *and* servant, the powerful and the less powerful, the ones who can pursue their interests almost without limits and the ones whose interests are primarily about demonstrating their functioning within the boundaries set by the system. It also requires an ideology which defines, explains and justifies this unequal and unjust relationship between (groups of) people. No social group could ever dominate if it did not have submissive groups beneath it. Managers, too, can only dominate when there are employees. The former's positions and prerogatives depend heavily on the latter's complementing worldview, thinking, actions and behaviour. Therefore, a theory of the dominance of managers is only comprehensive when it also considers how managers' power, interests and ideology are strengthened by their subordinates' power (or powerlessness), interests and ideology.

Subordinates are by definition less powerful than superiors—at least officially and publicly.[5] As the analysis in Chapters 3 through 5 has revealed, employees are made less powerful by managerialism. This is not a one-off situation, but an ongoing process of societal conditioning, professional socialisation, organisational routines and being managed. Employees are generally expected to demonstrate compliance and obedience, well-functioning and fear in their routines as well as guilt and confession in case of mal-functioning and under-performance. All these aspects are not really important *as such*—but have meaning and consequences. What they do is keep the employees busy and concerned, keep them weak and in the subordinate position. The well-functioning of the employees is meant to keep them comparatively powerless. At the same time (and this is equally if not more important), these functions and demonstrations strengthen the position of managers. They put the manager in charge of judging these demonstrations and underline managers' structural power. Employees, in return, are expected to express their desire to fit into "the family", group or teams, to demonstrate pro-active work attitudes, career and performance orientation, even to develop managerial skills and a calculative mind. These aspects could even be interpreted as making employees (more) powerful. And indeed, they empower people. At the same time, though, these traits empower managers as well. They re-affirm managers' management skills, underline their leadership and keep their overall prerogatives intact, if not strengthened. Put in a more cynical way, *whatever subordinates do within the boundaries of the social system, it will always strengthen their superiors' position.* Employees' empowerment is at the same time their dis-empowerment.

In this sense, it is not so much a question whether or not employees have got power. The more important question is probably whether or not they are aware of it and for which purposes they use it. As explained earlier, because of shifts in dominant social values and managerial concepts, employees nowadays use their power largely for the pursuit of individual, if not to say egoistic goals within the boundaries set by the system (just as managers do). It is *their interests* which are most reflected in the socially dominating value of 'calculative selfishness'—that strange combination of instrumental individualism, goal-oriented pragmatism, and narrowly defined functional rationalism. Constant provision, marketing and internalisation of the now dominating societal values of calculative selfishness have made it into one of most people's strongest *interests* within our contemporary societies and organisations. Subordinates *want* to care primarily about their own personal affairs and well-being within the system and, amongst other things, have largely lost interest in challenging managers' powers and unjust hierarchical systems. Most people primarily concentrate on functioning smoothly within institutional boundaries in order to gain individual advantages. This interest and behaviour plays into the hands of dominating groups and ruling classes. In the case of managerial organisations, it strengthens the dominance of managers. In return, the majority of employees actually gain considerable advantages in most managerial organisations, including

- psychological advantages (belonging to a greater, strong and successful entity which gives the subjective feeling of security or offers factual career perspectives),
- concrete advantages due to the division of labour (doing one's job more efficiently and with less input required),
- material advantages (usually higher wages, better overall remuneration packages and fewer working hours compared to other organisations or opportunities to earn a living) and even
- physical advantages (better health and safety policies).

Employees may benefit from these advantages *as long as they function within the boundaries of the system*. Hence, subordinates do not function because they are not 'conscious' and 'reflective' enough; on the contrary, most employees have *very explicit and conscious* interests in functioning smoothly because this is much more advantageous for them, and the pursuit of their interests, than to question or challenge managerial power and authority.

However, as is the case for managers, employees' power and interest would be hardly stable over a longer period of time if it were not based on, and supported by deeply held beliefs and worldviews, i.e. ideology. As just indicated, most employees' interests are reflections of the societal values of the well-functioning, well-performing, and—most importantly—well-behaving employee. Moreover, these societal values are a justification of employees' powerlessness and interest orientation; only a well-functioning employee is a good employee! Although daily routines and conditioning contribute a great deal to getting this message through to subordinates, they might be not enough. This is where ideology kicks in; it provides core cognitive, psychological and sociological functions which all help to direct subordinates' power and interests into a direction which does not threaten, in fact usually supports superiors' power and interests. It explains the (business) world people live in, it scares and frightens them with portraits of a threatening business environment, and provides security, reassurance and certainty for those who will believe in managerialism. The ideology of management provides subordinates with sufficient reasons and 'explanations' that it is in *their* interest—*and in their best interest*—to function smoothly within the managerial organisation, and that they should use their power (sic!) and energy to perform and excel, and to fit into conditions which make them subordinates. Hence, the ideology of management explains and justifies subordinates' tasks and duty of obedience while simultaneously explaining their superiors' dominant positions, prerogatives and privileges.

Overall, subordinates' contribution to the dominance of managers is also based on the mutual reinforcement of the three concepts of interests, power and ideology. Managers' dominance can be partly explained by employees' reduced and focused use of their power according to the principle of calculative selfishness. Employees' obedience is also an outcome of their pronounced interest in supporting and maintaining the hierarchical system of orthodox organisations, in actively contributing to the very social system which makes them subordinates. This might be even called a 'rational' interest and behaviour since there is a whole range of factual advantages for those who function. And thirdly, subordinates are willing to function because societal values portray smooth functioning and performing as ideal behaviour for the calculative actor. Against this backcloth, ideology has managed to convince people not only that they should and must obey managerial power and dominance, but that it is in their very own interest and to their own advantage to do so; functioning smoothly within the boundaries of the hierarchical, unjust, and oppressive social system of managerial organisations means great advantages for the individual. In this sense, it is the utmost form of selfishness and egoism. Seen in this way, the dominance of managers over subordinates is, again, quite a sophisticated combination of power, interest and ideology. It is the combination of anticipatory obedience and calculated acceptance of managers' prerogatives and power in order to increase one's own opportunities within the boundaries of the system which portrays this weird reality as the norm and normality. However competent and skilful the individual manager is, whatever the specific corporate culture, and however direct or indirect control happens via performance measurement and control systems, subordinates largely accept, indirectly strengthen or even actively support their superiors' dominance with their interest-driven acting mainly for individual advantages. Employees' power and interests mainly orbit around the ideology of calculative selfishness and, in doing so, support managers' power and interests and strengthen their structural and factual dominance.

SOCIAL SYSTEM—THE MANAGERIAL ORGANISATION AND HIERARCHICAL ORDER

As it may have become clear in the previous two sections, the power, interests and ideology of both managers and subordinates are not only defined and shaped by and within the same managerial system but complement each other to a high degree. Managers' application and demonstration of power is supported by their subordinates' powerlessness and calculated obedience. Both have vested interests in stabilising this unequal relation of power because it provides them with a known structure of opportunities to pursue their own interests. And managerial ideology provides more than sufficient "functional reasons" why managers' and employees' roles and interests within the hierarchical organisation are quite complementary. Managers' *and* employees' power, interests and ideology together represent a basis for the explanation and justification of managers' dominance. Moreover, they jointly contribute to its *stabilisation* and *persistence*; managers' dominance is, amongst other things, based on their subordinates' obedience. In this sense, superiors' and subordinates' power, interests and ideology create *a comprehensive and stable social system*—the *hierarchical system of the managerial organisation*. In return, the system shapes and strengthens people's power, interests and ideology—according to their position and roles within the system.

Managers have been extremely successful in gaining *power and control* over the hierarchy and bureaucracy of orthodox organisations and other hierarchical social systems—even 'post-modern' or (allegedly) 'non-bureaucratic' systems of work organisation. In addition to orthodox command-and-control systems, managers have introduced new forms of managerial power and control, e.g. indirect control via performance measurement and management systems, electronic systems, or de-centralised control amongst employees. Managers are so identified with hierarchical authority and social positions, bureaucracy, career and selection, responsibilities for resources, centralisation and de-centralisation, direct and indirect control that we are hardly able to think about organisations *without* these things, and, most importantly, *without* managers. Organisational structures and processes are *managerial* structures and processes through and through. They provide managers with power and control no one can or should challenge. The hierarchical social order / the managerial organisation make and keep employees *powerless*—in both relative and absolute terms. The main aim is to achieve a better fit of individual employees into the managerial / hierarchical system and to guarantee their uncritical functioning within those systems. This, of course, makes it so much easier for managers to manage and to rule without being questioned or challenged. And, because of life-long socialisation and conditioning, most employees are more than keen to function within the hierarchical frameworks of managerial organisations. They are quite eager to fit into the prevailing managerial systems of power. In doing so, they reinforce managers' power and the hierarchical structure of the social system via their daily actions and routines. The unjust social system of managerial organisations is, hence, institutionalised on a daily basis and, at the same time, provides the framework for these actions. Managerialism creates a social system in which both superiors and subordinates collaborate and co-exist—each at their place and according to the powers and possibilities ascribed to these social roles and positions.

It is therefore quite understandable that most managers have a strong *interest* not only in keeping and nurturing their roles and positions within that hierarchy but also in defending and maintaining the whole managerial system of power-and-control structures and processes of hierarchical organisations. Even when managers' interests clash—for example concerning the formulation of new strategies, major change initiatives, resource allocation or departmental budgets, they will nonetheless only compete with each other *within* the framework of organisational hierarchy and managerial ideology. Managers may challenge each other's positions and privileges but they will *never* challenge the social system as such, because they know very well that they can only pursue their interests and use their power and privileges as long as the hierarchical social system continues. The same is true for most subordinates and their interests. The organisation offers them advantages and opportunities that they also could not easily get somewhere else—at least seen from the perspective of employees who are very much trapped in their daily lives and routines, have to pay their bills, have their children in a particular school and have a certain standard of living. "Yes, there are also considerable downsides which come along with the job—it is sometimes boring, the paperwork increases more and more, the manager is ignorant and incompetent, and the guys in other departments are always late with their data." However, for the majority of employees, the hierarchy and social system of the managerial organisation are, all in all, at least acceptable. Employees, therefore have a vested interest in seeing the continuance of the hierarchical social system since it provides them—within limits and on balance—with purpose and order, with opportunities to meet their interests and with protection against some of the difficulties life can bring. This sort of calculative selfishness works well for *both* the employee *and* the manager *at the same time*. The employee develops strategies to get the most out of an organisation while reducing his or her input and possible frictions within the system to a minimum—and the manager can 'count' on this calculative behaviour—mainly because managers think and act in the same way. Both can use the other's calculative selfishness to their own advantage and to further their aims and ambitions. Managers' dominance depends to a great extent on this ability to count on calculative, and therefore predictable and manageable behaviour on the side of their employees. Both managers and employees have an active interest in fitting into and maintaining the system of managerial hierarchy for the sake of personal advantage. Although coming from different directions, managers and employees are somehow united in their interests in the social system. In addition to pursuing individual goals within the boundaries of the system, managers and employees have a *common interest* in maintaining the social system, and particularly the hierarchical system of orthodox organisations, *as it is*.

Finally, ideology plays an important role in stabilising the social system— predominantly from managers' perspective. The ideology of management defines and justifies managers' positions and responsibilities within the organisational hierarchy particularly, and it guarantees and secures their privileges and advantages. It justifies managers' prerogatives concerning decision-making, budget and resource responsibilities, or their tasks of leading and controlling. It is even more concerned with the ideological construction and justification of social structures and processes as *managerial* structures and processes, i.e.

- the political order of organisations (i.e. the existing hierarchy, power relations and mechanisms for decision-making),
- dominance (i.e. power and authority of particular individuals and groups over others),
- privileges and prerogatives of (a) certain group(s) (members of privileged groups are in a much better position to pursuit their own individual and group interests),
- social inequality (differences in life chances between social groups).

All of these are only justified when they are, or can be portrayed as 'managerial' and of 'functional necessity'. Equally important, the ideology of management explains to employees why the managerial organisation is structured and functions in the way it does: why managers are at the top and employees at the bottom of the hierarchy, why everyone gets what they deserve and why this all creates a cosmos and an order which is the best of all possible worlds. Ideology explains the managerial organisation as an order where the power and interests of different groups and people are in balance. Moreover, one of the main functions of managerial ideology concerning subordinates is to give them the impression that the social reality of hierarchical organisations is *normal*—that managerial organisations are how typical organisations look— and *should* look. Managerial organisation of business and work is the way things are, the way things should be and the way people *must* act, behave and even think (otherwise *they* are not 'normal').

Accordingly, managers' dominance and employees' obedience within the social system does not only stem from their relative positions, their respective interests in dominating or following and the ideology of management *as such*, but more importantly *in their combination*. Managers' power within and because of the hierarchical social system only contributes to managers' dominance because they also have vested interests in maintaining this system. If managers lost their interest in keeping the organisational hierarchy alive, the whole system would start to change. Or if a different kind of manager started to question the hierarchical structure per se, the system would also change. Organisational hierarchy ensures managers' dominance only as long as managers have the power *and* the interest *and* an appropriate ideological basis to maintain and justify this particular type of social system. And the same is true for employees and the way in which they function within, and contribute to, the maintenance of the social system.

ENVIRONMENT—INSTITUTIONAL EMBEDDEDNESS

Although most managerial dominance is based on intra-organisational aspects, there are also some factors within the organisational environment which contribute to it. These external factors can play an important role in managers' power, interests and ideology, since managers are not the most dominating group or class within society but "only" one amongst others. As indicated in Chapter 1, the emergence of management and the making of 'the manager' was a historical process which started in the midst of Manchester capitalism and is still continuing. Managers were already quite powerful in late capitalism. In the early 20th century, Scientific Management, the first business schools and management associations began to spread the word and changed the business world. However, the modern understanding of 'management' and the image of 'the manager' really only developed in the early 1980s, alongside larger socio-cultural trends within Western societies towards neo-conservatism, neo-liberalism and individualism (in the sense of egoism / calculative selfishness and individual success). It could be said therefore that the modern manager is not so much empowered by technical or organisational changes within organisations (although they are also important), but by epochal changes in the socio-cultural, political and value system of society. Managers nowadays are powerful not only because management is a widely accepted concept, but because 'the manager' is a highly appreciated social institution, supported (and made) by dominant socio-cultural and political values and belief systems. The concept is further institutionalised and secured by a whole universe of legal and regulatory frameworks, norms and quality standards.

In addition to these 'abstract' epochal trends and societal value systems, managers are embedded in concrete networks and alliances with strong and powerful external stakeholders at a more micro-level. There is a "constellation of interests" comprising institutional investors, banks, business organisations, consultancies and business schools. Some of these may have an interest in limiting, or at least controlling managers' decisions and actions. However, they are all basically very much in favour of management per se since it guarantees that organisations will deliver what these stakeholders want. Despite their possible differences, these highly influential and powerful institutions have a strong interest in seeing managers remain powerful and are more than willing to contribute to the (further) institutionalisation of management. Hence, management and managers can remain powerful as long as they achieve a high degree of isomorphism with the relevant socio-economic institutions and value systems of modern societies. At present, managers are so powerful and established that they do not even have to justify their power and existence *in principle* ('why do we have and need managers?') but only in a *technical* sense ('does the manager ensure that the organisation achieves its objectives?'). Against the current backcloth of extremely favourable and supportive socio-economic, legal and cultural factors, combined with social capital due to their close links to powerful stakeholders, managers are in a very strong and powerful position.

Managers are quite aware of this. They know that they can pursue their own interests best when they are closely linked to the external environment. It is even more in managers' interest to fit to the external factors which make them powerful. Hence, they are usually keen to demonstrate that their decisions and actions correspond with societal norms and values, legal and regulatory requirements, and with the expectations of powerful and influential stakeholders. And they are able to do so. In contrast to other dominant groups, one of managers' highest values is pragmatism—a pragmatic interest, action and result orientation. Amongst other things, this means that they regard their organisation's environment in fairly opportunistic terms. They know that they can achieve the best results and outcomes both for themselves and their organisation if they do not fundamentally challenge institutions in their environment but comply with them pragmatically. This pragmatism includes, for example, constant attempts from managers and business organisations to influence political decisions, legal frameworks, and societal values and discourses. As other interest-oriented people, managers are keen to have the most favourable conditions for the pursuit of their interests. Yet, at the same time, managers and managerial organisations are highly adaptable and can prosper in very different environments (as the history of market economy and managerialism demonstrates). As long as environmental conditions or external stakeholders do not seriously start to threaten their very existence and main objectives, managers will simply focus on the pragmatic pursuit of their interests, i.e. seeking opportunities and small changes in their favour, while leaving the larger frameworks unchallenged and untouched.

However, like other powerful groups, managers do not really need to meet the expectations of their environments or others—it often is enough that they give the impression that they do (and that others believe it). For example, managers may actively support the neo-liberal ideology of a free market economy and competition, while at the same time doing everything in their daily business to disable market forces and reduce competition. Managers may praise and demand democracy and liberty, while at the same time maintaining hierarchical organisations and imposing managerial power-and-control systems which oppress people and exclude employees from any meaningful participation in important decisions or decision-making processes. Managers may claim just and performance-related remuneration while systematically denying their employees a fair share of the profits they have generated, and agreeing their own pay deals which are hardly related to the actual performance of the organisation. To put it in a nutshell: *the managerial organisation is by its very nature an anti-democratic, anti-libertarian and unjust institution*[6]—*but its proponents have managed to make it look as if it fits into democracies, liberal and formally just societies!*

As so often the case, it is sufficient that the relationship between societal values and factual reality is constructed (and covered up) by rhetorical means. For this, ideology provides a suitable device, flexible enough to be adapted to even fundamental discrepancies and inconsistencies. The ideology of management has not only been successful in linking managers' power and interests with societal institutions and their socio-economic environment. It has been even more successful in creating the impression that 'the manager', 'management' and 'managerial organisations' fit into modern democratic societies. The impression created is that it is even a natural part of them, and provides the best organisational forms for employees, the pursuit of their interests and the development of their skills. In this sense, the relationship between the organisational environment and managers' dominance can be seen as another example of how interests, power and ideology interrelate and support each other.

However, *if* larger socio-economic trends and / or powerful institutions changed direction, the power basis of managers could shrink to a great extent. As history has shown, whole social classes have lost their dominance because of epochal changes. Also, if managers lost interest in complying with external requirements and expectations—even if it were only at the level of impression management—their power would be reduced almost immediately. Finally, managers' dominance is only secure as long as the ideology of management is successful in providing people with the impression that contemporary concepts of 'the manager' and 'management' are good for society and organisations, and that they are in line with societal norms and values. As soon as the majority of people started to realise how alien managerial organisations are to modern society, knowledge economies and educated employees, managers could no longer pursue their interests on the scale they do now and their power would be considerably reduced.

THE 'COSMOS' OF SOCIAL DOMINANCE OF MANAGERS

As the four sub-sections above have demonstrated, managers' dominance stretches over *all* relevant areas of social dominance. Managers have managed to

a) establish the roles, responsibilities and images, position and privileges of managers as the centrepieces of organisations,
b) achieve a situation where subordinates not only acknowledge managerial dominance but are keen to function and perform within the system set and run by managers,
c) transform hierarchical and bureaucratic social systems into managerial organisations and
d) establish isomorphic relationships with socio-economic institutions, epochal trends and powerful stakeholders.

The hierarchical relationship and interaction between managers and employees constitutes the social system of the managerial organisation in ways which fit to the larger institutional environment. Moreover, the four areas are strongly related, coordinated, and together fit into one comprehensive, multi-dimensional and multi-layered system of managerial dominance, which is held together and maintained by the mutually reinforcing factors of managers' power, interests and ideology. Together, the areas and factors create a *'cosmos' of social dominance*. The following figure illustrates this whole system or cosmos of managerial dominance.

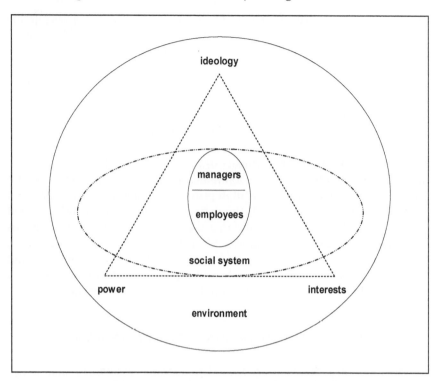

Figure 6.2   The 'cosmos' of social dominance of managers.

Whatever the perspective, *any* general investigation into persistent and comprehensive social dominance has to take this multi-dimensional system perspective into account. As references in Chapters 3 through 5 indicated, the theory developed here can be seen in the grand tradition of critical theory. It would require more space here to interrogate how exactly the 'theory of social dominance of managers' relates to other critical theories. But at least one comparison might help to illustrate it further. As demonstrated above, the theory addresses some of the same problems Marx's theory of capitalist production has addressed, if not to say revealed—particularly the unequal, exploitative and unjust relationships between social groups within the economic realm / sphere of production. Some of the main similarities and differences between the two theories might be briefly highlighted as follows:

Like Marx's approach, the theory of social dominance of managers also has a dichotomical view of the main parties involved and concerned (for Marx: capitalists and workers, here: managers and employees). However, Marx was more of the opinion that at that time this dichotomy was an approximately true reflection of organisational and societal reality (give or take a few other social groups). And he was probably right when one considers societies and organisations within such a divisive societal context as the era of Manchester capitalism. In contrast, in the theory developed here these two categories are only meant as *analytical constructs*. Contemporary organisational and social reality is much more differentiated, if not to say fragmented, than 19th-century class society. Hierarchical relationships can be found everywhere and stretch through a continuum (or patchwork) of groups, classes, social roles and positions. And they can be found within very different forms of organisations, in 'classical' hierarchies as well as (post-) modern types such as collegial or professional organisations, networks or partnerships.

Furthermore, Marx's famous analysis of the socio-economic conditions of capitalist production, even capitalist society, also comprised the three dimensions of power, interests and ideology. Although his theory is much more comprehensive, developed, far-reaching, and with many more implications than the theory developed here, Marx's concepts of power, interests and ideology are comparatively one-dimensional. In particular:

a) in his theory, superiors' (capitalists') power is mainly seen as stemming from their *property rights* (i.e. ownership of the means of production), as well as in their means to design, run, and use systems and mechanisms of direct control and punishment within organisations, particularly the factory system;

b) interests are mainly defined and analysed as *class interests*, i.e. as interests which primarily stem from one's modes of income earning (e.g. rent, profit or wage) and, hence, one's social position within society (i.e. landowner, capitalist or worker); and

c) ideology is seen as the *ideological superstructure* justifying the 'material basis' of society, production and its consequences (i.e. the unequal and unjust allocation of property, possession of means of production and, as a direct result, the unequal and unjust relationships between capitalists and proletarians). Ideology, as a set of societal norms and values, political and legal frameworks, is developed and maintained by institutions of the state (government, judiciary, educational sector, Army), political parties, the Church, and capitalist associations. Workers are only ever seen "at the receiving end" of the ideological superstructure and, hence, have little more than a 'false consciousness'.

One might therefore say that Marx's theory was very consistent in that he maintained both the dichotomical and the one-dimensional view concerning the concepts of power, interests and ideology. In contrast to Marx's theory, and as outlined in Chapters 3 through 5, the theory proposed here assumes that power, interests and ideology are multi-dimensional concepts. In addition, in Marx's theory power, interests and ideology are all more or less external forces, i.e. they are social and societal phenomena which have entered organisations. In contrast, the theory of social dominance of managers assumes that all three comprise external as well as internal aspects. They are not only present and embedded in the organisation's environment, but also in organisational functions, structures and processes, in the functional, (socio-) psychological, and sociological aspects of managers' and employees' views, decisions, attitudes and actions. In other words, all three aspects play their role in

- the constitution of individuals and groups as dominant social actors (managers),
- subordinates' more or less conscious and willing obedience (employees),
- the hierarchical and unjust design of the social system and (social system),
- its overall fit with its environment and epochal trends (environment).

According to the 'theory of social dominance of managers', the three concepts of power, interests and ideology together with the four areas of managerial organisations (managers, employees, social system, environment), create the comprehensive system of social reality of the managerial organisation. And together they create the societal cosmos of managers' dominance.

In this sense, the theory of social dominance is about how (groups of) people are related to each other within a particular social system and a certain environment. Typical aspects are that the dominant group is provided with, and uses (almost) any means in its powers to pursue its own interests, and that this is so deeply embedded in (almost) all aspects and affairs that it is hardly identifiable any more as ideology. Managers are responsible for the design of the organisational systems, structures and processes which provide them with the power and control mechanisms which they, as an elite minority, can use to pursue their own specific interests. And they have the rhetorical and intellectual tools on their side. The whole body of management knowledge is especially made for managers, tailor-made for *their* concerns and perspectives, designed for strengthening *their* position and dominance both within and beyond hierarchical organisations. It is an ideology specifically designed to portray managers' individual and group interests as the interests of the whole. In so doing, it institutionalises managers' power and interests as well as subordinates' duties to acknowledge managers' prerogatives and behave accordingly. Managerial language and discourses do not simply set the scene. They provide the moral justification and legitimisation of social reality which even praises unjust and unjustifiable inequalities. For managers, this is about justifying management and legitimising managers' authority and privileges—the imperatives of managing and the necessities of subordination and control. Managerial ideology provides explanations for how the world (of business and organisations) 'is' and how it should be, why managers are in charge, why others shall obey, and what managers and employees 'together' have to do in order to keep this system functioning and going.

Finally, the theory of managers' social dominance draws attention to the fact that managerial organisations incorporate many aspects which are typical for *all* hierarchical and unjust social systems. The dominance of managers investigated in this book is only one, albeit very important example of group-based dominance (Sidanius / Pratto 1999). If, e.g. one simply exchanged the word 'manager' for 'priests', 'aristocrats', 'capitalists' or 'apparatchiks' in the paragraph above (and equally 'managerial'), one would be not far away from a fair description of the hierarchical, oppressive and unjust systems of the Church, feudalism and monarchy, capitalism or communism. Managers' social dominance is just a further example of historical or contemporary forms of hierarchical social systems. In one word: it is made for the dominance of the few over many.

POWER, INTERESTS AND IDEOLOGY OF MANAGERS AS A GROUP AND AS A CLASS

So far, the terms 'managers' and 'group of managers' have been used in a more general sense. They simply indicate that a larger number of managers is a different entity compared to the individual manager. In doing so, we followed established conventions rather than an explicit analytical concept. At several points, the analysis of managers' dominance revealed that their power, interests and ideology actually has a lot to do with their position and status as a 'group' (amongst, together and against other groups). This collective dimension is an important component of managers' dominance, in fact of *any* social dominance within larger social systems, even dictatorships. The methodological discussion in this section therefore sheds some light on this collective / larger entity of managers. In fact, there are different ways of seeing managers as an entity:

- Firstly, we can talk about 'managers' in general, i.e. using quite a general term with no specific meaning or strong implications (e.g. whether managers have interests in common or not).
- Secondly, we may call them 'the managers'—which somehow implies a closer proximity for them, and already indicates some additional aspects, e.g. a consciousness of a distinction between 'those at the top' and 'those down there'.
- Thirdly, we might use the term 'group of managers'—which additionally implies common interests and beliefs, norms and values, cohesion and similarities, and gives the whole analysis a much more socio-psychological and sociological dimension.
- Finally, it is possible to talk about the 'class of managers'—which can simply be a neutral, logical and methodological term (e.g. 'class

of objects', 'classification').[7] However, used in a social context, and because of its historical background, 'class' usually adds societal, political, and moral-philosophical dimensions and views to the investigation (e.g. 'class struggle').

As with all definitions, there is no 'right' or 'wrong' concerning any of the four terms as such. But terminology defines, even makes and shapes (social) reality. Hence, it becomes very important when it concerns what we want to say and reveal—or *not* to say and to hide. For example, orthodox management and organisation theory largely talks about 'managers' or 'the managers'. As shown in previous sections, this is mainly due to the intention to portray management as a mere functional or technical necessity. However, it became clear that such a use of terms, and such a portrait of management and managers, captures only the smallest (and less important) part of the whole phenomenon. It is therefore insufficient for a comprehensive investigation of management. Even more, the use of such allegedly 'objective' and 'neutral' terms and language is precisely part of the unjust social systems and ideology these terms obscure. Hence, in order to understand the dominance of managers as a social and organisational phenomenon, and to address the societal implications and consequences of this problem, it is often more appropriate—and telling—to refer explicitly to the 'group' or 'class of managers', rather than simply talking about 'managers' or 'the managers'. The question, therefore, is whether or when it makes more sense to talk about 'group' or 'class'.

MANAGERS AS A GROUP

According to Social Identity Theory (Ashforth / Mael 1989, Tajfel / Turner 1979), a group can be defined as 'a collection of individuals who perceive themselves to be members of the same category, share some emotional involvement in this common definition of themselves and achieve some degree of social consensus about their group' (Tajfel and Turner 1979, cited in Hartley 1983, p. 16). It is about the distinctiveness of their group's values and practices compared to other groups, the attractiveness / prestige of belonging to that group, and the salience of out-groups (Ashforth / Mael 1989, pp. 24–25). This is definitely all true for managers and we therefore might talk about the 'group of managers'. Nonetheless, there also might be downsides to this.

The analysis in Chapter 3 demonstrated that much of managers' *power* stems from their roles and responsibilities, their positions and privileges as well as their abilities to influence, even define and shape organisational realities. These factors definitely vary considerably, largely according to managers' positions within organisational hierarchy. Due to the hierarchical level and related roles there can be considerable differences in the actual scope of managers' power. It often makes sense to at least differentiate between senior, middle, and lower management and regard these layers as different groups of managers. On the other hand, in a general sense managers' power is based largely on the same range of power and control tools. By definition, all managers have in common that they are superior to their subordinates. A manager, *every* manager is powerful because only they are empowered and allowed to make decisions which are directly relevant for others; only they have budget and line responsibilities; only they have access to increasingly important information and a whole range of systems and tools to control and punish others. Moreover, managers are powerful specifically because other members within the organisation are systematically excluded from these opportunities. For example, O'Brien / Crandall (2005, p. 1) draw attention to the fact that 'human societies tend to be structured as group-based hierarchies in which dominant groups possess a disproportionately large share of positive social value such as political authority, power, wealth, and social status, whereas the subordinate groups possess a disproportionately larger share of negative social values including low power, low social status, and poverty'. Hence, managers' power is defined by similar clusters of characteristics—particularly in relation to other groups. Levy et al. (2001, p. 2, similarly Feldman 2000, p. 624) made the point that 'management can be viewed as a set of practices and discourses embedded within broader asymmetrical power relations which systematically privilege the interests and viewpoints of some groups while silencing and marginalising others.' These asymmetrical power relations within hierarchical organisations, as well as the nature and characteristics of managers' power (particularly when compared to other groups) form typical patterns. The managerial organisation is a 'group-based social hierarchy' (Sidanius / Pratto 1999, p. 32) and, therefore, it is indeed possible to talk about the 'group of managers' (which may be further differentiated into sub-groups).

The same can be said about managers' *interests*. Again, as Chapter 4 revealed, individual managers can have very different personal interests and (career) objectives, and different understandings and ideas about their organisation, and, hence, may clash with each other. Within the group of managers, large differences can be identified due to hierarchical position ('vertical differences in interests') and departmental affiliation ('horizontal differences in interests'). However, many of their professional interests are relatively similar, mainly because of their roles as managers *as such*. Most of managers' concerns orbit around their prerogatives and privileges, roles and responsibilities, images and identities, job and career prospects, as well as their subordinates' roles and responsibilities, tasks and attitudes. Seeing themselves as superiors, managers have enough in common to develop some group coherence, some common or group interests (e.g. Swedberg 2005, p. 367, Ashforth / Mael 1989, pp. 22–24)—particularly in relation to other groups (e.g. professionals, workers' representatives, or external stakeholders). They share very similar sets of interests, specifically the further establishment, development and dissemination of management and its prerogatives, i.e. the privileged opportunities to pursue their specific individual and collective interests.

Finally, managers can have very different worldviews, perspectives, personal preferences and opinions. Quite often, it is possible to identify clashes of cosmologies amongst managers which can be traced back to differences in deeply held values and beliefs about the organisation's objectives and strategy, and how it should do its business. Nonetheless, most, if not all managers do not challenge or question the 'common wisdoms of management', i.e. management's basic rules and assumptions, functional concepts, models, and tools. In addition, most managers share very similar sets of values and beliefs: about themselves (and their employees); their image and description; their roles and responsibilities; their positions and privileges; and how organisations and business should function. There is a shared understanding about what management means, what it *should* mean—and who should be in charge of it. To sum up, (almost) all managers share the same ideology of management, at least the fundamentals of it.

All in all, because of these deeply embedded and strongly developed commonalities in power, interests and ideology, it definitely makes some sense to regard managers as 'a group'; "being a manager" at the same time means "belonging to the group of managers". It provides managers with a social identity (Elstak / Van Riel 2005, p. E2, Hogg/Terry 2000, p. 122) and a feeling of belonging to a "psychological group", i.e. 'a collection of people who share the same social identification or define themselves in terms of the same social category membership' (Turner 1984, cited in Ashforth / Mael 1989, p. 24).

However, there are also limits to this approach. Traditionally, the sociological term 'group' has been used primarily for a smaller number of people. Although interpersonal interaction, similarity, liking, and proximity are possible, but not necessary aspects of a group (Ashforth / Mael 1989, pp. 24–25), it nonetheless implies, or can imply, a specific number of people which (at least theoretically) could all be in direct contact, or inhabit the same physical or virtual space. This understanding of group is more about a local, identifiable type. In this case, the internal relations of such a group are usually seen as more intense, with strong socio-psychological identification between its members, e.g. intra-group cohesion, cooperation, intra-group altruism, internalisation of (some) group values and norms, homogeneity in attitudes and behaviour, and self-stereotyping depersonalisation (Ashforth / Mael 1989, p. 26). Hence, it is probably more appropriate to talk about the 'group of managers' when it is either about a *particular* group of managers within a certain organisation or perhaps even all of the managers in a *particular* organisation. And secondly, since the term 'group' has mostly socio-psychological and sociological implications, it might be used particularly when we are talking about managers' perceptions, organisational interests and objectives, decision-making, attitudes, behaviours and organisational politics.

MANAGERS AS A CLASS

This last point indicated that it might be questionable whether talking about the 'group of managers' captures the whole phenomenon, in particular that which has emerged since the early 1980s. As the analysis in Chapter 1 revealed, the appearance of the modern type of manager and the dominance of managers has not simply changed some aspects of some organisations: it has changed *all* types of organisations *fundamentally*. Even more, the sheer scale of the dissemination and institutionalisation of the ideas of 'management' and 'the manager' shows that this process has implications well beyond organisational boundaries. The proponents of managerialism and managers have extended their dominance way beyond the organisation they work for—it extends beyond whole industries or even the economy. In fact, managerialism has long exceeded the economic realm. As Alvesson / Willmott (1992a, p. 3) described: 'Established management discourse and practice tends to incorporate and 'swallow up' larger and larger domains of social and personal life, such as culture, conflict and even pleasure, . . .'. Managerialism is a *societal*, even a *global* phenomenon. It has put managers on the map of societal dominance in a way rarely seen before. Managerialism is about shaping and changing society—in particular the alignment of social norms and values, social reality and practices to managers' interests, power, and ideology. Hence, to talk 'merely' about the 'group of managers' fails to capture the full scope and magnitude of this epochal and global change; with the emergence and institutionalisation of managers, we have witnessed the emergence and institutionalisation of a new (ruling) *class*.

To refer to managers as *a class* is more than just a change in terminology. According to Weber's classical description (1921/1980, pp. 177, 531), the concept of class clusters people whose life chances share the same specific causal components, particularly with regard to socio-economic conditions. In contrast (or addition) to 'group' as a social category, the class concept refers particularly to individuals' whose positions in society are similar because of their occupation and their possession of similar resources to advance their ends (e.g. Aries / Seider 2007, p. 138, Hussain 2007, pp. 335–336). In addition to the socio-psychological and sociological dimensions of the group concept, 'class' particularly addresses the socio-economical and socio-cultural, social and even societal preconditions and consequences of differentiated and stratified social systems such as larger orthodox organisations and societies. In doing so, it reveals some of the historical and epochal circumstances of systematic inequality in life chances and differences in views amongst people. People belonging to the same class share the same or similar interests based on the modes of their earnings (ownership or gainful employment), the type and scale of power over goods or qualifications as means for earning a living, and their social position and worldviews stemming from it. In this sense, Weber's class concept *particularly refers to the interests, power, and ideology which people have in common because of their same or similar socio-economical conditions of existence* (Nesbit 2006, p. 174).

Following this interpretation one might say that managers constitute a social class because of similarities in their life chances which stem from their superior positions within organisational hierarchies. However, one must admit that these similarities are fairly general and are more meant *in principle*. The class of managers is not one coherent entity (as perhaps a more traditional understanding of the class concept may imply). As outlined in Chapter 2, managers are very different in many respects. Factual differences in their actual jobs, working for different organisations in different sectors and industries, and other strong societal values such as individualism, mean that managers do not have a common 'class consciousness' or convey 'collective actions'. And there are very strong differences between different levels of managers, such as senior, middle and lower management. In this respect, the contemporary concept of class is much 'weaker' than the historical class concept, in particular Marxist concept. All that the contemporary class concept can say is that because of similarities in their managerial power, their role-related interests and their shared ideology of management, managers have a societal relevance which suggests that they could be regarded as a social class.

In this sense, applying Weber's (weaker) class concept to managers adds something more to the group concept. It sheds more light on the fact that the dominance of managers *systematically* provides them with prerogatives and privileges, resources and opportunities from which others are *systematically* excluded. The class concept stresses that individual life chances stemming from conditions of systemic inequalities are not only *absolute* but *relative*. Class describes unequal social relationships between individuals and groups as representatives of their particular class ('stratification'); 'class is less a possession than a dynamic: a relationship between different people and groups divided along axes of power and privilege. So class differences play out in power relations' (Nesbit 2006, pp. 171, 175 referring to E. P. Thompson 1968). The life chances of one class of people are to a large extent shaped and influenced by the situation and interpretations, opportunities (or lack of opportunities) and actions (or non-actions!) of other classes. They may even depend heavily on the advancement or restriction of other classes' life chances. In the case of the class of managers, this primarily relates to their relative status and scale of life chances compared to employees, i.e. all subordinates without strategic and / or managerial responsibilities. Managers dominate within organisations because employees are systematically excluded from the sources of power. In addition, they do not have an interest in dominating and / or their ideology simply doesn't support such a notion. Employees' ideology and value system only suggests that they should function and behave well within the current system.

Managers' dominance as a social class can be also identified at a societal level. Managers have found very favourable historical conditions for becoming a privileged and powerful social class. Since the emergence and development of corporate capitalism in the late 19th century, larger organisations ('corporations'), and the ways they do their business have been playing an increasingly important and dominant part within modern economies and societies. The economy, and concerns about 'the economy' are now at the core of every industrialised nation, as well as most developing countries. Business, globalisation and trade, growth, product innovation, productivity, efficiency, and making (ever more) money are apparently almost everyone's greatest concern—and all of this (allegedly) can only be guaranteed by business corporations and, hence, managers. Their power, interests and ideology are now established in society:

1) These epochal changes in societal values and factual modes of production have meant that managers' *power and influence* have been expanded from organisations into society, into *every* part of modern societies. Managers direct the generation, exploitation, flow, allocation, use and disposal of resources, goods and services. They run not only networks of organisations but whole industries. They influence and shape the legal and regulatory frameworks for business, financial policies, private and public spending as well as politics. Gabriel (1999, p. 402) gave a vivid description: 'Managers currently constitute one of the largest occupational groups in industrialized countries, they control vast resources, they are rarely accountable to anyone other than their peers and the most famous among them acquire heroic status. More importantly, management has colonized every area of personal, group and social activity as well as the ways we think about them.' Because of their hierarchical positions and related privileges, managers have already accumulated power and influence within organisations in a way rarely seen before. But managers have extended their power and influence well beyond organisational boundaries. Due to the historical process of corporate capitalism, managers are now one of the most powerful, influential and established classes within most societies.

2) This process to a great extent involves *the universalisation of managers' sectional interests* (Hamilton 1987, p. 23, Shrivastava 1986, pp. 366, 369). Managers' sectional interests, values and objectives are portrayed *as the prime concerns of the whole social system*, i.e. as universal. Perhaps even more crucially, managers' major ideological interest is not only in the (further) institutionalisation of the 'primacy of management', but about the (further) institutionalisation of the 'primacy of managers' at a societal level. Whether it is private or public sector organisations, economy or culture, business or private lives—

literally everything must not only be managed, but shall be managed *by managers*. Meanwhile, in our societies it is generally accepted that managers, *and only managers*, do management. Therefore, only managers will be responsible for managing, for making all these important decisions concerning strategy, structures and processes, design and maintenance, functioning and control—whatever the system and whatever the purpose is. In having their personal and group interests accepted by society and institutionalised as the prevailing norms and values, managers have managed to establish themselves as a widely appreciated, even admired social class. The 'equation of management with managers' (Grey 1999, p. 567) together with the dissemination of management into all areas and activities of society is the "little detail" which is so relevant for managerial domination both within organisations and society.

3) The expansion of managers' interests and power into society has been supported by the emergence and expansion of the *ideology of management at a societal level*. Like the ideology of any powerful class, managers' ideology, at its core, is very simple. Basically it explains and justifies why managers dominate, why managers *should* dominate and why others have to accept this 'fact'. Within organisations, the ideology of management is very comprehensive and systematic, clear and specific about this (e.g. Pollitt 1990, p. 6, Hartley 1983, pp. 14–15). But, as indicated above, the ideology of management has gone well beyond organisational boundaries and has entered discourses in all areas of society. Claims about the necessity and superiority of management functions (covering managers' real interests and power behind these claims) can be found in all institutions, at all societal levels and with regard to every issue. Managerial ideology is in our daily routines, decisions, actions and social practices. Kirkpatrick et al. (2005, p. 3) drew attention to the fact 'that a new "hierarchy of legitimation" has emerged in which discourses of "managerialism and business" are now hegemonic.' The ideology of management is often so embedded in social practices that we are unaware of its presence. And if people became aware of its presence, they would see few reasons why they should give it a second thought. According to Hume's explanation of "naturalistic fallacy", i.e. the false assumption that things should be, because they are (O'Brien / Crandall 2005, p. 3), the dominance of management and managerial discourses are justified by their very existence. It is managers who selflessly look after organisations, the economy and society. For the sake of the whole, managers *must be* the ruling class—and should remain in charge.

This position becomes even stronger since managers are embedded in wider societal institutions and relationships. They have gained, secured and enlarged their social dominance against (but often with a great deal of support from) other social groups and classes—'managers are not alone in believing in managerial ideologies . . .' (Alvesson / Willmott 1992a, p. 7). For example, although quite different views and objectives do exist, Chapter 4 showed that managers are often successful in establishing common understandings and *interests* with external and internal stakeholders (Freeman 1983). They are aware of the image and expectations, fads and fashions within their organisation's environment and can shape the ways in which they, and their decisions and actions, are perceived and interpreted by others. In Chapter 3 it emerged that managers' *power* also stems from their close relationships with other actors representing powerful organisations, i.e. their 'social capital' (e.g. Gant et al. 2002, Nahapiet / Ghoshal 1998, Bourdieu 1983, Granovetter 1973). Finally, Chapter 5 revealed that the *ideology of management* has been developed and disseminated in ways which fit into the institutional rules of its environment (DiMaggio / Powell 1983, Meyer / Rowan 1977). The isomorphism which has been successfully established is not only about abstract systems and forces such as neo-liberal competition and managerial organisations, but also about actors' worldviews, including external powerful stakeholders' expectations and managers' own understanding and conduct of business. Managers are embedded in asymmetrical power relations within both organisations and society which 'systematically privilege the interests and viewpoints of some groups while silencing and marginalising others' (Levy et al. 2001, p. 2). This embeddedness in socio-economic structures supports the legitimacy of their roles and positions and *institutionally empowers* managers (Willmott 1987, p. 253, 1984, p. 350). In business and organisations, *managers are in the middle of a power web* which is a necessary precondition for their societal dominance.

Meanwhile, managers' overall power, interests and ideology are deeply embedded not only in organisational but also societal institutions. Based on Weber's class concept, it can therefore be said that managers are one of the new classes which have emerged in regulated capitalistic societies (Rowlinson et al. 2006, p. 691 referring to Galbraith 1967 and Chandler 1977). And managers are not only 'a' social class. In line with Social Dominance Theory (O'Brien / Crandall 2005, Sidanius et al., 2004) we are talking about a *dominant* social class. Burnham (1941, p. 155) defined "ruling class" as 'the group of persons which has (as a matter of *fact*, not necessarily of law or words or theory), as against the rest of the population, a special degree of control over access to the instruments of production and preferential treatment in the distribution of the products of those instruments'. Managers are privileged in both respects. They, indeed, have control over *all* instruments of production. That includes not only machinery and workforce, but also managerial concepts, organisation theory and business models, performance measurement and management systems, and organisational structures and processes. In addition, (most) managers also receive preferential treatment in every respect. They have the material privileges (high salaries, remuneration packages and annual bonuses with little or no relation to actual performances), intellectual privileges (participation in decision-making, access to information, and managerial tasks others are being excluded from), and social privileges (high status, self-image and societal discourses all underlying the importance of managers). Managers' prerogatives and dominance are endemic, systematic and comprehensive. Managerialism has reached *hegemonic* control and domination (Shrivastava 1986, p. 364).

CONCLUSIONS

The aim of this chapter was to bring together the results of the analysis carried out in Chapters 3 through 5 in order to establish the *theory of social dominance of managers based on power, interests and ideology*. The main aspects addressed were the following:

1) Managers dominate because their personal and structural power, their individual and group interests, and the ideology of management, fit together and jointly create a *comprehensive and multidimensional system of social dominance*. Within an organisational context, the system is based on a) roles and responsibilities, positions and privileges of managers / superiors, b) the functioning and obedience of their employees / subordinates, c) hierarchical and unjust organisational structures and processes, and d) isomorph relationships with socio-economic trends and powerful stakeholders within the environment. These four areas simultaneously constitute not only the managerial organisation but also the foundation and framework for managerial dominance. The 'theory of social dominance of managers' concentrates explicitly on the fact that managers have interests in dominating, that they have the power and control tools within hierarchical organisations to do so, and that both their interests and power are explained, justified, and concealed by an elaborated ideology of management.

2) The implications of such an approach go far beyond the individual manager. There are such strong and widespread commonalities amongst managers that it therefore often makes sense to use the 'group of managers' as the unit of analysis (which may be further differentiated into sub-groups of managers). However, the analysis revealed further common characteristics of managers which are highly relevant beyond organisational boundaries. There are good reasons for these including societal dimensions and consequences of the dominance of managers into the analysis. It then becomes appropriate to talk about the *class of managers*. Managers constitute a quite differentiated social class in themselves (in the Weberian sense). Their power, their

role-related interests and the commonly shared ideology of management create similar patterns exceeding the conditions of any specific organisational hierarchy, or responsibilities and positions within it. This result is of even greater importance because both the reasons for, and consequences of, managers' dominance can be identified within organisations *and* at a societal level.

3) Managers are not only a social class—we are talking about a *dominant* social class. Against the historical backcloth of corporate capitalism, managerialism, consumerism and globalisation, managers are now one of the most powerful, influential and established classes in most developed economies. Because their embeddedness in socio-economic structures supports the legitimacy of their roles and positions, managers are institutionally empowered.

All in all, the dominance of managers is of historical proportions. What we have witnessed on an epochal and global scale in the last decades is the *managerialisation* of our organisations, our societies, and our private affairs. This has taken place partly through the dissemination of the idea of management, and partly, but more importantly, through the creation of millions and millions of managerial positions. Managers dominate and are privileged not only as individuals or as special members of a particular organisation, but as a social class within society. In this sense, the dominance of managers as a class has the same society-shaping impact as the domination of earlier social classes. It differs little from the dominance and power of druids and priests in ancient societies, clergy and knights in medieval times, royals and aristocrats, landlords and merchants during feudalism, bourgeois and capitalists during capitalism or the political elites in communism or military regimes.

7 How Managers Create, Justify and Conduct Strategic Change in Their Organisation—A Case Study

> It is easy to persuade [the people] of a thing, but difficult to keep them in that persuasion. And so it is necessary to order things so that when they no longer believe, they can be made to believe by force.
>
> Machiavelli, in 'The Prince', 1513 (cited in Frank 2001, p. 476)

INTRODUCTION

This chapter uses a small case study to provide some evidence for the core aspects of managers' power, interests and ideology which have been analysed in the previous chapters. The case study is about a major strategic change initiative at a large Western European university—International University (IU)—which took place largely between 2002 and 2004.[1]

In 2002, a new Vice-Chancellor joined IU. She was keen to demonstrate 'leadership' and 'professionalism' and interpreted both concepts in an orthodox managerial way. Although the shift to managerialism had already been happening gradually over many years, it can be argued that this ideology was primarily introduced by the new Vice-Chancellor and her inner circle of senior managers. The plan was quite ambitious. Against the background of an allegedly more competitive and challenging business environment, IU should undergo major organisational changes in order to become a truly managerial organisation (e.g. Hellawell / Hancock 2001, p. 191). The prime objective of the strategic change initiative was the introduction of *New Public Management*, i.e. to make IU much more 'business-like'.[2]

This shift would involve changing IU's strategy, mission and vision, as well as its structures, processes, routines and outcomes. The new strategic orientation comprised various aspects, including rigorous student and market orientation, income and cost orientation, increasing efficiency, performance measurement and auditing systems. Moreover, the new strategy was meant to change how people did business and how they thought and acted. It was about changing people's worldviews and attitudes (e.g. Newton 2003, Ylijoki 2003, Martin et al. 2001, Austin et al. 1997). For example, Spencer-Matthews (2001, p. 52) described organisational change as 'the negotiation or the renegotiation of shared meaning about what is to be valued, believed in and aimed for'. In this sense, strategic change is (also) *cultural change*.[3] The whole strategic change initiative at IU was one more of the innumerable examples of the imposition of neo-conservative and managerial ideologies on large organisations (e.g. Aronowitz / Giroux 1985, pp. 163–183). The aim was to transform it into *a typical managerial organisation*. And it worked. This initiative was a fantastic opportunity to witness the ideology of management 'at work' and the (increasing) dominance of managers 'in the making'.

Officially, or at first sight, the strategic change initiative was based on the worldviews, perceptions and strategic understandings[4] of senior management. It was about how they perceived changes in IU's business environment and how the organisation should respond to these challenges. It was about how the organisation did, or should do business in order to be successful (e.g. McAuley et al. 2000, p. 88). However, a second look reveals that the usual buzzword games played at boardroom level were much more than mere strategy development; they were also, if not primarily about gaining, keeping and increasing dominance within the organisation. Change rhetoric was largely used to construct an ideological basis for claims of supremacy. The analysis reveals how its proponents justified and communicated the change initiative by using the usual rhetorical repertoire of ideology. However, behind this were the particular individual and group interests of certain senior managers, used ideologically to justify their particular individual ideas and aspirations. The new strategic change initiative was largely a tool for strengthening their position in clashes of cosmologies and internal organisational politics (e.g. Ferdinand 2004, Coopey / Burgoyne 2000, Burns 1961), in order to protect and increase their own power and spheres of influence at the expense of others—even at the expense of the whole. In this sense, the aims and objectives of this investigation are as follows:

1. To reveal the different perceptions, interpretations and understandings of IU's senior managers concerning issues of strategic importance
2. To understand how the introduction and implementation of new strategic objectives and managerialistic change management were explained and justified at senior level
3. To reveal the competing understandings and interests behind such concepts
4. To investigate how managerial terms and concepts are used for internal battles between senior managers in order to pursue their interests, increase their power and influence, and promote the adoption of their ideological convictions
5. To shed some light on the factual, intended and / or unintended consequences of the strategic change initiative

Because of the nature of the issues to be investigated, a qualitative approach was chosen. Twenty semi-structured interviews were undertaken with most of IU's academic and administrative senior managers (Vice-Chancellor, Pro-Vice-Chancellors, Deans of Faculties, senior managers of administration and service units) and one external consultant. These interviews took place between March and September 2004. The interviews were recorded, transcribed, qualitatively analysed, and the findings summarised. In addition, internal documents (strategy and vision papers, university and unit plans, minutes of academic bodies stemming from 1996 onwards, internal reports, reports from external consultants) provided further information and allowed many statements to be cross-checked. Finally, academic literature, in particular case studies on managers' perceptions and change initiatives at large organisations, allowed for triangulation of the data and a better foundation for the findings.

JUSTIFICATION OF THE NEW STRATEGY VIA COSMOLOGICAL RHETORIC—"SCARING PEOPLE HELPS"

Since the new strategic change initiative meant far-reaching changes for the whole organisation, the proponents were keen to justify the initiative as strongly as possible. Kezar / Eckel (2002, p. 299) point out that change 'often invites risk and an uncertain future or destination, so having a compelling reason for change and a proposed direction is crucial'. Usually, these 'compelling reasons' are "found" outside the social system because this draws attention away from the leaders and their power position and strengthens group coherence in the face of external threats.

In the particular case of IU, all senior managers seemed to be very aware of, and concerned with changes in IU's business environment. They shared the opinion that the Higher Education sector as a whole had become a much more difficult environment, and this meant that IU operated and had to survive in

> '. . . an environment that is much, much, much more competitive than it has ever been before.'

Because of this alleged increased pressure and competition and the much more challenging business environment (Newton, 2003, p. 428, Ellis, 1998, p. 231), proponents of the change initiative therefore argued that the decision to opt for the new strategy was not a *choice* (or *their* choice!) but an *unavoidable necessity.*

> Now, what you are going to do is make people realize that actually there is no real choice here. I mean we just have to change at the times, there are driving forces, there is a need for change.

IU *had to* change significantly. Moreover, the New Public Management strategy package at IU was based on the 'TINA principle'—'There is no alternative!' Famously introduced by the then British Prime Minister Margaret Thatcher as a very general principle, it is flexible enough to be used by ambitious leaders of all political colours and in many different settings. According to this principle, even if the proponents wanted to, they could not choose but to respond to the challenges in the particular way they suggest. They, and all others, have to accept 'reality'—or rather what *they* portray as 'the reality'. References to forces outside a social system which serve as explanations and justifications for (far-reaching) decisions are a typical sign of ideology. This is especially true when these forces are being portrayed as "natural" and "beyond humans' abilities to withstand or handle them". Suddaby / Greenwood (2005, p. 55) call this 'cosmological rhetoric'. According to them:

> an emphatic theme embedded in cosmological rhetoric is that the changes originate from a source more powerful than the affected community of actors and audiences and that resistance to such change is futile, if not outright dangerous. In contrast to teleological rhetoric, the model of change articulated here is not internally driven by the agency of immediate actors but is imposed from the outside as part of the natural unfolding of the universe.

As in most managerial rhetoric, in the case of IU, references to 'market forces' served as such a cosmological rhetoric; 'the market' (and the 'forces' at work there) explained and justified the necessity of the new strategy and the inevitability of decisions related to it. Like many other ideologies, the ideology of management portrays a *bad and dangerous* present. In belief systems like managerialism, it always helps to portray the environment as hostile, dangerous and frightening, and to have an 'enemy outside'—ideally one that threatens the survival of the whole. People who are scared are more willing to change, or at least to accept what the grand leaders suggest. According to Van Loon (2001, p. 297), 'major organizational change is really only likely in the face of a truly difficult situation. The people in the organization must be genuinely afraid for its survival if they are to support radical change.' Whether or not the (allegedly) irresistible and dramatic forces in the environment are real or not is not really important—*it is almost irrelevant whether the 'threat' or 'the enemy' really exists.* The crucial aspect is how convincingly and colourfully the threat is described, communicated and perceived (Bartunek, 1984, p. 364)—preferably as powerful, bad and dangerous as the 'bogie man' for children. If this is done successfully, this constructed social reality can serve as evidence—and justification—for the change proponents' plans to challenge peoples' existing values and interpretive schemes. It aims to put people in a permanent state of fear, alertness and worry. The 'enemy outside' then becomes internalised—an 'enemy in people's heads'. It creates ambiguity and uncertainty, and the need to find new schemata to cope with this new situation (Balogun / Johnson, 2004, p. 525). And, indeed, the fact that the top management of IU repeatedly portrayed the environment in a threatening way helped their cause immensely (Van Loon, 2001, p. 296, Whittington, 1992, p. 701, Bartunek, 1984, pp. 356–357).

ISOMORPHISM BETWEEN THE NEW STRATEGY, EXTERNAL EXPECTATIONS, TRENDS AND FASHIONS

As market-oriented as some of IU's leaders wished to appear, they were at the same time unwilling to take much personal risk. They used widely established and accepted business terms and management concepts to address the strategic or organisational issues. In fact, IU's top management based its whole change initiative on seemingly safe textbook approaches and used the usual mainstream business terminology. IU's Vice-Chancellor explained:

> I mean, I used basic business principles to evolve the priorities that we've got now and there is nothing very original about that. It's just an application of how you are doing your business . . . improving the management information, improving the people's understanding of how things work, improving people's discipline with respect to the market.

As the Vice-Chancellor said, there was nothing really original about the new strategy. It was a carbon copy of the neo-liberal / neo-conservative managerialism which dominates private sector organisations, and which has been introduced to public sector organisations all over the globe (e.g. Deem 2001, pp. 10–13, Vickers / Kouzmin 2001, pp. 109–110, McAuley et al. 2000, p. 89, Cohen et al. 1999, pp. 477–478). There are many reasons for this trend. One explanation is that management concepts are introduced to organisations 'not so much to execute their tasks more efficiently but to gain legitimacy or cultural support' (Staw / Epstein 2000, p. 524). Like many other universities in industrialised countries, IU is under the thorough scrutiny of external funding and auditing bodies (e.g. AACSB, AMBA, EQUIS, RAE). Its senior management is therefore keen to present the organisation to these powerful stakeholders in ways which address their concerns and meet their expectations. According to Coopey / Burgoyne (2000, p. 873), 'to achieve legitimacy an organization needs to mirror the institutional patterning generated in the environment, often in a variety of social fields. These effects result not only from direct control mechanisms (e.g. as exercised by central government) but also through constitutive processes created by environmental meaning systems.' In this sense, IU's new strategy could be seen as a link between its proponents' intentions and perceptions, and those external institutions which are highly relevant to the organisation (Pettigrew 2002, p. 105 referring to Wildavsky 1964).

Nonetheless, expectations from different external stakeholders can be variable and contradictory. There is, therefore, no automatic choice whatsoever concerning which strategy senior managers 'have to' adopt. Which issues they refer to, in what ways, and by which criteria they formulate an organisation's strategy is entirely at managers' discretion. The managerialistic strategy of IU was only one of many possible strategies. This is supported by the fact that at senior management level there were still claims for *alternative* strategic directions. For example, that the organisation should be more driven by research and teaching interests, and therefore by very different values and performance criteria than by the dictation of de facto or assumed market requirements.

> There is still a lot questioning whether those [financial figures, student numbers] are the primary metrics or the secondary metrics, whether the university is making money in order to thrive to do what it really should be doing, which is educating people.

> A number of academics who have been here for a long time were quite open about the fact that they don't see why we should be driven by student numbers and income. We should be driven by research, feeding into teaching, teaching about things that they considered to be strategically important, that can change policy, that can have an impact on practice, or, frankly, things they just enjoy working on.

Obviously, such positions do not correspond with the prevailing ideology of market orientation and management. Howie (2005, p. 7) summed it up: 'The language of quality is able to silence all that might be critical and suppress any disturbance on the calm waters of managerial unanimity by rendering the non-compliant individual as untrustworthy, incompetent and irrational.' Meanwhile, the official and dominant IU strategy seemed to be legitimized simply by "how the world is". *In the age of hedonistic individualism, market economy, profit-driven corporations, globalisation, neo-liberalism and the consumer society, who could be against such apparently self-evident business principles?*

IU's senior managers were acutely aware of all of these perspectives. The growing impression is that the proponents of IU's strategic change initiative followed managerial fads and fashions not only because these are dominant, but actually for the sake of their own personal interests; using the latest managerial concepts signals professionalism, a pro-active approach, even innovation and leadership. For both internal and external stakeholders, these are all crucial criteria for judging the quality of the management of an organisation. To 'do as the Romans do' ensures you not only a safe passage, but is also one of the most efficient routes to promotion and to increasing your own market value.

THE JUSTIFICATION OF LEADERSHIP

Although the development into a more managerialistic institution had already been happening at IU for some years, this latest change initiative was particularly introduced and shaped by the current Vice-Chancellor. As one senior manager commented:

The tone has been set from the Vice-Chancellor downwards and that's the way of thinking of things.

The (claimed) prerogatives of initiating 'strategic change', of interpreting the environment in certain ways, and of directing the change initiative all underline one crucial aspect; *leadership*. The rhetoric about strategy reflects and justifies not only senior management's responsibilities for leading the organisation, but the importance of management itself. In this sense, the top-down approach used by IU's new Vice-Chancellor and her inner circle of change proponents was just another example of aspirational management keen to demonstrate a certain type of "leadership"—*hierarchical leadership*.[5] According to *this* understanding of leadership, there are the selected few who know, and the many who do not know. "Naturally", the former have to guide the latter. For example, Austin / Currie (2003, p. 236) stress that 'it is important that leaders take the time to define for and communicate to their teams which things will change and which will stay the same'. Strategic change, therefore, is the prerogative of the (powerful) 'upper echelons' (e.g. Kezar / Eckel 2002, p. 298, Schwenk 2002, p. 179). Gill (2003, p. 309) concluded: 'If change is a process of taking an organisation (or a nation) on a journey from its current state to a desired future state and dealing with all the problems that arise along the journey, then change is about leadership as well as management'. IU's change initiative was based on this very hierarchical understanding of how change has to be managed. It was an 'invasionary' approach to change, whereby senior managers and other change experts push change initiatives into organisations (e.g. Clegg / Walsh 2004, p. 223, Brooks / Bate 1994, p. 185).

In addition to be hierarchical, leadership has to be *tough*. And, again, this toughness is claimed to be purely for the sake of the greater good (at least, this is how the proponents of change see it). Austin / Currie (2003, p. 236) provide a typical example of such thinking: 'One of the by-products of change is confusion, and without clear communication of what is and is not over, people are likely to do one of three things: not dare give up anything and burn out trying to do everything, make their own decisions on what to keep and give up, toss out everything that was done in the past.' In other words: If people dare to make their own decisions and / or try to do what *they* think is best, this could cause (serious) damage to the "grand plan" of the change initiative. More importantly, it could threaten superiors' dominance. In this sense, for the proponents of managerialism there is not only an 'enemy outside' but also an 'enemy inside', i.e. the people. Therefore, the proponents *have to* be tough, they *have to* get their agenda through in order to prevent 'damage' to the grand plan. The Vice-Chancellor made it very clear.

I mean, people have different approaches to strategy but we are absolutely fierce.

. . . we did actually force them through because we had to, we had no choice. And you get to a certain degree, but then you actually do have to force things through in my experience.

According to this view, *not one* of the new strategic priorities could be left out in the realisation of the change process and achieving the objectives. Another manager explained:

> And it would be very difficult to imagine that any one or two could be taken out and separated from the rest as important, because a lot of them have to be achieved in parallel. Otherwise it doesn't really matter whether they are achieved. . . . And many of them are really non-negotiable. That's not a question of, say, we'll do this and than we'll do that and then we'll do that. They have to be done in parallel.

Of course, if there can be only one right way, all the committees, meetings, communication and discussions, all the scenario planning, and all the drafts on strategy and vision do not really make any difference. The 'grand plan' is already decided. This is the second TINA principle. It is not only the environment that imposes the need for a particular change on the organisation; the organisation can change in only one way—the way the proponents of change, particular the leader(s)!, suggest.

Together, the hierarchical understanding of change management ('being clear') and the toughness with which it is justified, communicated, defended and implemented by its proponents ('being fierce'), are core parts of the conservative ideology of *hierarchical leadership*, i.e. the relationship between leaders who are allegedly knowledgeable, insightful and skilled—and those who aren't. This managerial rhetoric was used by the Vice-Chancellor time and time again not only to get her agenda through but also to underline and strengthen her position. IU's Vice-Chancellor was very ambitious and career-oriented. She had a track-record of tactical career-moves and battles at institutions where she had worked before. And she had learned to play the leadership card almost to perfection. The rhetoric of leadership plays automatically into the hands of superiors and strengthens their power-base because it communicates the socially constructed image of a strong leader. At the same time, (cynical) references to higher values and the sake of the whole shall conceal the personal and group interests of those using this rhetoric to their advantage. Conservative ideologies such as hierarchical leadership can be used by anyone with average intellectual capabilities and above-average "moral flexibility"—regardless of political colour, race, nationality, religion or gender.

THE REACTIONS AND VIEWPOINTS OF RELATIVELY POWERFUL OPPONENTS OF CHANGE

Initially, the proponents of the new strategic change initiative thought that rhetoric about an increasingly competitive environment and financial pressure as well as the use of 'tried and tested' mainstream strategy and management concepts would be sufficient to convince people of the necessity of change. Nonetheless, despite almost two years of internal "communication" at IU, the change initiative was still receiving few standing ovations, on the contrary; opposition and resistance emerged in various forms. As indicated above, the new strategic change initiative at IU was largely cultural. It was about re-designing the organisation according to the principles of the ideology of management. Of course, this was a very different set of values from, for example, the more traditional academic work ethos. In this section, we will first look at how some comparatively powerful opponents reacted. One or two of IU's senior managers voiced some fundamental criticism of the new approach and referred to a somewhat 'academic tradition'. One Dean stated that

> the university ought to be a kind of academic community, a self-regulating academic community in which academic freedom is paramount in relation to which management so to speak is seen as an intrusion and a bother, and that's its academic values and so on . . .

At IU, however, as in many other public sector organisations and even private sector organisations, these beliefs were already in sharp decline and had become too weak to compete for supremacy with the prevailing managerialistic ideology. References to an 'academic tradition' were no longer a consistent set of values but were rather based on personal beliefs and sentimental memories idealising a past which probably never was. If they had not already left the institution, people with such "non-managerial" views were usually simply ignored and marginalised. Worthington / Hodgson (2005, p. 98) explain this further:

> Those who do so, suggesting for example that the primary 'purpose of education is (or should be) to develop critical thought', find themselves framed not as radicals but as conservatives, whose views are thus seen as an attempt to preserve an outdated intellectual value-system that is incongruous to the needs of equity, consumers and the new global economy. Those who resist quality, in other words, are likely to be perceived as suffering from 'golden ageism', or, worse, as undesirables who are either unwilling or incapable of making the necessary changes and readjustments to university teaching and working practices deemed necessary to achieve service improvement.

The ideology of management and the dominance of managers were already quite prevalent at IU. With the new Vice-Chancellor's change initiative, they reached hegemonic status. This initiative was only the final, but decisive push—the last nail in the coffin. In most of our organisations, or even at societal level, there is barely any elaborated model or convincing alternative programme (anymore) which can really challenge and compete with the market / management ideology. As a consequence, in a longer period of strategic and structural changes like the one imposed by powerful leaders at IU, the momentum is on the side of the proponents. The opportunities to oppose it are therefore fairly limited. Most people, therefore, do not openly resist but have learned to cope with the prevailing ideology on a tactical / operational level. This was also the situation at IU. Some opponents criticised procedural aspects of how change had been managed and communicated at a very basic level:

> So, the need for change was there, definitely. I'm not suggesting it wasn't there, but I think the management of the process of change was poor. . . . , not enough people understanding what change meant, there wasn't a proper explanation of the benefits of change, and I thought that was poorly done and I hope the university learns from that, ...

Similarly, some managers questioned the quality of the information on which the change initiative was based. In particular, crucial data with regard to the market or other external developments were perceived as not entirely solid. Student markets were seen as quite volatile and the business environment in general as uncertain. As one senior manager indicated:

> It's too diffuse at the moment and it makes it difficult capturing exactly what the market is.

> You have to make the decision on the basis of very good information as to whether you are in a cycle or in a trend. And you can argue either. . . . I believe that we are in a cycle. . . . But that's a business gamble.

Although uncertainty is always the case (e.g. Diefenbach 2004, pp. 558–559), it was obviously used by managers to question some aspects of the new strategy. However, all of this criticism related to "technicalities" rather than the main rationale or fundamental assumptions of the change initiative. At senior management level, most discussions, if not clashes, were about different interpretations of numbers, their implications and which conclusions could be drawn from them (Bartunek 1984, p. 368). In most cases, the opponents did not get far with their doubts. A better chance for criticism was the validity of the data—particularly of the ones which were presented or used by the proponents of the change initiative.

> And I know from what I've heard talking to people that . . . the financial crisis is being manufactured. That it's a story being made up. People are massaging the numbers to try and create change that isn't really needed. And there is a lot of resistance to that change.

The atmosphere between senior proponents and opponents of the change initiative steadily deteriorated, leading to increasing mutual mistrust. What was "objective" data for one senior manager were "blatant lies", or at least "biased interpretations" for others. The allegedly 'objective' description of the organisation's environment was subject to interest-oriented interpretations and politicised debates about the meaning and implications for the organisation. As Waller et al. (1995, p. 964) explained: 'Knowing the environment is only a means, getting rewarded for performance happens internally and is an end in itself'. For all managers involved it was clear that numbers and evidence were used within the context of organisational politics, i.e. most argumentation was driven by personal interests and (relative) power of the parties involved. In the end, it was not markets or the welfare of the organisation, but internal politics and personal advantages which mattered most for most managers.

In this sense, some Deans even went a step further. On many occasions, they made a case for more empowerment and argued for the principle of subsidiarity with more autonomy and resources for faculties. It could even be argued that most Deans had a different business model in mind—a model in sharp contrast to the Vice-Chancellor's and other administrative senior managers' idea of an administered university. In contrast to the widespread portrayal of academics as comparatively 'action-averse', many Deans regarded themselves not only as *academic* managers but also as *business* managers, even as entrepreneurs. They saw their faculties as not only serving existing markets but as willing to enter or create new markets, and to launch new products—or so they claimed. For this, they not 'only' wanted the resources and support needed to carry out their daily business in an even more 'entrepreneurial' manner; they wanted autonomy, discretion and responsibilities to be institutionalised further down the management structure.

> I think one thing you've got to do is to give responsibility to people, like myself, who have an understanding of the overall strategic constraints but also have an understanding of the local subject-based systems, and dynamics. So, that argues for a much more federal type of government and management structures than we have at the moment. . . .

To a certain extent one could interpret these claims as "fundamental opposition" to the Vice-Chancellor's strategic change initiative and her understanding of leadership. And many, both proponents and opponents, probably saw it that way. However, these claims and discourses still took place within the ideology of management. The fundamental idea of the managerialistic change initiative itself was not questioned. Moreover, clashes and disputes between parties, fights and mistrust between superiors and subordinates, and opposition and resistance within organisational settings are some of the fundamental assumptions and rationales of a management ideology of management (as well as of neo-classical market theory, neo-liberal political theory and other conservative ideologies). In particular, senior managers are expected to (officially and publicly) fight for the units they are responsible for. This often fits nicely with personal interests such as career aspirations or psychological desires (or needs) to play the power game. As long as people are complaining about procedural aspects, questioning data and information, or even making (strong) claims for more empowerment, autonomy, discretion or responsibilities, they present no real problem or danger to the managerial system. On the contrary, they are behaving *exactly* as anticipated, even expected by their superiors. By following and realising this public transcript (Scott 1990), the opponents did not do much more than play into the hands of the proponents of the managerial change initiative. They simply played their part of it. As we explore in the next two sections, this is in fact understandable, since major organisational changes can have a considerable impact on people's position and future. There is simply too much at stake to make decisions (solely) on moral grounds or idealistic beliefs.

TO CENTRALISE OR NOT TO CENTRALISE?

This section provides a concrete example of the managerialistic notion of top-down strategic change and hierarchical leadership, as well as of the functional forms of opposition and resistance analysed above. It will show that these are not only rhetoric: ideology-, power- and interest-oriented controversies (can) have real consequences for all parties involved. At the centre of the disputes around IU's strategic change initiative, a functional or organisational issue emerged: centralisation. It became 'the battlefield' of the whole change process and the place where both proponents and opponents drew their lines in the sand.

From the proponents' (the Vice-Chancellor and her inner circle) point of view, the basic idea of centralisation sounded quite convincing. In a large organisation like IU, there is considerable duplication of effort in its units (faculties). Centralising activities which are crucial for the organisation as a whole as well as for its parts will reduce inefficiency, increase productivity and save money. In contrast, some Deans portrayed IU as an already centralised organisation and saw (further) shifts towards the centre not as a solution but as part of the problem. One Dean compared this trend of centralisation to what happened in Western European manufacturing in the 1960s. There was a strong feeling amongst Deans that the centre provided little support, and insufficient resources, subsidiarity and empowerment. They portrayed the relation between centre and periphery as too much top-down intervention. Many initiatives from the top were regarded with suspicion and interpreted as interference and restriction of faculties' elbowroom. These perceptions are consistent with empirical findings elsewhere (e.g. Newton 2003, p. 438, Newton 2002, p. 190, Cohen et al. 1999, pp. 473, 480). Several senior managers complained not only about 'technical' or 'managerial' constraints, but about increasing distrust between the centre and the periphery. It is probably not very surprising that the senior managers around the Vice-Chancellor saw this issue rather differently. But it is interesting to see how they responded to such complaints. There was not one consistent pattern, but several, quite different responses.

One strategy was to conceal the issue. A widespread pattern of response among senior managers which emerged during the interviews was the provision of statements in accordance with the official strategy and references to official documents. There were quite obvious attempts to avoid addressing the issue of power and control, and to deny tensions and differences between the centre and the periphery. This was especially true for senior managers at the centre of power, or those close to it or anxious to appear in accordance with the official party line.

In a second version, a few of these senior managers straightforwardly rejected the complaints that the centre was striving for more influence, power and control. They claimed

> . . . that we go for subsidiarity wherever possible.

In sharp contrast to this, a third position was to describe such struggles and the existence of different views as quite common for organisations.

> I think that exists in most organisations to some degree. Virtually every sizeable organisation has some sort of centre and periphery.

A fourth position was to lay stress on the fact that one is very aware of it, that it is acknowledged as a serious problem and that one is interested in structural reforms.

> That's one of the reasons we're looking at the faculty structure is that you want to allow faculty structures to make decisions without continual reference to the centre within broad policy frameworks, and at the moment we probably call in too many decisions to be made centrally.

Fifthly, one administrative senior manager was very clear.

> We can't have everybody doing what they want.

Obviously, there were different ideas about centralisation and de-centralisation, about a strong centre, empowered faculties and their relationship. On the one hand it was about 'real issues': 'technical problems' such as allocation of resources, financial contributions to the centre, support of faculties' initiatives, decision-making processes and subsidiarity. On the other hand, there were a range of relevant aspects coming into play.

One of the most far-reaching organisational change initiatives at IU had been the *centralisation of marketing*. Whereas faculties either had previously had their own marketing unit or no marketing at all, it was the idea of the proponents of change to create one single marketing unit responsible for (almost) all activities in this field throughout the whole university. One senior manager explained

> that there were over 100 staff spread all over the university often repeating parts of what other people were doing, . . . so, there was a clear line of development there to bring them together, to rationalise the work and to deliver services that we've never had before. . . . ., so that's one example where clearly centralisation, I think, will bring significant benefit across the university and give us a better marketing function, a more targeted marketing function than we had before and more universal, across all faculties and schools.

External consultants, who had been employed to assist the university in reviewing its marketing activities, recommended the centralisation of marketing.[6] The decision to centralise was made by the Vice-Chancellor immediately after (or perhaps before?) the presentation of their report in March 2003. However, in its first year, the new centralised marketing unit was busier organising itself, formulating strategies, gathering data, and producing reports about its activities than actually doing any marketing. One critical senior manager mentioned that

> it is much less marketing done than before. They seem to spend all of their time appointing staff and organising themselves. There seems to be much less effort of marketing of our faculty's courses. . . . And all of the other faculties are making the same complaint . . . Certainly for the first year it has made the situation worse. Whether this is temporary or not I have no idea . . .

At the same time there had been dramatic changes in student numbers.[7] In May 2000 'a 10% growth in student numbers from 1999 to 2000' and in July 2000 an 'assumed growth rate of 4% in student numbers' were reported. In December 2002 'first concerns were expressed at the inclusion of a target of 3–5% for student recruitment growth'. In January 2003 it became clear 'that recruitment of new students was below target'. In March 2003 the Vice-Chancellor reported 'that the University had not reached the student number target' in this year and again in December 2003 the Vice-Chancellor expressed 'a concern that student recruitment would not meet forecasts'. In 2004 the top management kept silent about the numbers: one Pro-Vice-Chancellor (Students) reported that he was 'confident that the University would be able to meet its current student recruitment targets this year (i.e. an increase of 3%)'. However, in March 2005 the Vice-Chancellor informed that 'current predictions indicated that the University would be 4.2% below its student recruitment target'. In June 2005 'the latest (June) forecast of student numbers indicated that the University was likely to have a shortfall of 6.3% on the 2004/05 target, with a shortfall of 12.2% for new students'. Although the numbers changed every week, it could be argued that centralising marketing had so far led to more *in*efficiency, i.e. the decrease in outcome was greater than a possible reduction of costs and effort. One of the major reasons for this development was seen in the reduction of the close relationship between faculty management and marketing people, which was previously a collaboration based on trust and joint sense-making:

> When there was a marketing group within the faculty before the changes, we were—as I call it—hard wired. The knowledge was local, there was responsibility within the unit for all aspects of marketing . . . and we also used to attend all sorts of committees, meetings and whatever. So we were very close to the academic community, administrative community, to the market place, and we were dedicated to the faculty. So, there was an easy knowledge interface. People exchanged information very easily and readily from the faculty, from the non-academics to the marketing staff.

The underlying rationale is the idea of the generation and use of local and socially embedded knowledge. One theory in knowledge management is that information should be interpreted and decisions should be made where the knowledge is, i.e. where people are situated in their daily context of work. In the face of a changing and more complex environment, it is, therefore, about *de*-centralisation, not centralisation. In sharp contrast, there was no shortage of other explanations for the above described change from 10% growth to a 6% or even 12% decline in student numbers—particularly from the Vice-Chancellor and the inner circle of top management who were behind the idea to centralise marketing. These explanations included that it is the government (Higher Education politics, 'the consequence of new fees and loan arrangements'), the markets (in which the university is operating), the competitors (strategy and fee changes introduced by other universities), the customers ('changing patterns of registration made forecasting difficult'), or *operational* reasons within the university ('There had been marketing problems and difficulties in translating reservations to registrations.'). Whatever the 'real' reasons for the decline, there were countless further suggestions for possible solutions, *all* at *operational* level. Moreover, top management and the marketing unit increased their activities to raise the profile about the marketing activities that had been launched. The information about the activities of the new centralised marketing unit increased almost as fast as the student numbers declined. Finally, the Vice-Chancellor made it clear that this was everyone's problem. 'The whole University community should work collegially over this issue since it affected the future of the University.' Well, not quite for all; the Marketing and Sales Director (who had been appointed in early 2001 to centralise marketing with all the support of the new Vice-Chancellor) had to leave in December

2004! Ironically, only three months before he left IU 'voluntarily', he told me in an interview:

> and some people fell out, they couldn't cope with the new structure, which you can expect in a change process because those that can't deal with it go elsewhere or drop out, and it's quite a normal model. So, it was encouraging to see one or two drop out, I'm not saying it personally was, but it meant that we were making sufficient change for it to be impactful in the way it needed to be.

At the same time, one Dean, who had criticised the centralisation of marketing the most, also left the university "voluntarily" in order to "have more time to spend with his family". The revolution eats its children . . .

There were also conflicting views on how marketing activities would develop in the future. The proponents were convinced that the backlash was only temporary and that the advantages had already started to gain momentum. In contrast, some of the Deans saw serious damage being done to their business, as well as to the whole university, and they believed that it would take years to repair this. Whatever the factual developments might be, there will be always different interpretations of possible reasons and implications. The 'facts', if any, do not count very much in such political battles—and neither do the theoretical principles of neo-liberalism and New Public Management. The proponents of managerialism choose their business strategy opportunistically from a range of inconsistent basic assumptions. Centralisation of IU's marketing had become a highly controversial and politicised issue. It had become the battleground for senior managers and their ideas about how IU was to be organised strategically. The 'technical' aspects of the problem were only of minor importance: the real issues were keeping or increasing power and control, protecting fiefdoms and spheres of influence. As one Dean explained:

> It has become more extreme in the last few years. And it has become more extreme under the current Vice-Chancellor. Primarily, I would argue because we had a financial crisis which [the Vice-Chancellor] used to access and gain greater power and control. So, it has been, in my opinion, manipulated to increase centralisation.

Hellawell / Hancock (2001, p. 192) also found that 'these VCs operated as though the universities were . . . originally designated as "power cultures"'. In the managerial organisation there are permanent tensions between the centre and the periphery, between units and departments, concerning authority, power, control over resources, or other key policy decisions (Kirkpatrick et al. 2005, p. 165). Rhetorical references to 'efficiency', 'economies of scale', 'market orientation' or similar buzzwords are only foils in those fights. '*Who runs the organisation?*' *is the real question.* There are, therefore, interests at stake that do not allow any of the parties involved to step back. So far, the centre has won the battle at IU.

'UNABLE' OR 'UNWILLING' CHANGE OPPONENTS—THE NEED FOR GUIDANCE

As the previous section indicated, the factual results of the new strategic change initiative were anything but convincing. Despite all the effort and resources put into the initiative, it took much longer—and delivered less—than had been promised and hoped for. However, as the proponents of managerialism had developed the new strategy and other ideas "by the book", in their views there could not have been any major problems with the objectives themselves or their implementation. The reasons, therefore, *must lie on the human side of the change process*. This section now focuses on the employees: how they had been perceived by the proponents of change and how they reacted to the change initiative as a whole. As one senior manager explained:

> Things have got to change and the pace of change is getting quicker, and people find that very difficult here. There isn't a change culture here. There is no culture of change here; they don't like change. Most people find it difficult, but there is a fundamental—it's not fear of change here—it's almost a feeling of indifference, nothing is really going to change, it's not really going to change, I'm never going to lose my job, little things will change, management will make some bad mistakes and then we'll go back to square one. It's unhealthy as an organisation in that respect.
>
> . . . we are in a very settled community. If you live in [name of the town] and you work in [name of the town] and come to your office every day it's not immediately clear to you that you should change.

According to the proponents of the strategic change initiative, people stayed too long in the same job at IU, felt too comfortable, and were therefore simply resisting necessary change because of indifference and apathy (e.g. Brooks / Bate 1994). From this point of view, resistance to change was cast as 'negative, backward looking, self-serving, and based on emotional, and thereby inappropriate, reactions' (Clegg / Walsh, 2004, p. 227). Nonetheless, for subordinates or less powerful people, turning their backs on it and keeping their heads down might be quite a sensible tactic. Opposing change creates personal risk and anxiety, but supporting change too openly, too enthusiastically, or simply too early, also bears risks—particularly if you take into account that the next strategic change initiative is already around the corner and power constellations might shift again. In this sense, people have simply learned to live with managerialistic change initiatives in pragmatic terms. They listen more or less carefully to all the change rhetoric, make up their own minds and find ways to bypass it in their daily routines. One practical, and very widespread, solution is to agree to all (change) rhetoric and initiatives but to try and avoid any direct consequences for one's own affairs. I call this form of indirect and hidden resistance *NIMBY tactics* ('Not in my backyard!'). For example, one Dean mentioned that

> it's relatively easy to get agreement that we need to change. It's actually pretty easy to get agreement in the fact that those people over there need to change, but it's damn near impossible to get agreement with the fact that my bit needs to change too.

NIMBY tactics can be seen as one of the rational responses of less powerful people to the TINA principle of forceful leaders. Now it could be argued that such tactics, attitudes and behaviour of many subordinates are not welcomed either by the proponents of the ideology of management in general, or managerial change initiatives in particular. For example, according to Ellis (1998, p. 227), 'Resistance to change and individual fear of the unknown are well documented and understood to be a major barrier to the introduction of cultural renewal and challenge'. Yet although it sounds paradoxical, 'unable' and / or 'unwilling', people actually fit very well into the managerial ideology of change management! They are simply yet another reason and justification for the change initiative. In fact they are a reason for *more* "initiative" and "management"; since people are obviously either unable or unwilling to change and adapt to the new order, it is therefore the leaders' responsibility to improve people's change capabilities (Karp, 2005, p. 88). The allegedly sluggish response of the many requires "clear" leadership and "determined" leaders. It is the leaders, and only the leaders, who see the wider picture. They know what is best for both the organization and the people, can develop a 'well thought-out acceptance management' (Bruch et al., 2005, p. 102), and are able to shape 'the sense-making activities of others' (Samra-Fredericks, 2000, p. 249). As Willmott, 1997, p. 1353 explained: 'Rubbishing the workforce as short-sighted and self-interested enables managers to secure and sustain their position and prerogative as the sole trustees and defenders of "business objectives" who, according to their self-serving rhetoric, are not "self-interested"'. The people's resistance is interpreted by the proponents of change management as evidence that change is right and necessary, that clear leadership and tough leaders are required, and that their opponents only need more 'guidance'. In this sense, blaming the people for their "resistance" serves simultaneously as a justification for the

- managerial ideology of change ('We have to change their attitudes because they are obviously not able to cope with today's challenges!'),
- paternalistic version of leadership ('They need guidance!') and

- privileged roles and positions of the leaders ('Since we are the only ones who really know and have understood the grand plan, it is us- and only us!—who can guide the people!').

Moreover, the idea of providing 'guidance' means overcoming resistance, coping with unable or unwilling people and getting them to do things they otherwise would not do. At the same time, it is about "educating" and changing people: to make them able and willing to behave as expected and to 'enthusiastically' and 'pro-actively' support the new agenda. In this sense, IU's new strategic change initiative didn't simply cut deeply into its organisational structures and processes. It was possibly even more about changing (parts of) people's schemata, their mindsets, beliefs and attitudes. It was about changing how people think and act. As one senior manager explained:

> . . . this is a gradual change process over two or three years about at- titude, behaviour, ways of thinking, ways decisions are made. It's a culture change.

> It is about hearts and minds and beliefs . . . Really leading institutions, the real winners, tap into their staff's emotions and not just their ratio- nal thinking, ...

Hence, under the leadership and guidance of the change proponents, people *have to* change, regardless of whether they are 'unable' or 'unwilling'. And they have to change in a particular way.

> . . ., how do you live the brand? And if a brand's about being modern, about being responsive, about being flexible, about being seen exter- nally as being that, then the kind of behaviour you'd expect people to model would be behaviour in which people were more outward- focussed, people were more willing to part with other institutions, on the phone people were more responsive, people were more willing to perhaps go the extra mile . . . .

It requests *additional* effort from people—to do more, to do better. People need to develop (almost) entrepreneurial attitudes—of course, under the guidance and surveillance, command and control of the change leaders. *People not only have to function well within the managerial organisa- tion—they have to (publicly) live the ideology of management.*

Because of the ideology of management's hegemonic status and the dom- inance of managers, most subordinates have no choice but to buy into the ideas of the change initiative, behave and act accordingly, and to adapt to the new order. If they are not willing to change (or at least are not able to pretend to do so!), they have to face the consequences. At the same time, managers are expected to do everything in order to 'minimize the effects of this resistance'. Techniques such as effective communication of the justification behind the changes or involvement strategies are typical of the positive measures that have been used. More negative approaches might include threats, punishment or disciplinary action for 'the resisting organization members' (Ellis, 1998, p. 228). During the process of change at IU, some of 'the usual suspects' and their associates were identified (i.e. those who either could not cope with the change or were openly against it). They left the organisation or were forced to do so. Ellis (1998, p. 232) made it absolutely clear: 'The old adage, "if you can't change the people you have to change the people", is one that may hold the answer in this case.' A change process that delivers victims is a healthy one. In this sense, people have no alternative: the choice is either 'Yes' or 'No' to change, (pretend to) adopt or go. In the sense of traditional logic there is no third alternative ('tritos non datur!').

> . . ., and some people felt out, they couldn't cope with the new structure, which you can expect in a change process because those that can't deal with it go elsewhere or drop out, and it's quite a normal model. So, it was encouraging to see one or two drop out, I'm not saying it personally was, but it meant that we were making sufficient change for it to be impactful from the way it needed to be.

Given that the 'new vision' further emphasised the "people-are-our-greatest-value" sentiment of the organisation, the 'adopt-or-go' policy is very cynical. It goes without saying that not everyone had to change. Those who were in favour of managerialism, or those who successfully pretended to be didn't need to change their worldviews or attitudes. There were a few at senior management level who had to either adopt or go when they openly questioned the new strategic initiative. But beside these usual 'boardroom battles', pressure stemming from managerial concepts and conduct 'is usually projected "down" the organizational hierarchy, and rarely "upwards". Very rarely is the accusation of "resistance" laid at the door of senior managers' (Clegg / Walsh 2004, p. 226). It's not only history which is written by the winners (and leaders of successful change initiatives) but also the right ways of thinking. It is the losers—a few at senior level, more among the rank and file—who have to either change or go elsewhere.

One interesting aspect revealed in this analysis is that it makes almost no difference how subordinates or comparatively less powerful people react to the introduction of managerial concepts. Whether they oppose them openly, remain indifferent, use NIMBY tactics or demonstrate other "problematic" behaviour, (almost) all reactions are perceived and interpreted by their superiors in ways which suggest a need for (more) guidance and "appropriate" responses from the proponents of the ideology of management. By doing so, they once more underline their superior positions, responsibilities and interests. However, the proponents of managerialism are also always keen to have at their disposal 'tougher' measures such as silencing, marginalising or sacking people—and to make people clearly aware of these possibilities. Since the proponents obviously put a great deal of effort into 'scaring people into their world', apparently *even they* aren't very convinced of the attractiveness of their ideology—an aspect we will interrogate in more detail in the following two sections.

WHAT ARE ORGANISATIONAL CHANGE AND ITS MANAGEMENT REALLY ABOUT?

It is generally assumed that managers opt for a (new) strategy 'neither as a habit nor as a mindless repertoire . . .' (Stubbart, 1989, p. 330) but because of particular reasons and on the basis of (what people regarded as) facts. These are conscious decisions—though this does not necessarily mean that they are objective or rational. As indicated in the introduction and first sections of this chapter, the proponents of IU's strategic change initiative provided several *official* reasons for managerial change. These were to address challenges and changes in the business environment, to increase efficiency and reduce costs, to increase profits and growth, to become more business-like and to secure the survival of the organisation—you name it!

All these claims might be true one way or another. Many managers truly believe what they say and work very hard to achieve the changes and results proclaimed. However, behind such claims there can be more subtle reasons and drivers which are mentioned less often, if at all. Despite all management assurances that the new agenda is solely driven by rational strategies and functional aspects, the reality of organisations and management suggests otherwise. For example, according to one senior manager the financial pressure at IU

> was inflated, without doubt. And it was all about what is a suitable weapon to gain control. And, unfortunately, it is being used in a manner which I find very questionable to what in taking the organisation forward. It has changed the culture of the place to where I would say is uncomfortable.

More senior managers particularly know from their experience that strategic change initiatives, and their formulation, communication and implementation, provide excellent opportunities for gaining, keeping or increasing influence, power and control—or for losing it. IU's strategic change initiative developed into an arsenal of weaponry for internal battles, between on the one hand, the Vice-Chancellor and her inner circle ('the centre'), and on the other, some of the Deans and lower managers. For a social system, organisational change is primarily about power and control. It is about dominance and supremacy—whose access to resources will be enlarged or reduced, who can stay and who has to go.

Strategic change initiatives usually have far-reaching internal consequences for organisations as well as for the parties involved. For example, senior managers are well aware of the fact that initiating strategic change can, *irrespective of the factual outcomes for the organisation*, increase *their* credibility (Staw / Epstein, 2000, p. 551), by increasing their market value outside the organisation and their position and influence inside the organisation. 'Observers may perceive that managers are well qualified and of high ability when they are using the latest techniques, such as TQM, empowerment, or teams. Because these techniques are popular, leaders using them are assumed to be competent, regardless of their actual degree of effectiveness' (Staw / Epstein, 2000, p. 528). In this sense, managers make decisions on quite a rational basis—seen from *their* perspective, their struggles for supremacy, power and control are strongly related to their *personal interests*. This became very obvious during the change process at IU. In particular, the controversy about the centralisation of marketing at IU very soon developed into an intense controversy between groups of senior managers. Centralisation became the internal centrepiece of the new change initiative and, hence, highly politicised. The stakes were high. Both sides knew that the outcome of this battle would decide the war. And so it did.

However, despite the fact that the ideas of individualism and self-interest are deeply embedded in Western cultures, senior managers are well aware that they cannot be seen to base their strategic decisions on their personal interests and ambitions. It would be social suicide. The same is true for their group interests. Although senior managers have a very high status in both their organisations and in our society, they still *have to* refer—at least officially—to the dominant values in these social systems, and have to explain and justify their 'visions' and decisions accordingly. On the other hand, senior managers are powerful and influential. It is they who largely define and shape a social system's leading principles—its values, visions, objectives and the criteria against which everything else is judged. Managers, therefore, often want to impose 'their' version, their interpretation of how the world "is" and what the organisation should be doing—because they know very well that determining 'meaning' will influence everything else. Walsh (1995, p. 290) drew the attention to the fact 'that the struggle for power in an organization is often a struggle to impose and legitimate a self-serving construction of meaning for others.' For example, managerialism legitimates 'the interests of management in how organisations are managed, stressing the role and accountability of individual managers and their positions as managers' (Lawler / Hearn 1996, cited in McAuley et al., 2000, p. 95). The introduction of the ideology of management at IU via a strategic change initiative was just such an attempt: the Vice-Chancellor and her inner circle were imposing a new system of values and principles on a social system. Although it took three years and failed to deliver the promised results, they were in fact very successful; IU had become a managerial organisation.

As in the IU case, it can be said that strategic change initiatives and other management issues provide excellent opportunities for senior and middle managers to keep, gain or increase their internal power and influence. It allows them to strengthen their roles and positions, to pursue their very own individual and group interests (even more), and to make the ideology of management part of an organisation's primary strategic objectives and principles—which in return further strengthens their position and supports their interests.

WHAT PEOPLE REALLY RESIST

Despite all of the IU senior management's efforts and tactical manoeuvring—possibly in fact because of it—the strategic change initiative failed to create consensus. As one senior manager described:

> it was a recipe for conflict, and that's exactly what happened. The people got very upset . . .

The question here is why many people were so upset, and what it was they were really resisting. There is a general perception—which is also deeply held by the proponents of the ideology of management and organisational change—that human beings do not change easily. According to this view, one thing many people therefore resist is the idea of change itself—people do not like change, *any* change. In most people's assessment of their situation, a strong preference for stability and continuity is usually quite dominant. For better or worse, the notion of 'feeling comfortable', being familiar with the known and fearing the unknown is widespread. Proponents of change interpret this as indifference and passive resistance.

Of course, 'feeling comfortable' isn't bad as such. On the contrary, most organisation studies and management approaches assume that only people who feel comfortable within their work conditions (amongst other things) can and want to perform. Moreover, investigations of human and social capital as well as organisational and individual learning show that organisational change can damage or hinder many people's efficient use of the experiences, skills, routines and networks which they have developed over time. These are crucial factors in higher productivity and above-average performance. Yet our age seems to have produced an ideology of change where change is portrayed as good per se; organisations and individuals, processes and products *must* change constantly. This assumption is highly questionable since there may be very good reasons for preserving and nurturing things which are worth keeping.

But even if people within an organisation do feel so comfortable that necessary change cannot happen, it is still questionable whether the ideology of managerial change can provide the right answers. One of its basic assumptions, perhaps even its very nature is that concepts and methods should be implemented in an organisation top-down and only in the way its proponents have planned. Such a paternalistic approach is quite alien to most, at least to educated people. People are perfectly capable to judge the situation they are in on their own and in collaborative ways. And they are experienced enough to do so. People change many things on a daily basis, but preferably according to *their* terms and from *their* point of view. They may even change their own situation dramatically, but only when both the pull- and push-forces are *so* strong that people *themselves* see no other solution than to change. An allegedly "much more challenging" business environment and a "vision" of a "much more business-like" organisation (or whatever) are definitely not sufficient to convince employees to change daily routines at their workplace. People have their own minds! They know their job (it's what they get paid for), they know how to do things and they don't like it if someone else tells them what to do and how to do it because he or she thinks they know better. IU's senior managers were simply not able to see that their understanding of change is not other people's understanding of change.

Another issue people are quite sensitive about are the 'technical' aspects of change initiatives, i.e. how change is introduced, communicated and discussed. They care whether and how their viewpoints are not only heard but taken into account, and to what extent they are really involved. In the case of IU, because of its governance structures, boards and committees (as well as its tradition and core values as a democratic and participatory organisation), it seems that previously there had been sufficient communication and information—at least, pro forma. However, it is the very nature of managerial change management to be hierarchical. This means that all important decisions are made at the top and communicated down and sanctioned by formal hearings and proceedings sometime later. This is simply not good enough. Most people nowadays do not really feel involved by official rhetoric, formal meetings and a new branding. Creativity, engagement and involvement seek their own ways—but this is exactly what superiors fear.

A third area of concern was the very idea of managerialism—the language of the market and efficiency, of accountability and performance measurement—and the intended and unintended consequences which come with these principles and methods. Although the ideology of management and the dominance of managers have reached hegemonic status, many people are (still) of the opinion that an organisation is—or should be—much more than simply a profit-generating, efficiency- and productivity-oriented machine. First and foremost, an organisation is a social system, a place in people's lives where they spend a large amount of their time. People have their own values and expect much more from an organisation than just the monthly pay check and ludicrous "We are one big family" rhetoric. Such values and convictions can be quite deeply embedded in an organisation's culture and in people's attitudes. Any change initiative has to take this into account. 'There is a significant body of literature that draws attention to the difficulty of changing organisational culture on the grounds that culture is deeply ingrained in the underlying norms and values of an organisation and cannot be imposed from above' (Parker / Bradley 2000, p. 137). In this sense, many people seem to be against top-down, paternalistic approaches, the ideology of hierarchical leadership, centralisation of power and control, and the dominance of managers. However, because of the reasons stated above, the ideology of management does not allow independent mindsets and alternative values. It therefore comes as no surprise that most people switch to work-to-rule attitudes as soon as they face management-speak.

Perhaps what many people resist most is the cynical use and misuse of 'grand' ideas for personal and group interests. People are fed up with ambitious (senior) managers who join organisations they don't know, get on everyone's nerves with their buzzword ideas and are only interested in furthering their own career and in increasing their market value. They often mess around for a couple of years with a few change management initiatives and then leave the organisation in a state worse than before, rewarded with a golden handshake. People are fed up with incompetent and ignorant managers and socalled leaders who have only little understanding of the social and human sides of business, who do not care for the ideas and needs of their employees and who are even prepared to sacrifice them if it looks good on paper. People are tired of managers who pretend to be busy and important, even vital for the survival of the whole, but who are only after personal advantage and mostly interested in securing and strengthening their own position and influence.

All in all, most employees are not against change *per se, but they are against managerialistic change-management initiatives and a paternalistic ideology of leadership which primarily serves the personal and group interests of a few*. During a strategic change initiative or organisational change, whatever the specific issues may be, people in general start to resist. Often it is not that there is resistance first which managerialism then has to overcome. It is the other way round; managerialism *produces* resistance (Kirkpatrick / Ackroyd 2000, p. 524)—as well as a whole range of other negative outcomes. The ideology of management and managerial concepts are often the cause of the problem, not the cure. The case of IU is a further empirical example of this.

THE MANAGERIALISTIC IDEOLOGY
OF CHANGE MANAGEMENT

The way in which the latest change initiative at IU was instigated and implemented is a fairly typical example not only of the introduction of New Public Management in public sector organisations, but also of the introduction of managerialistic concepts in larger organisations in general. The main characteristics of this kind of managerial understanding of change management might be summarised as follows:

Table 7.1 The Managerialistic Ideology of Change Management

1. Because of an allegedly more challenging environment, proponents of the change initiative argue that a new strategy is not a choice but an unavoidable necessity (first part of the TINA principle). Even if the proponents wanted to, they could not decide otherwise. They, and all others, have to accept 'the reality'.

2. The environment is portrayed as hostile, dangerous and frightening ('the enemy outside')—ideally so threatening that (allegedly) the survival and future existence of the whole group, organisation or nation is at stake.

3. There is a need for leadership. Notions of 'business-like' leadership and change management are a hierarchical and paternalistic understanding of leaders who are knowledgeable, insightful and skilful and their relations to those who aren't.

4. The organisation can change in only one way—the way the proponents of change suggest (second part of the TINA principle).

5. For the proponents of managerialism there is not only an 'enemy outside' but also an 'enemy inside'—the people. It is they who are either not able or not willing to adapt to the new order.

6. People's resistance is therefore interpreted as evidence that change is not only right and necessary, but that clear leadership and tough leaders are required—and that the opponents simply need (even more) 'guidance'.

7. The notion of providing 'guidance' is about overcoming resistance and putting people in a state of fear and dependency. It is about changing people; to make them able and willing to behave (as expected) and to enthusiastically and pro-actively support the new agenda. It is about changing mindsets and attitudes, how people think and act.

8. People have either to adapt or go. Only a change process that produces victims is a healthy one. It is evidence that the change initiative progresses and that the change proponents are true leaders.

IU's managerialistic approach towards change meant much more than just making the organisation more "business-like" and "efficient". This so-called new vision packed with the latest buzzwords and based on the TINA principle provoked the NIMBY principle and similar responses. The initiative led the organisation into a process of intense organisational politics—which seem to be an integral part of managerial approaches—where different cosmologies and belief systems clashed with each other. Most of the proponents of the change initiative probably deeply believed in the necessity for change and in the convincing logic of their position. The same is true for the opponents who either saw a need for protecting IU's tradition or had a very different, "non-managerial" business model in mind. The advocates of change claimed that the necessity for change was the reality. The critics saw it as artificially created and imposed on the organisation for other reasons. Both camps made their claims for moral authority, at which point the controversy led into a spiral of increasingly hardening positions. Whereas the discussion had started with more or less rational arguments, it soon developed into a fundamental disagreement. At this stage, the 'blame game' and personal attacks started and gained momentum. The proponents of the initiative were blamed for damaging, if not destroying the organisation. The opponents were portrayed as apathetic, as sticking to an old model of academia that was no longer valid and as being unable or unwilling to read the writing on the wall and to act accordingly. The proponents' conclusion was to break the (passive) resistance by imposing increasing pressure, and the opponents' conclusion was to bypass the change initiatives by playing the game without any real conviction. On both sides, the last resort was seen as getting rid of (some of) the other side. Overall, the effects of managerialistic change management on IU's corporate culture (and, as a consequence, on its market position and performance as a whole) were far more negative than positive. However, the more important point is that the proponents of managerialism and hierarchical leadership were able to initiate a game *according to their rules*—and that the following processes had been managerial, too. *This* is what such (change) initiatives are really about. In this sense, IU's strategic change initiative was a great success.

CONCLUSIONS

The data presented in this case study demonstrate that the ideology of management / New Public Management does not provide the silver bullet for managing and changing (public) organisations. In fact they cannot do so as a matter of principle. There are several reasons for this.

Firstly, the ideology of management is not a consistent concept or set of solutions (as explained in Chapter 5). As the case of IU has revealed, the proponents of change talk about market orientation and business-like behaviour, and try to achieve this through regulations, procedures and policies. They simultaneously make the case for de-centralisation, flexibility, and subsidiarity and centralisation, standardisation, and authority. They demand lean management while strengthening bureaucracy. They praise trust and empowerment while actually installing more control systems and implementing more rules. They claim to be people-oriented but at the same time put more pressure on employees. They say "We are all one family" but solely pursue their own sectoral interests. IU's strategic change initiative was an odd combination of contradictory principles such as marketisation and centralisation, standardisation and flexibilisation, control and empowerment (e.g. Apple 2005, p. 11, Hoggett 1996, p. 18). These and other inconsistencies allow senior managers to take almost any position and to claim whatever suits them best. This is probably a further reason why managerial concepts are so attractive to managers. Many (senior) managers refer to and use fads, ideologies and buzzwords in a perfectly pragmatic manner, i.e. based on situative requirements and for their own interests and advantages. But what is good for them is not necessarily good for the organisations or units for which they are responsible.

Secondly, in contrast to their alleged or expected positive outcomes, managerialistic approaches usually raise more questions and problems for organisations and the people working for them than they solve. Some of the problems they cause include

- a narrow and opportunistic perception of an organisation's environment primarily based on numbers and interpreted mostly in ways which suit a few powerful stakeholders and their particular interests,
- a so-called business-like strategy that bulldozes values and ideas, convictions and attitudes that are non-managerial,
- increased tensions, pressure and battles between organisational units and individuals,
- negative effects on morale and motivation, a harsher working climate and more distrust between people.

There is empirical evidence that the assumption of a much more challenging business environment and the implementation of orthodox management concepts lead to much more challenging *internal* environments and working conditions (Newton 2003, p. 434). The corporate culture and working climate at IU have greatly suffered *because of* the strategic change initiative. However, most of the devastating effects of change management initiatives are not officially recognised within organisations and do not become publicly known. The negative impacts and consequences of managerialism for organisations, people and whole societies are much worse than we can actually know from the data available. There seems to be little awareness amongst its proponents that the ideology of management not only fails to cope with problems but *that it is the problem*!

What is less clear is whether or not the proponents of the change initiative were fully aware of what they were really doing. On the one hand, according to Austin / Currie (2003, p. 230), proponents of the ideology of management seem to be quite naïve and surprised when change goes wrong: 'They think they are executing this change by the book, using all the correct project management and business planning models. Still the organisation does not move with the efficiencies and speed bespoke by these models, . . .' Many proponents of managerialistic change seem to be puzzled by the fact that there is often widespread resistance to their plans, that people are not overly enthusiastic about the new agenda and the changes coming with it. On the other hand, it is widely known that company-wide, top-down initiated and introduced change programs simply do not work. Therefore, the question remains why so many (senior) managers use the same managerial concepts time and time again.

IU's case might provide some clues. As the case study revealed, in some respects such change initiatives work very well. Some of its proponents may well have a real and genuine belief that it is for the sake of the organisation, and that adopting 'business-like' methods—whatever this actually means—will lead to improvements. Despite all assurances by the proponents of New Public Management that it's really about "technical" issues, the empirical evidence suggests otherwise. When change happens, there are always strong personal and group interests at stake. It's all about gaining or increasing power and control, dominance and supremacy, social position and influence. It's about whose responsibilities and access to resources will be enlarged or reduced, and who can stay and who has to go. 'Change' is primarily not a technical but a political issue (Goia / Thomas, 1996, p. 378). The managerial methods within the ideology of management are simply tools to pursue and cover up these very personal and sectoral interests. As an ideology, it remains primarily about managers' power and control, dominance and supremacy. It is 'the modernist project which has as its heart the transcendence of professional management as a means of achieving control in organizations' (McAuley et al. 2000, p. 87). Unsurprisingly therefore, (senior) managers want to get this ideology adopted as the organisation's primary strategic objectives. 'At issue here is the question of organizational discourses: which agenda is seen to hold sway?, Whose interpretations are defining organizational reality?' (Cohen et al. 1999, p. 492). This is the real nature of change management. It is not primarily about making organisations more efficient in a technical sense. It is about gaining, keeping, and increasing influence and supremacy, and enhancing the prerogatives and privileges of powerful parties.

It is also about misleading people about the true nature of, and reasons behind, all this management and change hysteria. As Willmott (1996, p. 325) explained: 'If "subordinates" can be persuaded that managers simply perform a role, task or function within the division of labour that is necessary to maximize efficiency and effectiveness, resistance to managerial authority appears to be irrational and anti-social—it threatens to undermine the capacity of management to do what, allegedly, is in the universal interests of everyone concerned.' As long as the whole game is about that particular understanding of management, the proponents will stay on top of the game *whatever the real outcomes are*. Most of the proponents of change are more or less fully aware of the downsides that will accompany it. But these are seen as either unimportant side effects of the game, or even as a sign of approval indicating "progress". It is not the case that most of the proponents of managerialistic change initiatives are simply unaware or just naïve about the unintended and hidden consequences. *They do know, but they don't care!* It may be a cynical worldview but it works—at least, in *that* sense and *for them.*

8 Critique of Management and Orthodox Organisations

> Simply because something is everywhere doesn't mean it is good or necessary, . . .
>
> Martin Parker (2002, p. 2)

INTRODUCTION

As the previous chapters have revealed, the dominance of managers is based on a comprehensive system of mutually reinforcing interests, power and ideology. Even more, it is supported by a whole range of powerful and influential groups and institutions, such as business organisations, institutional investors, consultancies, media and orthodox business school academics—not to mention accordingly socialised and submissive employees. Managers' dominance and influence have long exceeded organisational boundaries, and managers have become a societal institution—on an increasingly global scale. Managers have become one of the most influential social classes of our time. In many societies, the notion of management and the dominance of managers have long reached *a hegemonic stage*.

The ideology of management has shaped organisational and societal reality to an extent similar to other grand ideologies (e.g. Christianity, monarchy, capitalism, or communism). It is so embedded in organisational and societal institutions and internalised by people to such an extent that it is no longer even recognised as ideology. The ways in which organisations—particularly hierarchical organisations with their elaborated systems of managerial position and privileges, roles and responsibilities—currently function and are managed have become the norm and normality. The dominance of managers and the ideology of management seem to be a normal part of organisational and societal reality—they *are* the norm and normality. Because of this, managerial dominance is neither questioned nor challenged anymore. Managers *and* non-managers alike perceive and interpret organisational 'reality' only in managerial ways. The vast majority of people are no longer able or willing to reflect critically on the current state of affairs. According to Gramsci (1971, referred to in Stoddart 2007, p. 201),

> hegemonic power works to convince individuals and social classes to subscribe to the social values and norms of an inherently exploitative system. It is a form of social power that relies on voluntarism and participation, rather than the threat of punishment for disobedience.

Hegemony appears as the 'common sense' that guides our everyday, mundane understanding of the world.

We can no longer imagine organisations, business, even society *without* managers and management, or talk convincingly about organisational affairs without using management-speak and the latest buzzwords. It has become increasingly difficult to make the case for fundamentally alternative concepts—organisations and society *without* privileged and powerful managers have simply become *unthinkable*. In *this* sense, managers' dominance is thorough, comprehensive and total.

Putting people in such mental cages is the usual 'strategy of normalisation' (Braynion 2004, p. 458) used by dominating groups and classes. If it works, people are not only unable and unwilling to see alternatives anymore, but they accept the status quo because it seems to them natural and normal (Akella 2003, p. 47). They even believe that the current state of affairs is in their own best interest. This is crucial, as Brookfield (2005, p. 44) has explained so strikingly:

> The ideas and practices of hegemony—the stock opinions, conventional wisdoms, and commonsense ways of behaving in particular situations that we take for granted—are part and parcel of everyday life. It is not as if these are being forced on us against our will. The dark irony, the cruelty of hegemony, is that adults take pride in learning and acting on the beliefs and assumptions that work to enslave them. In learning diligently to live by these assumptions, people become their own jailers.

That powerful managers are responsible for the management and development of our organisations and society is not only portrayed and seen as the norm (and normal), but expected and welcomed by almost everyone—managers and owners, investors and bankers, consultants and academics, even employees and professionals alike.

As indicated in the introduction, this book has two main purposes. One was to develop a 'theory of the social dominance of managers' in order to analyse comprehensively and systematically managers' power, interests and ideology. The second was to simultaneously use this analysis as a polemic against managers' dominance, against hierarchical order such as the managerial organisation. This final chapter puts the main aspects of this critique of management and orthodox organisations together. The following three sections are about these ideas:

1. Criticism: what are the main negative aspects and consequences of the dominance of managers and the managerial organisation?
2. Critical management and organisation studies: how can we develop our understanding of (contemporary) organisations?

3. Change and alternatives: how can the status quo be changed fundamentally?

CRITICISM OF THE MANAGERIAL ORGANISATION

Orthodox management is actually only an example of 'a' dominant ideology and managers for 'a' prevailing class in our contemporary complex societies—they are not 'the' dominant ideology and not 'the' dominant class. Future generations will probably identify calculative selfishness ('individualism') and materialism ('consumerism') as the most influential and dominating ideologies of our time, and complex networks of different types of people and professions as 'the' power elite and ruling class. More importantly, the managerial organisation and society, the ideology of management and the dominance of managers are much better and less harmful for both managers *and* employees than many other ideologies and governance systems mankind has witnessed so far. *On average*, managerialism causes comparatively less damage to society, organisations and individuals than many religions, unregulated capitalism, monarchy, fascism or communism. Although comprehensive, multi-dimensional and designed primarily for the pursuit of a particular group's interests and power, the ideology of management is a total, but *not* a totalitarian ideology. However hierarchical and unjust managerial organisations might be, brutal physical terror and punishment, famine, systematic psycho-terror and crude indoctrination are simply not in their nature.[1] This is mainly due to the fact that managerialism is based on the ideas of pragmatism and result orientation, not fundamentalism—management (and managers) *must deliver*. And they can only deliver if they, amongst others, improve organisational structures and processes, employees' conditions and the organisation's relations with its environment. There are strong principles and mechanisms within the ideology of management (albeit of secondary importance) which contribute to the ongoing improvement of organisational, social and environmental affairs. As the analysis has shown, one of the main pillars of management dominance is to use comparatively cunning and subtle forms of power and control, and even to provide (within limits) a whole range of positive incentives and opportunities for individuals. In this sense, managerial ideology is in many respects much closer to Huxley's 'Brave New World' than to Orwell's '1984', and people are usually much better off under the former. The dominance of interest- and power-oriented managers is definitely better and more bearable than the ruling of hypocritical clerics, narrow-minded royals and aristocrats, or ideologically deformed radical politicians.

Nonetheless, Chapters 3 through 6 revealed that the downsides do outweigh the positive aspects by far and are serious. This is mainly due to the fact that managerialism and orthodox management concepts are based on the same idea as many other group-based hierarchies—specifically the *idea of a hierarchical, unequal and institutionalised relationship between superior and subordinate, leader and follower, master and servant.* It is the very rationale of such hierarchical social systems that advantages, prerogatives and privileges increase the higher up the system one goes. In this sense, the position and status of managers are synonymous with *hierarchical authority and prerogatives. This* is the core of the ideology of management and the dominance of managers. And *this* is also the core reasons for its many serious faults. The main ones are the following:

1) It is a characteristic of hierarchical organisations that the right to make decisions is allocated in accordance with the social position within the hierarchy. Superiors have exclusive right to make the decisions their subordinates are not allowed to make. Positions higher up an organisation's hierarchy provide the role-holder with an increasing amount of power, prerogatives for making decisions, more tools for hierarchical domination and control of subordinates—and with less and less control from below. This nature of hierarchical organisations produces almost automatically the tendency that role-holders will be keen to accumulate more and more prerogatives and responsibilities. Over time, the more important decisions will be located higher up the hierarchy. This is a self-reinforcing and self-stabilising process. Decisions are not discussed and agreed collectively, but made at the top and communicated downwards. In this sense, managerial organisations are based on *un-democratic* governance structures and decision-making processes. The ideology of management and the dominance of managers *are alien to the ideas of democracy and democratic society*; they are anti-democratic by definition.

2) The same principle of unequal allocation applies to information and knowledge. Because leadership and the privileges and responsibilities which come along with it are hierarchical, people are provided with better and more important information the higher up they are positioned within the organisational hierarchy. They also have much better (often exclusive) access to sources and types of information which can be used to strengthen their own role and position. Accordingly, subordinates are only provided with fairly operational, task-oriented information so they can only use and develop their knowledge in limited ways. In this sense, organisational information systems, structures and processes further deepen the division between those who think (about the grand themes and important issues) and those who carry out pre-defined and tightly controlled tasks and operations. In such a system it remains largely unknown how much knowledge, experience and skills cannot be used by subordinates because of the pre-defined division between managerial and non-managerial competencies. Hence, the hierarchical domination and control of subordinates by managers leads to *an inadequate use, allocation, distribution and*

development of skills and knowledge. This is particularly worrisome in view of the fact that we live in knowledge economies and information societies, with a majority of highly educated, well-informed and creative citizens.

3) As indicated, the organisational hierarchy provides role-holders with different and clearly distinguished bundles of roles and responsibilities, privileges and prerogatives. Every hierarchical social system comes with elaborated systems of artificially created and enhanced differences. According to the ideology of management, managers do not only have a higher status than employees but they *must have* (and deserve) higher status. Managerialism is a social stratification system based on the principle of hierarchical segmentation. In this sense, the notion of orthodox management and managerial dominance are based on the same old ideology of a hierarchically differentiated society—the ideology of social differentiation between 'those at the top' and 'the people'. Accordingly, the managerial organisation creates a comprehensive micro-cosmos of social positions and their unequal hierarchical relations. It is a class society in miniature. The ideology of management is just another concept, and useful tool, for the *systematic (re-) production, cementation and intensification of social inequalities.*

4) Because of the un-democratic decision-making processes, the uneven allocation of and access to information, and social inequalities, superiors cannot trust subordinates, and subordinates cannot trust superiors. And since mistrust is endemic to hierarchical authority, managerial dominance can only function on elaborated systems of control (and punishment). Generally speaking, inequalities in social systems require the permanent control of subordinates by their superiors. Therefore, an increasing number of people higher up the organisational hierarchy need to be provided with more and increasingly sophisticated tools for controlling subordinates. Organisational systems, structures and processes create a panopticon through which superiors control subordinates along the lines of hierarchy. Without these tightly elaborated regimes of control there would be no managerial organisation. Managerial dominance and the managerial organisation are based by *necessity* on *comprehensive, systematic, multi-dimensional and thorough control systems.*

5) Un-democratic decision-making procedures, unequal allocation of information and knowledge, systematic inequalities in social status and elaborated control systems are sufficient to create and secure managerial dominance and the "iron cage of hierarchical authority". However, this oppressive regime becomes fully comprehensive and even more efficient when the external mechanisms of social differentiation become internalised. For this, a paternalistic approach is used. According to this idea, 'to manage people' means to use the same

spectrum of psychological means which parents use for the education of their children; to scare and frighten, to calm anxieties and fears, to provide security and reassurance, to motivate and encourage, to punish and to show boundaries. Shaping employees' identities, beliefs, emotions, attitudes and behaviour via top-down ideologies, comprehensive power and control systems, and direct intervention is nothing else but intense socialisation, indoctrination and conditioning towards conformity and obedience. And it works! Over time, the external stimuli will be largely internalised and channelled into unconscious functioning, calculative selfishness and even a pro-active willingness to support the very order which oppresses. In this sense, the dominance of managers has contributed to the (further) *infantilisation and deformation of adults on an industrial scale*. The mainstream understanding of managerial dominance and leadership is very paternalistic.

6) Behind all of this is one main driving force: managers' interests. What are portrayed as organisational necessities is, in fact, pure ideology which serves and advances the individual, sectional and group interests of managers. Managers are keen to secure, if not to increase, their superior position, power and influence within asymmetrical power relations. This is about the primacy of management and managers, managers' prerogatives and privileges, fiefdoms and egos, personal advantages and well-being. And it is about institutionalising their personal and group interests as organisations', even society's primary objectives, norms and values. Their very sectoral interests are being portrayed as universal interests. The ideology of management means the universalisation of sectional interests—which is, in fact, nothing more than the *egoistic pursuit of individual and group interests at the expense of others and the whole social system.*

7) Proponents of managerial dominance may even acknowledge the truth of the above statement, although they might rephrase it in a much more positive light. They would certainly try to explain that this is all justified for the sake of the greater good. The ideology of management talks primarily about (increased) efficiency, cost-effectiveness and productivity, customer orientation and value for money, better service and quality, sustainable competitive advantage and corporate social responsibility, empowerment and intra-preneurship. Such references to higher values are one of the typical rhetoric and strategies of ruling groups and classes. The dominance of managers is portrayed as being good for the whole; their decisions and actions, even their privileges and prerogatives are explained and justified as advantageous and necessary for the very existence of the whole social system. The pursuit of managers' individual and group interests is not only covered up by management-speak but is explained as 'serving the community'. However, factual changes in the managerial organisation together with the

cynical use of rhetoric for the promotion of sectoral interests has led to a massive destruction of social and ethical values, including business ethics, morale and integrity; altruism and civic virtues; social justice, fairness and equality; empowerment and citizenship; democratic institutions and representation; public welfare and liberty. In summary, the dominance of managers has led to a *(further) demolition and deterioration of social values*.

All in all, the dominance of managers and the managerial organisation come with the following negative aspects and consequences *with necessity*:

1) Un-democratic governance structures and decision-making processes
2) Insufficient use, allocation, distribution and development of skills and knowledge
3) Systematic (re-) production, cementation and intensification of social inequalities
4) Comprehensive, systematic, multi-dimensional and thorough control systems
5) Infantilisation and deformation of subordinates at an industrial scale
6) Egoistic pursuit of individual and group interests at the expense of others and the whole
7) (Further) demolition and deterioration of social values

In this sense, the dominance of managers is not only based on a comprehensive and multi-dimensional system of social dominance established and driven by their power, individual and group interests, and an elaborated ideology of management. The system itself is based on highly questionable assumptions and *by necessity* generates highly negative consequences for individuals, organisations, business and the society. The managerial organisation has a bizarre socio-political order (hierarchy and power relations), systematically nurtures inequalities (domination of particular individuals and groups over others) and permanently (re-) produces social injustice (privileges and preferential treatment of certain group interests). To sum up, *the ideology of management, the dominance of managers and the managerial organisation are anti-democratic, exploitative, inhumane, unjust and class-centred.* If people were free, they would not choose this type of organisation.

There are no 'functional' necessities whatsoever which could justify managers' prerogatives and power, and the current state of affairs is simply not acceptable. The widespread embeddedness and establishment of managerial ideology and managers' dominance within both our public and private organisations goes against the ideas of democracy and enlightenment. They are in sharp contrast to the ideas of modern societies and citizenship, participation and empowerment, knowledge workers and organisational learning. They even contradict ideas of organisational efficiency and market orientation. The question, therefore, is what can we do? Or what should we do?

CRITICAL MANAGEMENT AND ORGANISATION STUDIES

The investigation carried out in this book concentrated on the analysis of managers' dominance within organisations. In relation to this, the dominance of the functional approach was mentioned several times. Generally speaking, orthodox management concepts and methods have also reached hegemonic status. The theories and models developed and used by business schools, business and management consultants are (almost) all made for managers, address their concerns, describe organisational problems from a managerial perspective and recommend managerial solutions. Because of this, management and organisation studies are largely functional, management-oriented, conservative, biased and narrow-minded. Such a 'focused' approach is not helpful in the light of multi-dimensional environments, differentiated information societies, changing industries, global markets, complex organisations and a largely well-educated and knowledgeable workforce. Management, organisations and managers, therefore need to be investigated and provided with theories and concepts in much more challenging, reflective and enlightened ways. This particularly means the need to (Brookfield 2005, Feldman 2000, Alvesson / Willmott 1992a)

- investigate not only functional aspects and means-ends relationships, but also the ends and interests behind such aspects of and within social relations and socio-productive systems such as organisations,
- illuminate omissions, distortions and falsities in current management thinking,
- identify and criticise unfair and oppressive institutions and management practices,
- reveal dominant ideology and mechanisms for convincing people that privileges and social differences are the norm and normality of social affairs and
- challenge and change the institutionalised unjust conditions of prevailing management discourses and practices.

As the French philosopher Denis Diderot outlined in the preface to the famous Encyclopaedia in 1752 (cited in Kramnick 1995, p. 18): '*All things must be examined, debated, investigated without exception and without regard for anyone's feelings*'. The following sub-sections give some ideas which particular areas and aspects management and organisation studies need to address in the context of (managerial) organisations, the dominance of managers, and the ideology of management.

The Purpose(s) of Organisations and Management

As just mentioned, orthodox management and organisation studies are largely about functional aspects, the technical and financial dimensions involved in making profit. Milton Friedman's famous / infamous statement (cited in Goshal 2005, p. 79) very poignantly reflects this: 'Few trends could so thoroughly undermine the very foundations of our free society as the acceptance by corporate officials of a social responsibility other than to make as much money for their stockholders as possible'. According to this spirit, management is portrayed as simply fulfilling roles and carrying out functions *allegedly* in order to make organisations more efficient and productive, performance- and cost-oriented, competitive and customer-focused (e.g. Diefenbach 2005, Haque 1999, p. 469). People, organisations, and even society are being instrumentalised for the pursuit by a small minority of people of their sectoral interests.

In sharp contrast to this narrow-mindedness, we must remind ourselves that management and organisations are *social systems*. They, therefore, necessarily fulfil a whole range of purposes: the financial and technological purposes described by orthodox management and organisation studies, but also purposes of welfare, sense-giving and sense-making, being and self-development, social justice and workplace democracy, equality, humanity, citizenship, communitarian values and others (e.g. Kirkpatrick et al. 2005, p. 48, Haque 1999, p. 468, Hoggett 1996, p. 14). There is only a tiny fraction of people who regard profit making, if not to say profit maximisation as 'the', even 'the only' purpose of organisations (i.e. some radical economists or extremists amongst shareholders and managers). In reality, even amongst senior managers one can easily identify very different understandings, convictions, perceptions and business models. Also, most entrepreneurs do not (solely) start a business in order to make "massive" profits, but to earn a decent living, to realise their dreams of 'being their own boss', to see their product innovation materialising and / or being in a better position to combine work and private life. And of course, almost all employees do not work for organisations for the purpose of profit maximisation but, again, for a whole range of reasons and purposes. Hence, for realistic and appropriate management and organisation studies it is important to be aware of the whole spectrum of purposes, of *competing* objectives, values and belief systems, *clashing* schemata and cosmologies within organisations. And it is even more important to understand that all of these different purposes are of some value and need to be put into perspective. Non-financial and non-functional values especially are not just 'nice-to-haves' (if at all) but of the highest importance in their own right as well as in their relevance for the organisation and business.

Such an approach is not only realistic in the context of organisations, but is also much more capable of including the multi-dimensional links between the individual, organisation, and society. It would much better address the embeddedness and responsibilities of organisations not only within markets, but within society and a wider civilisational context, i.e. within global and national political economies, societal institutions, private households and natural environments (e.g. Grey / Willmott 2002, p. 415, Zald 2002, p. 383, Jacques 1996, p. 8). To include these areas is *not* a task for specialised areas within management and organisation studies, such as business ethics, international business, human resource management, or marketing. We need to go 'beyond the established specialisms and disciplines of management' (Grey / Willmott 2002, p. 415). Alvesson / Willmott (1992a, pp. 3–4) were quite clear about this: 'As a counterweight to technical (or technocratic) images and ideals of management—in which a narrow focus on the improvement of means/ends relationships is predominant—there is a strong case for advancing sociological, historical, philosophical and critical studies of management'. In this sense, management and organisation studies have to be redesigned and further developed as a truly *social science* (Diefenbach 2003).

Interests concerning and within organisations

Realistic management and organisation studies also try to look harder "beyond the obvious", i.e. to identify the driving forces behind organisations, business and management which contribute to explanations of their functioning (or mal-functioning). Since organisations are social systems, many key drivers can be found at the level of individuals and groups (within institutions), i.e. motivational factors relevant for attitudes, decision-making and (social) action. Many of those can be subsumed under 'interests' in the broadest sense. According to Hindess (1986, p. 116), 'interests appear to provide an explanatory link between action and social structure. On the one hand they provide actors with reasons for action and on the other hand they are derived from features of social structure'. In this sense, questions arise such as what are the interests behind x?, whose interests are (best) served by x?, which interests clash with each other in what ways?, and what are possible solutions for complying with different and differing interests? These interests form patterns along the lines and stratification of social structures and processes.

Firstly, it is about *prevailing and privileged* interests—the interests of the ruling class and dominant groups, the partiality of their interests and how they conflict with the public interest which they allegedly represent (Baker 2005, p. 692). For example, Willmott (1984, p. 361–362) explained that 'the political economic perspective, in contrast, reveals how organizational structures are designed to secure and advance the interests of a ruling class whose interests they chiefly (but not exclusively) represent'. In order to develop truly efficient and just organisations we need to reveal how damaging and cynical the sectoral interests of the powerful really are.

Secondly—and equally, if not more importantly—it is about *suppressed and ignored* interests, i.e. the interests of subordinates and all other stakeholders which are portrayed as of secondary importance, irrelevant and often neglected. Realistic management and organisation studies would reveal the whole cosmos of people's interests and how organisations and business relate to them. For example, when people work for an organisation, their interests are much more multi-dimensional and far-reaching than simply fitting into pre-conceived, pre-designed and pre-formulated tasks and routines (and getting paid for doing so). It is therefore worth thinking about how we can design organisations around the needs and aspirations of individuals, not the other way round, i.e. making people fit into the iron cage.[2]

The pursuit of both privileged and suppressed interests draws attention to 'agency' and to the fact that people are responsible (and can be held responsible) for their actions (or non-actions). In an organisational context this would particularly relate to managers and other dominating actors. Realistic management and organisation studies would reveal that such actors do not simply and impartially carry out technical functions and are not only the servants, if not to say the victims of 'quasi-natural objective forces' (Jacques 1996, p. 15) such as 'the market' or 'technology'. It would demonstrate how managers' pursuit of their individual and group interests impacts negatively on the larger social systems. And it would hold actors more accountable. 'We need to ask: who are the people, what are the organizations promoting the reorganization of capitalism? Where do they operate? Can we name them and do they have an address?' (Newman 1994, cited in Brookfield 2005, p. 169).

Finally, systematically including all possible interests in the analysis of management and organisations necessitates a multi-dimensional stakeholder approach. Such an approach would enable us to better see the clashes as well as possible links between different interests—as well as how the design, governance structures and management of organisations does, can and should encompass these differences. According to Alvesson / Willmott (1992a, p. 6), we need to ask and analyse whose purposes and interests organisations serve (e.g. owners, managers, employees, or consumers), how these relate to each other and how organisations and work can and should be organised accordingly (e.g. autocratically, bureaucratically, managerially or democratically).

Power and Control in Organisations

Just as with interests, power and control have been either largely neglected by orthodox management studies (e.g. Lacey 2007, p. 131) or are portrayed (read "covered up") as more or less functional managerial routines and organisational systems. In contrast, realistic management and organisation studies put power and control issues into the centre of its analysis, as Critical Management Studies already does (e.g. Clegg et al. 2006). Approaching management and organisations from a power-and-control perspective suggests they should be regarded as fundamental factors in the constitution and maintenance of social systems such as organisations. Corporations, therefore, are seen as political organisations and much more attention is drawn to their internal politics. (Burns 1961, pp. 258, 260). In this sense, we can talk about *competing* paradigms of governance, power and control—between and within social groups and classes. For example, strategic organisational outcomes, such as official mission and vision statements, strategy and strategic decisions, performance management and measurement systems, structures and processes, 'are viewed as reflections of the values and cognitive bases of powerful actors in the organization' (Hambrick / Mason 1984, p. 193). Power and control are largely about dominance, i.e. which (and whose!) belief system reigns. Significantly, dominance is only partially based on 'discourses' or 'rhetoric'. It is in fact about how individuals, groups and classes attempt to gain, keep and extend their real power and control over resources, social structures and processes.

In an organisational context, therefore, managerial dominance is about managerial elites, their institutional and societal power and how they secure their positions and privileges through organisational politics, centralisation and during change management initiatives (Diefenbach 2005). For example, both in orthodox and post-modern organisations (e.g. networks, projects, teamwork) managers have managed to keep and even extend their dominance (e.g. Kärreman / Alvesson 2004, Akella 2003, Courpasson 2000, Willmott 1997). According to Alvesson / Willmott (1992a, p. 12), 'Top management is routinely privileged in decision-making and agenda-setting and in defining and shaping human needs and social reality'. Realistic management and organisation studies would identify and analyse these mechanisms, and could 'challenge the centrality and necessity of the dominant role of elites in defining reality and impeding emancipatory change' (ibid., p. 12).

Where there is power, there is also powerlessness. Superiors do not exist without subordinates, social dominance does not exist without social oppression and control. We therefore need to study in much more depth (and from a much more critical perspective) how power and control are exercised on a daily basis. We need to analyse how surveillance takes place not only via auditing and performance measurement systems but also leads—in combination with other mechanisms—to self-discipline, self-surveillance and even self-censorship amongst subordinates (Brookfield 2005, pp. 45, 126, 134 referring to Foucault). We need to reveal how power is embedded in the structures and processes of social oppression, and how allegedly objective organisational structures and processes have institutionalised imbalances of power and continue to systematically generate asymmetrical relationships (Pettigrew 1992, Willmott 1984, p. 361). And we need a better understanding of the reasons for, and mechanisms of, subordinates' compliance, obedience and un-critical functioning.

Ideologies about management and organisations

People's individual values, beliefs, perceptions, interests and power are to a certain extent linked to, and shaped by collectively held norms, values and beliefs (Hamilton 1987, p. 38), i.e. ideologies. Furthermore, (managerial and organisational) reality is largely made and shaped by ideology, by 'the system of beliefs, values, and practices that reflects and reproduces existing social structures, systems, and relations' (Brookfield 2005, p. 68). It has always been a primary objective of critical theory to reveal the ideologies which underpin social practices and discourses (Humphrey 2005, p. 240), and support institutions as well as 'mere' functional systems, structures and processes. Realistic management and organisation studies, therefore, must reveal and identify ideology behind and within managerial and organisational reality, and shed light on why individuals or groups of people have vested interests in producing or justifying ideologies. The aim should be to investigate much more thoroughly the origins of epochal ideologies, what are their sources, where are their producers and contributors? Who is behind these grand narratives, who benefits from them, and how?

Just as interests and power do, ideology follows societal and social faults. It therefore makes sense on the one hand to concentrate on the *ideology of superiors* or *dominant* ideology (Brookfield 2005, p. viii) which represents 'the beliefs which dominant groups hold and disseminate' (Abercrombie et al. 1980, p. 130). In the case of organisations, this is largely managers. So Critical Management Studies should particularly investigate how managerialism 'privileges managers' views of the world above that of other groups' (Watson 2001, p. 387), and how this shapes organisations for better or worse. Even more, we need to question and challenge managers' ideological claims for, and justifications of, authority, responsibility, prerogatives and privileges, as well as the alleged need for employees' subordination and control.

On the other hand, the *ideology of subordinates* is also of interest. These ideologies are primarily designed to complement and support the dominant ideology. They explain and justify 'the way things are', why they will not change and why they should not change (Jost / Hunyady 2005, p. 260). The ideology of subordinates is largely designed for guaranteeing the smooth functioning of subordinates within institutions—the so-called work ethos and work attitudes. In this respect it helps a lot that the notion of smooth functioning corresponds quite nicely with human psychological needs to cope with, and avoid uncertainty, ambiguity as well as needs for order, structure, and closure (Jost / Hunyady 2005, pp. 261–262). Moreover, if these needs do not already exist 'naturally', then ideology provides enough tools to create and nurture such needs artificially, e.g. through systems of threats and punishments, reassurances and rewards.

The endless process of human socialisation, if not to say indoctrination and conditioning, is largely based on ideologies, which promote the externally initiated and supported internalisation of dominant values and beliefs by new and becoming members of a particular group or social system. Realistic management and organisation studies reveals, investigates and critically challenges both superiors' and subordinates' ideology. It also interrogates how they complement each other and jointly establish, justify and secure the continuation of a hierarchical and unjust social order.

The Privileged and the Disadvantaged

Orthodox management and organisation studies are about managers and their problems, as well as organisational aspects seen from a managerial and functional perspective. In simple terms, they contribute to the further dominance of managers. However, superiors are sufficiently privileged by organisational and societal realities. They are perfectly able (and institutionally enabled) to pursue their individual and group interests, and to use and extend their power to shape, (re-) construct and interpret reality in their favour by use of an elaborated repertoire of dominant ideology. Since managers are in these comparatively strong positions, there is certainly no need for academics to (further) strengthen their privileges by academics via providing yet another managerial concept. We need exactly the opposite! We need *more* critical investigations of the privileged. For example, Michael (2005, p. 102) is right when he commented that 'it is usually the weak that get "named and shamed" rather than the powerful'. We need to challenge the status, privileges and prerogatives of dominant classes and elites (Alvesson / Willmott 1992a, p. 12). We need to question their real worldviews and codes of conduct as well as their factual actions or non-actions. We also need to interrogate more thoroughly the socio-philosophical, ethical, and ideological basis on which such claims for social dominance and privileges are being made, defended and justified. And we need to criticise where privileges and prerogatives are not ethically justified, or when they contradict values such as democracy, justice, freedom or equality.

The same is true of the disadvantaged. Simply because people are subordinates does not make them better citizens. Many subordinates also develop different strategies and tactics to turn social reality to their favour, to gain advantages and privileges within social structures and social processes. And they, too, have developed ethical and moral systems and ideology which explain and justify social reality and social action. Subordinates' actions and ideologies can and must be seen not only in functional ways, but also in critical and reflective, and sympathetic ways. However, one of the differences between the advantaged and disadvantaged, the powerful and the powerless is that the possibilities of the latter are often limited, sometimes to a dramatic extent. One major area of social and organisational discrimination is the opportunities for participation, particularly in decision-making processes and discourses. Most employees for example, are systematically excluded from (strategic) decision-making, and organisational communication is largely top-down. Academic investigations into management, organisations and business are mainly manager-oriented and address work-related issues in rather functional terms. Alvesson / Willmott (1992a, p. 8) therefore demand that we pay more 'attention to various interest groups and perspectives that are under-represented or silenced in mainstream writings and in corporate talk and decision-making'. We need to give the disadvantaged, the repressed and marginalised a voice and speak out for the mistreated (e.g. Antonacopoulou 1999, p. 3, Jermier 1998, p. 240).

Perhaps even more importantly, a realistic management and organisation studies needs to address the *institutional* foundations of systematic discrimination, i.e. the institutionalisation of injustice and inequalities, of advantages and disadvantages, privileges and prerogatives. We need to further analyse the unjust conditions which not only produce but maintain, and often even increase, social differences and inequalities. We need to reveal the whole system whereby 'more powerful groups and individuals reap the benefits of participating in processes through which less-powerful people and the natural environment are mistreated' (Jermier 1998, p. 236). And this is particularly necessary for managerial organisations since these are some of the most unjust and oppressive institutions in modern economies and societies. It is about critically examining and criticising the unjust allocation of privileges, the power relationships within hierarchical organisations and at the workplace, and what can and should be done about them (Jacques 1996, pp. 8–9). According to Horkheimer (1972, cited in Jermier 1998, p. 238), 'the project of the critical theorist is to think in the service of exploited and oppressed humanity and to work for the abolition of social injustice'. In this sense, realistic management and organisation studies is about revealing the conditions and perspectives of the disadvantaged and under-privileged, about making 'a commitment to the victims of corporate power' (Adler 2002, p. 390) and actively seeking to fight oppression, and to end exploitation, injustice, and bigotry (e.g. Brookfield 2005, p. 10, Antonacopoulou 1999, p. 3).

To summarise, despite all its inconsistencies, flaws and negative consequences, the ideology of management is not presently being challenged. According to Whittington (1992, p. 708) management research should 'investigate how individual leaders constitute and sustain their authority within different social systems, . . .' Up until now, the issues of power and politics, and ideology and interests have received too little attention in the field of management and organisation studies (Ferdinand 2004, p. 435, Coopey / Burgoyne 2000, p. 869). If we really want to understand what keeps organisations going, why they are the way they are, and the reasons behind managers' and employees' positions, decisions and behaviour, we need to address these issues at the outset:

a) The purpose(s) of organisations and management
b) Interests concerning and within organisations
c) Power and control in organisations
d) Ideologies about management and organisations
e) The privileged and the disadvantaged

Everything else can be seen within or in relation to this framework.

THE NEED FOR CHANGE AND ALTERNATIVES

It is relatively easy to criticise things. The challenge is to come up with something better—to show how the current state can be changed and the future state can be achieved (and sustained). But that's exactly the idea of all critical theory. Fournier / Grey (2000, p. 16) made the point that 'to be engaged in critical management studies means, at the most basic level, to say that there is something wrong with management, as a practice and as a body of knowledge, and that it should be changed'. Critical Management Studies aims to provide people with the knowledge and skills necessary to free themselves from any kind of oppression. It can be seen in the tradition of one of Marx' most famous statements, his eleventh thesis on Feuerbach: *"The philosophers have only interpreted the world in various ways—the point is to change it!"* Ruling out unlawful and non-democratic ways of change, this means demonstrating either how existing social systems and institutions, in our case organisations, can be transformed or how new alternative organisations can be created. This must take place within the current framework of legal, economic and social institutions, i.e. the very same institutions which largely support and protect the status quo and fight far-reaching alternatives (Burnham 1941, p. 169).

This seems to be an even more challenging task when considering how comprehensive and thorough the dominance of orthodox management and managers is. As the analysis in this book has demonstrated, managers are institutionally empowered. Their positions, areas of responsibilities and influence are created and protected by several, very strong institutions (e.g. organisational structures, governance, external bodies and stakeholders, societal values). The dominance of managers and the ideology of management (as well other capitalistic ideologies such as consumerism, calculative selfishness and the overall economisation of the lifeworld) have reached hegemonic status. Managers *and* employees—*all* social classes—have learned not only to accept unjust social order but to see it as the norm and normality. Worse still, many people (after appropriate socialisation and conditioning) see unjust social order largely as being in their own and best interest. It is in superiors' interest to keep and even extend their power and control, privileges and prerogatives, and it is also in subordinates' interests to take advantage of the system under the cover of smooth functioning. There are quite some advantages to managerialism and the managerial organisation and people are very aware of these. *By and large*, people get a lot out of the organisation they are working for, and, hence, have various interests in continuing to do so. Of course, the job comes with a lot of downsides, but who cares? Most people live and work in 'comfortable, smooth, reasonable, democratic unfreedom' (Marcuse 1964, cited in Brookfield 2005, p. 188). Quite understandably, the processes of socialisation conditioning and the daily rat-race do their work on all of us. People look for the next possible treat or advantage and come to the conclusion that their jobs are, overall, "not too bad". *Why should they challenge the status quo? Why should they change the very foundation on which they can make their own little career steps?*

Moreover, there is no need to come up with ideas for change. Orthodox management has developed 'change' as one of its own core rationales; strategic change, change management, organisational and individual learning are bread and butter for both managers and employees in the face of an ever-changing and increasingly challenging business environment. Managers are 'change facilitators', employees are 'change agents'. Although *almost all* change initiated by orthodox economics or management studies never really changes anything (i.e. it is mostly technical, rarely fundamental change), the rhetoric of change and innovation is enough to provide people with the impression that things change, develop, and improve all the time. In this respect the ideology of management is rather different from other orthodox ideologies. Whereas the latter see change as evil, the former regards change as the panacea for keeping things stable.

On the other hand, *social change has happened*—even the currently dominant classes, ideologies and practices have not always been around but came into existence through social change. The history of mankind is a history of social change. In this sense, it is not unrealistic to think about real alternatives and how we can really change contemporary management and organisations. First therefore, we need to draw employees' as well as managers' attention to the fact that managerial organisations (as well as other social systems and realities) are *not* the norm—nor are they based on, or function in accordance with 'natural laws'. They are all man-made, i.e. designed, shaped and kept going by our interests and decisions, social actions or omissions. Social institutions can be changed and modified according to a wealth of different principles and values, purposes and needs. This 'opening up' of our views on social reality enables us to see it in a much more differentiated light.

However, this is only the first step. We need to draw people's attention to all that is (still) missing, largely neglected and oppressed in managerial organisations, e.g. democracy, justice and freedom—the whole range of ethical and social values our societies are so (rightly) proud of in public. We also particularly need to make people more aware of the *whole* price they pay—both managers and employees!—for smooth functioning within the managerial organisation. We must ceaselessly highlight the *fundamental* flaws of the dominance of managers and managerial organisations, together will all the injustice, inequalities, inefficiencies and narrow-mindedness that come with these social institutions. We need to draw attention to the poor and narrow-minded conditions in most of these organisations which stifle people's thoughts and creativity, prevent them from realising their full potential, from making decisions about their own concerns, or hinder them from following their ideas and dreams.

Making people aware of what is missing lays the foundation for, and contributes to, the development of what Marcuse (referred to in Brookfield 2005, p. 54) called a 'rebellious subjectivity' of people. *It is about our cognitive, intellectual, psychological, sociological, ethical, legal and technical abilities to fundamentally question and challenge social reality.* People can, *and should,* expect much more from their working life and their involvement in organisational affairs than simple smooth functioning and a few material advantages. And we need to make clear that these expectations should not be portrayed as "illegitimate demands" or "plain nagging" but as the basic humanity which people can *rightfully* expect in and from every social system. *It is a fundamental human right to criticise oppressive systems and to expect as well as to strive for circumstances which enable individuals to live to their full human potential!*

In this sense, criticism is also one of the necessary preconditions for social change. As Brookfield (2005, p. 69) explained: 'When people really believe that they "mustn't grumble," then the system is safe. Grumbling, on the other hand, challenges the system. If enough people grumble, they might start to hear each other's low rumbling sound of protest and decide to seek each other out in order to do something. If "mustn't grumble" is ideology in action, then "must grumble" is the start of ideological critique'. In this sense, we need to encourage people to criticise contemporary oppressive social systems, undeserved privileges and prerogatives, and inhuman working conditions.

The idea that change is possible and necessary is completed by the demonstration of *positive alternatives.* We need to provide existing positive examples or develop new concepts of true alternatives to managerial organisation and the dominance of managers. Probably the most important, and definitely the most difficult, part of any critical enterprise, is to provide an *elaborated and realistic* positive alternative to the status quo (e.g. Doane 2003, p. 616, Walsh / Weber 2002, p. 409, Jermier 1998, p. 237).[3] Such alternatives can still be developed within contemporary managerial discourses. The aim is to put into practice 'more humane forms of management', i.e. to improve the working conditions of employees within hierarchical organisations (Fournier / Grey 2000, p. 23). Such approaches usually lead to more and better human resource management, different forms of collaboration at operational levels (e.g. teamwork, flexible hours), and a whole range of employee-oriented policies and procedures. Those people who have worked for organisations which seriously practice 'Investors in People' standards, e.g., know that such policies make a real difference. The managerial organisation is comparatively open to change and can be stretched towards (some of) the ideals of the learning organisation.

However, what the managerial organisation will never allow is a change of its fundamental principles (e.g. profit orientation, dominance of managers, hierarchy etc.). There is therefore an even greater need for *fundamentally* different alternatives to managerial organisations and the dominance of managers, i.e. forms of organisations and social systems which are no longer based on the orthodox, unjust and exploitative superior-subordinate relationship. With reference to some of the most important founders of Critical Theory (particularly Horkheimer, Adorno, Marcuse, Fromm and Habermas), Alvesson / Willmott (1992b, p. 435) summarised this notion: 'A fundamental claim of the proponents of CT is that social science can and should contribute to the liberation of people from unnecessarily restrictive traditions, ideologies, assumptions, power relations, identity formations, and so forth, that inhibit or distort opportunities for autonomy, clarification of genuine needs and wants, and thus greater and lasting satisfaction (. . .).'

Throughout the whole period of capitalism, there have been alternatives and there are many examples of successful alternative businesses out there. For example, types of organisations such as the 'democratic organisation' (e.g. partnerships, co-operatives, employee-owned companies) take the idea of empowerment and workplace democracy very seriously. They comprise ideas like worker participation in strategic and operational decision-making, autonomous work groups, profit-sharing, co-partnership and share ownership (e.g. de Jong / van Witteloostuijin 2004, Wagner 2002, Wilson 1999, Wunderer 1999, Case / Bianchi 1993, Kelly / Kelly 1991). Enabling workplace democracy actually does 'increase efficiency, innovativeness, and productivity' and at the same time has 'beneficial consequences of developing the individual, the organization, and consequently the wider society' (de Jong / van Witteloostuijin 2004, p. 54). There is increasing empirical evidence that an organisation's 'democratic structures and procedures help to develop and sustain organizational adaptation and learning capabilities and competencies which are critical to a knowledge- and service-based economy' (ibid., p. 54). With the help of such examples, we can demonstrate and explain how these alternative forms of organisations function and how they can be developed even further. They also clearly demonstrate that it is not simply about a decision between "material advantages *or* democratic organisations" but that both can be combined in forms of economically successful organisations which at the same time enable people to develop their full potential. If people are truly engaged in organisational affairs (i.e. discursively *and* materially), both the organisation and the individual will benefit. Democratic organisations provide convincing solutions to the problems of managerial dominance, excesses in hierarchical decision-making processes, and the prevalence of managerial ideology and rhetoric. They also resist the exploitation, conditioning, and de-motivation of employees. Democratic organisations are *a real as well as realistic alternative to managerial organisations.*

Nonetheless, democratic organisations are no panacea. They can only correct some of the major flaws in the design and governance of managerial organisations. Even the most developed forms of democratic organisations are anything but problem-free. For example, democratic decision-making processes do not diminish organisational politics; on the contrary, they might even enhance such behaviour. In addition, the majority can still exercise oppressive forms of control and conditioning in a democracy (Brookfield 2005, p. 64)—Fromm even refers to a 'tyranny of the majority'. Most of the socio-psychological and social problems humans face or generate will not disappear simply because an organisation is no longer managerial. And in some ways, they are more demanding—participative structures and processes require different values and additional effort from people. As Brookfield (2005, p. 177) rightly said, 'participatory democracy is hard work. It does not allow you to sit back and let others do your thinking, talking, and deciding for you'.

These points indicate that the project of enlightenment and emancipation is far from over. The overall goal might be the establishment of a truly free society, i.e. to free human beings from the conditions and power relations that enslave them (Horkheimer 1976, referred to in Carr 2000, p. 211, see also Fournier / Grey 2000, pp. 19–20) and to work toward an utopia where societies, organisations and social relations are free from exploitation, oppression and social injustice (e.g. Jermier 1998, p. 237, Alvesson / Willmott 1992b, p. 432). This striving for freedom has been (mis-) interpreted by some key proponents of Critical Theory as well as many opponents of the idea of enlightenment as "free of any constraints, structure and leading principles"—i.e. anarchy. Indeed, social systems based on such a notion are either hopelessly unrealistic or horribly immoral. Thus when we talk about the idea of truly free individuals, organisations and society, we need to search for, interrogate and discuss the validity and usefulness of *other* values and principles, i.e. those which can help to achieve freedom for people as well as better and more just social and societal structures and processes. Only then do they represent true alternatives to all the orthodox types of organisations and societies we have seen so far. In this sense, we need to take the concept of the democratic organisation even further: we must analyse which additional alternative value orientations and principles might be useful. These might include general welfare, equality and social justice, civic virtues, community norms, communitarian values and citizenship (e.g. Brookfield 2005, p. 10, Kirkpatrick et al. 2005, p. 41, Michael 2005, p. 105, Skålén 2004, p. 251, Gabriel 1999, p. 404, Hoggett 1996, p. 14, Pollitt 1990, p. 60). Jermier (1998, p. 237) captured this idea rather poignantly:

> Critical theory also has a normative component that stresses not what is but what could be or should be. It encourages reflection on the possibilities of a future society and cultivates the utopian imagination. This is important because utopian images are the foundations of critique: they shape social definitions of mistreatment. It is also important because part of the critical theory project involves working toward utopian states that are free from exploitation, oppression, and social injustice.

Most of what has been said about present managers and employees is also true for *future* managers and employees. The current status of teaching and research at business schools is highly disappointing. Management and organisation studies are too often narrow-minded, tunnel-visioned and politically partial (Alvesson / Willmott 1992a, pp. 3, 5). They are predominantly concerned with the development and provision of concepts, techniques and technologies about and for contemporary management practices seen from a management perspective (Yanow 2007, p. 176). Worse still, most teaching and research provided by business schools is largely designed to produce, on an industrial scale, future employees, lower and middle managers who will function smoothly. They will do their utmost, and even take pride in fitting into managerial organisations and re-producing existing social order and power relations. It is sad to see the extent of intellectual capabilities, talent, time and energy which are wasted in attempts to fit into existing unjust and ill-designed systems. It is depressing to see the continuing "business-fication" of business schools, and the deeply anti-academic and anti-intellectual climate that accompanies this worldwide trend. For this, future generations will rightly blame us.

We therefore need to particularly remind ourselves what academia stands for. It is "the" place—*and the only* social institution—where people have the time and resources to think freely about society and social institutions, and to critically reflect on past, present and future issues in a systematic and comprehensive manner. Academics have to become aware once more of 'the political implications of academic work' (Jermier 1998, p. 236). In the case of management and organisations, this especially means to see them from a broad, multi-purpose, multi-value, differentiated, critical, enlightened and utopian perspective. It means seeing the relations between individuals, groups, organisations and societies in more than mere functional and / or economic terms. For this, philosophical, ethical, social and environmental concerns must be *at the core* of the management and organisation studies' curriculum, not only as peripheral 'nice-to-haves' (or even politically correct 'must-haves'). This is the important 'distinction between education *for* management or business, and education *about* business and management' (Watson 2001, p. 386). On a more practical level, this means two things.

One is that we need to contribute to students' development in becoming *citizens*, not managers—particularly in today's diverse, multi-faceted knowledge economies and information societies. Students need to be able to see things from a critical perspective, to question and to challenge everything, especially dominant ideologies, and to ask the questions that are never or rarely raised (Doane 2003, p. 618). Students need to become critical and reflective practitioners. Brookfield, who has written one of the best, if not the best, book on Critical Theory for adult learning and teaching, summarised the task excellently (2005, p. 39) as learning to recognize and challenge ideology that attempts to portray the exploitation of the many by the few as a natural state of affairs, learning to uncover and counter hegemony, learning to unmask power, learning to overcome alienation and thereby accept freedom, learning to pursue liberation, learning to reclaim reason, and learning to practice democracy.

And secondly, we must provide students with positive alternatives and convincing ideas for building a better world in the future (Goshal 2005, p. 87). It is about implanting in students' hearts and minds the desire and openness to search for new and better forms of organisations and their management, for truly democratic organisations and social systems and an enlightened, just and equal society. If we don't do this as academics, we are not much more than the paid servants of power and contemporary foolishness.

CONCLUSIONS

This whole book has been about the dominance of managers, and the ideology of management and managerial organisations. It has examined power, interests and management ideology, and how devastating many of their effects are for organisations, individuals and our society. It has shed some light on the pathology of (some) managerial institutions and their malfunctions. Too much harm has been done in the name of management. Our private and public organisations are run in appallingly inefficient and unjust ways by managers who are at the same time both offenders and victims of the system—not to mention the anonymous employees. "There is something rotten in our private and public organisations!" The social dominance of managers is *not* a convincing solution for organisations, the managerial organisation is *not* the norm; it is *an anomaly within democratic society*.

It is high time for us to change this. This change could happen within existing business practices without any contribution from academics, the media or politicians. Social reality is sufficiently dynamic and flexible enough that it can and does change itself without any 'theoretical' input whatsoever. We cannot say whether and how social change will happen. But we can try to change and re-design social reality consciously for the better. And *we can*, and therefore *must*, develop management and organisation studies which are capable of coping with the requirements as well as possibilities of modern societies. This final chapter has outlined some of the most important and pressing issues we need to address more thoroughly. There are possibly more issues which need to be tackled. But those mentioned here indicate the direction which realistic management and organisation studies might take as their core. Generally speaking, realistic management and organisation studies should be able to keep the notion of fundamental critique and utopian alternative alive without being or becoming an esoteric pastime of insiders. At the same time, it can contribute to real-world problems in a realistic manner without becoming the servant of prevailing ideology and the dominant order. As shown above, it is possible to tackle both problems and, in doing so, develop serious and convincing alternatives to managerialistic mainstream thinking. We are in the 21st century: the fact that the ideology of management is less dreadful than many other radical ideologies does not mean that we should stop searching for better, more democratic and just alternatives. Our primary task is to end unjust social dominance in order to improve our institutions and organisations in accordance with the democratic principles and ethical values of our society. In this sense, realistic management and organisation studies is nothing new—it simply fits into the long-lasting tradition of critical theory and enlightenment.

There is a real need for more critique and criticism in management studies (Apple 2005, p. 17). We need to strengthen approaches and research that

a) contribute to a better understanding of how management and organisations *really* happen and function,
b) investigate the causes, explanations and consequences of power, interests and ideologies such as managerialism and
c) provide managers *and* employees with critical and emancipatory alternatives to the neo-liberal and managerialistic ideology.

The probably most important task is to come up with alternatives to current forms of managerial and organisational dimensions of power and control—*in collaboration with* managers but, if necessary, also *against* established practices and establishment. As David MacMichael (1984, cited in Frank 2001, p. 629) put it: 'The essence of power for these people is that they control the vision of reality. When you put forward an alternative to that, they get very angry because you are breaking an essential monopoly'. This is the real task of our time—we must make some people angry.

Notes

NOTES TO CHAPTER 1

1. As well as other groups of people whose business and professional activities are related to a great extent to management, i.e. business and management consultants, business organisations, business school academics, business- and management-oriented media and professions.
2. Quite interesting and telling insights into the mindsets of this new breed of all-purpose managers can be found in Zaleznik 1989.
3. If one sees Babbage's book 'On the Economy of Machinery and Manufacturers', which was published in 1832, as the written evidence for the emergence of modern management. For some history of management / the making of managers see, e.g. McKinlay / Wilson 2006, Burrell 2002, Fournier / Grey 2000, Jacques 1996, Barley / Kunda 1992, Reed / Anthony 1992, or Abercrombie et al. 1980.
4. For critical reflection on this, see e.g. Grey 1999, Townley 1993, Alvesson / Willmott 1992a, Willmott 1984.
5. With a few welcomed exceptions such as Clegg et al.'s 2006 'Power and Organizations' and several contributions particularly within Critical Management Studies.

NOTES TO CHAPTER 2

1. 'Class' is meant here solely in a methodological sense. In Chapter 6 there will be a discussion about whether managers can be seen as either a social group or a social class. This discussion then is more a sociological or socio-philosophical one.
2. Some of the in-group (or intra-class) differences between managers will be addressed in Chapters 3 through 5.
3. Quite often even the title doesn't really help. Because of its attractiveness, the title of 'manager' has become so widespread that it sometimes has lost all its meaning. A quick look at job advertisements reveals that team leaders, operational staff (such as salespersons or back-office employees) are also often called 'managers'. Even secretaries, shop-floor assistants and apprentices sometimes have the title of a manager.

NOTES TO CHAPTER 3

1. There is one concept within neoclassical economics / orthodox management studies which copes explicitly with power and control: the principal-agent

or agency theory (e.g. Grossmann / Hart 1983) as part of new institutional economics (North 1991, Williamson 1975, Alchian / Demsetz 1972, Coase 1937). However, because of its game-theoretical nature and very strong, unrealistic assumptions (e.g. rational behaviour, Pareto optimum, negative image of humans, opportunism only on the side of the agent), it does not contribute much to the investigation of factual power within real organisations.

2. For outlines and application of Critical Management Studies and the concept of 'organisational politics' see e.g. Diefenbach 2007, Clegg et al. 2006, Brookfield 2005, Balogun / Johnson 2004, Walsh / Weber 2002, Courpasson 2000, Cohen et al. 1999, Willmott 1997, Alvesson / Willmott 1992a, b, Pettigrew 1992, Willmott 1987, Mintzberg 1985, Knights / Willmott 1985, Burns 1961.

3. For example, Robert A. Dahl's classic definition of power (1957, cited in Lukes 1974, pp. 11–12) is very similar to Weber's understanding: 'A has powers over B to the extent that he can get B to do something that B would not otherwise do'.

4. For outlines and application of linguistic, post-modern and constructivist concepts see e.g. Sillince 2007, 1999, Clegg et al. 2006, Vickers / Kouzmin 2001, Alvesson / Kärreman 2000, Isabella 1990, Daft / Weick 1984, Giddens 1976, 1984, Berger / Luckmann 1966.

5. However, this chapter will not address primitive forms of power such as physical force and punishment or with extreme forms of control such as slavery, imprisonment or Orwellian forms of control. This is not to deny that these forms still exist even in parts of industrialised nations or in developing countries—often in the most appalling and horrendous forms. But this chapter concentrates on what is portrayed, perceived and accepted as the use of "normal" forms of power and control in "normal" organisations, i.e. forms of power and control which are largely not questioned and challenged but part of our daily (organisational) lives and routines.

6. This idea of leadership can be also seen in a slightly more cynical, quite funny, but nonetheless very telling way, as Bolchover (2005, p. 84) demonstrated:

> Being a leader of your common-or-garden large company is generally very easy. At least, it is at present. You get paid loads, everyone looks like they are having the best sex of their life every time you open your mouth, and you can indulge every middle-aged [wo]man's fantasy of listening constantly to the sound of your own voice by pontificating ad infinitum about the future of your industry or your own company strategy. You either retire a demi-god, or get sacked, receive a huge pay-off and take the gravy train to your next destination, where yet more sycophants shake their heads in sheer disbelief at your incisive brilliance.

Nonetheless, the problem of 'leadership'—particularly its hierarchical understanding—is much more serious than "only" flattering and pampering egos.

7. This doesn't exclude subordinates' (and superiors') widespread unofficial and hidden activities such as taking advantage of, or playing the system, shirking, cheating, or even subversive behaviour (what Scott 1990 described and analysed as 'hidden transcripts'). On the contrary: every oppressive system to a certain degree takes into account such behaviour (because no control can be absolutely complete and comprehensive), even needs to provide some 'un-controlled' space to its subordinates as a 'safety valve-function'.

8. Again, there can be a whole range of psychological reactions on the side of subordinates. However, since this section overall is about compliance and managerial dominance, tactics of the individual of *not* complying, leaving or even fighting the whole system—as interesting as these might be—will not be investigated further.

NOTES TO CHAPTER 4

1. However, James / Rassekh (2000) rightly draw the attention to the fact that by reducing him to this position and misrepresenting him as a supporter of egoism and selfishness, Adam Smith has been much misinterpreted. For a differentiated discussion of the principle of self-interest and Adam Smith's interpretation see also Suttle (1987).

2. Since this is not a philosophical discussion we do not need to consider whether or where to draw a line *within* the human race (e.g. if and when unborn or newborn babies, coma patients, mentally ill or heavily disabled people have got, or can have interests) or *between* humans and other living beings, i.e. where the class of interest-oriented animals ends (e.g. most higher developed mammals seem to be able to have interests and to develop some form of tactical behaviour to reach their objectives)—or whether it is possible at all to draw a line in such grey areas.

3. However, this is not a general claim but limited to societies in which the individual is more or less free and able to make decisions. In a dictatorship, strong hierarchical organisations or other oppressive forms of interpersonal relations, the room for making use of personal freedom can be limited or even absent.

4. For example, Moore / Loewenstein (2004, p. 190) differentiated between automatic, relatively effortless and unconscious processes on the one hand, and controlled, more effortful and analytical processes on the other hand.

5. Of course, organisations also can, and often want to influence their environment. The larger and stronger an organisation is, the more its managers might be interested in (and capable of) influencing its value chains, industry-specific issues such as standards and / or the image of their business, even political and regulatory issues. However, even the large corporations argue (rightly or wrongly) that they are under the Damocles sword of global changes and national regulations; i.e. that they have to understand, accept and find answers to the challenges and changes happening in their business environment.

6. This is not the place to investigate where such ideologies come from, how they enter and shape business practices and who gets what out of the fads-and-fashions industry. Parties involved are international organisations (e.g. Organisation for Economic Co-operation and Development [OECD], World Bank, International Monetary Fund), government and politicians in general, governmental organisations, think tanks, pressure groups, the media and fashion-setters, management consultants, popular business publications (management gurus, business mass-media publications) and academics (e.g. Bolchover 2005, pp. 8–11, 75, Pina / Torres 2003, pp. 334–335, Abrahamson 1996, pp. 254, 264, Willmott 1996, p. 326).

7. And it is not only politicians of national political parties. It is also (senior) representatives of supra-national institutions (such as the World Bank, the Organisation for Economic Co-operation and Development [OECD], the International Consortium for Financial Government Management, and the International Monetary Fund), think tanks and business organisations who have vested interests in collaborating with powerful managers (e.g. Pina / Torres 2003, pp. 334–335, Haque 1999, p. 470).

8. In return, those business schools and academics who behave properly and contribute to the further legitimisation and justification of big business, hierarchical organisations and managers' dominance get larger support from the business community (Rosen 1984, p. 319). As Rosen explained further (ibid.):

   > Support primarily derives from large corporations or individual capitalists, who 'donate' money to build office and class buildings, fund chairs, support research, support consulting and executive education

fees, send some of their members to part and/or full-time M.B.A. programmes, hire the bulk of undergraduate and graduate business school students, and so on. When the explanatory product of a group of theorists significantly diverges from the interests of these practitioners, particularly when this product no longer functions to legitimate and mystify the capitalist power order, its bases of power and relations of domination, this theory is not surprisingly backgrounded.

9. When all analysis is done, in Chapter 6 we will have a more detailed (methodological) discus-sion whether managers can be seen as a group or perhaps even as a social class. We will see that this has important implications for a 'theory of managers' social dominance'.

10. Chapter 5 will analyse some of the ideological cover-up of the egoistic pursuit of personal advantages.

NOTES TO CHAPTER 5

1. With this 'actor-oriented perspective', questions emerge such as: Where do epochal ideologies come from? Who's behind them? Who benefits from them and how? How do ideologies emerge? How do ideologies come into actions? What are the interests of the initiators and users of an ideology? Why do they produce it, and to what ends? And how do they use ideology for the pursuit of their own interests? Are there differences in all of this or is it always the same? This section can only address a few of these, highly relevant questions.

2. As discussed in Chapter 1, that dichotomy is to be understood more as an analytical tool for understanding the complex hierarchical structure and vertical differentiation of managerial organisations which, in fact, represent more a continuum than a dichotomy.

3. However, forms of employees' resistance will not be included in the analysis. For example, Scott (1990) provided quite a comprehensive analysis of both open and hidden forms of subordinates' resistance.

4. And the ones either not willing or not able to understand these systems of 'normal' functioning will be looked after and handled as deviants in complimentary systems within the social, educational, health or legal system.

5. Brookfield (2005, p. 52) called it 'automaton conformity'.

6. Willmott (1996, p. 325) explained this phenomena from a slightly different angle; 'If subordinates can be persuaded that managers simply perform a role, task or function within the division of labour that is necessary to maximize efficiency and effectiveness, resistance to managerial authority appears to be irrational and anti-social—it threatens to undermine the capacity of management to do what, allegedly, is in the universal interests of everyone concerned.'

7. To make this absolutely clear: this reference to psychological needs for stability is not meant to argue for conservatism. Human psychology can point into many directions. Moreover, in a social context, human psychology is always related to sociological, philosophical, legal, cultural and economical aspects. Hence, there might be also many (good or not so good) reasons and individual interests to change a given social order.

NOTES TO CHAPTER 6

1. Similarly, with their Social Dominance Theory Sidanius / Pratto (1999, p. 304) also 'suggest that group-based hierarchy is not only the product of psy-

chological, contextual, and institutional forces, but also the product of the mutually reinforcing interactions among these forces.'

2. After all the analysis carried out in the previous chapters, it might be clear that 'element' here is not understood as a single entity. From a system perspective it is meant in a methodological sense, i.e. every system is constituted by at least two elements and their relation. However, this also means that, if the analysis requires it, every element can be divided into further elements and their relations.

3. The term 'group' is used here in a mere colloquial sense. Further we will enter into a methodological discussion whether managers can be seen as a group or class, if not to say dominating group or class.

4. It must not be necessarily the case that 'the reality' corresponds with individuals' or a group's view. There is a wealth of empirical examples of small groups (e.g. policy-makers), larger groups (e.g. religious orders) or even whole nations which had developed quite distorted opinions about the world they lived in—and in some cases continued to exist in 'their reality' over a longer period of time till, fortunately or unfortunately, a more or less disastrous end stroke.

5. Throughout the whole book we abstract largely from interpersonal and dialectical power relationships in which subordinates, indeed, can be the more powerful actor.

6. Although, one must admit, comparatively 'moderate' compared to truly authoritarian and oppressive organisations and regimes like the Church, the Army, and prisons—or some despotic systems in individual private or public sector organisations or parts of them.

7. Such work-oriented classification schemes (here: occupational scales) which measure the social status and positions of different occupations have considerable analytical and even explanatory power (e.g. Weeden / Grusky 2005).

NOTES TO CHAPTER 7

1. This chapter is based on two papers published previously: Diefenbach, T. (2007) 'The Managerialistic Ideology of Organisational Change Management', *Journal of Organisational Change Management*, 20 (1): 126–144, and Diefenbach, T. (2005) 'Competing Strategic Perspectives and Sense-making of Senior Managers in Academia', *International Journal of Knowledge, Culture and Change Management*, 5 (6): 126–137. For copyright please refer to the publishers.

2. 'New Public Management' was first introduced to public sector organisations in the late 1970s (Adcroft / Willis 2005, p. 389, Dent / Barry 2004, p. 7, Clarke / Clegg 1999, Cohen et al. 1999, p. 477, Wilenski 1988, p. 213). It is a set of assumptions and conclusions about how public sector organisations should be designed, organized, managed and should function in a *quasi-business* manner. The basic idea of New Public Management is to make public sector organisations, and the people working in them, much more 'business-like' and 'market oriented', i.e. oriented toward performance, cost, efficiency and audit (e.g. Deem / Brehony 2005, Deem 2004, Newton 2003, Shattock 2003, Kezar / Eckel 2002, Deem 2001, pp. 10–13, Spencer-Matthews 2001, Vickers / Kouzmin 2001, p. 109–110, Gruening 2001, McAuley et al. 2000, p. 89, Cohen et al. 1999, pp. 477–478).

3. Sometimes this is called 'transitional change' (Austin / Currie 2003, p. 232), 'second-order change' (Bartunek 1984, p. 356), or corresponds with Argyris and Schön's (1978) 'double-loop learning'.

4. In this chapter, no particular term for managers' worldviews is being used. Mostly they are referred to as 'perceptions', 'schemata', 'ideologies' or 'cosmologies' (e.g. Grant et al. 2005, Schwenk 2002, Staples et al. 2001, Samra-Fredericks 2000, Cohen et al. 1999, Coopey et al. 1997, Waller et al., 1995, Meindl et al. 1994, Melone 1994, Isabella 1990, Stubbart, 1989, Daft / Weick 1984, Hambrick / Mason 1984). In academic literature there is not one single term that is widely accepted but many different terms. The most common ones are 'schemas' or 'schemata' (Balogun / Johnson 2004, Harris 1994), 'belief structures' or 'knowledge structures' (Walsh 1995, 1988), 'cognitive maps' (Schwenk 2002) or 'sensemaking, cognitive frameworks, mental models' (Kezar / Eckel 2002).

5. Moreover, the example also reflects a common and global trend in Higher Education: 'the emergence of the entrepreneurial, market-centred university vice-chancellor in the more traditional collegial university . . .' (McAuley et al., 2000, p. 97).

6. By 2000 external consultants had carried out a 'value for money' study on marketing. *This* study suggested that IU should develop a student focus and that this could *not* be achieved by having one large centralised marketing department. A more cynical observer would interpret the second invitation of external consultants as a tactical move to get a decision through or to justify it ex post that was already made by senior managers long before.

7. In internal minutes of IU's Governance bodies, in May 2000 a '10% growth in student numbers from 1999 to 2000', and in July 2000 an 'assumed growth rate of 4% in student numbers', were reported. In December 2002 'first concerns were expressed at the inclusion of a target of 3-5% for student recruitment growth'. In January 2003 it became clear 'that recruitment of new students was below target', in March 2003 the Vice-Chancellor reported 'that the University had not reached the student number target' in this year and again in December 2003 the Vice-Chancellor expressed 'a concern that student recruitment would not meet forecasts'. In 2004 the top-management kept quite silent about the numbers, one Pro-Vice-Chancellor (Students) reported that he was 'confident that the University would be able to meet its current student recruitment targets this year (i.e. an increase of 3%)'. However, in March 2005 the Vice-Chancellor informed that 'current predictions indicated that the University would be 4.2% below its student recruitment target'. In June 2005 'the latest (June) forecast of student numbers indicated that the University was likely to have a shortfall of 6.3% on the 2004/05 target, with a shortfall of 12.2% for new students'.

NOTES TO CHAPTER 8

1. These are core aspects of the 'Manchester capitalism' or 'unregulated capitalism' which we had seen in Europe in the 19th century and are now witnessed particularly in most countries of the former Soviet Union and many countries in East Asia. But these horrific conditions and crimes against humanity are definitely not constituting factors of managerial capitalism.

2. Interests are described and grouped here according to a two-class, dichotomous model only for the sake of clarity and simplicity. The organisational as well as societal reality is, of course, much more complex and needs differentiated analysis.

3. There are far fewer critical thinkers contributing to the enterprise of drafting a positive, if not to say utopian alternative—mainly because it is indeed the most difficult aspect (e.g. Adler 2002, p. 388). It can also go horribly wrong, as history has shown time and again.

Bibliography

AACSB International (2007) *Impact of Research*, Draft for Comments, The Association to Advance Collegiate Schools of Business, Tampa, Florida.

Abercrombie, N., Hill, S., Turner, B.S. (1980) *The Dominant Ideology Thesis*, London: Allen & Unwin.

Abrahamson, E. (1996) 'Management fashion', *Academy of Management Review*, 21 (1): 254–285.

Abrahamson, E., Eisenman, M. (2001) 'Why management scholars must intervene strategically in the management knowledge market', *Human Relations*, 54, 67–75.

Adcroft, A., Willis, R. (2005) 'The (un) intended outcome of public sector performance measurement', *International Journal of Public Sector Management*, 18 (5): 386–400.

Adler, P. (2002) 'Critical in the name of whom and what?', *Organization*, 9 (3): 387–395.

Akella, D. (2003) 'A question of power: How does management retain it?', *Vikalpa*, 28 (3): 45–56.

Alchian, A.A., Demsetz, H. (1972) 'Production, information costs, and economic organization', *AER*, 777–795.

Alexander, I.F. (2006) 'A Taxonomy of Stakeholders—Human Roles in System Development', retrieved 04/10/2006 from http://easyweb.easynet.co.uk/~iany/consultancy/stakeholder_ taxonomy/stakeholder_taxonomy.htm

Alvesson, M., Willmott, H. (1992a) 'Critical Theory and Management Studies: An Introduction', in Alvesson, M., Willmott, H. (eds.) *Critical Management Studies*, London: Sage Publications, 1–20.

Alvesson, M., Willmott, H. (1992b) 'On the idea of emancipation in management and organization studies', *Academy of Management Review*, 17 (3): 432–464.

Alvesson, M., Kärreman, D. (2000) 'Taking the linguistic turn in organizational research: Challenges, responses, consequences', *Journal of Applied Behavioral Science*, 36 (2): 136–158.

Alvesson, M., Willmott, H. (2002) 'Identity regulation as organizational control: Producing the appropriate individual', *Journal of Management Studies*, 39 (5): 619–644.

Antonacopoulou, E.P. (1999) 'The Power of Critique—Revisiting Critical Theory at the End of the Century', paper presented at the *1st International Critical Management Studies Conference*, UMIST, Manchester, 14–16 July 1999.

Apple, M.W. (2005) 'Education, markets, and an audit culture', *Critical Quarterly*, 47 (1–2): 11–29.

Argyris, C., Schön, D. (1978) *Organisational Learning: A Theory of Action Perspective*. Reading, MA: Addison-Wesley.

250 Bibliography

Aries, E., Seider, M. (2007) 'The role of social class in the formation of identity: A study of public and elite private college students', *Journal of Social Psychology*, 147 (2): 137–158.

Aronowitz, S., Giroux, H.A. (1985) *Education under Siege—The Conservative, Liberal and Radical Debate over Schooling*, London: Routledge & Kegan Paul.

Aronowitz, S., Giroux, H.A. (1991) *Postmodern Education—Politics, Culture, and Social Criticism*, Minneapolis: University of Minnesota Press.

Ashforth, B.E., Mael, F. (1989) 'Social identity theory and the organisation', *Academy of Management Review*, 14 (1): 20–39.

Austin, J. et al. (1997) 'Guiding organizational change', *New Directions for Higher Education*, 98: 31–56.

Austin, J., Currie, B. (2003) 'Changing organisations for a knowledge economy: The theory and practice of change management', *Journal of Facilities Management*, 2 (3): 229–243.

Azeem, M.A. (2005) 'Effectiveness of managers: A study of public and private sector organizations', *Global Business Review*, 6 (1): 41–54.

Baker, C.R. (2005) 'What is the meaning of "the public interest"? Examining the ideology of the American public accounting profession', *Accounting, Auditing & Accountability Journal*, 18 (5): 690–703.

Baldridge, D.C., Floyd, S.W., Markoczy, L. (2004) 'Are managers from Mars and academicians from Venus? Toward an understanding of the relationship between academic quality and practical relevance', *Strategic Management Journal*, 25 (11): 1063–1074.

Balogun, J., Johnson, G. (2004) 'Organizational restructuring and middle manager sensemaking', *Academy of Management Journal*, 47 (4): 523–549.

Barjot, D. (ed.) (2002) *Catching up with America. Productivity Missions and the Diffusion of American Economic and Technological Influence after the Second World War*, Paris: Presses de L'Université de Paris-Sorbonne.

Barley, S., Kunda, G. (1992) 'Design and devotion: Surges of rational and normative ideologies of control in managerial discourse', *Administrative Science Quarterly*, 37: 363–399.

Bartunek, J.M. (1984) 'Changing interpretive schemes and organizational restructuring: The example of a religious order', *Administrative Science Quarterly*, 29: 355–372.

Beer, M. et al. (1990) 'Why change programs don't produce change', *Harvard Business Review*, 68 (6): 158–166.

Benders, J., van Veen, K. (2001) 'What's in a fashion? Interpretative viability and management fashions', *Organization*, 8 (1): 33–53.

Berger, P., Luckmann, T. (1966) *The Social Construction of Reality: A Treatise in the Sociology of Knowledge*, New York: Anchor Books.

Biddle, B.J. (1979) *Role Theory. Expectations, Identities, and Behaviour*, New York: Academic Press.

Biddle, B.J. (1986) 'Recent developments in role theory', *Annual Review of Sociology*, 12: 67–92.

Blau, P.M. (1970) 'A formal theory of differentiation in organizations', *American Sociological Review*, 35 (2): 201–218.

Boddy, C.R. (2006) 'The dark side of management decisions: Organisational psychopaths', *Management Decision*, 44 (10): 1461–1475.

Bohman, J. (2005) 'We, heirs of Enlightenment: Critical theory, democracy and social science', *International Journal of Philosophical Studies*, 13 (3): 353–378.

Bolchover, D. (2005) *The Living Dead—Switched off, Zoned out. The Shocking Truth about Office Life*, Chichester: Capstone.

Bontis, N. (2001) 'Assessing knowledge assets: A review of the models used to measure intellectual capital', *International Journal of Management Reviews*, 3 (1): 41–60.

Bourdieu, P. (1983) 'Ökonomisches Kapital, kulturelles Kapital, soziales Kapital', in: Kreckel, R. (ed.) *Soziale Ungleichheiten. Soziale Welt*, Sonderband 2, Göttingen: Schwartz Verlag, 183–198.

Bowler, S., Donovan, T., Karp, J.A. (2006) 'Why politicians like electoral institutions: Self-interest, values, or ideology?', *Journal of Politics*, 68 (2): 434–446.

Boyer, R. (2005) 'From shareholder value to CEO power: The paradox of the 1990s', *Competition and Change*, 9 (1): 7–48.

Bracker, J. (1980) 'The historical development of the strategic management concept', *Academy of Management Review*, 5 (2): 219–224.

Braynion, P. (2004) 'Power and leadership', *Journal of Health Organization and Management*, 18 (6): 447–463.

Bresser-Pereira, L.C. (2001) 'Self-interest and incompetence', *Journal of Post Keynesian Economics*, 23 (3): 363–373.

Brookfield, S.D. (2005) *The Power of Critical Theory for Adult Learning and Teaching*, Maidenhead: Open University Press.

Brooks, I., Bate, P. (1994) 'The problems of effecting change within the British Civil Service: A cultural perspective', *British Journal of Management*, 5: 177–190.

Brown, D.M., Laverick, S. (1994) 'Measuring corporate performance', *Long Range Planning*, 27 (4): 89–98.

Brown, G., Lawrence, T.B., Robinson, S.L. (2005) 'Territoriality in organizations', *Academy of Management Review*, 30 (3): 577–594.

Bruch, H. et al. (2005) 'Strategic change decisions: Doing the right change right', *Journal of Change Management*, 5 (1): 97–106.

Burnham, J. (1941) *The Managerial Revolution*, New York: The John Day Company.

Burns, T. (1961) 'Micropolitics: Mechanisms of institutional change', *Administrative Science Quarterly*, 6 (3): 257–281.

Burrell, G. (2002) 'Twentieth-century quadrilles—Aristocracy, owners, managers, and professionals', *International Studies of Management & Organizations*, 32 (2): 25–50.

Butterfield, R., Edwards, C., Woodall, J. (2004) 'The New Public Management and the UK Police Service', *Public Management Review*, 6 (3): 395–415.

Butterfield, R., Edwards, C., Woodall, J. (2005) 'The New Public Management and managerial roles: The case of the police sergeant', *British Journal of Management*, 16 (4): 329–341.

Carr, A. (2000) 'Critical theory and the management of change in organizations', *Journal of Organizational Change Management*, 13 (3): 208–220.

Carroll, W.K. (2007) 'From Canadian corporate elite to transnational capitalist class: Transitions in the organization of corporate power', *Canadian Review of Sociology and Anthropology*, 44 (3): 265–288.

Carson, P.P. et al. (1999) 'A historical perspective on fad adoption and abandonment', *Journal of Management History*, 5 (6): 320–333.

Case, J., Bianchi, A. (1993) 'A company of business people', *Inc.*, 15 (4): 79–89.

Casey, C. (1999) 'Come Join Our Family: Discipline and Integration in Corporate Organizational Culture', *Human Relations*, 52 (1): 155–178.

Chandler, A.D. (1977) *The Visible Hand: The Managerial Revolution in American Business*, Boston: Harvard University Press.

Chiapello, E., Fairclough, N. (2002) 'Understanding the new management ideology: A transdisciplinary contribution from critical discourse analysis and new sociology of capitalism', *Discourse & Society*, 13 (2): 185–208.

Clarke, T., Clegg, S.R. (1999) 'Changing paradigms in public service management', *Administrative Theory & Praxis*, 21 (4): 485–489.

Clarke, T., Clegg, S.R. (2000) 'Management paradigms for the new millennium', *International Journal of Management Reviews*, 2 (1): 45–64.

Clegg, C., Walsh, S. (2004) 'Change management: Time for a change!', *European Journal of Work and Organizational Psychology*, 13 (2): 217–239.

Clegg, S.R., Courpasson, D., Phillips, N. (2006) *Power and Organizations*, London: Sage Publications.

Coase, R.H. (1937) 'The nature of the firm', *Economica*, 386–405.

Cohen, L., Duberley, J., McAuley, J. (1999) 'Fuelling discovery of monitoring productivity: Research scientists' changing perceptions of management', *Organization*, 6 (3): 473–498.

Coleman, J.S. (1988) 'Social capital in the creation of human capital', *American Journal of Sociology*, 94 (suppl), 95–120.

Collinson, D.L. (2003) 'Identities and Insecurities: Selves at Work', *Organization*, 10 (3): 527–547.

Considine, M. (1990) 'Managerialism strikes out', *Australian Journal of Public Administration*, 49: 166–178.

Contu, A., Willmott, H. (2005) 'You spin me round: The realist turn in organization and management studies', *Journal of Management Studies*, 42 (8): 1645–1662.

Coopey, J., Burgoyne, J. (2000) 'Politics and organizational learning', *Journal of Management Studies*, 37 (6): 869–885.

Coopey, J., Keegan, O., Emler, N. (1997) 'Managers' innovations as "sense-making"', *British Journal of Management*, 8: 301–315.

Courpasson, D. (2000) 'Managerial strategies of domination: Power in soft bureaucracies', *Organization Studies*, 21 (1): 141–161.

Courpasson, E.L., Clegg, S.R. (2006) Dissolving the iron cages? Tocqueville, Michels, bureaucracy and the perpetuation of elite power, *Organization*, 13 (3): 319–343.

Currie, G., Procter, S.J. (2005) 'The antecedents of middle managers' strategic contribution: The case of a professional bureaucracy, *Journal of Management Studies*, 42 (7): 1325–1356.

Cyert, R.M., March, J.G. (1963) *A Behavioral Theory of the Firm*, Englewood Cliffs, NJ: Prentice Hall.

Daft, R.L., Weick, K.E. (1984) 'Toward a model of organizations as interpretation systems', *Academy of Management Review*, 9 (2): 284–295.

Darke, P.R., Chaiken, S. (2005) 'The pursuit of self-interest: Self-interest bias in attitude judgment and persuasion', *Journal of Personality and Social Psychology*, 89 (6): 864–883.

de Jong, G., van Witteloostuijin, A. (2004) 'Successful corporate democracy: Sustainable cooperation of capital and labor in the Dutch Breman Group', *Academy of Management Executive*, 18 (3): 54–66.

Dearborn, D.C., Simon, H.A. (1958) 'Selective perception: A note on the departmental identifications of executives', *Sociometry*, 21 (2): 144–150.

Deem, R. (2001) 'Globalisation, new managerialism, academic capitalism and entrepreneurialism in universities: Is the local dimension still important?', *Comparative Education*, 37 (1): 7–20.

Deem, R. (2004) 'The knowledge worker, the manager-academic and the contemporary UK university: New and old forms of public management?', *Financial Accountability & Management*, 20 (2): 107–128.

Deem, R., Brehony, K.J. (2005) 'Management as ideology: The case of "new managerialism" in higher education', *Oxford Review of Education*, 31 (2): 217–235.

Dent, M., Barry, J. (2004) 'New Public Management and the Professions in the UK: Reconfiguring Control?', in Dent, M., Chandler, J., Barry, J. (eds.) *Questioning the New Public Management*, Aldershot: Ashgate, 7–20.

Diefenbach, T. (2003) *Kritik und Neukonzeption der Allgemeinen Betrieb-swirtschaftslehre auf sozialwissen-schaftlicher Basis*, Wiesbaden: DUV Gabler Verlag.

Diefenbach, T. (2004) 'Different meanings of intangible assets and knowledge— And their implications for management and innovation', *International Journal of Knowledge, Culture and Change Management*, 4: 553–567.

Diefenbach, T. (2005) 'Competing strategic perspectives and sense-making of senior managers in academia', *International Journal of Knowledge, Culture and Change Management*, 5 (6): 126–137.

Diefenbach, T. (2006) 'Intangible resources: A categorial system of knowledge and other intangible assets', *Journal of Intellectual Capital*, 7 (3): 406–420.

Diefenbach, T. (2007) 'The managerialistic ideology of organisational change management', *Journal of Organisational Change Management*, 20 (1): 126–144.

DiMaggio, P.J., Powell, W.W. (1983) 'The iron cage revisited: Institutional isomorphism and collective rationality in organization fields', *American Sociological Review*, 48 (2): 147–160.

Doane, A. W. (2003) 'Confronting Structures of Power: Toward a Humanist Sociology for the 21st Century', *Humanity and Society*, 27 (4): 615–625.

Donaldson, L. (2003) 'Organization Theory as a Positive Science', in Tsoukas, H., Knudsen, C. (eds.) *The Oxford Handbook of Organization Theory. Meta-Theoretical Perspectives*, Oxford: Oxford University Press, 39–62.

Doucouliagos, C. (1995) 'Worker participation and productivity in labor-managed and participatory capitalist firms: A meta-analysis', *Industrial and Labor Relations Review*, 49 (1): 58–77.

Drucker, P.F. (1954) *The Practice of Management*, New York: Harper & Row.

du Gay, P. (2005) 'Which is the "self" in "self-interest"?', *The Sociological Review*, 53 (3): 391–411.

DuVal, G. (2004) 'Institutional conflicts of interest: Protecting human subjects, scientific integrity, and institutional accountability', *Journal of Law, Medicine & Ethics*, 32 (4): 613–625.

Edvinsson, L., Brünig, G. (2000) *Aktivposten Wissenskapital. Unsichtbare Werte bilanzierbar machen*, Wiesbaden: Gabler Verlag.

EFQM (2003a) *Introducing Excellence*, Brussels: European Foundation for Quality Management.

EFQM (2003b) *The Fundamental Concepts of Excellence*, Brussels: European Foundation for Quality Management.

Ellis, S. (1998) 'A new role for the Post Office: An investigation into issues behind strategic change at Royal Mail', *Total Quality Management*, 9 (2–3): 223–234.

Elstak, M.N., Van Riel, C.B.M. (2005) 'Organizational identity change: An alliance between organizational identity and identification', *Academy of Management Best Conference Paper* 2005 MOC: E1–E6.

Fayol, H. (1949) *General and Industrial Management*, London: Pitman.

Feldman, S.P. (2000) 'Management ethics without the past: Rationalism and individualism in critical organization theory', *Business Ethics Quarterly*, 10 (3): 623–643.

Ferdinand, J. (2004) 'Power, politics and state intervention in organizational learning', *Management Learning*, 35 (4): 435–450.

Ferraro, F., Pfeffer, J., Sutton, R.I. (2005a) 'Economics language and assumptions: How theories can become self-fulfilling', *Academy of Management Review*, 30 (1): 8–24.

Ferraro, F., Pfeffer, J., Sutton, R.I. (2005b) 'Prescriptions are not enough', *Academy of Management Review*, 30 (1): 32–35.

Fincham, R. (1992) 'Perspectives on power: processual, institutional and "internal" forms of organizational power', *Journal of Management Studies*, 26 (9): 741–759.

Finkelstein, S. (1992) 'Power in top management teams: Dimensions, measurement, and validation', *Academy of Management Journal*, 35: 505–538.

Fleetwood, S. (2005) 'Ontology in organization and management studies: A critical realist perspective', *Organization*, 12 (2): 197–222.

Floyd, S. W., Wooldridge, B (1992) 'Middle management involvement in strategy and its association with strategic type: A research note', *Strategic Management Journal*, 13: 153–167.

Floyd, S.W., Wooldridge, B (1994) 'Dinosaurs or dynamos? Recognizing middle management's strategic role', *Academy of Management Executive*, 8 (4): 47–57.

Fournier, V., Grey, C. (2000) 'At the critical moment: Conditions and prospects for critical management studies', *Human Relations*, 53 (1): 7–32.

Frank, L.R. (ed.) (2001) *Random House Webster's Quotationary*, New York: Random House.

Freeman, R.E. (1983) 'Strategic management: A stakeholder approach', *Advances in Strategic Management*, 1: 31–60.

Freiberg, A. (2005) 'Managerialism in Australian criminal justice: RIP for KPIs?', *Monash University Law Review*, 31 (1): 12–36.

Friedman, V.J., Lipshitz, R., Popper, M. (2005) 'The mystification of organizational learning', *Journal of Management Inquiry*, 14 (1): 19–30.

Gabriel, Y. (1999) 'Beyond Happy Families: A Critical Revaluation of the Control-Resistance-Identity Triangle', *Human Relations*, 52 (2): 179–199.

Galbraith, J.K. (1977) *The Age of Uncertainty*, London: BBC.

Gant, J., Ichniowski, C., Shaw, K. (2002) 'Social capital and organizational change in high-involvement and traditional work organizations', *Journal of Economics & Management Strategy*, 11 (2): 289–328.

Gawthrop, L.C. (1999) 'Public service and democratic values: The moral interface', *Administrative Theory & Praxis*, 21 (4): 427–432.

Gentile, E. (2004) 'Fascism, totalitarianism and political religion: Definitions and critical reflections on criticism of an interpretation', *Totalitarian Movements and Political Religions*, 5 (3): 326–375.

Giddens, A. (1976) *New Rules of Sociological Method*, London: Hutchinson University Library.

Giddens, A. (1984) *The Constitution of Society, Outline of the Theory of Structuration*, Cambridge: Polity Press.

Gill, R. (2003) 'Change management—or change leadership?', *Journal of Change Management*, 3 (4): 307–318.

Gioia, D.A., Thomas, J.B. (1996) 'Identity, image, and issue interpretation: Sensemaking during strategic change in academia', *Administrative Science Quarterly*, 41: 370–403.

Goshal, S. (2005) 'Bad management theories are destroying good management practices, *Academy of Management Learning & Education*, 4 (1): 75–91.

Granovetter, M.S. (1973) 'The strength of weak ties', *American Journal of Sociology*, 78 (6): 1360–1380.

Granovetter, M. (1985) 'Economic action and social structure: The problem of embeddedness', *American Journal of Science*, 91 (3): 481–510.

Grant, D. et al. (2005) 'Guest editorial: Discourse and organizational change', *Journal of Organizational Change Management*, 18 (1): 6–15.

Grey, C. (1996) 'Towards a critique of managerialism. The contribution of Simone Weil', *Journal of Management Studies*, 33 (5): 590–611.

Grey, C. (1999) '"We are all managers now"; "We always were"; On the development and demise of management', *Journal of Management Studies*, 36 (5): 561–585.

Grey, C., Willmott, H. (2002) 'Contexts of CMS', *Organization*, 9 (3): 411–418.

Griffin, R. (2006) 'Ideology and culture', *Journal of Political Ideologies*, 11 (1): 77–99.

Gröjer, J.-E. (2001) 'Intangibles and accounting classifications: In search of a classification strategy', *Accounting, Organizations and Society*, 26: 695–713.

Grossmann, S.J., Hart, O.D. (1983) 'An analysis of the principal-agent problem', *Econometrica*, 7–45.

Gruening, G. (2001) 'Origin and theoretical basis of New Public Management', *International Public Management Journal*, 4: 1–25.

Hales, C. (1999) 'Why do managers do what they do? Reconciling evidence and theory in accounts and managerial work', *British Journal of Management*, 10: 335–350.

Hambrick, D.C. (1989) 'Putting top managers back in the strategy picture, *Strategic Management Journal*, 10: 5–15.

Hambrick, D.C. (2007) 'Upper echelons theory: An update', *Academy of Management Review*, 32 (2): 334–343.

Hambrick, D., Mason, P. (1984) 'Upper echelons: The organization as a reflection of its top managers', *Academy of Management Review*, 9: 193–206.

Hamilton, M. (1987): 'The elements of the concept of ideology', *Political Studies*, 35 (1): 18–38.

Haque, M.S. (1999) 'Ethical tension in public governance: Critical impacts on theory-building', *Administrative Theory & Praxis*, 21 (4): 468–473.

Harris, S.G. (1994) 'Organizational culture and individual sensemaking: A schema-based perspective', *Organization Science*, 5 (3): 309–321.

Hartley, J.F. (1983) 'Ideology and organizational behaviour', *International Studies of Management & Organization*, 13 (3): 7–34.

Hassard, J., Hogan, J., Rowlinson, M. (2001) 'From Labor Process Theory to Critical Management Studies', *Administrative Theory & Praxis*, 23 (3): 339–362.

Heames, J. T., Harvey, M. (2006) 'The Evolution of the Concept of the `Executive' from the 20th Century Manager to the 21st Century Global Leader', *Journal of Leadership and Or-ganizational Studies*, 13 (2): 29-41.

Hellawell, D., Hancock, N. (2001) 'A case study of the changing role of the academic middle manager in higher education: between hierarchical control and collegiality?', *Research Papers in Education*, 16 (2): 183–197.

Hendry, J. (2005) 'Beyond self-interest: Agency theory and the board in a satisfying world', *British Journal of Management*, 16: S55–S63.

Hindess, B. (1986) '"Interests" in Political Analysis' in Law, J. (ed.) *Power, Action and Belief. A New Sociology of Knowledge?*, London: Routledge & Kegan Paul, 112–131.

Hogg, M.A., Terry, D.J. (2000) 'Social identity and self-categorization processes in organizational contexts', *Academy of Management Review*, 25 (1): 121–140.

Hoggett, P. (1996) 'New modes of control in the public service', *Public Administration*, 74: 9–32.

Hood, C. (1991) 'A public management for all seasons?', *Public Administration*, 69: 3–19.

Hopwood, A.G. (1987) 'The archeology of accounting systems', *Accounting, Organizations and Society*, 11 (3): 207–234.

Howie, G. (2005) 'Universities in the UK drowning by numbers—Introduction', *Critical Quarterly*, 47 (1–2): 1–10.

Huddy, L. (2004) 'Contrasting theoretical approaches to intergroup relations', *Political Psychology*, 25 (6): 947–967.

Humphrey, M. (2005) '(De)contesting ideology: The struggle over the meaning of the struggle over meaning,' *Critical Review of International Social and Political Philosophy*, 8 (2): 225–246.

Hussain, W. (2007) 'The ethical dimension of class society', *Social Theory and Practice*, 33 (2): 335–344.

Ingram, P., Clay, K. (2000) 'The choice-within-constraints new institutionalism and implications for sociology', *Annual Review of Sociology*, 26: 525–546.

Isabella, L.A. (1990) 'Evolving interpretations as change unfolds: How managers construe key organizational events', *Academy of Management Journal*, 33 (1): 7–41.

Jacques, R. (1996) *Manufacturing the Employee—Management Knowledge from the 19th to 21st Centuries*, London: Sage Publications.

James, C. (2003) 'Economic rationalism and public sector ethics: Conflicts and catalysts', *Australian Journal of Public Administration*, 62 (1): 95–109.

James, H.R., Jr., Rassekh, F. (2000) 'Smith, Friedman, and self-interest in ethical society', *Business Ethics Quarterly*, 10 (3): 659–674.

James, O. (2005) 'The rise of regulation of the public sector in the United Kingdom', *Sociologie du travail*, 47 (3): 323–339.

Jermier, J.M. (1998) 'Introduction: Critical perspectives on organizational control', *Administration Science Quarterly*, 43 (2): 235–256.

Jermier, J.M., Clegg, S.R. (1994) 'Critical issues in organization science: A dialogue', *Organization Science*, 5 (1): 1–13.

Johnson, G., Scholes, K., Whittington, R. (2006) *Exploring Corporate Strategy*, 7th enhanced media ed., Harlow: Pearson Education Limited.

Jost, J.T., Elsbach, K.D. (2001) 'How Status and Power Differences Erode Personal and Social Identities at Work: A System Justification Critique of Organizational Applications of Social Identity Theory', in Hogg, M., Terry, D. (eds.) *Social Identity Processes in Organizational Contexts*, Philadelphia: Psychology Press, 181–196.

Jost, J.T., Hunyady, O. (2005) 'Antecedents and consequences of system-justifying ideologies', *Current Directions in Psychological Science*, 14 (5): 260–265.

Kanter, R.M. (1989) 'The new managerial work,' *Harvard Business Review*, 67 (6): 85–92.

Kaplan, R.S., Norton, D.P. (1992, January–February) 'The Balanced Scorecard—Measures that drive performance', *Harvard Business Review*, 71–79.

Karp, T. (2005) 'Unpacking the mysteries of change: Mental modelling', *Journal of Change Management*, 51: 87–96.

Kärreman, D., Alvesson, M. (2004) 'Cages in tandem: Management control, social identity, and identification in a knowledge-intensive firm', *Organization*, 11 (1): 149–175.

Kelly, J., Kelly, C. (1991) '"Them and us': Social psychology and 'the new industrial relations', *British Journal of Industrial Relations*, 29 (1): 25–48.

Kerr, S., Jermier, J.M. (1978) 'Substitutes for leadership: Their meaning and measurement,' *Organizational Behavior and Human Performance*, 22 (3): 375–403.

Kezar, A., Eckel, P. (2002) 'Examining the institutional transformation process: The importance of sensemaking, interrelated strategies, and balance', *Research in Higher Education*, 43 (3): 295–328.

Kieser, A. (1997) 'Rhetoric and myth in management fashion', *Organization*, 4 (1): 49–74.

Kirkpatrick, I., Ackroyd, S. (2000) 'Transforming the archetype? The new managerialism in social services', *Public Management Review*, 5 (4): 511–531.

Kirkpatrick, I., Ackroyd, S., Walker, R. (2005) *The New Managerialism and Public Service Professions*, New York: Palgrave Macmillan.

Knights, D., Willmott, H. (1985) 'Power and identity in theory and practice', *Sociological Review*, 33 (1): 22–46.

Kramnick, I. (ed.) (1995) *The Portable Enlightenment Reader*, New York: Penguin Books.

Krauss, S. (2006) 'Does ideology transcend culture? A preliminary examination in Romania', *Journal of Personality*, 74 (4): 1219–1256.

Kraut, A.I. et al. (2005) 'The role of the manager: What's really important in different management jobs' reprinted from 1989, 3 (4), *Academy of Management Executive*, 19 (4): 122–129.

Lacey, R. (2007) 'Introduction', *International Public Management Journal*, 10 (2): 131–135.

Landrum, N.E., Gardner, C.L. (2005) 'Using integral theory to effect strategic change', *Journal of Organizational Change Management*, 18 (3): 247–258.

Lawrence, P.R., Lorsch, J.W. (1967) *Organization and Environment: Managing Differentiation and Integration*, Boston: Harvard University.

Lazonick, W. (1992) 'Controlling the market for corporate control: The historical significance of managerial capitalism', *Industrial and Corporate Change*, 1 (3): 445–488.

Lee, E.W.Y., Haque, M.S. (2006) 'The New Public Management reform and governance in Asian NICs: A comparison of Hong Kong and Singapore', *Governance*, 19 (4): 605–626.

Levy, D.L., Alvesson, M., Willmott, H. (2001) 'Critical Approaches to Strategic Management', paper presented at the Critical Management Studies Conference, conference stream: Strategy, 11–13 July 2001, Manchester.

Lieven, A. (2005, 20 October) 'We do not deserve these people', *London Review of Books*, 27 (20): 11–12.

Lukes, S. (1974) *Power: A Radical View*, London: Macmillan.

Maesschalck, J. (2004) 'The impact of New Public Management reforms on public servants' ethics: Towards a theory', *Public Administration*, 82 (2): 465–489.

March, J.M., Simon, H. (1958) *Organizations*, New York: John Wiley & Sons.

Martin, R.R. et al. (2001) 'The self-study as a chariot for strategic change', *New Directions for Teaching and Learning*, 113: 95–115.

Mascarenhas, R.C. (1993) 'Building an enterprise culture in the public sector: Reform of the public sector in Australia, Britain, and New Zealand', *Public Administration Review*, 53 (4): 319–328.

McAuley, J., Duberley, J., Cohen, L. (2000) 'The meaning professionals give to management . . . and strategy', *Human Relations*, 53 (1): 87–116.

McKinlay, A., Wilson, R.G. (2006) 'Small acts of cunning': Bureaucracy, inspection and the career, c. 1890–1914', *Critical Perspective on Accounting*, 17: 657–678.

Mechanic, D. (1962) 'Sources of power of lower participants in complex organizations', *Administrative Science Quarterly*, 7 (3): 349–364.

Meglino, B.M., Korsgaard, M.A. (2004) 'Considering rational self-interest as a disposition: Organizational implications of other orientation', *Journal of Applied Psychology*, 89 (6): 946–959.

Meindl, J.R., Stubbart, C., Porac, J.F. (1994) 'Cognition within and between organizations: Five key questions', *Organization Science*, 5 (3): 289–293.

Melone, N.P. (1994) 'Reasoning in the executive suite: The influence of role, & experiences-based expertise on decision processes of corporate executives', *Organization Science*, 5 (3): 438–455.

Meyer, J.W., Rowan, B. (1977) 'Institutionalized organizations: Formal structure as myth and ceremony', *American Journal of Sociology*, 83: 340–363.

Michael, B. (2005) 'Questioning public sector accountability', *Public Integrity*, 7 (2): 95–110.

Miles, R.E., Snow, C.C., Miles, G. (2007) 'The ideology of innovation', *Strategic Organization*, 5 (47): 423–436.

Miller, D.T. (1999) 'The norm of self-interest', *American Psychologist*, 54 (2): 1053–1060.

Miller, S.J., Hickson, D.J., Wilson, D.C. (2002) 'Decision-making in organizations', first published in 1996, reprinted in Salaman, G. (ed.) *Decision Making for Business*, London: Sage Publications, 74–92.

Mintzberg, H. (1973) *The Nature of Managerial Work*, Harper & Row.

Mintzberg, H. (1979) *The Structuring of Organizations: A Synthesis of the Research*, Englewood Cliffs, NJ: Prentice Hall.

Mintzberg, H. (1985) 'The organization as political arena', *Journal of Management Studies*, 22 (2): 133–154.

Mintzberg, H. (1994) 'Rounding out the managerial job', *Sloan Management Review*, 36 (1): 11–26.

Mitchell, N.J. (2005) 'Calculating and believing: Ideological norms in the cradle of utility maximization', *Social Justice Research*, 18 (3): 243–256.

Moore, D.A., Loewenstein, G. (2004) 'Self-interest, automaticity, and the psychology of conflict of interest', *Social Justice Research*, 17 (2): 189–202.

Morley, L. (2005) 'The micropolitics of quality', *Critical Quarterly*, 47 (1–2): 84–95.

Musson, G., Duberley, J. (2007) 'Change, change or be exchanged: The discourse of participation and the manufacture of identity', *Journal of Management Studies*, 44 (1): 143–164.

n.a. (2007) 'Social Dominance Theory', retrieved 29/05/2007 from http://en.wikipedia.org/wiki/ Social_Dominance_Theory.

Nahapiet, J., Ghoshal, S. (1998) 'Social capital, intellectual capital, and the organizational advantage', *Academy of Management Review*, 23 (2): 242–266.

Nesbit, T. (2006) 'What's the matter with social class?', *Adult Education Quarterly*, 56 (3): 171–187.

Newman, J. (2002) 'Managerialism and Social Welfare', reprint in: Salaman Graeme (ed.) (2002) *Decision Making for Business, Sage Publications*, The Open University: 233–253.

Newton, J. (2002) 'Barriers to effective quality management and leadership: Case study of two academic departments', *Higher Education*, 44: 185-212.

Newton, J. (2003) 'Implementing an institution-wide learning and teaching strategy: Lessons in managing change', *Studies in Higher Education*, 28 (4): 427–441.

Nollmann, G., Strasser, H. (2007) 'The Twofold Class Concept: Traditional Limitations and New Perspectives of Class Research', *Canadian Journal of Sociology*, 32 (3): 371–398.

Nonaka, I. (1991, November–December) 'The knowledge-creating company', *Harvard Business Review*, 96–104.

Norreklit, H. (2000) 'The balance on the balanced scorecard—A critical analysis of some of its assumptions', *Management Accounting Research*, 1 1: 65–88.

North, D.C. (1991) 'Institutions', *Journal of Economic Perspectives*, 5 (1): 97–112.

O'Brien, L.T., Crandall, C.S. (2005) 'Perceiving self-interest: Power, ideology, and maintenance of the status quo', *Social Justice Research*, 18 (1): 1–24.

OECD (1997) *Organisation for Economic Co-operation and Development, Issues and Developments in Public Management: Survey 1996–1997*, OECD.

Page, S. (2005) 'What's new about the New Public Management? Administrative change in the human services', *Public Administration Review*, 65 (6): 713–727.

Palmer, D., Barber, B. (2001) 'Challengers, elites and owning families. A social class theory of corporate acquisitions in the 1960s', *Administrative Science Quarterly*, 46: 87–120.

Parker, M. (2002) *Against Management: Organisation in the Age of Managerialism*, Cambridge: Polity.

Parker, R., Bradley, L. (2000) 'Organizational culture in the public sector: Evidence from six organizations', *International Journal of Public Sector Management*, 13 (2): 125–141.

Perrow, C. (2000) 'An organizational analysis of organizational theory, *Contemporary Sociology*, 29(3): 469–476.

Petit, T.A. (1961) 'Management ideology: Myth and reality', *California Management Review*, 3 (2): 95–103.

Pettigrew, A.M. (1992) 'On studying managerial elites', *Strategic Management Journal*, 13: 163–182.

Pettigrew, A.M. (2002) 'Decision-making as a Political Process', first published 1973, reprinte in Salaman, G. (ed.) *Decision Making for Business*, The Open University: Sage Publications, 97–107.

Pfeffer, J., Fong, C.T. (2002) 'The end of business schools? Less success than meets the eye', *Academy of Management Learning & Education*, 1 (1).

Pina, V., Torres, L. (2003) 'Reshaping public sector accounting: An international comparative view', *Canadian Journal of Administrative Sciences*, 20 (4): 334–350.

Pollitt, C. (1990) *Managerialism and the Public Service—The Anglo-Saxon Experience*, Oxford: Basil Blackwell.

Pollitt, C. (2000) 'Is the emperor in his underwear? An analysis of the impacts of public management reform', *Public Management*, 2 (2): 181–199.

Poole, M. et al. (2003) 'Britain's managers over twenty years: A focus on ownership, control and stakeholder interests', *Journal of General Management*, 28 (4): 1–14.

Protherough, R., Pick, J. (2002) *Managing Britannia—Culture and Management in Modern Britain*, Edgeways, Denton: Brynmill Press.

Rai, S. (2004) 'Values, culture and organisation: The relevance', *International Journal of Human Resources Development and Management*, 4 (3): 297–311.

Ramsey, H. (1996) 'Managing Sceptically: A Critique of Organizational Fashion', in Clegg, S.R., Palmer, G. (eds.): *The Politics of Management Knowledge*, London: Sage Publications, 155–172.

Reed, M.I. (1984) 'Management as a social practice', *Journal of Management Studies*, 21 (3): 273–285.

Reed, M. (2003): 'The Agency/Structure Dilemma in Organization Theory: Open Doors and Brick Walls', in Tsoukas, H., Knudsen, C. (eds.): *The Oxford Handbook of Organization Theory. Meta-Theoretical Perspectives*, Oxford: Oxford University Press, 289–309.

Reed, M.I. (2005) 'Reflections on the 'realist turn' in organization and management studies', *Journal of Management Studies*, 42 (8): 1622–1644.

Reed, M., Anthony, P. (1992) 'Professionalizing Management and Managing Professionalization: British management in the 1980s', *Journal of Management Studies*, 29 (5): 591–613.

Roberts, J. (1984) 'The moral character of management practice', *Journal of Management Studies*, 21 (3): 287–302.

Rosen, M. (1984) 'Myth and reproduction: The contextualization of management theory, method and practice', *Journal of Management Studies*, 21 (3): 304–322.

Rothschild, J., Ollilainen, M. (1999) 'Obscuring but not reducing managerial control: Does TQM measure up to democracy standards?', *Economic and Industrial Democracy*, 20: 583–623.

Rowlinson, M., Toms, S., Wilson, J. (2006) 'Legitimacy and the capitalist corporation: Cross-cutting perspectives on ownership and control', *Critical Perspectives on Accounting*, 17 (5): 681–702.

Ruane, S. (2004) 'It's a Leap of Faith, Isn't it? Managers' Perceptions of PFI in the NHS', in Dent, M., Chandler, J., Barry, J. (ed.) *Questioning the New Public Management*, Aldershot, Ashgate: 129–140.

Rutledge, R.W., Karim, E.K. (1999) 'The influence of self-interest and ethical considerations on managers' evaluation judgments', *Accounting, Organizations and Society*, 24: 173–184.

Ryle, R.R., Robinson, R.V. (2006) 'Ideology, moral cosmology, and community in the United States', *City and Community*, 5 (1): 53–69.

Samra-Fredericks, D. (2000) 'Doing 'Board-in-Action' research—An ethnographic approach for the capture and analysis of directors' and senior managers' interactive routines', *Corporate Governance—Empirical Research-Based and Theory Building Papers*, 8 (3): 244–257.

Sanderson, I. (2001) 'Performance management, evaluation and learning in 'modern' local government', *Public Administration*, 79 (2): 297–313.

Sarker, A. (2005) 'New Public Management, service provision and non-governmental organizations in Bangladesh', *Public Organization Review*, 5 (3): 249–271.

Saunders, M. (2006) 'The madness and malady of managerialism', *Quadrant*, 50 (3): 9–17.

Savage, G.T., Nix, T.W., Whitehead, C.J., Blair, J.D. (1991) 'Strategies for assessing and managing organisational stakeholders', *Academy of Management Executive*, 5 (2): 61–75.

Scherer, A.G. (2003): 'Modes of Explanation in Organization Theory', in Tsoukas, H., Knudsen, C. (eds.): *The Oxford Handbook of Organization Theory. Meta-Theoretical Perspectives*, Oxford: Oxford University Press, 310–344.

Schwenk, C.R. (2002), 'The Cognitive Perspective on Strategic Decision-making', first published in 1988, reprinted in Salaman, G. (ed.) *Decision Making for Business*, London: Sage Publications, 179–191.

Scott, J.C. (1990) *Domination and the Arts of Resistance: Hidden Transcripts*, New Haven: Yale University Press.

Scott, J. (2003): 'Transformations in the British Economic Elite', in Dogan, M. (ed.) *Elite Configurations at the Apex of Power*, Leiden: Brill, 155–173.

Shapiro, B., Matson, D. (2007) 'Strategies of resistance to internal control regulation', *Accounting, Organizations and Society*, 33 (2–3): 199–228.

Shattock, M. (2003) *Managing Successful Universities*, Maidenhead: Society for Research into Higher Education & Open University Press.

Shenhav, Y. (2003): 'The Historical and Epistemological Foundations of Organization Theory: Fusing Sociological Theory with Engineering Discourse', in Tsoukas, H., Knudsen, C. (eds.): *The Oxford Handbook of Organization Theory. Meta-Theoretical Perspectives*, Oxford: Oxford University Press, 183–209.

Shrivastava, P. (1986) 'Is strategic management ideological?', *Journal of Management*, 12 (3): 363–377.

Sidanius, J., Pratto, F. (1999) *Social dominance: An intergroup theory of social hierarchy and oppression*. Cambridge: Cambridge University Press.

Sidanius, J., Pratto, F., van Laar, C., Levin, S. (2004) 'Social Dominance Theory: Its agenda and method, *Political Psychology*, 25 (6): 845–880.

Sillince J.A.A. (1999) 'The Role of Political Language Forms and Language Coherence in the Organizational Change Process', *Organization Studies*, 20 (3): 485–518.

Sillince J.A.A. (2006) 'Resources and organizational identities: the role of rhetoric in the creation of competitive advantage', *Management Communication Quarterly*, 20 (2): 186–213.

Sillince J.A.A. (2007) 'Organizational context and the discursive construction of organizing', *Management Communication Quarterly*, 20 (4): 363–394.

Sim, S., Van Loon, B. (2004) *Introducing Critical Theory*, Royston: Iconbooks.

Simon, H.A. (1957) *Administrative Behaviour*, 2nd ed., London: Macmillan.

Simon, H.A. (1960) *The new science of management decision*, Englewood Cliff, NJ: Prentice Hall.

Simon, H.A. (1979) 'Rational decision making in business organizations', *American Economic Review*, 69: 493–513.

Simon, H.A. (1991) 'Bounded rationality and organizational learning', *Organization Science*, 2 (1): 125–134.

Skålén, P. (2004) 'New Public Management reform and the construction of organizational identities', *The International Journal of Public Sector Management*, 17 (3): 251–263.

Smallman, C. (2006) 'In search of relevance: Conventional or critical management inquiry?', *Management Decision*, 44 (6): 771–782.

Smircich, L., Stubbart, C. (2002) 'Strategic Management in an Enacted World', originally 1985, reprint in Salaman, G. (ed.): Decision Making for Business, The Open University: Sage Publications, 141–154.

Spencer-Matthews, S. (2001) 'Enforced cultural change in academe. A practical case study: Implementing quality management systems in higher education', *Assessment & Evaluation in Higher Education*, 26 (1): 51–59.

Spierenburg, P. (2004) 'Punishment, power, and history: Foucault and Elias', *Social Science History*, 28 (4): 607–636.

Staples, D.S., Greenaway, K., McKeen, J.D. (2001) 'Opportunities for research about managing the knowledge-based enterprise', *International Journal of Management Reviews*, 3 (1): 1–20.

Starbuck, W.H. (2003): 'The Origins of Organization Theory', in Tsoukas, H., Knudsen, C. (eds.): *The Oxford Handbook of Organization Theory. Meta-Theoretical Perspectives*, Oxford: Oxford University Press, 143–182.

Starr, M.A. (2004) 'Reading *The Economist* on globalisation: Knowledge, identity, and power', *Global Society*, 18 (4): 373–396.

Staw, B.M., Epstein, L.D. (2000) 'What bandwagons bring: Effects of popular management techniques on corporate performance, reputation, and CEO pay', *Administrative Science Quarterly*, 45 (3): 523–556.

Steger, M. (2005) 'From market globalism to imperial globalism: Ideology and American power after 9/11', *Globalizations*, 2 (1): 31–46.

Stewart, J., Kringas, P. (2003) 'Change management—Strategy and values in six agencies from the Australian Public Service', *Public Administration Review*, 63 (6): 675–688.

Stoddart, M.C.J. (2007) 'Ideology, hegemony, discourse: A critical review of theories of knowledge and power', *Social Thought and Research*, 28: 191–226.

Stubbart, C.I. (1989) 'Managerial cognition: A missing link in strategic management research', *Journal of Management Studies*, 26: 325–345.

Suddaby, R., Greenwood, R. (2005) 'Rhetorical strategies of legitimacy', *Administrative Science Quarterly*, 50 (1): 35–67.

Suttle, B.B. (1987) 'The passion of self-interest: The development of the idea and its changing status', *American Journal of Economics and Sociology*, 46 (4): 459–472.

Sveiby, K.E. (1998) *Wissenskapital, das unentdeckte Vermögen: immaterielle Unternehmenswerte aufspüren, messen und steigern*, Landsberg/Lech: verlag moderne industrie.

Swedberg, R. (2005) 'Can there be a sociological concept of interest?', *Theory and Society*, 34 (4): 359–390.

Tajfel, H., Turner, J. C. (1979) 'An Integrative Theory of Intergroup Conflict', in Austin, W.G., Worchel, S. (eds.) *The Social Psychology of Intergroup Relations*, Monterey, CA: Brooks/Cole, 33–47.

Taylor, F.W. (1911/1967) *The Principles of Scientific Management*, New York: Norton & Company.

Therborn, G. (1980) *The ideology of power and the power of ideology*, London: Versons Edition and NLB.

Thomas, P. (1998) 'Ideology and the discourse of strategic management: A critical research framework', *Electronic Journal of Radical Organization Theory*, 4 (1).

Thompson, V.A. (1961) 'Hierarchy, specialization, and organizational conflict', *Administrative Science Quarterly*, 5 (4): 485–521.

Thrift, N. (2002) '"Think and act like revolutionaries": Episodes from the global triumph of management discourse', *Critical Quarterly*, 44 (3): 19–26.

Torres, L. (2004) 'Trajectories in public administration reforms in European Continental countries', *Australian Journal of Public Administration*, 63 (3): 99–112.

Tourish, D., Robson, P. (2006) 'Sensemaking and the distortion of critical upward communication in organizations', *Journal of Management Studies*, 43 (4): 711–730.

Townley, B. (1993) 'Performance appraisal and the emergence of management', *Journal of Management Studies*, 30 (2), 221–238.

Turner, J.C. (2005) 'Explaining the nature of power: A three-process theory', *European Journal of Social Psychology*, 35 (1): 1–22.

Turner, J.C., Reynolds, K.J. (2003) 'Why Social Dominance Theory has been falsified', *British Journal of Social Psychology*, 42: 199–206.

Tyler, T.R. (2005) 'Introduction: Legitimating ideologies', *Social Justice Research*, 18 (3): 211–215.

Ullrich, J., Wieseke, J., Van Dick, R. (2005) 'Continuity and change in mergers and acquisitions: A social identity case study of a German industrial merger', *Journal of Management Studies*, 42 (8): 1549–1569.

Van Dijk, T.A. (2006) 'Ideology and discourse analysis', *Journal of Political Ideologies*, 11 (1): 115–140.

Van Loon, R. (2001) 'Organizational change: A case study', *Innovative Higher Education*, 25 (4): 285–301.

Van Vugt, M. (2006) 'Evolutionary origins of leadership and followership', *Personality and Social Psychology Review*, 10 (4): 354–371.

Vickers, M.H., Kouzmin, A. (2001) '"Resilience' in organizational actors and rearticulating "voice"', *Public Management Review*, 3 (1): 95–119.

Voronov, M., Yorks, L. (2005) 'Taking power seriously in strategic organizational learning', *Larning Organization*, 12 (1): 9–25.

Wagner, K.-R. (Hrsg.) (2002) *Mitarbeiterbeteiligung. Visionen für eine Gesellschaft von Teilhabern*, Wiesbaden: Gabler Verlag.

Waller, M.J., Huber, G.P., Glick, W.H. (1995) 'Functional background as a determinant of executives' selective perception', *Academy of Management Journal*, 38: 943–974.

Walsh, J.P. (1988) 'Selectivity and selective perception: An investigation of managers' belief structures and information processing', *Academy of Management Journal*, 31: 873–896.

Walsh, J.P. (1995) 'Managerial and organizational cognition: Notes from a trip down memory lane', *Organization Science*, 6 (3): 280–321.

Walsh, J.P., Weber, K. (2002) 'The prospects for Critical Management Studies in the American Academy of Management', *Organization*, 9 (3): 402–410.

Watson, T.J. (1982) 'Group ideologies and organisational change', *Journal of Management Studies*, 19 (3): 259–275.

Watson, T.J. (2001) 'Beyond Managism: Negotiated Narratives and Critical Management Edu-cation in Practice', *British Journal of Management*, 12: 385-396.

Watson, T. (2006) *Organising and Managing Work*, 2nd ed., Harlow: Pearson Education Limited.

Weber, M. (1904/1993) *Die protestantische Ethik und der „Geist" des Kapitalismus*, Bodenheim: Athenäum Hain Hanstein.

Weber, M. (1921/1980) *Wirtschaft und Gesellschaft*, 5., revidierte Auflage, Tübingen: J.C.B. Mohr (Paul Siebeck).

Weeden, K.A., Grusky, D.B. (2005) 'The case for a new class map', *American Journal of Sociology*, 111: 141–212.

Weick, K.E. (1979) *The Social Psychology of Organizing*, Reading, MA: Addison-Wesley.

Whitley, R. (1989) 'On the nature of managerial tasks: Their distinguishing characteristics and organisation'. *Journal of Management Studies*, 26 (3): 209–224.

Whittington, R. (1992) 'Putting Giddens into action: Social systems and managerial agency', *Journal of Management Studies*, 29 (6): 693–712.

Wilenski, P. (1988) 'Social change as a source of competing values in public administration', *Australian Journal of Public Administration*, 47 (3): 213–222.

Williamson, O.E. (1975) *Markets and Hierarchies*, New York: The Free Press.

Willmott, H.C. (1984) 'Images and ideals of managerial work: A critical examination of conceptual and empirical accounts', *Journal of Management Studies*, 21 (3): 349–368.

Willmott, H.C. (1987) 'Studying managerial work: A critique and a proposal', *Journal of Management Studies*, 24 (3): 249–270.

Willmott, H.C. (1996) 'A metatheory of management: Omniscience or obfuscation?', *British Journal of Management*, 7 (4): 323–328.

Willmott, H.C. (1997) 'Rethinking management and managerial work: Capitalism, control and subjectivity', *Human Relations*, 50 (11): 1329–1359.

Wilson, E.O. (1975) *Sociobiology: The new synthesis*, Boston: Harvard University Press.

Wilson, F.M. (1999) 'Alternative organizational ownership forms: Their effect on organizational behaviour', *Organizational Behaviour*, 171–181.

Winter, J.A. (1991) 'Religious belief and managerial ideology: An exploratory study of an extrapolation from the Weber thesis, *Review of Religious Research*, 33 (2): 169–175.

Worthington, F., Hodgson, J. (2005) 'Academic labour and the politics of quality in higher education: A critical evaluation of the conditions of possibility of resistance', *Critical Quarterly*, 47 (1–2): 96–110.

Wunderer, R. (Hrsg.) (1999) *Mitarbeiter als Mitunternehmer*, Neuwied: Luchterhand.

Yanow, D. (2007) 'Power, politics, and science in the study of complex organizations', *International Public Management Journal*, 10 (2): 173–189.

Ylijoki, O-H. (2003) 'Entangled in academic capitalism? A case-study on changing ideals and practices of university research', *Higher Education*, 45: 307–335.

Zald, M.N. (2002) 'Spinning disciplines: Critical Management Studies in the context of the transformation of management education', *Organization*, 9 (3): 365–385.

Zaleznik, A. (1989) *The Managerial Mystique—Restoring Leadership in Business*, New York: Harper & Row.

Zammuto, R.F., Gifford, B., Goodman, E.A. (2000) 'Managerial Ideologies, Organization Culture, and the Outcomes of Innovation', in Ashkanasy, N.M., Wilderom, C.P.M., Peterson, M.F. (eds.) *Handbook of Organizational Culture & Climate*, Thousand Oaks, CA: Sage Publications, 261–278.

Zeitlin, M. (1974) 'Corporate ownership and control: The large corporation and the capitalist class', *American Journal of Sociology*, 79 (5): 1073–1119.

Index

T - #0022 - 230425 - C0 - 229/152/15 [17] - CB - 9780415443357 - Gloss Lamination